ADVANCE PRAISE

As sales of recorded music plummet, live shows are supposed to save the music industry. Maybe so. But who will save the fans — beleaguered by scalpers, high ticket prices and insane "service" fees? Budnick and Baron explain how we got to this sorry pass, and what will have to happen before we get through it. Music lovers both, they're on the side of concert goers, who pay the bills and deserve more for their dollars and devotion.

— Anthony DeCurtis, contributing editor, *Rolling Stone*

Ticket Masters manages to cover forty years of the concert business and tell a series of complicated, interlocking business stories with the speed and clarity of a thriller. Reading this book won't make you any happier about spending four hundred bucks to go to a rock show, but you'll understand how it happened and who's to blame.

— Bill Flanagan, executive vice president and editorial director of MTV Networks, author *Evening's Empire, A&R*

For anyone who's ever suffered rock concert sticker shock — and we all have — Dean Budnick and Josh Baron's *Ticket Masters* is the best seat in the house to the show behind the show: an inside look at those inexhaustible high-wire artists, corporate jugglers and ringmasters who are always chasing one more deal, one more concession, one more buck in the empire burlesque that is the multi-billion-dollar rock concert business.

— Fred Goodman, author *Fortune's Fool* and *The Mansion on the Hill*

When community meets commerce, things get complicated. In *Ticket Masters*, Josh Baron and Dean Budnick take you behind the box office and explain, for the first time, the real reasons a good seat costs so damn much.

— Alan Light, former editor-in-chief, *Vibe* and *Spin* magazines

Dean Budnick and Josh Baron brilliantly chronicle the storied history of ticketing, providing a front row seat to the back room drama. A must-read for any music business enthusiast.

— Shirley Halperin, music editor, *The Hollywood Reporter*

Who turned concert ticketing into a monstrous machine for bleeding music fans dry? Dean Budnick and Josh Baron chronicle the rise of the Ticketmaster juggernaut — and hell-spawn like Clear Channel, StubHub, and Live Nation — by following the money with the dogged persistence of detectives and a knack for turning bottom-line history into engaging narrative. Along the way, you'll meet a rogues' gallery of aspiring tycoons, proud parasites, and mavens-on-the-make, along with visionary tech-heads and beautiful dreamers like the Grateful Dead's crew of "wooly freaks" who managed to turn a homegrown mail-order ticketing operation into a way of generating and rewarding good karma. If you wonder why you're paying ten times as much for overblown, cross-promoted spectacles that are one-tenth as satisfying as the rock and roll of your youth, you need to read this book.

— Steve Silberman, editor, *Wired* magazine

TICKET MASTERS

THE RISE OF THE CONCERT INDUSTRY
and HOW THE PUBLIC GOT SCALPED

DEAN BUDNICK *and* JOSH BARON

ECW Press

Dean: To my gold circle: Leanne Barrett, Caroline Budnick, Quinn Budnick, Alfred Budnick and Janet Budnick

Josh: To Rachel: Thank you for enduring my frequent absences during our first year of marriage and for being my biggest champion through your ceaseless encouragement.

Published by ECW Press
2120 Queen Street East, Suite 200, Toronto, Ontario, Canada M4E 1E2
416-694-3348 / info@ecwpress.com

LIBRARY AND ARCHIVES CANADA CATALOGUING IN PUBLICATION

Budnick, Dean
Ticket masters: The rise of the concert industry and how the
public got scalped / Dean Budnick, Josh Baron.

Includes bibliographical references.
ISBN 978-1-55022-949-3
ALSO ISSUED AS:
978-1-55490-949-0 (PDF); 978-1-55490-941-4 (EPUB)

1. Ticket brokerage. 2. Performing arts—Ticket subscription.
3. Performing arts—Ticket prices. 4. Ticket scalping.
I. Baron, Josh II. Title.

HD9999.T522B83 2011   381'.4579   C2010-907123-9

Developing Editor: Jennifer Hale
Cover Design: David Gee
Text Design: Tania Craan
Production and Typesetting: Troy Cunningham
Printing: Lake Book Manufacturing 1 2 3 4 5

PRINTED AND BOUND IN THE UNITED STATES

ECW PRESS
ecwpress.com

Table of Contents

The Summer of Their Discontent

THE CHAIRMAN HAD SPOKEN.

On the evening of August 3, 2010, Irving Azoff, whose role as chief executive officer of Ticketmaster had recently expanded following an industry altering merger that furnished the new title of Live Nation executive chairman, bypassed the company's publicity firm to offer his first direct message to ticket buyers via the social networking service Twitter.

Azoff's comments fell in the midst of what looked to be the most miserable U.S. summer concert season on record. Weak ticket sales had forced the cancellation of numerous high-profile performances, starting with a series of stadium shows by Azoff's longtime management client the Eagles on a bill with country superstars the Dixie Chicks and Keith Urban. In the weeks that followed a number of "recession-proof" acts did the same, as the Jonas Brothers, Rihanna and Lilith Fair all canceled multiple dates. Limp Bizkit scrapped its U.S. amphitheater tour and Christina Aguilera soon followed suit, citing "prior commitments." Even the annual American Idols Live! outing, which had blown out tickets in prior years, was forced to scale back its itinerary, dropping seven shows and rescheduling many others.

Entertainment reporters and Wall Street pundits alike took particular interest in the flagging amphitheater sales figures since most of these "sheds" were under the control of Live Nation. The summer of 2010 represented the first official go-round for the blended company after the government had approved the union of the world's largest live event promoter, Live Nation, with the world's largest ticketing agency, Ticketmaster (which had recently acquired the world's largest artist management firm, Azoff's Front Line).

The Department of Justice's ruling had been preceded by nearly eleven months of inquiry and two congressional hearings. In February 2009, shortly after the corporations announced their intent to unite, Azoff had been summoned to Capitol Hill in a moment that echoed former Ticketmaster CEO Fred Rosen's 1994 appearance before Congress in the wake of a public dustup with Pearl Jam. However, unlike the earlier inquiry, which in many respects resulted from the fight over a nickel, by 2009 billions of nickels were in play. As a result, both the House Subcommittee on Antitrust and the House Subcommittee on Courts and Competition Policy elected to weigh in on the matter.

Ultimately though, it fell to the Obama White House and his Department of Justice to determine whether to block the merger as an illegal restraint of trade. The federal government eventually granted its permission over the strident objections of opponents, who charged that the mega-company would raise prices and inhibit the development of new musical artists.

By August 2010 a growing segment of the financial community began offering its own criticism, as initial optimism regarding the prospects of Live Nation Entertainment was falling in tandem with the rate of ticket sales.

Over the course of the summer the company had taken a series of increasingly desperate measures to draw audiences into its amphitheaters. Package deals that offered coupons for a free soda and a hot dog gave way to mid-June's "No Services Fees" promotion, which proclaimed, "Your summer concert tickets at Live Nation amphitheaters now have No Service Fees" (even as an asterisk qualified, "Parking, shipping and other non 'service fee' costs may apply").

In late July the company instituted a $10 ticket program, which dropped prices even lower, scrambling to achieve a short-term financial benefit that led some prior ticket holders to grouse about their decision to purchase seats during initial sales at much greater expense.

When the expected windfall wasn't realized, Live Nation then outfitted employees with sandwich boards and paraded them through its venues, tickets in hand, hawking the cheap seats for future shows. Yet despite all of this, sales figures remained low as audiences were uncomfortable with the overall price structure of the concert experience.

In the face of these events, at 10:53 p.m. on August 3, Executive Chairman Azoff shared his sentiments with the public via the immediacy of Twitter.

"So if you want ticket prices to go down stop stealing music."

Seemingly absolving his company of responsibility, Azoff placed the burden squarely on the overburdened shoulders of consumers. This wasn't the first time he had conveyed such a message. A few weeks earlier, at *Fortune* magazine's Brainstorm Tech conference in Aspen, he had shared similar thoughts about his customer base with the magazine's managing editor: "If they could figure out a way to steal the tickets they would, just like they steal movies and music. But so far they haven't figured out how to do that."

The declining sales of recorded music held deep significance for Azoff, who in addition to running Front Line Management had previously headed both MCA and Giant Records. Still, few concertgoers appreciated his sentiment, flustered and frustrated as they were by parking costs, concession prices, $5 add-ons for the "luxury" of a short, ordered line into the venue, as well as the very price of tickets themselves, with their vexing array of fees. Consumers pointed, for instance, to Lady Gaga's Monster Ball tour, in which a single $20 lawn ticket could cost nearly $50 after a "facility charge" ($12), "convenience charge" ($10.05), "order processing fee" ($5.20) and "TicketFast Delivery," i.e., print-at-home ticketing ($2.50).

The sheer magnitude of it all had led one would-be concertgoer to profess in an online forum, with equal measures of humor and irritation, "Screw Live Nation, I'm grabbing these tix *after* the show."

Other music fans were baffled by their attempts to ascertain the fundamentals of concert ticket pricing. What is included in a service fee, they wondered, and why does the cost of that service vary with the price of a ticket? Who profits from these extra charges? Why are tickets sold online with impunity for five times their face value? Aren't there laws to protect consumers? Are musicians really scalping their best seats? And what's up with these VIP packages? Where do they find those front row tickets, and who reaps the benefits? Just what is a facility fee, and if the public is paying for renovations of some sort, shouldn't all the amphitheaters be recast in platinum by now? And just how did ticket prices get so *high* anyhow?

The story is complex, the players dynamic, the motives varied.

It all began with the simple, elegant notion that tickets could be marketed and sold more efficiently with the aid of a computer.

That eureka moment unfolded in the midtown Manhattan of the 1960s.

CHAPTER 1

A Few Reservations

THE LAST THING HARVEY DUBNER needed was another idea man.

He'd seen his share of them parade though his Madison Avenue office at New York City's Computer Applications Incorporated (CAI). As vice president of system design, Dubner occupied a unique role at the software house, serving as CAI's lone hardware expert. Most anyone who was pitching a potential project ultimately was funneled to Dubner, who gauged its viability.

Lately this had meant deflating any number of computer-enhanced caviar dreams. Ever since CBS News had enlisted the newly minted UNIVAC to provide analysis of the 1952 U.S. presidential election, the mainframe computer had become increasingly mainstream. Over the years that followed, the public grew fascinated with electronic data processors and their seemingly limitless potential. Although computing power remained cost-prohibitive, with price tags for the larger systems running well into the millions by 1966, there was no shortage of dreamers (and schemers) who sought to put mainframes to use.[1]

This was where "service bureaus" came into the picture. CAI, then the largest such entity on the East Coast, created custom software solutions packaged with the appropriate computer host. Typically this meant developing programs for businesses such as Western Union, TWA and even NASA. However, most any potential client with financial means would be considered if the technical feasibility of the proposed project passed muster. In many cases such determinations fell to Dubner, and in this particular week in early 1966, his lunch hours had been filled with wide-eyed entrepreneurs eager to enlist the company to develop algorithms capable of countering the house odds in Las Vegas or anticipating fluctuations in the stock market.

Dubner's latest visitor had an altogether different goal in mind. Jack Quinn, a seasoned "start-up man" in his mid-forties, sought CAI's assistance with his plan to utilize a mainframe to sell Broadway theater tickets. Dubner would have none of it.

"You have it all wrong," the weary, famished VP responded. "This is not the type of problem that requires a big computer. Your main problem is servicing terminals. I wouldn't want to touch that with a big computer."

It also became apparent to Dubner that Quinn had no sense of the cost associated with developing such a system. Quinn didn't blink when Dubner explained that the mainframe he coveted could cost $7 million and didn't demonstrate any sense of relief when Dubner suggested a $120,000 alternative.

Looking back more than forty years later, Dubner laughs, freely recalling his initial encounter with Jack Quinn, the man he now credits for giving him the credibility and confidence he needed to branch out on his own and create Dubner Computer Systems in 1970. "I was not in the sales mood. I kept making trouble by telling him he was out of his mind. He'd say something and I'd knock him down. All I knew is that the guy wanted a computer system and had no concept of how much this thing could cost. That was on a Thursday. On Friday he called me up and said, 'Can you come to my office? I like your ideas.' I said, 'Uh-oh.'"

Dubner was wary of wasting his time, but Quinn was only a few blocks away, so he consented.

Dubner arrived on Friday afternoon to discover that Quinn's surroundings were somewhat Spartan and not even his own. Instead the president of the proposed new venture was occupying a corner desk in the office of another individual. The fact that the space was owned by Broadway producer Hal Prince mollified him only slightly, if at all.

Dubner took a seat, and Quinn jumped back into their exchange of the day prior.

"I like what you're telling me. I like the concept of a small system. I like your approach. You're an engineer, not a programmer. I'm very unhappy with programmers. They tend to do things wrong."

Dubner found himself warming to the guy.

"It's going to cost a lot of money. Not seven million, but a lot of money."

"What's a lot of money?"

Dubner pulled a number out of midair.

"Two million dollars."

Quinn didn't hesitate.

"Okay."

"Okay?"

"Yes, no problem. How fast will it take you to build?"

"Well . . ." Dubner briefly sputtered before putting his mind to the task. "We should start with a pilot system. If we move on this right away, I would imagine that in three or four months we can have something running with two or three terminals."

On Monday morning Harvey Dubner received a call. Quinn was prepared to move forward with CAI, provided that Dubner would serve as project manager. By the week's end Dubner would have men and a dedicated machine set to create the first "computer-controlled communication service" on behalf of Ticket Reservation Systems, Inc.

From the vantage point of four decades on, Dubner grins at his memory of the initial encounters. "That's how it all began," he says. "I didn't want to have anything to do with Jack Quinn when he first walked into my place. I described how I would do the job, but I was not selling him because I didn't believe him. It was not a sales meeting; it was a free-flowing technical discussion. All I knew is here's a guy who starts saying the right words, saying he likes me, and I start liking him. And then he jumped on it. I still had no idea where he was getting his money."

TWO MONTHS INTO THE JOB, Dubner had ceased wondering about Quinn's capital resources, not only because he was being paid regularly but also because he had finally discovered the source of Quinn's cavalier attitude toward finances. Ticket Reservation Systems was being bankrolled by an investment fund that controlled the world's largest distillery, which in 1965 became the first such company to exceed the $1 billion annual sales mark. The fund's principal was Edgar M. Bronfman, the scion of Seagram's owner Samuel Bronfman and himself head of the company's U.S. operations.

Samuel Bronfman was born in Russia and immigrated to Canada as an infant in 1891 with his parents who were escaping anti-Semitic pressures in their homeland. His father, Yechiel (soon anglicized to Ekiel), entered a variety of businesses, including horse-trading, before purchasing a series of hotels, where the bars proved particularly lucrative, despite the brief interlude of Canadian Prohibition from 1916 to 1919. Sam took note of his father's success with liquor and in 1924, five years after Yechiel passed away, broke ground on a family-run distillery. The company found swift success, aided in no small part by its practice of exporting liquor to the United States, which was then in the midst of its own Prohibition. Three years later, the Bronfmans acquired their rival, Joseph E. Seagram & Sons, and the resulting Distillers Corporation-Seagrams would become the pre-eminent worldwide producer and distributor of alcohol.

Edgar, the oldest male of Sam's four children, was born in 1929. Known for his strong will (at Trinity College School, which he attended through twelfth grade, he was identified as "the boy who was caned the most"), Edgar asserted his interest from an early age in the position that he assumed would be rightfully his, that of his father's successor. By 1957 the elder Bronfman deemed Edgar worthy of heading Joseph E. Seagram & Sons, the U.S. subsidiary of the company, soon to be based in midtown Manhattan's new Seagram Building.[2]

While living in New York City, Edgar took an increasingly active role in the arts.[3] The 120th season of the New York Philharmonic opened on September 26, 1961, and the *New York Times* listed Edgar and his wife Ann as prominent box holders in attendance, along with Vanderbilts, Guggenheims and Rockefellers. Edgar's interest in the entertainment realm soon moved beyond that of a socialite. Over the years he would serve as an angel investor on Broadway, quietly fronting money for shows.

Edgar also had Hollywood aspirations, and in early 1967 he cofounded Sagittarius Productions with the intent to create films for U.S. television, which then could be released theatrically in foreign markets. Looking back on that venture in 1998, he wrote, "I'd always loved entertainment, and this was my chance to get my hand in the business. More than that, it provided an outlet for my creative drive. Indeed, while there were easier ways to make money than investing in the motion picture/TV industry (or Broadway, as I also found out), participating in an artistic endeavor proved to be uniquely satisfying."

Later that same year Bronfman guided his Cemp Investments fund to acquire a stake in MGM amounting to eighteen percent of the venerable film studio. In 1951 Sam Bronfman had created Cemp (an acronym for his children's first names: Charles, Edgar, Minda and Phyllis) as a means to protect their interest in his company and also to build for their future. Mr. Sam, as he was called by his employees, seeded Cemp with a majority of the Distillers Corporation shares, along with additional funds from his children's trusts. His son's MGM stock purchase unsettled Sam to the point where he made a rare closed-door office visit. As Edgar recounts in his biography, *Good Spirits*, his father inquired "whether we were buying all that stock so that I could meet girls." To which Edgar assured him, "Father, nobody has to spend $56 million to get laid."

Edgar's ambitions in the entertainment world found another early outlet with the formation of Ticket Reservation Systems (TRS), funded by Cemp and incorporated on May 4, 1965. The timing seemed fortuitous, as on May 23, *New York Times* chief drama critic Howard Taubman wrote a piece entitled "How To Civilize Ticket Sales." Taubman's prescription was "a computerized ticket system," whereby "what is beyond doubt is that the process of acquiring tickets would become infinitely easier and pleasanter." TRS intended to become the first company to initiate such a process and on July 13 trumpeted its plans for "a countrywide electronic system, starting with the 1966–67 season."

By the fall of 1966, however, TRS still had nothing to show for itself beyond an estimable board of directors. Part of the problem was focused, capable leadership. The company remained a sidelight for Bronfman, who had a liquor company to run and was beginning his push into film. Broadway producer George W. George, who had taken an exploratory role via a feasibility study that led him to pitch a computerized ticketing system to Bronfman, found himself swallowed up by George's vocation, with *Happily Never After*, *The Great Indoors*, *Ben Franklin in Paris* and *Any Wednesday* all on the boards during this time period.[4] The Ultronic System Corporation had been tapped as a programming partner for TRS but, lacking steady direction, soon committed all available resources to its new global stock quotation service.

So, despite the company's pedigree, TRS might have remained a well-funded abstraction had Bronfman not approached Jack Quinn in early October 1966. Quinn, who was then forty-five years old, possessed experience with start-ups as well as a general technical understanding of the issues brought to bear by the undertaking.[5] Quinn had spent the 1950s at Kimball Systems, Inc., where he rose to vice president and marketing director while developing a perforated sales tag that functioned as an early version of the present-day bar code (one highlight was a cold call at the Sears Tower that eventually led the company to place the tags on all Sears garments at the point of manufacture). He would become the driving force that brought TRS online.

When Bronfman approached him, Quinn, who had recently left his post as VP at Litton Automated Business Systems, recognized not only the business opportunity but also the potential returns for his wife and eight kids. Quinn's wife, Jane (like many of the unnamed spouses to follow, as this was still an era of "Mad Men"), deserves her share of credit. She recalls the initial days after he took the position: "Jack spent that entire weekend at our dining room table on the first business plan. I was running a second corporation, which was a family of eight children. I spent all weekend making sure they were busy to keep them away from Daddy because he had a big project. But he was able to concentrate in the middle of the chaos. That weekend he wrote the first attempt at a business plan and drew the first sketches to be used for the patent [which was eventually granted]."

Quinn recognized that, to launch TRS, he needed to focus simultaneously on three essential elements: outlets, clients and a system (not necessarily in that order, as it would become something of a tightrope act, providing assurances to everyone while working to achieve what he represented as a fait accompli). So began the saga of Jack Quinn, which a few years later at his farewell party, one of "Jack's Guys" committed to rhyme. The poem opens:

Listen employees, a tale I shall spin
Of the four year ride of a Jack named Quinn.
On the fifteenth of October in '66
He started in doing his Ticketron Shticks.
He started with nothing – like the man in the barrel
A little cash from Edgar and a little Cash named Carol [his secretary was named
   Carol Cash]
And a passionate feeling deep down in his genes
That folks would buy tickets from funny machines.

Responsibility for the "funny machines" was left to Harvey Dubner, who made some decisions that would have long-term repercussions for the fate of TRS. As he had initially suggested to Quinn, rather than using a mainframe, he opted for a minicomputer. Not quite as compact as the personal computers that would arrive in the 1970s, minicomputers were closer in bulk to large office desks. The creation of the integrated circuit allowed these machines to be more manageable in size and a bit less temperamental in their maintenance needs. In *A History of Modern Computing* Paul Ceruzzi writes, "One could obtain a minicomputer and not feel obliged also to get a restrictive lease agreement, a climate-controlled room or a team of technicians whose job it seemed to be keeping users away."

The computer that would remain at the heart of the TRS system for well over a decade was the Control Data 1700. In the summer of 1957 Bill Norris, head of the UNIVAC division at Sperry Rand, resigned along with many other key employees, including the eccentric, virtuoso engineer Seymour Cray. They soon founded the Control Data Corporation, setting up shop in downtown Minneapolis.[6] By the middle of the 1960s, with IBM swiftly gaining traction to the point where the industry was described as IBM and the Seven Dwarves (Control Data, Sperry Rand, Honeywell, RCA, General Electric, Burroughs and NCR), Norris's company distinguished itself and rose to number two in worldwide sales by focusing on niche markets, building machines for scientific and military applications. The "Big Box," the CDC 6600, which Cray designed, exceeded any IBM machine in terms of performance and price point. As something of an afterthought, Cray, who worked in his own Chippewa Falls, Wisconsin lab nearly 100 miles away from corporate headquarters, also created a smaller computer to service input and output functions for a larger machine. This device soon inaugurated a line of minicomputers that would prove lucrative, even if much of CDC's focus would remain on the so-called supercomputers, where it dominated the market.

Here is where many critics of Ticket Reservation Systems and its successor, Ticketron, would later get things wrong. It is certainly true that Control Data made its name on mainframes and would remain in that business well into the 1980s, long past the point when this represented prudent business sense. However, the computer that Dubner placed at the center of the new system was slightly larger than an office copier from the 1990s. The CDC 1700 appears with Bill Norris in a photo that ran alongside an October 2, 1965 *Business Week* feature on the new machine, "Control Data Widens Line," and one can find matching equipment in the TRS marketing brochure.

Unlike the IBMs, which typically ran on the company's own operating system and software (which is how IBM ensconced itself in the business market until the PC era), the CDC 1700 was a bit more pliable. So Dubner and half a dozen CAI employees under his watch took the 1700 and made a series of modifications, crafting a custom operating system.

Larry Littwin ran computer operations after Dubner and CAI completed their work.[7] He explains: "Most systems today and then came with an operating system, but an operating system is inherently inefficient because it's meant to handle any case that you might want to run on the computer. So Dubner and CAI wrote their own which was much smaller, more efficient and much faster than the standard operating system. The performance of the system was such that it could do a lot more than people ever thought because it was running a very application-specific software custom tailored to do just the job it was doing."

Dubner's operating system required only 5,000 words of memory and would achieve a transparency that he would describe in the title of a paper he delivered at a computer conference in 1970: "Ticketron — a successful operating system without an operating system."

While that operating system may have been the height of efficiency, the corresponding equipment provided to the remote outlets did not share that designation. The "agent sets," as described in the initial TRS brochure, did not provide visual support through a cathode ray tube (CRT) monitor. Instead outlets were provided with a ticket printer, a Teletype printer and a "latched keyboard" on which the keys remained depressed after someone typed each entry until manually released (an article written shortly after TRS commenced operations described the units as "accordion-like teletype machines"). While the CRT-free system may have been a relatively cost-effective way for TRS to place its systems in multiple remote locations, it limited users' ability to glean info at a glance, and the clatter of the Teletype was not altogether suitable for retail settings.

What's more, for the first few years, the ticket printing process had its quirks. For efficiency's sake each printer received bursts of information in thirds. The system then briefly polled other units, occasionally creating hybrid Frankentickets that mixed and matched various orders. The printers themselves also could be erratic, and Bill Schmitt, who eventually joined Ticketron as company president in the early 1970s, shares one situation in which the company took extreme steps to ensure reliability: "There was an early demonstration of the system for the press, and while I can't vouch for this personally, I heard as a rumor that they hired a midget to push out tickets."[8]

Returning to the poem at Jack Quinn's farewell dinner, some of these initial challenges were referenced in couplets:

Then Jack sold the pilot: in the New Theatre they'd stick it;
(And it took just two minutes to print out one ticket).
But the show was a smash and business was fine
And a lady had twins while waiting in line.
So back to the drawing boards; once more they began
With Tinkertoy printers they bought from Di/An.

Di/An Controls had been enlisted to create the second batch of printer units. However, TRS soon turned to Control Data to assist with the next round, a decision that further entwined the futures of the two companies.[9]

With system development now in motion (a motion that proved nearly perpetual in the first few years), Quinn set his sights on an outlet network. Given the company's initial focus on Broadway ticketing, he gravitated toward banks and travel bureaus to host the "Electronic Box Office Terminals." By the time of TRS's formal launch, its outlets would be found at American Express offices, Chase Manhattan, Broadway Bank and Temple Travel Services. Quinn and his team also pitched retail stores, emphasizing not only the added foot traffic but also, initially, the additional source of revenue. TRS's approach can be seen in a 1967 *Supermarket News* article that emphasized that, although agents would pay "a $150 monthly equipment rental and miscellaneous overhead," they would earn twenty-five cents per ticket fee. If they sold "two hundred tickets daily, they could gross $1,250 per month."

A few retailers did eventually sign on, with Grand Union supermarkets and Abraham & Straus department stores among the initial partners. The flagship retailer, however, was Gimbels, which committed its iconic Herald Square store (the setting of the 1947 film *Miracle on 34th Street* and a frequent shopping destination of Lucy Ricardo and Ethel Mertz). The announcement of Gimbels' participation carried a degree of star power as Edgar Bronfman himself appeared for a rare company photo op alongside a Gimbels executive.

As it turned out, the initial commission projections far exceeded the actual monthly revenue. These numbers would rise in the early 1970s once TRS moved beyond Broadway and into the world of rock music. However, that higher volume would be accompanied by bigger heartache.

Kurt Devlin, another early TRS employee (and the iron man of computerized ticketing, now in his fourth decade in the business, working for the Shubert Organization), notes: "The department stores came to view ticketing not as a profit center but mostly as a crowd attractant. So they would put it in the furthest, most obscure back part of the store, so that when you went in you had to walk through the entire store, with the hope you would stop and buy something. They liked that business but they hated some of the rock business. When they had to sell the Grateful Dead or Jethro Tull, they didn't like the people coming through the store."

Matt Whelan, who joined Ticketron in the mid-1970s, adds: "I had a lot of dealings with Sears and Roebuck. We sold it to them as a way to get people into their stores. The executives at Sears sort of liked the concept, but then you had the little old lady behind the counter. In the early days sometimes the computers ran smoothly and sometimes they didn't. If the lady went on lunch and you put Led Zeppelin on sale, well, she didn't care about Led Zeppelin; she cared about lunch."

In the spring of 1967 Jack Quinn wasn't fixated on rock music either. In fact the company as a whole took little interest in the genre, as evidenced by its brochure, which didn't specify rock concerts among the TRS targets: theater, sports, motion pictures, summer stock, supper clubs, non-profit and college events and "all other reserve seat spectator attractions." So Quinn occupied himself in making the rounds from theater office to theater office, attempting to enlist any producers or theater owners willing to commit their ticket inventory to the new, untried system. Edgar Bronfman took a hand as well, tapping into his many networks (and presumably offering up occasional complimentary cases of Crown Royal).

The proposed TRS business model directed nearly fifty cents of gross income from every ticket into company coffers. The tickets themselves typically carried a service charge of twenty-five to fifty cents, half of which would return to the outlet. TRS also would collect a twenty-five cent "inside charge" from the theaters, producers and sports teams who utilized the system. This amount would not be generated from an additional expense to the consumer but would be contributed by the TRS client. In addition, venues paid a monthly rental fee for each box office terminal (somewhere in the neighborhood of $150) and a monthly service charge based on the total volume of seats sold, an expense that typically reached $500 to $1,000.

This approach resulted in some tensions regarding the price point of the service charges added to each ticket. TRS clients accepted the expense of the service in the belief that the inside charges would be more than offset by the overall increases in ticket sales. Part of these calculations took into consideration the ultimate cost to the consumer. As a result, the facilities resisted even the smallest of incremental increases to the service charges, which yielded no direct financial benefit while potentially alienating ticket buyers.

Ultimately a single Broadway theater production, an off-Broadway show and a soon-to-be-defunct sports team were willing to participate in the launch, for which TRS waived its fees to clinch participation. On July 6, 1967, TRS finally debuted its self-described pilot project (an earlier announcement had proved premature). *I Do! I Do!* produced by David Merrick and starring Mary Martin and Robert Preston, was then seven months into its run at the 46th Street Theater and in need of a ticket sales jolt. Also signing on was *Drums in the Night*, then appearing in Greenwich Village at the Circle in the Square Theater, as well as the National Professional Soccer League's New York Generals, who had already started their first (and only) season in the NPSL.

The debut of TRS was mostly successful in that tickets were indeed sold from remote locations, although there were still a few kinks, which again were reflected in the poetic serenade to Jack Quinn:

> They sold tickets at Gimbels; while half of the troops
> Were back at the office, counting the dupes.
> When clients complained, with a smile on his mug
> Jack would buy them a drink, and say "It's a bug!"
> But no matter the problems, he just kept on goin',
> And told bigger whoppers to Merrick and Cohen.

A few instances of double-sold seats provided only a minor distraction for TRS, which otherwise basked in the media's fascination with its operations. The *New York Times* reported somewhat breathlessly (for the *New York Times*, that is) on the TRS pilot, with an account from Gimbels on the opening day of ticket sales. The article quoted Quinn's assertion that "TRS is the first major innovation in 100 years in the sales of reserved seat tickets for entertainment events." Drama reporter Louis Calta marveled at the technological achievement whereby "automated machines called terminal units are hooked up by telephone lines to a central computer at 15 East 26th Street, which has been programmed to handle ticket requests." National papers also took interest in TRS and television soon followed suit.

One morning in mid-1967 news of the TRS launch reached Los Angeles, where Roy Bellman watched a report on NBC's *Today Show* that provided remote coverage of the "world's first computerized ticketing system." He felt as if the floor had dropped out beneath him: "I thought *we* were developing the world's first computerized ticketing system."

ON JUNE 10, 1966, a self-described "automation consultant" named Walter T. McHale made a presentation in the El Segundo, California offices of the Computer Sciences Corporation. CSC had been founded seven years earlier by Fletcher Jones and Roy Nutt, who met in an IBM user group while each worked in data processing for the aerospace industry. The pair correctly anticipated that the future of computing would rely increasingly on independent software. CSC swiftly secured its first contract, creating a business language compiler called FACT for Honeywell, translating a higher level of programming language into a more accessible one. By 1965 Computer Sciences had become the largest company in the United States exclusively producing software, and the thirty-two-year-old Jones was among the entrepreneurs solicited for advice in a *Time* magazine cover story entitled "Millionaires: How They Do It."

Before a team of junior CSC executives, McHale, who had previously run a data processing division at Security National Bank, outlined "The Teleticket Concept." His introductory materials explained, "The Teleticket system was designed to update the ticket distribution function of the entertainment industry by application of the latest techniques of automation. The basic concept is all seats to all events within a geographical area (such as Southern California) are stored in a central electronic file. This total inventory of available seats is accessible through 200 to 300 outlets via a ticket printing terminal. Total transaction time is measured in seconds. Under this concept, promoters of events will contract with the Teleticket Corporation for storage of their seating information in the central computer. The Teleticket Corporation will provide the network of distribution outlets."

McHale told the increasingly interested CSC representatives that he had been developing "the Teleticket concept" over the previous fifteen months. During this period he had approached a number of potential customers, indicating that both the ownership of the Los Angeles Dodgers and the Los

Angeles Rams "have been especially influential, helpful and encouraging." In addition, "the system has been presented to a major Los Angeles bank with more than 300 branches, a major supermarket chain and a number of large industrial organizations. In all cases there has been enthusiastic response to the suggestion that they serve as ticket distribution outlets for the system. Extensive work also has been done with the IBM Corporation. They have contributed a substantial amount of time to the development of the ticket printing terminal and verifying the feasibility of the technical concept." Best of all, he proclaimed, the field was wide open and ripe for the taking. No other companies would challenge the manifest destiny of the Teleticket Corporation.

McHale estimated that it would take twelve months to develop, sell and install the system in Southern California. He projected gross revenue for the Teleticket Corporation to be $1.8 million in Los Angeles alone the first year after the launch (based on gross ticket sales of $32 million). McHale then exhibited a bravado liberally spiked with delusion in explaining that six months after operations began in Los Angeles, "all other cities in the United States will be installed. In addition, significant commitments will be made for operations in Germany, France, England, Japan, Canada, Italy."

Computer Sciences Corporation bought into McHale's idea, quite literally, investing $13 million over the next four years (although no one made it to the Trevi Fountain). Much of this expense came from the hardware committed to the project. Unlike the Control Data minicomputers used by its as-yet-undiscovered competitor, CSC committed not one but two IBM mainframes to the task. Roy Bellman, who would soon come aboard to design and test the ticketing software, recalls: "You're talking millions of dollars for the mainframes. We had two 360/50s in the computer room, and at that time they were about as big as it gets. The disc drives used the big multi-layered discs that had handles, and you loaded packs of discs from the top. We had one of the 360/50s backing up the other as a hot spare. Everything that happened on one computer happened on the second as well. One computer controlled everything and was the system of record, but if it crashed for any reason, the other one kicked right in so that in the field you didn't even know that anything had happened. And that wasn't heard of in those days. You didn't have a hot spare. If it goes down, it goes down."

The "network terminal" differed substantially from the TRS "agent sets" as well. Rather than a latched keyboard, CSC utilized a CRT monitor, which made it easier to look at the screen and determine the status of a particular transaction at a glance. This proved helpful in retail situations, as often the person handling the ticketing transaction was multitasking, balancing ticket sales with regular job responsibilities. The unit as a whole, including the console and the ticket printer, also doubled as a desk. This design aspired to take into account the various steps associated with selling tickets. In its brochure for potential clients, the company cooed, "Each sturdy unit is handsomely custom-finished with a counter top of durable, wood-grain Formica. There is ample counter space for check writing, change making, etc. The compact ticket printing module has its own built-in, partitioned, lock-and-key cash drawer."

The name Teleticket hadn't lasted much beyond McHale's pitch meeting. Ten days following his presentation, an interoffice memo circulated, indicating "from now on, the project will be referred to as 'Computicket.'" This selection reinforced a Computer Sciences brand that had achieved a new level of success with its Computax software program. The Computicket logo featured a ticket stub affixed to the quintessential mid-1960s image of a computer with a reel-to-reel tape drive and a bank of lights. An early ad hailed the service as "the new computer way to buy great seats."

By contrast, starting with its name, Ticket Reservation Systems downplayed any association with new technology, likely for fear of intimidating its projected Broadway ticket buyers. The same held true for the TRS logo, which featured a row of theater seats, with the two in the middle marked in red as reserved.

Despite Computer Science's technical know-how, it lacked a meaningful connection to the entertainment world. On July 19, 1967, more than a year after commencing operations, CSC unveiled Computicket at a press conference that identified Ralphs Grocery as its first outlet partner. However, Computicket still could not boast of a single client commitment. In response the company approached Nick Mayo, a former Broadway actor turned theater director and producer, who had spent the previous few years building and managing a theater in the round in the San Fernando Valley.

Mayo's Rolodex and his entrepreneurial spirit proved well-suited to Computicket. He provided the company with a catalyst akin to Jack Quinn's efforts at TRS. Originally hired as a consultant, Mayo had his role upped within a month to vice president and director of marketing (he eventually succeeded to president). Mayo had graduated from Los Angeles City College in 1937 at age sixteen and eventually relocated to New York, taking on some minor theater roles and then serving as stage manager for a number of productions. In this capacity he met Hollywood actress Janet Blair, who had been handpicked by Richard Rodgers and Oscar Hammerstein to perform the lead in the touring production of *South Pacific*. The two married in 1952 and settled down outside L.A. to raise a son and daughter while continuing their respective careers.[10]

In the early 1960s the Mayos partnered with Bob Hope, Art Linkletter, Danny Thomas and others on the Valley Music Theater, which opened on July 6, 1964, with Blair starring in *The Sound of Music.* To Mayo's deep disappointment, the VMT closed its doors after three seasons for lack of local support (his son Andrew remarks, "My dad was ahead of his times by ten years on a number of his projects").

In his new role at Computicket, Mayo set to work drawing on his existing professional relationships. He hired a number of friends and former associates with common entertainment backgrounds, such as actor and sports reporter Mario Machado (best known later as newsman Casey Wong in all three *RoboCop* films), Broadway performer and producer Howard Erskine (who would become a fixture in Woody Allen's repertory company) and Faye Nuell, a former actress and employee at the Valley Music Theater (she was also a close friend of Natalie Wood and served as Wood's double in *Rebel Without a Cause*).

Mayo lent a box office perspective and a theatrical air to the job as well. In describing the necessity of computerized ticketing, he pronounced: "Here we are dealing with the most perishable commodity on earth, a ticket to a seat to a specific performance, and handling it in the same way it was handled in great-grandfather's time. We put every roadblock possible between what we're trying to sell and the willing customer."

Computicket's sales brochure also reflected Mayo's prior occupation. The opening "Dedication" page (a rarity in materials of this sort) flashed back to his days at the Valley Music Theater. It burbled, "Dedicated to the brave and lonely event promoter, who sticks his career neck out every time he puts his money where his idea is, with the knowledge that Computicket can contribute substantially to his greater success . . . and serenity."

This overwrought expression of empathy may well have assisted with an initial sale, as Computicket soon received a commitment from the Los Angeles Music Center. The system's very first operation, however, was not to dispense tickets but to notify customers of a play's postponement. In February 1968 Mayo explained, "When *Happy Time* was postponed a week, it only took six hours to dispatch 32,000 letters to season subscribers. It would have been impossible to handle this manually in such an incredibly short period of time." Through Mayo's industry connections, the Hollywood Bowl, the Dorothy Chandler Pavilion and the Ahmanson Theatre also signed on to utilize Computicket's "Master Patron File and Subscription Mailing Service," even as equipment delays precluded a full system install.

While Mayo may have anticipated technical difficulties, shortly after he settled into his new role he was confronted with a complication of greater consequence. The existence of Ticket Reservation Systems had been known to a few Computer Science executives for some months, but they had adopted a policy of willful blindness toward TRS, hoping that the rival company would fizzle out.[11] Mayo was not briefed regarding TRS when he took the position at Computicket, and colleagues recall his distress upon learning of the other company.

BY EARLY 1968 THE BATTLE was pitched. From the outset both companies' business plans had hinged on market exclusivity. Faye Nuell Mayo (she married Nick Mayo in 1981, two years before he died of cancer) remembers that the discovery of TRS "threw our projections completely out the window because they were done with a single company, basically a monopoly, but it needed to be that way because you couldn't have two companies selling the same theater tickets." Over on the TRS side, Littwin recalls that the common understanding was: "You have to be a monopoly in this business to make money, so the question was how long do you have to survive to be a monopoly? That was really what it was all about, who was going to survive longest." A March 23, 1968 article in *Business Week* titled "No SRO at Computer" affirmed that "both companies are sure only one will survive."

A March 31 *Los Angeles Times* piece, "Computers Poised to Solve Sports Ticket Problems," compared the two services, casting Computicket in a generally positive light, with an accompanying image of Mayo and Nuell examining the "Tickets of the Future." However, in a discussion about end users, Computicket West Coast Marketing Director Jack Tobin acknowledged, "We have yet to offer a contract," adding somewhat lamely, "but we plan to start within two weeks. Right now we have a crowded calendar of demonstrations."

This is not to say that everyone recognized the nature of the competition. In his lighthearted column, "A Loaf of Bread . . . a Jug of Wine . . . and 2 Tickets to a Dodger Game?" the *Los Angeles Times*' John Hall described the impending arrival of "a national ticket service" at Ralphs Grocery but conflated the competitors, likely unaware that two independent entities existed: "The name of the organization is Ticket Reservation Systems Inc. — to be known to the short-cutters as 'Computicket.'"

With their very survival at stake the two companies couldn't tolerate such market confusion and pushed aggressively to distinguish themselves. "Polite, edgy hostility marks the comment(s) by the executives of each company about the other," observed the Associated Press. An April 1, 1968 *Newsweek* article captured the growing enmity, describing "some of the bitterest competitive infighting in American business in years. . . . Last week Nick Mayo said the TRS system, based on Control Data Corp. 1700 computers, doesn't have a fraction of the capability of his system. A TRS spokesman acidly replied that 'the only difference between their system and ours is that theirs doesn't exist.'"

TRS then brought the tussle to Computicket's backyard. Jack Quinn flew to Los Angeles to supervise the opening of a particularly swank West Coast branch. In an effort to emphasize its deep pockets and staying power, TRS set up shop at the Beverly Hilton Hotel. Rather than just its marketing executives, Quinn also opted to place the company's technical team as well as a ticket outlet in the high-profile real estate. Kurt Devlin has fond memories of this era, clocking in each day at the intersection of Wilshire and Santa Monica boulevards. "The computer room had a huge plate glass window at ground level on Wilshire Boulevard," he says. "That would be taboo in today's world. The offices overlooked a small swimming pool and sunbathing courtyard. There was always something big going on at the hotel, with Bentleys parked near the entrance and many celebrity sightings." (Jack Lemmon and Jack Palance were among the repeat ticket customers.)

These efforts soon yielded a major new client, as TRS secured the rights to the Los Angeles Forum. In an effort to twist the knife a bit, the company shared this development with a flourish via a full-page advertisement in the *Los Angeles Times* Calendar section. The ad crowed, "Jack Kent Cooke announces the newest, most efficient ticket service in the world . . . computerized ticketing by Ticket Reservations Inc." In addition it puffed up the facility (albeit in a self-serving manner) by hailing "Another First For The Fabulous Forum."

Six weeks earlier Control Data had purchased a full-page ad of a similar tone in the *Wall Street Journal*. With no small measure of grandiosity the text proclaimed, "It is inevitable that the computer will someday revolutionize the whole business of seat reservations and ticket sales . . . 'Someday' is May 1st!" CDC then highlighted the addition of Chicago, the third hub "plugged into the transcontinental network." The three systems, each designed to handle the load for a third of the country, were linked so that a customer could have access to all of TRS's ticket inventory. The dense, thirteen-paragraph advertisement then explained, "Pre-printed tickets are a thing of the past. Seat inventories exist only in the memory banks of the Control Data computers. And remote 'electronic box offices' can spring up wherever there are telephone lines for computer hook-up. In effect a 'ticket' is everywhere simultaneously. A West Coast Musical enthusiast can buy seats for the Broadway show he plans to see on his next trip with as much ease as a native New Yorker."

The TRS Chicago office was located in Marina City, the sixty-five story dual circular building complex that boasted the tallest reinforced concrete structures in the world (and rooms devoid of right angles). Peter

Schniedermeier — in some respects computerized ticketing's Forrest Gump, given his proximity to so many developments in the field over the years to follow — was an early hire. The nineteen-year-old German immigrant was recruited as a junior developer while still a student at a local technical school, and he remembers being awed by the sense that, "I get to be in the entertainment industry." This impression was reinforced by the presence of local sports figures such as Bobby Hull and Leo Durocher, who occasionally stopped in because they were accounting clients of Regional Vice President Harvey Wineberg. Another TRS executive docked his boat below the towers and hosted office parties, all of which contributed to the conviviality and glamour. Schniedermeier's other memory of the era is that, "The day we went live, a bunch of reporters came in with their big flash cameras. When we flipped the switch and the reporters started taking photos of the computer center, the computers all went down because of the camera flashes. But we brought them back up, eventually."

No such drama accompanied the premiere of Computicket, which finally arrived in the fall of 1968. The Ahmanson Theatre, UCLA football and the American Basketball Association's Los Angeles Stars were among the first to offer tickets. Mayo's stage connections also proved fruitful, as within a few weeks more than a dozen New York City theaters had agreed to participate. Computicket shared this news with its own full-page *Los Angeles Times* advertisement: "New York bound? Take your Broadway theatre seats with you! Computicket — the great new way to see the best on Broadway! Before you leave for New York you can pick up your tickets to these great Broadway shows at the Computicket outlet in your neighborhood."

Computicket also sought to match its rival's high style. The executive offices in Los Angeles soon were adorned with an art collection that led programmer Roy Bellman to observe, "They probably could have financed the company on the paintings." Computicket mirrored TRS's earlier move by establishing a beachhead on the opposite coast. With TRS by then having secured new digs in Seagram's corporate home, Computicket leased pricey real estate in the Paramount Building.

There was only one hitch to all this escalating opulence. Neither company was generating significant revenue.

ONE OBSTACLE WAS THE SHEER cost of doing business. When Computicket launched in Los Angeles, it did so with significantly fewer outlets than initially announced. Whereas it once had projected that 150 area terminals would roll out at the start (with fifty-two in Ralphs Markets alone), by the spring of 1969 only twenty-nine were in place (spread out among Ralphs, Bullock's department stores and Wallach's Music City). The individual units proved far more expensive to produce than expected, while the costs of renting dedicated phone lines similarly exceeded projections. Prior to a single ticket sale, Computicket had committed $6 million to equipment and development, while TRS's total was $10 million and rising.

Despite the significant investments, neither company was generating substantial revenues from ticket sales. Computicket came to grips with this rather quickly, in modifying its service charges from what it had announced would be a flat fifty cents per order regardless of how many tickets were purchased to thirty-five cents per ticket in Los Angeles and fifty cents in New York. From this the company ultimately pocketed about four percent of any ticket sales, which on average amounted to just over thirty cents. This would have represented a relatively robust figure if Computicket's gross sales approached even the $2.5 million per month projected for Los Angeles alone, but the numbers for the company as a whole fell shy of this figure, and ongoing monthly deficits exceeded half a million dollars.

What both Computicket and TRS failed to anticipate was that their clients were only willing to commit a fraction of available ticket inventory to computerized sales. In its marketing brochure Computicket extolled the fundamental virtues of its system: "All network terminals have equal access to the seating inventory of each theater, area or stadium. . . . They are direct extensions of the main box office — not separate box offices with individual or limited allocation of their own." This was not, in fact, the case. In practice, the main office did retain its own inventory (and in some cases also still utilized traditional hard ticket outlets), while the computerized services received only a limited allocation.

This reality was reflected at the close of the laudatory *New York Times* piece that covered the first day of ticket sales at Gimbels. Sisters from Massachusetts had attempted to purchase "medium priced seats" for two theater performances. They were denied tickets at their chosen price point. In response, "Bernard B. Zients, executive head of Gimbels, picked up the tab for the special occasion and presented a delighted Miss Sami with two $9.90 tickets to 'I Do! I Do!' and two $4.35 tickets to 'Drums in the Night.'" It's fair to assume that after *Times* reporter Louis Calta retreated, so did Zients, along with any similar offers.

Roy Bellman recalls that the theaters' decisions to limit ticket allocations affected Computicket negatively on two levels: "One thing that shocked everybody was that the venues themselves were not willing to give up much of their inventory. They were reluctant to change the way they had been selling tickets, so they would give most of their inventory to their traditional distribution points and maybe give us ten to thirty percent of the venue. That's such a small amount of tickets to be selling, and we're advertising,

'Come to us and we're going to give you the best available seats.' But it wasn't true because we didn't have best available. So we had credibility problems from the get-go, and we also started to worry almost immediately that the volume of sales wouldn't be enough to keep the doors open."

George W. George, the theater producer who funded the original study that paved the way for TRS, later lamented that given the limited inventory, Broadway was "only paying lip service to the service." In 1976, when the *New York Times* asked him to assess the quality of the system he helped facilitate, George responded, "Personally, I've never bought Ticketron tickets because I know I can get better seats through the house."

PRIOR TO THE ADVENT OF TRS and Computicket, Broadway theater tickets were distributed in three ways. Patrons could walk up to the box office and purchase hard tickets that were stored on the premises in racks. Mail order was a second option, as someone could send in a request along with a check and typically receive a voucher to be exchanged for tickets at the box office on the night of the performance. Ticket agencies provided the final choice, as these firms were registered with the city and typically granted a direct allotment of seats by the theaters. The agencies commonly worked out of hotels and were permitted by New York law to add an additional $1.50 fee per ticket for their efforts.

During this juncture Michael Myerberg, owner of the Brooks Atkinson Theater, estimated, "I allocate twenty-five percent of my tickets to brokers, twenty-five percent to mail orders. The rest are sold over the window. The brokers get the tickets two weeks in advance. The tickets that don't sell are returned to the box office by seven o'clock on the night of the performance and sold over the window."

The problem for would-be theatergoers, particularly when it came to high-profile events, was that the best seats commonly found their way into the hands of "sidewalk men" profiteering just outside the premises (sometimes just steps away from the box office) and into the mitts of "speculators," often working in the back rooms of the registered agencies, who flaunted their disregard for the $1.50 statutory limit.

In 1964 Hal Prince and David Merrick had become so frustrated with the brokers' inflated prices that they decided to send a message by briefly eliminating the middlemen. Sensing strong demand prior to the openings of *Hello, Dolly!* and *Fiddler on the Roof*, the pair terminated their sanctioned broker allotments, focusing exclusively on mail-order and box office sales. Eventually, however, with pressure brought to bear by their business partners, minimal allocations were restored to maintain a steady flow of sales from these additional points of purchase.

Ticket scalping, however, was by no means a recent phenomenon, as it plagued Charles Dickens during his second tour of America in 1867–68. The author's manager, George Dolby, estimated that just before the Boston box office opened in November, "by eight o'clock in the morning, the queue was nearly half a mile long and about that time the employers of the persons who had been standing in the streets all night began to arrive and take their places." A frenzy soon ensued, leading contemporaries to decry "the horrid speculators who buy all the good tickets and sell them again at exorbitant prices." Dickens himself responded in a letter to his sister-in-law: "We are at wits' end how to keep tickets out of the hands of speculators. . . . The young under-graduates of Cambridge have made a representation to Longfellow that they are five hundred strong and cannot get one ticket. I don't know what is to be done, but I suppose I must read there, somehow." When tickets went on sale in New York, Dickens reported that "speculators went up and down offering twenty dollars for any body's place. The money was in no case accepted. But one man sold two tickets for the second, third and fourth nights; his payment in exchange being one ticket for the first night; fifty dollars and a 'brandy cock-tail.'"

This matter was of particular concern to Dickens, not only because he wanted to satisfy everyone's interest, but also because frustration led to intimations that he was in league with the resellers. "We cannot beat the speculators in our tickets. We sell no more than six to any one person for the course of four readings; but these speculators who sell at greatly increased prices and make large profits will employ any number of men to buy. One of the chief of them — now living in this house, in order that he may move as we move! — can put on fifty people in any place we go to; and thus he gets three hundred tickets into his own hands."

Yet Dickens was not the first to find himself traveling with ticket scalpers. His predicament echoed the events of 1851, when the "Swedish Nightingale," singer Jenny Lind, toured the United States. An article entitled "The Jenny Lind Fracas" outlined a combustible situation in Hartford, Connecticut. "It appeared very evident, as early as Friday afternoon, July 4th, that there was much dissatisfaction on the part of a majority of our citizens, in consequence of the tickets to the concerts getting unfairly into the hands of speculators. . . . [When tickets went on sale after a fifteen-minute delay] there was a rush for the ticket stand. It was soon discovered that a very large number of tickets for the very best seats in the house had already been disposed of; and in the course of an hour and a half every ticket in first hands was sold, and yet hundreds, perhaps thousands who wished to procure tickets, were not supplied. The next morning large painted signs were floating from four different places around the State House Square, with the words, "Jenny Lind tickets

for sale here." The regular price of the tickets was three and four dollars.
The speculators demanded four and six dollars. . . . The general belief that
[Lind's] agents and speculators were in fact bona fide partners in the swindle
— for they travel together from place to place — raised the indignation of
our citizens to an unnatural degree."

Collusion between resellers and insiders was long suspected and often
documented. A letter to the editor in the April 5, 1908 *New York Times*,
signed by Grandpa, related his attempts to attend the circus at Madison
Square Garden with his family. Upon arriving at the facility, "The box office
man smilingly informed me 'All sold out.' And at my elbow stood the bar-
gain speculator. 'Saturday afternoon, sure!' and from his well filled satchel
he produced a bunch of tickets and showed how well he was stocked. . . .
The speculator was cheek by jowl with the management, for he stood well
into the lobby, only a few feet from the box office. I suppose this condition
of affairs will endure as long as fools continue to buy tickets from speculators but there should be some pretense of protection for people like me who
can't help themselves."

Over the following decades, local, state and even national officials looked
into doing just that. In 1927 New York City resident and newly appointed
United States Attorney Charles H. Tuttle hosted hearings on the matter.
Producer Arthur Hammerstein testified to the corruption and graft of
"gougers and ticket brokers." The investigation swiftly revealed that box
office workers were funneling tickets to agents in exchange for monetary
kickbacks, with individuals often attaining $50,000 to $75,000 per year. The
prevailing "commission" at that time was a dollar per ticket for primo seats
that otherwise would be held by the box office, which led to the early closing
of the show *Yours Truly*, when brokers eventually refused to accept the $1.50
charged by the musical's George Buck, who soon came to be known on
Broadway as "Buck and a Half."

The situation hadn't changed considerably by the time of a 1949 probe initiated by John M. Murtagh, commissioner of New York City's Department
of Investigation. Two pieces of industry jargon soon captivated reporters and
entered the public parlance. The word "digger" described those individuals
who had once vexed Charles Dickens, hired by brokers to wait in line when
tickets first went on sale. "Ice" was the term for the money directed to box
office officials by the agencies to ensure a steady flow of choice tickets to
popular shows. However, other than the proliferation of such colorful language, little came of Murtagh's efforts.

The same held true for the public hearings initiated by New York Attorney
General Louis Lefkowitz in December 1963, which affirmed "the existence
of a Broadway black market in theater tickets involving millions of dollars

annually." Producer Leland Hayward indicated that the annual traffic in ice likely exceeded $10 million. Little could be definitively determined, though, because in the face of the investigation most of the parties proved tight-lipped. On December 23, for instance, twenty-five of the twenty-eight box office treasurers and staffers subpoenaed invoked their Fifth Amendment rights and refused to testify.

A July 17, 1964 *Time* magazine piece titled "Broadway: The Icemen Melteth" surveyed the landscape (and tortured a metaphor along the way): "The annual take in ice has been estimated at more than $10 million. Among major icemen, box office employees have always had the longest tongs, which goes a long way toward explaining why they have always behaved with such freezing contempt toward the wretched public that lines up to buy ice-free tickets at the wicket. Brokers testified that they regularly delivered envelopes to box offices containing checks covering the list price of tickets plus agreed amounts of extra cash, usually about $5 to $7 for an orchestra seat."

It was in this climate that representatives of Computicket and TRS approached many of the same individuals who had failed to testify for fear of self-incrimination and attempted to pitch them on an inventory control system that would usher in a new era of transparency and accountability. Most of the conversations were brief.

As one TRS employee, involved in many such abrupt exchanges, recalls: "At times it seemed like the wealthiest people in the world were the treasurers in New York City theater box offices because everything was a cash business. You walked up with your voucher thinking you were in Row F. Well, they could just swap out your seats because they got a better deal from somebody else. And there were plenty of better deals to be found."

Craig Hankenson's interest in computerized ticketing began at the San Francisco Opera in 1962 and then continued at the Saratoga Performing Arts Center in the late 1960s, where he offered his assistance to the TRS programmers as they developed a user-friendly interface for amphitheaters (Edgar Bronfman was on the SPAC Board of Directors).[12] Hankenson remembers the resistance of his colleagues then working on Broadway: "The biggest obstacle was the accounting because the system could account to the penny, and at that time the New York City box office managers were earning salaries of about $25,000 a year, but they all lived on Long Island and drove Cadillacs. There was something that was called breakage with the comp tickets, and the trick there was to sell a ticket to people and mark it as a comp on the books. Every show in Manhattan was always maxed out for allowable comps. The truth was, hardly any comps were ever distributed; the box office managers simply pocketed the cash from the selling of the comp tickets."

Both Computicket and TRS promoted their systems as a means to limit scalping. The TRS marketing brochure included a number of recommendations for future users in a section called "Unions" (the box office treasurers' union was notoriously tenacious). "Experience has shown that 'block seat allotments' that cannot be sold (accessed) by the box office and that require non-positive audit trail procedures for accounting will jeopardize the good audit procedures and even the accuracy of the box office statement. Therefore, TRS applies and recommends the general rule of 'all seats must be available to the box office machine' and thereby requires box office machines (automatic ticket printers) be installed for any seats available to the TRS 'broad network of outside selling terminals.'"

There also was a section called "Diggers" that acknowledged the challenges of inhibiting such individuals. However, the brochure emphasized, "there are probably more positive factors working against the 'digger' with the TRS system than under the preprinted ticket system of today. . . . To begin with, the remote selling machines will not be able to sell more than eight tickets per transaction (larger quantities required by the buyer are directed to the box office or to the mail order). Secondly, the number of seats assigned to a particular area may be limited by the box office in cases where the 'digger' has potential (the hit show). Thirdly, the TRS system will increase advance sales if management directs an increase in advance sales inventory, and in this way, the 'digger,' or his benefactor, must risk capital for much longer periods of time."

Ultimately, as they canvassed Broadway producers and theater owners, the Computicket and TRS representatives discovered that few prospective clients were inclined to disrupt the status quo. A symbiotic relationship existed whereby even if the treasurers benefited from a second source of income that they kept *entirely* to themselves (a big if), the treasurers' efforts still often resulted in a steady stream of ticket sales. Larry Littwin likens it to "the bartender in partnership with the owner of the bar. If the bartender can find a way to make the bottle go further, if it's supposed to have twenty drinks and he gets twenty-two out of it, then the money from the last two goes into his pocket."

TRS was able to secure a limited number of contracts with Manhattan playhouses. However, these were smaller theaters and off-Broadway auditoriums hoping to benefit from marketing opportunities. Even when TRS systems were installed in the larger houses, the initial allocations numbered in the dozens, not the hundreds, as the box offices opted to retain control of most inventory.

Computicket, by contrast, scrambled to find one way to penetrate the Broadway market when it announced a partnership with the largest ticket agency in the city. Tyson-Sullivan branches were located in hotels (including the Plaza, the Waldorf-Astoria and the St. Regis). In this setting Computicket raised its service charge to the maximum legal allowance of $1.50. Paul Dano, president of Tyson-Sullivan, explained that his interest in working with Computicket was expanding his reach to "outlying areas of greater New York and elsewhere."

TRS and Computicket increasingly directed their energies toward signing larger venues and professional sports franchises. The two competitors made particularly aggressive appeals to baseball teams, which had up to then printed their entire season's worth of tickets in advance and held the seats for all eighty-one games in massive racks. While both companies emphasized that baseball clubs could save $50,000 in printing costs, the teams were reluctant to commit. The Montreal Expos were the first Canadian adopters of the TRS system, but not so coincidentally, the team was owned by Charles Bronfman, Edgar's brother, a relationship not emphasized in the press release. Some teams expressed doubt regarding the computerized services' ability to handle both single game ticketing and season ticket packages. Other clubs saw the opportunity to make the most of the competition between the two businesses, and in Los Angeles, where TRS hoped to issue a knockout blow, Jack Quinn groaned, "Walter O'Malley of the Dodgers is asking for an arm and a leg." (TRS would eventually provide the donation and win the contract.) Meanwhile, the Philadelphia Spectrum, the Anaheim Convention Center and the Long Beach Arena hedged their bets with a course of action that proved satisfying to neither suitor: they directed small portions of inventory to each of the systems.

By the summer of 1969 the pressure to turn a profit ultimately led to a change in ownership at TRS. Ever since the company had launched, its founder had faced detractors who raised an issue echoed by the *New York Times*: "As Edgar M. Bronfman, president of Joseph E. Seagram Sons, the nation's largest distiller, makes headlines with his incursion into other fields, some people have been asking, 'Who's running the store at Seagram's?'" In August Bronfman opted to lighten his load, selling Control Data a fifty-one percent interest in TRS for $6.9 million — not a shabby sum for a company that as per CDC's own calculations had a negative net worth of $3.9 million.

Following the purchase Ticket Reservations Systems was no more. Given the nature of its own business operations, Control Data decided to emphasize the computer connection. Another CDC acquisition from this era was the American Research Bureau, which the parent company then renamed after one of ARB's services, Arbitron. So much as the Computer Sciences Corporation had once done, Control Data opted to build on a sense of familiarity in rebranding — TRS was now Ticketron.

The following months saw additional upheaval. Control Data sought to interest bankers in a Ticketron public stock offering but was told that until the company "could produce a positive cash flow and demonstrate a capability for steady growth in revenues and earnings, the automated ticketing concept itself was in question." Under Control Data's watch, Ticketron cut back expenses by moving into significantly less glitzy offices. Nevertheless, in late December 1969 the *Chicago Tribune* reported on "the red ink flowing over the new company's books." Finally, in late March 1970 Ticketron decided to reduce its workforce considerably, eliminating more than half of its marketing positions and many of its technical ones, with a shared understanding by the senior staff that the future of the company was in jeopardy. These personnel moves were to be announced the first full week of April.

However, after a few years as an also-ran, Computicket finally achieved a first.

On Friday, April 3, 1970, the Computer Sciences Corporation announced that its ticketing enterprise would be the first one to fold. Computicket's remote terminals had been operational for a little more than eighteen months, yet it had burned through $12.7 million. Nick Mayo had come to the conclusion that the bout with Ticketron had taken its toll and that another $10–$12 million would be required before reaching the potential for profit. So he had summoned the CSC executives and explained, "This is just not what I had anticipated. Given the current state, you won't see a profit in three years. It'll be more like five at the earliest, and even then it'll be difficult."

Today Faye Mayo says, laughing, "He was always very good at talking himself out of great jobs. He did it several times in his life. He was so honorable that he wouldn't keep taking a paycheck."[13]

Although Computicket shut its doors in 1970, its tangible legacy endures. In early 1969 Percy Tucker, who had founded South Africa's Show Service hard ticketing bureau, flew to America to examine the potential for moving his inventory online. He found himself particularly taken with the Computicket system after Mayo "convinced me that it was by far the most sophisticated . . . and could quite easily be adapted to South African requirements." Tucker and his investors purchased the software along with a 360/50 and Computicket remains active in South Africa to the present day.

As for Ticketron, over the weekend of April 4 and 5, 1970, its employees were given a reprieve. The company was small enough that most everyone knew of the impending dismissals to be handed down on Monday. After details of the CSC's decision to scrap Computicket filtered in on Friday evening, Ticketron executives made a flurry of phone calls that weekend sharing news of the demise, now sanguine about the future.

This optimism proved short-lived. Even without the competitive pressures from Computicket, communication costs remained high, service fees low and ticket inventory inadequate. By September 1, 1970, Ticketron had borrowed $16.6 million against a line of credit (with $12.2 million guaranteed by Control Data and $4.4 million by Cemp). Ultimately, Control Data decided that a change in leadership was needed, and Jack Quinn was asked to resign.[14] Quinn's successor, Ted Helweg, would be on the job for a month when he called Control Data Vice President Bob Price to inform him, "The only way I can have Ticketron lose less money is to walk down the street and, every time I see somebody trying to use one of our terminals, hit him over the head with a two by four, because every time we sell a ticket, we lose money."

The company closed its Chicago center, consolidating the region with its computers back east. In early 1973, despite Ticketron's reporting an annual loss that exceeded $5 million, the parent company decided to stay the course and quietly attained full ownership, exchanging nearly $6 million of its own stock for all outstanding Ticketron shares. The Bronfmans were out.

Still, despite mounting debts and record losses, Ticketron could take cold comfort in the fact that it had the market to itself.

This wouldn't last long.

DOROTHY MCLAUGHLIN COULDN'T BEAR TO look.

As she approached the front gates of Sun Devil Stadium, she tugged on her husband Mike's arm.

"I can't go in there."

McLaughlin was not anxious about the fate of the Arizona State football team, which was set to take the field for its home opener on that Saturday, September 23, 1972. The ASU squad was fresh off a top ten season under longtime coach Frank Kush and led by future All-Americans (and NFL stars) Danny White and Mike Haynes. Yet McLaughlin, a steady Sun Devils booster, couldn't even wrap her head around the challenge posed by the opposing Kansas State Wildcats. Instead she fixated on what might occur a few yards beyond the field.

"We've double-sold every seat. I'm sure of it."

McLaughlin's husband wrapped his arm around her waist, gave her an affectionate squeeze and steered her toward the turnstiles.

"Everything will be fine. We're going to go in and we're going to sit down."

Perched well above the fifty yard line, Dorothy McLaughlin relied on her binoculars. But rather than directing her attention to the field, where the Sun Devils drubbed the Wildcats 56 to 14, McLaughlin spent the entire game focused on the aisles. There, the woman who had written the software that supplied tickets for everyone in attendance discovered she'd had a winning day as well.

Sun Devil Stadium was a fitting setting for the debut of Select-A-Seat, the company McLaughlin had founded with her sister Margie Bliss and brother-in-law, Bill Bliss. A year earlier the three had hatched their plans while attending a minor league football game. Bill, an electrical engineer, was then facing the prospect of a cross-country move mandated by his boss at Hewlett Packard. As the family lamented the potential relocation to Vermont, they began discussing alternative employment options, at first fancifully and then with animated vigor. The tenor of the conversation shifted after Margie Bliss contributed her perspective from the box office of the Arizona Veterans Memorial Coliseum. The team of three (McLaughlin's husband remained supportive from the sidelines) swiftly became convinced that they had the complementary skill sets needed to make a push into the realm of computerized ticketing.

McLaughlin remembers: "We were sitting at the game just talking about what the three of us could do together. And when computerized ticketing came up, we all got really excited. My sister had ticketing knowledge. Bill knew about screens and felt we could probably get a printer. I knew about the programming. I remember sitting there saying to Bill, 'You know, we could put a map on the screen so that people could actually see what seat they wanted to sit in.' He said, 'Can we do that?' I said, 'Sure we can.' So the basic concept of picking your own seat came from the very first discussion we had that night, which is why our company was called Select-A-Seat."

The new entity adopted a technical approach that varied from its predecessors on a number of levels, perhaps none more so than in the staffing of its programming department. Whereas Ticketron and Computicket had relied on teams of software engineers working on pricey machines from corporate confines, Select-A-Seat rested its hopes on a lone woman sitting in her living room at night, dialing in to a timeshare computer via a Teletype. Moreover, while the Ticketron and Computicket staffers programmed in a "low-level" language utilizing commands similar to their machines' internal code, Dorothy McLaughlin wrote the Select-A-Seat software in BASIC, the same introductory computer language taught to high school freshmen.

McLaughlin, a pioneer in computerized ticketing who would soon one-up Ticketron by delivering viable season ticketing software, had only two years' experience as a programmer when she created the Select-A-Seat system. She hadn't even seen a computer until 1969, when happenstance led the former junior high math teacher to General Electric's process control division.

In the fall of 1968 the twenty-six-year-old McLaughlin and her husband, a fellow educator, had committed to a two-year stint at a government school in Guam. The couple took the opportunity "because we could get a trip around the world on the second year for dirt cheap, and we really wanted to travel." However, a few months after arriving on the island, their son took ill, necessitating a return to the U.S. mainland.

"So we came back in October, and I didn't want to start teaching in the middle of a semester. I had done that before and had gotten bad classes. One day in a grocery store I met a friend of mine I had gone to school with, who was working as a programmer at General Electric. He asked me what I was going to do. I told him I wasn't sure, and he said, 'You would really be a good programmer. You need to go to GE and apply for a job.' I said, 'That's ridiculous but I will.'

"So I went to General Electric and about two and a half minutes into the interview the guy said, 'Do you know anything about computers?' I told him I didn't, and he said, 'Why are you here?' And I explained that my friend Bob, who I knew he knew, thought I would be a good programmer. Then he said, 'There's no point in interviewing you. Do you want to go see a computer?' So he took me down, showed me a computer, gave me an aptitude test, and about a month later I was hired.

"Now they were talking to somebody who had never even seen a computer before. But basically what they did was to put you with a really good programmer who knew what he was doing, and then you would find out the hard way what programming was all about. I never took a course because they didn't have any classes. It was all on-the-job training. The programs I wrote went to an oil refinery, and they were data-linking IBM computers with GE computers. There were about fifty-nine other programmers in the room and only one other woman."

By January 1972 she had become the lone individual responsible for the Select-A-Seat software. Bill Bliss had been able to raise some initial funding and soon gave notice to his employer. Margie Bliss remained in her position to maintain a handle on the ticketing business (along with a steady paycheck). A few weeks of intense late nights on the Teletype after tucking her children into bed led McLaughlin to determine that she would need to commit to the project full-time, so she resigned from GE.

McLaughlin's approach was informed by her sister's bias: despite sharing an ownership stake in the computerized ticketing company, Margie Bliss was not particularly fond of computers. In an effort to anticipate resistance from Margie's box office colleagues, McLaughlin sought to monitor some real-time transactions in order to draft a program tailored closely to the practical needs of box office personnel — "what they really did, not what they were *supposed* to do." Bill approached the Phoenix Suns and the Arizona State University Athletic Department, asking permission for McLaughlin to observe their behavior. The two organizations agreed (after meeting with each other to confirm their mutual assent), granting her the access so that she could develop a program that, she remembers, "really tried to be user-friendly. It sounds like an old term now, but it wasn't then. We wanted something that a ticketing person could put their arms around and know right away."

Since McLaughlin's knowledge base developed from two settings that relied heavily on season ticketing, Select-A-Seat successfully grappled with a challenge that Ticketron could never quite lick in offering standard software applicable both to individual seat sales and season ticket packages. Nearly forty years later and two decades retired from the business, McLaughlin can still rattle off its features: "Our season ticketing programs kept track of names and addresses, but you could also put in a seat location and it would come back and tell you who was in that seat. It did receipts, billings, mailing labels, alphabetical listings, holding, unholding, assigning, unassigning. We had programs for people who buy season tickets late or change their season tickets. And between the single events, it kept all the auditing straight, so when you ran a report, you knew how many season tickets you sold, how many single seats you sold and all the dollar values for that."

What makes McLaughlin's achievement all the more remarkable is that she developed her software via a dial-up modem using the simplest of all programming languages, the Beginner's All-purpose Symbolic Instruction Code, BASIC.[1]

McLaughlin acknowledges: "Everybody laughs when we say we wrote the system in BASIC, but I think at that time it was probably the very best thing we could do because I could write programs fairly quickly, it had a really good debug capability and we could be online as soon as I finished. I mean I could turn out some programs in thirty minutes and have them available right away."

Ticketron architect Harvey Dubner remains incredulous on the topic of developing such a ticketing system in BASIC. "You couldn't do it. BASIC is a slow language. I wouldn't even use Fortran for the communication system. A higher level language is based on the fact that it's taking over the computer for a given period of time, and there would be too many things going on at once. It had to be designed, not sewn together. You can't do real-time stuff in BASIC, handling too many terminals simultaneously while printing a different number of tickets. The system is going to stop doing what it's doing and you'll have to start it up again. The question is how many terminals was she handling at once and how do you handle a thousand?"

Indeed this was the point. Select-A-Seat didn't aspire to store a nation's worth of ticket inventory. Instead the company pursued a localized approach, intending to sell systems that would serve a particular venue or municipality. Early on Bill Bliss contracted with Tom Poulter, himself a recent émigré from Hewlett Packard, to supply the Select-A-Seat hardware. Poulter's company, Basic Timesharing Inc., provided a modified HP minicomputer tailored to local communication. Rather than create a network of branded ticket outlets, once its Arizona operations were up and running, Select-A-Seat's goal was to install systems and provide support without requiring clients to use the Select-A-Seat name.

Of course this was all predicated on securing end users. In the early spring of 1972 Select-A-Seat welcomed the Arizona State University Athletic Department to its corporate offices for the first official demo of its fledgling system. At the time the Select-A-Seat corporate offices occupied the Bliss family dining room, and this modest base of operations reflected the company's direct, folksy approach. Besides, McLaughlin explains, "We never thought they'd go for it, but we figured they would be ideal to demonstrate the system to because we'd get a lot of really good feedback."

As it turned out, the feedback exceeded expectations. The demo itself proved quite successful, other than a slight gaffe caused by a misaligned printer that spat tickets all over the floor.

Despite the airborne ducats, ASU athletic department ticket manager Terry Wojtulewicz was sold. He recognized what Select-A-Seat could offer his box office. "It was evident that they could serve our needs," he says. "At the time we had a very large number of season ticket accounts. The football team was doing quite well, and the season ticket portion was pretty labor-intensive and prone to errors because of the manual ways things were being done. At the same time we had locations that sold tickets for us and we would bundle up tickets every week and take them out. Then on Saturday morning prior to the game, we had a guy who drove around, picked up the ones that didn't sell and dropped off the next week's tickets."

Select-A-Seat had secured its first client.[2]

Following ASU's commitment, the company achieved a new momentum. Bob Machen, the business manager of the Phoenix Suns, was equally impressed with McLaughlin and her system. "Ticketron, they had a lot of very smart computer programmers, but Dorothy did this by herself and did a better job. She could think through the whole process as well as anybody I've ever been around in my life."

Machen brought it to his boss, Jerry Colangelo. The team's general manager sat behind his desk and remained impassive while Machen made the case for aligning with the start-up. After Machen wrapped up his pitch, Colangelo paused and then leaned forward and asked, "How strongly do you believe in it?"

"I believe in it a lot."

"Now, Bob, you can do it, it's your decision, but it'll probably cost you your job if it doesn't work out. So do you still want to do it?"

"I do."

Machen held onto his job, although he acknowledges: "The ticket printers didn't always work the way you wanted. You needed to load the machine precisely with everything lined up, in order to have the ticket spit out into the tray." Still, he speaks with deep affection of his time working with McLaughlin: "She was a super lady and just so calm and cool."

After the Suns, Select-A-Seat signed contracts with the Western Hockey League's Phoenix Roadrunners and the Phoenix International Raceway. Margie Bliss then left her position at the Arizona Veteran Memorial Coliseum to join her husband and sister on a full-time basis as business manager. Select-A-Seat also locked in an outlet network via Hanny's, a local department store focusing on menswear. Starting in the fall of 1972, tickets to all available events would be offered at Hanny's with a service charge of a quarter, fifteen cents of which would be retained by the outlet.

Given the limited geographical ambit, Select-A-Seat was able to provide its outlets with a more full-featured system. At a time when Ticketron still wasn't providing cathode ray tube monitors to its customers, Select-A-Seat offered monitors capable of displaying rows of seats with codes to identify availability. In keeping with the founders' original vision (and the company's name), ticket buyers were given the ability to identify their own seat locations. Paper maps were placed on the counter as aids, while a "quick sell" option was available to make suggestions akin to Ticketron's "best available." The system also permitted patrons to name their preferred section and row, which would then be displayed on the screen. One downside of all this customer choice was extended transaction times. In the days following the system's debut at Hanny's, dozens regularly queued up, some of whom merely wished to experience an interaction with the computer, while McLaughlin worked to improve sluggishness on the technical response side.

Dorothy McLaughlin's last-minute jitters aside, Select-A-Seat's first event went off with minimal hitches on that September day in Sun Devil Stadium. Aside from the single instance of double-seating later attributed to box office error, one small hiccup had occurred a few hours before kickoff: "They had sold all their seats, and Terry called me to say, 'Dorothy, I've got to have some standing room only seats.' Now you have to understand I didn't know ticketing. I didn't know what standing room only was, and I thought I could make it a general admission section. I did that, but I didn't have any programs to add sections onto events while they were being sold. Well, I did it anyway, and I destroyed the auto report for his first football game. When I realized what was happening, we had to stop selling tickets because it ruined the file. I was in tears, and I called Terry and said, 'I just ruined your auto report. We can't sell any more tickets.' And you know what he told me? 'That's okay, Dorothy. We've sold enough tickets anyway.' So he didn't get upset, and we got through that first game."

As Select-A-Seat moved forward, it soon shared common ground with both Computicket and Ticketron in coming to recognize the challenges of maintaining a significant revenue stream with minimal service charges. "We decided that if the box offices didn't want to charge the customer a big service fee, then they were going to have to give us some money," McLaughlin explains. "So we'd charge them for the storage of season ticket holders' names and addresses. We charged them setup fees for their events, based on the total number of seats. We charged them for their terminals. We charged them for the paper stock they used. Nowadays, you might say we nickel-and-dimed them to death, but we didn't, and that gave us stable monthly income, even if we never sold tickets at an outlet."

Within a few years the struggle to stay afloat, while simultaneously pushing into new markets with attendant hardware costs, yielded an improbable new parent firm. The Arizona Cattle Company, eager to move into a new business realm, acquired the majority stake in Select-A-Seat, while contracting with the principals to remain on board. This curious turn of events was the culmination of a three-year run in which Select-A-Seat moved forward much quicker than anticipated with new rollouts, along with some crippling setbacks.

Originally, Bill Bliss's plan had been to operate for three years in Phoenix before expanding into additional markets. However, in mid-1973 a new opportunity presented itself. The Omni Coliseum, then the largest arena in the Southeast, had opened a year earlier in Atlanta and signed on as a Ticketron client. However, during a period of internal upheaval, a trio of Ticketron staffers contemplated striking off on their own, feeling that given the right set of circumstances, they could make inroads. This group, which included Peter Schniedermeier (who had moved with TRS/Ticketron from Chicago to Los Angeles and then finally to New York), learned of Select-A-Seat. Schniedermeier and his colleagues flew to Arizona for a meeting with Bliss and came away impressed.

Schniedermeier acknowledges: "The three of us conspired behind the scenes at Ticketron and said, 'We can do better.' So we flew down to see Select-A-Seat and thought it was really cool. They were using Teletype input, no freaking punch cards. We formed a partnership with them and then approached the folks we knew out of Atlanta who owned the Omni and had the Hawks and the Flames. We said, 'Why don't you guys open your own ticketing system?' Then we showed them the system we had in Phoenix and they decided to do it. We ended up leaving Ticketron, replicating the system and putting it into the Omni."

So despite his initial intent to strike a more methodical pace, Bill Bliss agreed to sell the rights to the Select-A-Seat software, which was rebranded as SEATS (Southeastern Advance Ticketing Service). This installation proved successful and was followed by system sales in Norfolk, Denver, San Diego, Chicago, Kansas City, Seattle, St. Louis and Minneapolis.[3] An arrangement with the Montgomery Ward Auto Club also led Select-A-Seat to handle all of the U.S. ticketing fulfillment for the 1976 Montreal Olympics.

However, in the midst of all this activity, Select-A-Seat felt obligated to levy legal charges against a competitor. In early 1974 the company discovered via phone logs that someone had used Basic Timesharing Inc.'s password, called into the Omni and copied the software. (At that time McLaughlin phoned in at night and made any requisite changes to the various systems while they were backed up.) Soon afterward Select-A-Seat found itself on the outs in both Denver (although the company would be called back in for a reinstallation a few months later) and Chicago (a somewhat dubious situation, in which the client, who had run into financial hardship, claimed that the hardware did not perform properly and seized it until Select-A-Seat pursued legal remedies and the equipment was returned). What then became clear to the Select-A-Seat team was that, particularly given the hazy state of intellectual property rights as applied to computer programming, unscrupulous entrepreneurs had taken an active interest in appropriating the Select-A-Seat system.

This all reached a boiling point when Dorothy McLaughlin attended the annual convention of the International Association of Assembly Managers (IAAM). There she strolled past the booth of a new company that was demoing its system. McLaughlin gave the computer screen a quick glance and immediately circled back for a second look. She gaped at what appeared to be a mirror image of the Select-A-Seat program. Waiting until the booth was unoccupied, McLaughlin hustled over and began typing in control characters to see how the system would respond. She swiftly became infuriated, convinced that the similarities were no coincidence: Bay Area Seating Service was running her stolen software.

IT MIGHT BE FACILE TO describe Jerry Seltzer and Hal Silen as the Odd Couple, but they sure as heck were an *odd* couple. Not in the romantic sense, although San Francisco was their base of operations and their personal and professional relationship spanned marriages and business endeavors.

Silen describes their partnership with a dollop of good-natured self-effacement: "Jerry is the visionary, the idea man. I've often laughingly said that Jerry will come up with about 100 ideas in a day, and about eight of them are good. But he's thinking all the time and he's doing things. Our arrangement was he'd run ideas by me and we'd talk about them and he'd look at them a little more carefully, and then he'd just pull the trigger and go ahead."

The two met in 1959, two years after Silen had graduated from the University of California's Hastings College of the Law. Then working in a small San Francisco practice, Silen was engaged by Seltzer to assist with some corporate filings (the attorney was selected as much for his modest fee as his steady, earnest approach). Seltzer, who had landed on the West Coast relatively recently after completing studies at Northwestern, was looking to register a new entity under the unassuming name of Bay Promotions. After Silen completed the paperwork, it was official: the modern Roller Derby had been incorporated.

Jerry Seltzer was legacy. In 1933 Jerry Seltzer's father, Leo, who then owned three movie theaters in Portland, Oregon, moved his infant son and family to Chicago. There, in the midst of the Great Depression, he filled local venues with the stunt events of the day, including walkathons and ice sitting contests. Two years later, after reading a *Literary Digest* article that indicated ninety-three percent of Americans had roller-skated at some point in their lives, Leo Seltzer developed a new marathon competition.[4]

More than 20,000 spectators made their way to the Chicago Coliseum on August 13, 1935, to witness the debut of Leo Seltzer's Transcontinental Roller Derby. As originally envisioned, teams of skaters circled the track, seeking to complete 57,000 laps, which roughly corresponded to the distance between San Diego and New York. A map of the United States served as the scoreboard, with lights marking each team's progress. Following his local success, Seltzer brought the Derby on tour, where three years later in Miami, sportswriter Damon Runyon permanently altered the nature of the competition. After he observed some blocking, shoving and escalating physical exchanges among the players, Runyon suggested, "You know, Seltzer, you ought to incorporate that into the game." Leo took his advice and the Derby entered national consciousness. By the early 1950s Roller Derby enjoyed a three-year ABC television contract, a collection of sponsors (perhaps not so surprisingly, Blatz beer was at the fore) and even a Mickey Rooney film with a Derby setting (1950's *The Fireballer*, whose posters exclaimed "Rooney runs riot on the roller race ways!").

However, the Roller Derby that Jerry Seltzer inherited was moribund. Despite drawing 82,000 fans to Madison Square Garden for a five-day championship in 1951, eight years later Leo contemplated shutting it all down. ABC had oversaturated the airwaves with Derby programming, and no network proved willing to pick it up after the contract lapsed. (CBS, "The Tiffany Network," turned its nose at the "pulchritude and pugnacity.") The game had lost its allure, and a West Coast relocation did little to revive interest. Roller Derby remained on life support until Leo transitioned operations over to his newly married son, who had returned from the Korean War and joined the venture, initially in sales at the in-house Roller Derby Skate Company.

As it turned out, Jerry Seltzer was a born promoter. Leo's boy helped usher in a Roller Derby renaissance. (The name of the sport, incidentally, is properly capitalized, and Jerry took the time to write letters of correction whenever he saw it published otherwise.) One of the significant changes he instituted was a modification to the revenue model. Rather than relying on television licensing fees, he used the medium to stimulate ticket sales. Seltzer ultimately syndicated the Derby to more than 100 stations for little or no money. While ABC had once paid $5,000 per week, Jerry now asked for a $100 licensing fee per one-hour program. He then used that exposure to support live appearances, in many cases offering the program for free in exchange for a few minutes of air time to hype upcoming tour stops. Frank Deford, who wrote a 1969 *Sports Illustrated* article on the Derby that he later expanded into a book, *Five Strides on the Banked Track*, characterized the profit structure as "upside down. . . . It is constructed, in fact, like a pyramid balancing on its point." Seltzer also often routed his tours based on interest gauged from fan correspondence in conjunction with local air times. This resulted in a typical tour itinerary with the following order of stops: Providence, Boston, Worcester, New Haven, Dayton, Canton, Steubenville, Cleveland, Chicago, Richmond, Norfolk, Greenville, St. Louis, Peoria, Moline, Dayton, Hammond, Boston, Worcester, Providence and on around one more time. This approach led Deford to observe: "Obviously the order of the trip makes no sense whatsoever. It winds, goes back and forth, up and down, here and there and doubles back again, thirteen cars and a semi-trailer in search of an arena." However skewed it might have been from a geographic perspective, it all made perfect business sense to Seltzer, whose instincts proved true, as the crowds swelled, ultimately peaking on September 15, 1972, when 50,118 fans turned out at Chicago's Comiskey Park.

Since he controlled the entire league, as opposed to owning a single franchise, Seltzer had the freedom to tinker as he saw fit. To satisfy demand after the Bay Bombers became the marquee team, he split the roster into two squads, the Oakland Bay Bombers and the San Francisco Bay Bombers, each featuring an equal share of star players, thereby allowing him to secure twice the bookings. Prior to then, he routinely "relocated" teams — which in practice simply meant renaming them — so that when the Derby came to town, one group of skaters would don the jerseys of the host city while the other would be identified as a rival metropolis (and these designations might well be reversed at the next tour stop).[5]

Meanwhile, back in Seltzer's hometown, he did what he could to antagonize his own local adversary, Oakland A's owner Charlie Finley. Seltzer had lost out on his ownership bid for the NHL's Oakland Seals to Finley, at least in part, because baseball was deemed to be more respectable than the Derby. (Seltzer remembers that one of the owners fell asleep during his presentation to the league. "That by itself did not worry me. . . . But I knew we were in trouble when no one bothered to wake him up.") So Jerry took particular joy, for instance, in countering Finley's "Farmers' Night" at the ballpark by hosting a competing "Farmers' Daughter Night" and drawing a larger crowd. When asked whether the Roller Derby would be held in higher esteem if it were more like baseball, Seltzer responded, "That's definitely true but hard as I try, I can't convince our skaters to chew tobacco and scratch themselves." After the Derby moved into the Coliseum on July 4 for successive Bay Bomber Bombastic events, drawing more than 28,000 fans in 1970 and nearly 35,000 in 1971, Jerry derided what he perceived as Finley's need to lure spectators with freebies, by describing the 1970 Derby crowd as "the largest one at the Coliseum this year when something was not given away."

Ultimately, however, for Seltzer and the Roller Derby, it became a case of live by the tour, die by the tour. Despite great success in terms of gate receipts, expenses continued to rise, and one could never be sure what the next season might bring. The Oil Crisis of 1973 proved the league's ultimate undoing. Seltzer recalls: "Gas prices weren't the factor so much as there was no gasoline. You'd get up early in the morning and go to a gas station and stand in line, and arenas were shutting down in winter and people weren't willing to travel to games. What had always been so successful for us had been our Eastern and Midwestern road trips, which we started in September, but that year it was dark and we basically ran out of money." In the face of such hardship, on December 7, 1973, Seltzer issued a seemingly sudden statement that had been in the works for some time, explaining that as of the next day, "Roller Derby as we know it will cease to exist."

Hal Silen, who had been in-house counsel for a few years, helped pay off the creditors and returned to his general law practice in Marin County. However, Seltzer recalls, "the arena world was a very small one," which resulted in a business proposition that led him to computerized ticketing: "Atlanta had opened an independent ticket system, and whereas Control Data had a computer that could land somebody on the moon, this was a small stand-alone system. I was approached by a guy in Chicago who had gone bankrupt and offered us the HP system that had been used in Atlanta."

Seltzer contacted Silen, who agreed that there seemed to be an opportunity. But after the Derby closed, the two had vowed never to rely solely on their own resources. So Silen began to raise funds: "I got our insurance agent, our accountants, my then-wife's OB/GYN . . . My mother-in-law at that time became a pretty big investor. I also went to a number of law clients who I knew had invested in crazy operations. They liked me and I liked them, so they went along with it." By the summer of 1974 the pair had the money in place to commence operations as the Bay Area Seating Service with Hal as president and Jerry as chairman of the board.

Given Dorothy McLaughlin's strident belief based on her observation at the IAAM convention that the BASS system was purloined, the provenance of its initial software does appear somewhat suspect. Indeed, Seltzer acknowledges, "By the time the guy shows up with the software package on tape, I had heard rumors that it had been stolen." So to make sure that things were on the up and up, Seltzer went outside the company and approached one of the attorneys representing a potential BASS client, asking him to hold onto the tape. The lawyer agreed but added, "Just remember, you're supposed to be operating within the next eight weeks.'"

While scrambling to find a solution, someone suggested that perhaps they could hire a programmer to create new software. It seemed like a near impossible task given the time constraints; however, this hypothetical computing whiz would have some help. Peter Schniedermeier now joined the BASS team along with Dan Deboer, who would work in computerized ticketing for the decades to follow. The two were available to describe the basic functions of the system, including the interactions between the minicomputer, terminal and ticket printer.

A young attorney employed in the office that was storing the software tape suggested that Hal and Jerry contact a former college classmate of his, Bruce Baumgart, who was then completing his computer science Ph.D. at Stanford. Baumgart's résumé was devoid of any ticketing experience, and his Stanford studies were in artificial intelligence, a field altogether unrelated to the project at hand. However, the BASS founders were swayed by Baumgart's Harvard undergraduate degree and the stellar reputation of Stanford's AI program. Bruce was also something of a celebrity, having appeared in *Whole Earth Catalog* founder Stewart Brand's lengthy 1972 *Rolling Stone* article about competitive computer gaming among the geniuswonks in the nation's top computer labs, entitled "Spacewar: Fanatic Life and Symbolic Death Among the Computer Bums." The piece included an image taken by Annie Leibovitz of a radiant, grinning Baumgart, his hair cascading well past his shoulders, above the caption, "Bruce Baumgart, winner of the Five-Man Free-For-All at the First Intergalactic Spacewar Olympics, brandishing control buttons in triumph."

The Spacewar champ mulled over the offer to reverse-engineer the ticketing system, considered the short-term nature of the project and took the gig. Baumgart was motivated less by the challenge than by the carrot he offered himself at its completion: he would use his paycheck to purchase a home computer. Looking back, he now believes, "People on planet Earth with home computers in 1974 numbered in a single digit. I was not the first and I was likely not the tenth or greater."

BASS had found their man. "He was a strange guy," Seltzer concedes, "but absolutely fucking brilliant. Never said hello or goodbye because it was unnecessary. Did you ever see the movie *Tron*? And what they [Select-A-Seat] could never believe is that while they worked for two years to develop their software, Bruce did it in five-and-a-half weeks."

Schniedermeier remembers: "Bruce was a young guy with a ponytail and a very kinetic energy, but he didn't want to work when anyone was around the office. So he'd show up at eleven o'clock at night and I had to change my whole routine and come in and show him how event ticketing systems worked — how strings of seats and sections and price breaks were set up. I literally laid it out on a blackboard."

Following a six week "work blitz binge," Baumgart had earned his prize: a small machine from the Digital Equipment Corporation, a PDP-1105. "My house cost $26,000; the computer to go in the house was $4,000. I sold the house decades later for upward of a million and I sold the computer for about $4,000 three years later." Baumgart, who initially had harbored no significant interest in computerized ticketing, would later write additional ticketing programs as the founder of Softix.

Now that BASS had operational software, Seltzer set his sights on the competition. As his earlier goading of Charlie Finley suggested, when Jerry identified an opponent, he did not shy away from gamesmanship ("shy" being a word long struck from the Seltzer glossary). Ticketron earned Seltzer's ire in May 1973, and the sentiment would never abate.

After drawing 50,000 to Comiskey Park the previous September, Seltzer had looked to top these numbers over Memorial Day weekend 1973. He had scheduled a triple-header "World Championship for the Gold Cup" to take place at New York's Shea Stadium on Saturday, May 26, 1973. When he contacted Ticketron on the morning of May 25, he was told that advance sales were just north of 27,000. When he followed up on the day of the event, the ticket count was exactly the same. More than a little flummoxed, he discovered that the system had been down for nearly seventy-two hours.

"Of course we were furious," he recalls with a lingering irritation. "This doesn't have to be a big secret. If you had told us this, we could have made other arrangements. We could have gotten hard tickets to Macy's or whatever. They said, 'Well, the whole Eastern Seaboard was down.' I told them, 'Well, that doesn't make me feel any better.'"

One of the lessons he would take from this incident was the recognition that BASS could distinguish itself from its much larger rival through a personalized approach. "Jerry's theory, carried out to the end," Silen explains, "was that sales and marketing were identical. The people who worked with him were always visiting the clients, making sure the clients were happy, finding out what more they wanted."

"Having been a promoter," Seltzer adds, "and realizing that people were evaluating Ticketron's service by the computer they used and not their customer service, which was nil, we started signing up everyone we could using our promotion techniques. We hired a PR person and started sending out newsletters and calendars every week to show what was playing in town. This way our clients had the perceived idea that we were trying to help them sell tickets. And they'd hear from us all the time. We had our sales people out, while most of Ticketron's clients never saw a salesperson. Our approach was: Know the clients, call on them, call on accounts that we don't have — and the good part is if we don't have them, there's no reason you can't call them again the next week because we don't have them."

The story he tells to emphasize this point involves the Harlem Globetrotters. Both Leo Seltzer and his son had a relationship with the team, as they shared information about venues and swapped dates on occasion. The Globetrotters had been a longtime Ticketron client, but heeding his own mantra, Jerry kept applying his brand of friendly pressure: "I went to Los Angeles to meet with Joe Anzivino, who I knew very well, and I told them all the things we could do. I said, 'I know how you work in each city and we can send out press releases and so forth.' Finally they said, 'You know, that sounds great.' So after they signed with us, they got a call from [Ticketron senior vice president] Bob Gorra, who started off, 'We have served you well and done well with you over the last fourteen years.' And there was a pause, and Joe said, 'I'm so glad to hear your voice. It's the first time I've heard it in fourteen years. . . .'"

Many years later this memory still elicits a boisterous, chuckle from Jerry. "You see, I come at it old school, which is 'make the customer happy.' Computerized ticketing has nothing to do with the computer. The computer is a device that you utilize. It's the company and what you decide to do with it. We had fun with it. We had T-shirts that said, 'Put your seat in our hands.' And while Ticketron had kind of a computer symbol for their company, we had Mr. BASS in a tuxedo because he was not a scary computerized figure."

With its methodology and technology in place, all the Bay Area Seating Service needed to make a go of it was a high-profile client. And this is where the Roller Derby Magnate met the Rock Impresario.

NEARLY TWO DECADES AFTER HIS death Bill Graham looms large as a mythic figure, a role he also occupied in his lifetime. Graham was the first modern rock promoter, defining and then redefining the concert experience.

A child of the Holocaust, Bill Graham was born as Wolodia Grajonca in 1931. ("Wolfgang's Vault," the name of the memorabilia website founded by Minnesota businessman William E. Sagan after he purchased the Graham archives in 2003, references the promoter's German nickname.) His father passed away shortly after Graham's birth, while his mother was killed in a Nazi concentration camp. Graham became a refugee during the war, spending time in a French orphanage before the Red Cross placed him on a ship bound for the United States. A German Jewish children's aid group then took responsibility for the ten-year-old until a foster family in the Bronx agreed to raise the boy (he anglicized his name in 1949, later explaining that he picked Graham out of a phonebook because it was close in spelling to Grajonca).

Graham served in the Korean War and then as a Catskills maître d' before relocating to the Bay Area in the early 1960s. There the aspiring actor quit his "straight job" as a regional office manager for Allis-Chalmers (a manufacturer best known for its tractors) and took on the role of business manager with the radical San Francisco Mime Troupe. In late 1965, after members of the troupe were arrested and later convicted for performing without a park permit, Graham staged a benefit to defray legal costs. The response to the sold-out event, which included a set from Jefferson Airplane (a group Graham would soon manage), proved eye-opening. A follow-up took place a month later in a larger hall located for the occasion, the Fillmore Auditorium. (*San Francisco Chronicle* columnist Ralph Gleason reported: "At 9:30 there was a double line around the block outside. Inside a most remarkable assemblage of humanity was leaping, jumping, frigging, fragging and frugging. . . . The costumes were free-form Goodwill *cum* Sherwood Forest.") An invitation soon followed for Graham to produce the Trips Festival at the Longshoreman's Hall in San Francisco, featuring Ken Kesey and the Merry Pranksters, the Grateful Dead, Big Brother and the Holding Company and an ample supply of high-grade LSD. The promoter discovered, as he later recalled in an atypically understated manner, that he "seemed to have a knack for it." There was no looking back.

Graham broke ties with the Mime Troupe, took over the Fillmore lease and began hosting "dance concerts" with live music. He blended an appreciation for the scene in all its electric hues with the organizational skills in evidence at Allis-Chalmers. The Grateful Dead's Jerry Garcia first laid eyes on Graham at the Trips Festival in the midst of "total, wall-to-wall, gonzo lunacy." There, to the guitarist's amusement, he noticed "this guy running around with a clipboard. . . . I mean in the midst of total insanity." Graham learned on the fly while moving into progressively larger clubs, eventually traversing the nation and becoming bicoastal in 1968 with the Fillmore West and Fillmore East, venues with legal capacities of 2,200 and 2,700, respectively. In the spring of 1971 he announced he was closing both Fillmores, citing burnout, his contempt for competing arena shows and an antipathy toward the increasingly corporate nature of the rock scene — a charge that now seems quaint. However, he returned to his vocation within six months, moving into many of the same facilities he had decried and sometimes on past them, as with the Days on the Green summer concert series, which he inaugurated in 1976 at the Oakland Coliseum baseball stadium.

The mercurial and complicated promoter was able to balance two oft-contradictory impulses that facilitated his success. On one hand it never escaped him that he was running a business venture, doing whatever he could to keep show costs down while maximizing revenues. Longtime lighting designer Chip Monck claims that early on Graham would tamper with the ticket count to bypass building codes and mask receipts from the artists themselves: "Bill would stand at the top of the stairs at Fillmore West with a little basket in his hand, taking tickets. But he wouldn't tear the ticket. He would just put it in the basket. Then he would rush downstairs and hand them all to the box office person and they would sell the same little ticket again."

San Francisco Examiner critic Phil Elwood, who covered the Bay Area music scene for half a century before he passed away in 2006, received a call from an agitated Graham after he reported on the overflow capacity of a Janis Joplin show at the Fillmore West. "I remember he phoned me on a Friday morning and exploded at me, saying, 'Where did you get those figures?' It was one of the few times over the years that I was on the receiving end of one of Bill's intemperate screaming phone calls, and he let me have it. It probably made him feel better to blow off steam once in a while, although it didn't make me feel any better. It was an unnerving experience to be lambasted by Bill Graham for five minutes." Elwood assumed the promoter acted that way because "he was fearful that the law-enforcement people or the fire department would consider he was overfilling the hall." It's likely that Graham didn't wish any booking agents or managers to read it, either.

Hyatt Hotel heir John Pritzker, whose family would later enter the ticketing realm with their purchase of Ticketmaster, remembers: "I went to a Grateful Dead concert at Winterland [a 5,400 capacity converted ballroom that Graham began booking in 1971] when I was about eighteen with a buddy, and we got there probably five minutes into their first set. You could hear the music outside the door. We pulled up to the corner and there was a guy with his back to us, and I rolled down the window and said, 'Excuse me, are there any tickets left?' And Bill Graham turned around. For me, it was like looking into the face of God. He said, 'How many you need?' I said, 'Two.' He said, 'Go in and talk to Sherry [Wasserman] and tell her I said you need two tickets.' And I turned to my buddy, slapped him on the arm and said, 'See that? Anybody else would have sold this thing out months ago. He holds tickets out for idiots like us.' We go to the show. . . . Literally twenty years later I'm in the shower and it occurs to me that Graham is backdooring the tickets. That's why he had two tickets for the next six hundred people. That was my first understanding of how ticketing *really works*."

However, while Graham remained focused on the bottom line, he constantly looked up from the balance sheet, viewing his efforts as a means of personal expression. He never played an instrument onstage (save perhaps when a Grateful Dead crew member dosed him with acid and he ended up on cowbell), yet his presence could be felt throughout a facility, even when he was absent. Plus, in many respects it was all a performance to him, particularly when it came to his notorious short fuse — as when, genuinely aggravated, merely posturing or yelling purely for sport, Graham could go from zero to sixty decibels in a few seconds. Pritzker adds: "Bill gave the fans more than they paid for. I would go to New Year's shows and they'd serve breakfast. Who serves breakfast? Who hands out apples? Who makes sure that there's more security, not to bust anybody, but to make sure the crowds are more comfortable? That was Graham's ethos." So whether it was the barrel of apples that greeted concertgoers with the note "Take One or Two," the stylized event posters offered free to attendees, the balloons and volleyball nets provided to occupy early arrivals or the familiar soothing tones of "Greensleeves" that serenaded departing concertgoers, a Bill Graham production was an event.

Graham also prided himself on the creativity of his concert bills, later musing wistfully on the days when "we were able to put on Howlin' Wolf with Janis Joplin or two one-act plays by Leroi Jones at a Byrds concert at the Fillmore. To see the faces of Grateful Dead fans listening to Miles Davis; to watch a roomful of really hyper Who fans being blown away by Woody Herman. Turning the houselights on with Aretha Franklin and Ray Charles and the King Curtis band, and the band went into twenty minutes of laying down this incredible beat, and Aretha and Ray both stopped playing and singing, and Aretha just held Ray's arm, and the two of them rocked back and forth on stage. That was pretty much nirvana."

Meanwhile the major booking agencies were still coming to grips with rock music. Initially the old guard believed that it was all a fad and devoted minimal resources, if any, to the genre. This left the field wide open for pioneers such as Frank Barsalona, who left the General Artists Corporation, where he had started in the mail room, to form Premier Talent in 1964. Within a few years Barsalona's booking roster included Led Zeppelin, The Who, J. Geils Band and Herman's Hermits. (Premier later added Bruce Springsteen, U2, Tom Petty and Van Halen.)

As Dave Marsh wrote in 2002: "Frank Barsalona virtually invented the rock concert business. When he started out, it was package shows with fifteen-minute, five-song sets in buildings without sound systems or decent lights, for fly-by-night promoters who often cheated them. Rock was, as Frank put it, 'the asshole of show business, lower than the rodeo.' Three years after Barsalona formed Premier Talent, the first talent agency to represent rock acts exclusively, bands were playing in far better setups and they were getting paid. Yet nobody outside the concert world knows who Barsalona is. They think all the innovations came from Bill Graham or out of the clear blue sky (or the orange sunshine)."

Barsalona became known as the godfather of the rock tour industry. This point was underscored at the 2005 Rock and Roll Hall of Fame ceremony, where the agent was honored in the Lifetime Achievement category. Steve Van Zandt inducted Barsalona in the persona of his *Sopranos* character, Silvio Dante, taking the podium alongside co-stars James Gandolfini (Tony Soprano) and Steve Schirripa (Bobby Baccalieri).

Van Zandt, who benefited from Premier Talent's stature and might as a member of Springsteen's E Street Band, also saluted Barsalona on a special edition of his *Underground Garage* radio show. There he explained: "Among the many things that Frank did to change the business was coming up with one simple concept. He felt a band's live performance was as important and maybe more important than their records. This was unprecedented and totally radical thinking." Van Zandt hailed Barsalona's efforts during an era "when agents were agents, baby."

Looking back on the occasion of Premier's twentieth anniversary, Barsalona reflected: "When I first started to become an agent, contemporary music was the armpit of the business. You used a hit record as, at most, a first stepping stone to television or motion pictures. And that wasn't just at the agencies — that was also the thinking of even the managers. A hit record was useful only to get you bookings on *The Ed Sullivan Show*, at The Copa or in casinos."

Like many in the industry, Barsalona seized his opportunities early on when the financial terms were far less standard. He acknowledges that at the time he relished calls from twenty-somethings who fancied themselves rock promoters: "If I got a call from a new kid who had some bread and wanted a show, I would sell him whatever I could sell him — for however much money I could get. And then if there was any money left, I would call my buddy at William Morris or Associated Booking: 'I got a live one — here's who you should call.' And they would do the same for me."

Bill Graham acted similarly from the other side of the table. One story that made the rounds among agents in the 1970s and 1980s was that when a visitor complimented Graham on the size and beauty of his home, he smiled and responded, "Flat deals at the Fillmore." In other words, rather than sharing the proceeds of the show in some predetermined split, with X percent of the total receipts going to the artist and the remaining X percent to the promoter (as would soon become standard), whenever possible, Graham gave the acts a guaranteed sum and pocketed the remainder. Such arrangements were soon to become obsolete, at least among the major acts and booking agents. Rather than taking the short, guaranteed money, Barsalona and agents such as Tom Ross began striking deals that acknowledged the full profit potential of superstar artists, often with lower advances but aggressive upsides that yielded up to eighty percent of gross ticket sales (with much more yet to come).

Graham always received some measure of deference when it came to negotiations, particularly early on, since he controlled prestigious rooms on both coasts and also functioned as a tastemaker, whose booking decisions carried clout with other talent buyers. Ross, who worked for the prestigious APA (Agency for the Performing Arts) before moving to two other industry powerhouses, CAA (Creative Artists Agency) and ICM (International Creative Management), remembers, "Bill Graham would come down to book his schedule for the Fillmores, and at the time, the true test of whether you were making it in the music world was if you played the Fillmore East and West."

Barsalona, in a November 1970 *Billboard* interview, added: "He brought a sense of professionalism into the promotion business. Prior to Bill, the music scene was not concerned with stage presence. It was forty minutes and off. No light shows, no good sound system. Graham made other promoters compete with him, greatly raising the professional standards of that end of the business. The Fillmore was the first to try for that professional touch. He is fun to deal with but no one will get rich by booking groups with him. The fact is that groups want to play the Fillmore because of the audience and because of the professional surroundings he has brought there."

By the early 1970s, to develop a healthy tour base for the acts that were gaining renown through FM radio and the nascent rock press, booking agents became less interested in swindling young people who sought to purchase talent and more concerned with nurturing them. Barsalona's prescription for developing his acts at Premier was to maintain a steady dialogue with record labels, artist management and an emerging crop of younger promoters.

Barsalona later explained: "To me, one of the most important things about Premier is not just the acts, but that we developed the rock promoters as well. Unlike the agencies before, who went to the established promoters, we developed new promoters, young promoters . . . people who did nothing else but rock, and who knew the music, liked the music, heard about the music."

Local fiefdoms began spreading across the country where neophytes proved themselves and developed industry relationships that would endure for decades. As rock music exploded out of clubs and into arenas during the 1970s, these promoters were positioned to accompany the acts on the journey. Larry Magid, who was fresh out of Temple University when he joined forces with the Spivak brothers in a converted tire warehouse that became known as the Electric Factory, also credits Barsalona: "When I started in the business, Premier said, 'We're going to start these young promoters that understand the music.' They helped these promoters develop their talent, and in turn, the promoters also developed." Many of them would become industry lifers, including Jack Boyle (DC area), Arny Granat and Jerry Mickelson (Chicago), Barry Fey (Denver), Jules and Mike Belkin (Cleveland), Steve Schankman and Irv Zuckerman (St. Louis), Alex Cooley (Atlanta), Steve Sybesma and Dave Lucas (Indianapolis), Don Law (Boston) and Frank Russo (Providence).

Ticketing became more complex over time as shows moved from the general admission club setting into reserved seating theater and arena realms. Promoters were required to secure a manifest of the seating plot from the box office, outsource to a company that printed hard tickets, break those down into sections and rows, distribute the tickets to whatever outlet system was in place and keep in steady contact with the overall network, not only to ensure that tickets were not sold out at a particular location, but also to move inventory from one outlet to another as mandated by the flow of sales. Then, as the show approached, one needed to collect the unsold tickets and place the remainders at the box office, while reconciling the final count and the cash proceeds with the outlets.

Barry Fey recalls that his initial distribution would take an entire day: "My ex-wife and I would put the baby in the car seat, and we'd start at Miller Music in Colorado Springs at eight o'clock in the morning. We'd wind our way to the south, do all the Denver outlets and then go to Boulder. We had three outlets within fifty yards in Boulder, but they all catered to different personnel. Then we would take what was called the Longmont Diagonal [highway] to Longmont Music, ending up in Fort Collins at Bach or Rock, and that was at six o'clock at night."

Keith Krokyn, Jack Boyle's point person for tickets at the Cellar Door, remembers: "You had to be very fluid in terms of where you put your seats because if the store in Georgetown was selling well but the store in Baltimore wasn't selling well, and you were starting to find your sales for this act were going to be in Washington, then why would you want to have the seats up in Baltimore sitting there doing nothing? So I would have to send somebody up there to pull them out of those outlets and bring them all down here."

Charlie Ryan ran a hard ticketing service for over a decade in Memphis, beginning in the late 1970s. At that time "tickets were always an afterthought. They were just a mechanism." He likens his efforts back then on the night of a show to "a Chinese fire drill because you had to run around town and grab all the tickets, take them to the coliseum, count them and pay the checks." During the weeks leading up the event, he was required to provide promoters with a daily sales update. "Every morning we'd get in at eight o'clock, and I'd have to hand count all my ticket stock to make sure that the shows balanced. At any time we had five or six shows on sale and we had to audit them. Every ticket outlet did too. So by eleven o'clock you were expected to call every outlet, having had them go through their rack to count how many tickets they had left for the Rolling Stones, and write it down. Then you were supposed to have a report by noon for the promoter, so he would know what his ticket sales were yesterday. And of course record store employees, they might be crawling in at the crack of eleven. It was such a cowboy deal."

The ongoing communication and redistribution could be trying. Frank Russo looks back: "You have to keep in mind, a lot of these people did it as a sidebar. It was not their core business. So you'd have to call and get a report. Let's say Roth Ticket had 500 tickets. I'd call and say, 'Lou, how many tickets have you sold?' And after he got through chewing his stogie he'd report, 'I sold 304. I got 190-something left.' So then I'd ask, 'What locations did you sell?' And he'd say, 'I don't know, I'm too busy. I got Yankees tickets to sell here, I'm selling Red Sox tickets . . . What do you want from me? I'm selling your tickets, aren't I?'"

Jerry Seltzer had been through much of the same rigmarole while on the road with the Roller Derby, often juggling tight deadlines and multiple destinations, which is why he knew he could lighten the load (and pad Graham's wallet at the same time).

UNLIKE BILL GRAHAM, JERRY SELTZER never groveled for an encore from a recalcitrant Crosby, Stills, Nash & Young holed up in their dressing room (nor achieved that goal by sliding cutesy notes and $100 bills under the door). He also never received a birthday "present" onstage from the Grateful Dead: the nickname Uncle Bobo, which aggravated Graham for years. However, Seltzer and Graham did share a common promoter's perspective. So Jerry's initial pitch emphasized BASS's advantages as best articulated by someone who had traveled from city to city, collecting and reconciling tickets from independent outlets, while storing inventory within the trunk of a light green 1955 Cadillac (which belonged to box office manager Peggy Brown — she occasionally stuffed $10,000 to $20,000 in there as well "because we weren't always in areas that had a bank").

Yet Seltzer offered more than mere words to win Graham's favor. Jerry and Hal Silen met with Bill and enlisted him as a BASS customer by presenting a tantalizing tangible bonus: cash. They proposed to raise the service charge of each ticket slightly, so that it would hover around the fifty cent mark, and then rebate a quarter of the proceeds to Graham's company. The promoter was swayed.

Much would be made later of Fred Rosen changing the game at Ticketmaster via his revenue sharing model with the introduction of a wider and more lucrative range of service charges. However, the first computerized ticketing company offering such an arrangement on a permanent basis was the Bay Area Seating Service to its flagship client — Bill Graham.

Seltzer casts himself back to that discussion: "Bill had the most wonderful words when we first met. He said, 'You know, I've heard a lot about you, and everybody says you're a very square guy, so let's give each other an honest con.' And we did."

The BASS system became operational in December 1974. With Graham on board the initial outlets maintained a music focus: Warehouse Records, Tower Records and Pacific Stereo. Sears eventually signed on but again proved an ill fit. "That was a bad mistake," Seltzer recalls. "They hated the kids. They were pushed around in the stores. I met with the manager and I said, 'Don't you realize that one day these are your customers, even if you don't think they are now?' Sears decided that they wouldn't sell certain rock shows. I told them we can't have an outlet system that doesn't sell everything that we have."

Jerry had learned this lesson the loud way after an outlet refused to sell a Grateful Dead ticket to a fan who then complained to Graham. The promoter became incensed, phoning Seltzer and shrieking: "Get your fucking machines out of my places and throw them in the streets! You're not taking care of my kids!" (This was a common refrain, as Seltzer opines: "What made Bill Graham so good for the Bay Area was he'd walk in and look at the first four or five rows for any event, and if he saw any people who worked for him, worked for BASS, the record company, anybody he knew, he'd go nuts, and I'd hear from him the next day: 'The kids have to get the tickets! The kids have to get the tickets!' That wasn't true everywhere else in the country.")

At times, Graham being Graham, the promoter delivered mixed messages. Doug Levinson had been on the job as VP of operations for just three months when BASS implemented a new policy for a Bruce Springsteen on-sale, where numbered wristbands would be distributed, with one number randomly selected as the starting point and all other wristband holders then lined up sequentially. Wishing to observe one of the busier outlets, he was directed to Warehouse Records in San Rafael, having been forewarned that the promoter lived nearby.

"So here I am on a Sunday morning with my stupid little three-piece suit, and he walks in dressed like a bum. I introduce myself, and I'm literally shaking, but he's so nice and sweet. Then, after we announce the first number, some of these kids start grumbling. Meanwhile, Bill is talking to me, talking about the virtues of the wristband policy, just giving me a little history lesson. I'm soaking it all in, but we can hear these kids getting louder. So Bill says, 'Excuse me one second,' turns to one of them in line, picks him up by his sweatshirt, slams him against the wall and starts screaming, 'Don't tell me what to do with my tickets!' Remember, this is someone who had just been preaching about wonderful customer service. Well, this kid's legs are dangling in the air, swinging back and forth. Then Bill literally drops him dead in his tracks and starts back to me. I'm sweating and thinking, 'What is this guy going to do?' Well he comes back and says, 'Now, where were we?' and keeps right on going with the conversation. I didn't know if this was an act, but I came to realize that this was just Bill Graham."

BASS's client base consisted initially of just Bill Graham, as the company had approached San Francisco's symphony and ballet and opera companies but was met with resistance. After wearing them down over a few years, they would become clients, but initially, as Silen recollects, "They didn't care for us much because everyone thought we were the rock and roll people." Some of BASS's identity was also tied in to the Roller Derby, and not just because of its founders' prior association but also because many of its positions were filled by former Derby employees, including Peggy Brown and a variety of skaters.[6]

Although it took a while for BASS to win over the area's performing arts companies, Seltzer had more success with nightclubs such as the Boarding House, where Steve Martin recorded much of his debut album, *Let's Get Small*. Seltzer met with owner David Allen, who was reluctant at first, explaining that his big shows on Friday and Saturday had already sold out. "I said, 'Fine,'" Seltzer recalls, looking back on a moment that captures his spirit and sales technique. "'Then give me large allocations of Thursday and Sunday, and give me a small allocation of Friday and Saturday.' So we would sell out of Friday and Saturday and have a message that said 'Additional tickets may be available at the box office, good seats available Thursday and Sunday.' And we found out that his non-good nights were selling out in advance. You can't sell out a Thursday night ticket on a Saturday night, but you sure as hell can sell it ahead of time, and then you can add Wednesday."

Seltzer's philosophy regarding the relationship between sales and marketing led him to apply data in a way that still eluded other ticketing companies: "We divided northern California into areas and with each event determined the percentage of tickets that were sold in each area. At that time Bill Graham was advertising very heavily on the AM and FM stations and the San Francisco newspapers. So I called him one day and said, 'Let's talk.' I went in, brought the sheets, and I asked, 'When you play acts like Bachman-Turner Overdrive, what percentage of your audience lives within fifteen miles of San Francisco? He answered, 'Between fifty and sixty percent.' I said, 'How about fifteen percent? And fifty percent comes from the San Jose area.' So he started buying radio in San Jose and cutting back on the more expensive stations. We also used this with the baseball stadiums, so they could see what percentage was coming from Sacramento. Our clients appreciated it, and of course it helped our ticket sales."

Jerry also applied Roller Derby-inspired guerilla marketing, "where you connect the dots when you don't have a lot of money." He brokered deals that offered concert tickets to Pacific Stereo in exchange for space in the store's print ads, which mentioned the event in question and noted that tickets could be found at Pacific Stereo's BASS outlets. "So we'd go to a client and say, 'Pacific Stereo is going to run an ad for your shows, and all it's going to cost you is some tickets for Wednesday night.' Then we'd go one step further. When we found out an act was coming, we'd call Tower and ask if the record label was doing any co-op [allocating funds to promote touring acts' new albums]. Remember, there used to be a lot of that. So we'd ask, 'Is there any reason when they do their promotion on the radio or newspaper or television that they can't put in there, "Tickets are on sale at Tower Records?"' That way we could show the clients that they didn't even have to buy the ad."

This is not to say that everything went smoothly. Because of limited ticket inventory, tight margins and technical upgrades, there was not an immediate path to profit. Not all of Jerry's (many) ideas proved successful. For instance, the proposed fleet of limousines to be used for wooing clients ended at one car, and that lone vehicle, which offered a full-on light show, was sold at a loss.

Doug Levinson, who eventually assumed the mantle of president, remarks: "Jerry was a wonderful human being, a heart as big as the world, but he would drive us nuts. He was ADHD on steroids, your classic salesman entrepreneur. He talked in phrases because his mind was constantly racing, and he could not talk in complete sentences. He would do a thousand things at once, go off in a million directions, and what was a priority today wasn't even top twenty tomorrow, and then it would come back up two weeks later."

Silen echoes: "Jerry is a very anxious sort of guy, and things have to be done immediately, which could stir up an office. If the machines went down, he knew it before anyone else, and he would drive everyone nuts, in his positive way, to get in and do something."

Seltzer admits: "I preferred not to know anything about the technology, so when I asked the programmers to do things and they told me they couldn't, I didn't know what they were talking about [and encouraged them to figure it out]. That was always my philosophy."

The technology was an early stumbling block. BASS soon overextended a system originally intended for only a limited number of applications. When BASS opened in 1974, only twenty-four ports were available outside the box offices, capping the remote terminal usage at two dozen. Meanwhile, with the modems operating at 1200 baud, Jerry recalls: "You literally could see the numbers and letters going across the screen. At night we shut off the box offices that were only open nine to five and switched those ports to places that had performances at night to try to give us the impact of thirty or so. We took phone reservations, but we couldn't do credit cards online, and we'd have to turn around and enter them later when we had available ports. It was a real dance." BASS turned to Bruce Baumgart once more, and he orchestrated a new system on a Digital Equipment Corporation minicomputer that more than doubled the available ports, exceeding even what DEC thought possible.

Baumgart would later acquire the rights to this system, which he marketed elsewhere under the Softix banner after a BASS Worldwide venture went belly up in 1979, following installations in Toronto, Vancouver, Houston, Miami and Orlando (BASS stood for *Best Available* Seating Service in those cities). Silen remembers: "Jerry was going all over the world. We even went to Hawaii and all of these were busts. We just didn't have the money and the people sufficiently trained to take them around. Eventually these places all became part of something else, but originally they were part of BASS Worldwide." The founding company remained in business, however, as BASS continued to thrive in Northern California, even as the steadily reducing price of computers drew new players onto the landscape.

IN 1978 THE FOTOMAT CORPORATION, with its collection of nearly 4,000 drive-through kiosks, viewed itself as a natural fit for a ticketing network. Just as customers could drop off film and return a day later to retrieve finished photos without exiting their vehicles, so too, the company theorized, could they purchase tickets with relative ease. Fotomat initiated a series of motion studies to confirm the feasibility of such an endeavor.

In seeking out industry expertise, Fotomat approached the Computer Sciences Corporation. CSC in turn enlisted former Computicket programmer Roy Bellman to handle the technical specifications. Bellman formed Leisuretime Reservation Systems Inc. (the name oddly echoed his one-time ticketing rival, TRS) and assembled a team to develop Fototicket.

On its face the plan made perfect sense. As outlined in the Fototicket Executive Summary, the virtues included these:

- Fotomat has three to four times the number of outlets of all the current market participants combined.
- Fotomat's outlets are much more convenient for the ticket buyer than any of the current market participants.
- Fotomat's ticket sellers are Fotomat employees. No one else has ever been able to justify the expense required to put a full-time company employee at the outlet. Current market participants have to settle for someone else's employee who has little motivation to properly represent the ticket seller.

As for revenues, the business model was to emulate Ticketron, with both an inside charge (to the promoter) and a per ticket fee. However, unlike Ticketron, since Fototicket would not be outsourcing outlet sales but rather utilizing its own employees (the fair and friendly "Fotomates"), "Fotomat gets to keep more of the service charge. Current market participants have to pay up to 50 percent of the service charge collected from the customer to the company providing the outlet. Operating the outlet is apparently more profitable than operating the system." The summary then concluded, "From conversations with both the promoters and consumers, we have found that the current charges by Ticketron are considered reasonable for the service offered. Based on this fact, Fotomat can reasonably expect to receive $1.00 for each ticket sold. About $0.25 will come from the promoter and about $0.75 from the ticket buyer." One significant lesson gleaned from the Computicket experience was that Fototicket would not settle for partial ticket inventory but rather would require 100 percent of the allocation to any event.

The system itself would be based on Computicket, providing "the ability to avoid an expensive reinvention of the wheel in getting Fototicket up and running." Rather than using a mainframe, though, Bellman designed the Fototicket software to run on a Tandem NonStop minicomputer.[7] A beta test was planned for Colorado with a national rollout expected to follow.

However, Roy Bellman and CSC were foiled yet again. This time the culprit was the videocassette. In an era before national chains like Blockbuster, Fotomat hoped to establish itself as the alternative to the mom and pop stores, with customers making video requests to be filled the next day. Bellman's recollection of the events remains sour: "The president of the company thought they could strike deals with the studios to get first-run movies. He believed they could compete against the movie theaters. So he started taking meetings with the big movie moguls. It was a complete ego trip." Ego trip or not, it consumed company resources as Fotomat began filling warehouses with videocassettes in an all-out (failed) bid to win market dominance. Fototicket lost favor and was discontinued in 1979.

Things weren't much better for Dorothy McLaughlin and Select-A-Seat. The Arizona Cattle Company brought a lawsuit against BASS on behalf of Select-A-Seat, charging wrongful appropriation of its software. However, a court-appointed master compared the source code and ruled in BASS's favor. Meanwhile, McLaughlin relates, "The Cattle Company way overspent, trying to spread the system all over the place, because you have to remember we were only charging the public twenty-five cents a ticket." In early 1977 Select-A-Seat filed for bankruptcy.[8]

Part of Select-A-Seat's legacy is that it provided a source of inspiration for Arizona State grad student Albert Leffler. The recipient of an internship in arts and administration, Leffler had been the box office manager for a season at the Santa Fe Opera, following a stint at the University of New Mexico's Popejoy Hall. In both instances he'd worked with hard tickets and was intrigued by the Select-A-Seat system installed at ASU's Gammage Auditorium. One day in late 1974, while speaking with his wife's brother regarding his potential plans after his internship expired the following year, Leffler, who anticipated he would pursue a managerial role with a theater or a symphony orchestra, made an offhand remark about the field of computerized ticketing. A few days later Leffler's wife, Kathy, received a call from her brother's childhood friend, Gordon Gunn, who had recently left a sales position at IBM to start his own company, UniSystems Corporation. Gunn held an Original Equipment Manufacturer (OEM) license from the Digital Equipment Corporation, which allowed him to sell their minicomputers.

Despite his brother-in-law's recollection of their conversation, Albert had little more than a vague sense that an opportunity existed. However, the affable grad student returned the call. "I talked to Gordon for a little bit, having never met the fellow, and here was the interesting catalyst," he enthuses today. "He said, 'I've heard of this brilliant programmer working at ASU. I've met his dad somewhere along the line. If I can find him, he might be a resource we can use to see about this idea of yours.'"

Gunn located Peter Gadwa, whose family had moved from Minnesota to Arizona almost a decade earlier. A focused if somewhat socially awkward individual, Gadwa had recently returned to the state after receiving his master's in computer science from Stanford. He also held an undergraduate degree and a master's in mathematics from ASU, where he was then providing software support for the ASU psychology department.

"So he managed to track down this individual," Leffler continues, "and the three of us got together. I had them over for dinner at this little duplex Kathy and I were renting adjacent to campus, and we talked about the possibility of starting a company to do computerized ticketing, of which none of us really knew much."

They didn't really know each other either but decided to throw their fortunes together — metaphorically speaking, as they all lacked capital — and set out to launch a computerized ticketing company.

One major hurdle was they lacked a computer and the means to purchase one. Over the course of 1975 Gunn took on that responsibility, while simultaneously running his other company to support his wife and four kids. Albert chipped in on the market research side, developing documentation for the business plan. Peter started thinking about the technical requirements for their new system, which would build on the Select-A-Seat approach but would place much more processing ability in the ticket printer to speed up transaction time.

By midsummer Leffler remained frustrated by his inability to fashion a suitable name for the company. At the time they were still operating under the generic placeholder Computer Ticket Service. The issue was heavy on his mind one Sunday afternoon as he drove his silver 1972 Cutlass Supreme back home after visiting family in New Mexico with his wife and two-year-old daughter. The Lefflers began volleying potential names back and forth.

"You know," Kathy offered, "there's this dry cleaner in El Paso. It's called Master Cleaners. I always liked the sound of it. What do you think about Master Ticket?"

Leffler paused, mulled and countered.

"What about Ticket Master?"

IN A STERILE CONFERENCE ROOM on Wilshire Boulevard filled with banquet tables and fold-up chairs, the company that would come to dominate the computerized ticketing industry for decades to follow was prepared to make its Southern California debut. It was Sunday morning, March 27, 1983, and the occasion was the initial on-sale for the US Festival. Fifty phone operators were on hand to take orders for the event, which would present David Bowie, Van Halen, the Clash and twenty other acts over the Memorial Day weekend in San Bernardino. There was only one thing missing from the Ticketmaster phone room: any semblance of computer technology whatsoever.

Instead, with sharpened pencils and order forms at the ready, operators were primed to record any ticket requests. These in turn would be fulfilled with the same preprinted tickets scheduled to become available the following Friday at any of the forty-five "Ticketmaster Ticket Centers" at Sportsmart, Music Plus and Federated Group stores. The arrangement with the US Festival had come together too quickly for Ticketmaster to install any equipment, meaning that the company's first foray into this significant market, then dominated by Ticketron, would be as a traditional hard ticket company.

All of this sat quite well with US Festival founder Steve Wozniak. The co-creator of Apple Computer had been inspired by a screening of the *Woodstock* concert film "to do a kind of Woodstock for my generation." He achieved this goal within a year, creating the music festival in 1982 with its accompanying Technology Exposition and funding the entire undertaking out of his own pocket. That pocket became about $12 million lighter when the final numbers had been tabulated, and Wozniak's accountants led him to believe this stemmed from a discrepancy between the ticket count and the actual attendance. He decided to give it a go again in 1983 but vowed that "this time we'll have supertight controls and make sure everybody has a ticket." As a precaution, he dropped Ticketron, which had handled the prior year's sales, and committed to the upstart. When informed that because of timing issues, Ticketmaster would need to operate without its online network, Apple's original vice president of research and development replied, "That's great. We want hard tickets. We don't trust the computers."

Ticketmaster's connection to the US Festival came through the individual who would soon become the company's new vice president, Jerry Seltzer. After BASS Worldwide closed in 1979, Seltzer initially kept his focus on his lone remaining operations in Northern California. However, to his mind, "Ticketron still didn't get it. Why weren't they trying to sign statewide contracts with the circus and others that play various arenas?" So he hired a researcher from Stanford to survey the Los Angeles market and assess its vulnerabilities. In the process of doing this, a friend mentioned that a new team backed by the Chicago-based Pritzker family had taken over Ticketmaster and was considering making a play for the region. Simultaneously, through his connection with Bill Graham, who had booked the first US Festival, Seltzer learned of the opportunity to displace Ticketron. He pushed his case for a strategic alliance with Ticketmaster's new CEO, Fred Rosen.

Rosen would soon revolutionize the business of ticketing, but initially he was hustling to make whatever he could of what he later described as "the leavings." After initial success in Chicago (where the Pritzker family possessed enormous footprints), the New York native was hoping to gain traction back east. He had discovered, however, that to make it work in the Tri-State Area, he'd need to land three of the six major clients: Nassau Coliseum, Meadowlands Sports Complex, Madison Square Garden, Radio City Music Hall, the New York Mets and the New York Yankees. Rosen received some initial interest from Nassau and the Mets but couldn't attain critical mass. In lieu of this he decided to head west, recognizing that the US Festival with its six-figure advertising budget would provide something of a "free peek into the market" with maximum visibility. So he opted to move forward without his computers while also utilizing a third-party vendor, Chargit, to assist with phone sales.

A full-page US Festival ad in the Sunday, March 27 *Los Angeles Times* heralded the relationship: "Ticketmaster Joins 'Us!'" That same morning, a phone room full of part-time employees gathered on Wilshire, anticipating their call to action.

As nine o'clock in the morning approached, Pat Moore, who managed the
center, basked in the moment of debut as he stood before his staff and the
fifty phones that had been daisy-chained together. He announced, "Let me
and at the first operating position so you can watch how it goes."

At the top of the hour the initial call arrived.

"Good morning. Thank you for calling Ticketmaster/Chargit. What
can I help you with?"

re was precisely one event on sale.

re listened intently.

no, I'm sorry. There's no José here."

minutes of silence followed.

gradually, orders started to trickle in.

uch an awkward start, one would be hard-pressed to anticipate
to follow.

E TICKETMASTER SYSTEM HAD its advocates, over the preceding
the company as a whole had not posed a credible national threat
computerized ticketing services.

nclusion was reached by the team developing Fototicket, which
n October 1978: "Ticketmaster is another system operating out
x, Arizona. CSC [Computer Sciences Corporation] has not been
t much data on this company although we understand they are not
ch. At a recent promoter's show in Kentucky their booth had no
it and no people in it."

master had been inching toward its goal of becoming a major
er since Albert Leffler and his wife collaborated on the name of
any during their family car trip. As for that name, it began as one
h the T and M both capitalized, but over the company's first few
d succession of investors), the M gradually became lower-case.
ial logo, which Leffler designed, was a simple representation of the
elled out in the Optical Character Recognition font and photo-
d. The OCR typeface (created in 1968 as a style that could be read
ines and humans alike) evoked the computer connection at a glance
t being too overbearing about it.

a period of time the logo represented only an idealized connection
computer realm as Ticketmaster was unable to afford any hardware.
on Gunn's sights were set on the Digital Equipment Corporation
-11, a minicomputer he knew quite well, as he had sold his share of them
igh his license from the company. (One of his clients was Arizona State
ersity, where Ticketmaster programmer Peter Gadwa had spent time
he machine.[1]) Although somewhat similar in size to the CDC 1700 that

was still running the Ticketron system, the PDP-11 was far more advanced from a technological standpoint and, perhaps more germane, significantly less expensive. However, despite Gunn's ability to secure a bottom-line price, the PDP-11 was still about $10,000 out of reach.

Until the Pritzkers entered the picture a few years later, Ticketmaster would endure cycles of economic hardship. However, the most frustrating of these came at the outset, when Leffler, Gunn and Gadwa researched the available ticketing systems, increasingly confident in their alternative.

Leffler remembers: "It was a start-up from scratch, no ties to anything else, just three guys trying to invent a better mousetrap. I will give Select-A-Seat full credit for having the vision to break away from what was really a bad example with Ticketron. They were able to have a consolidated package that wasn't designed to support a thousand terminals but was a citywide operation that had incorporated both single ticket sales and subscription sales. One of the big differences we had was that part of what Pete Gadwa had envisioned was trying to offload as much of the work as possible to the ticket printer. At that point in time a ticket printer had very little smarts to it; it was just a machine. But we buffered all that with a lot of stuff in a very early miniprocessor."

"Albert had invited me in to Grady Gammage Auditorium to inspect Select-A-Seat," Gunn affirms. "It was based on Hewlett-Packard minicomputer hardware, and it had many good features, but the biggest problem was throughput. The time it took to complete a ticket transaction created a bottleneck. But I knew we could overcome that with the power of the PDP-11 with its multi-user, multitasking and multiprogramming operating system."

If only they could afford one.

Finally, impatience, self-assurance and insight into the delivery question allowed Gadwa to begin development. The programmer recalls: "The order was placed in January of 1976, and there was no hope of receiving the computer before May. This was a good thing since none of us had the money to pay for the computer." In the interim Gadwa was permitted to work on a machine at the DEC sales office.

Before the final bill came due, Gunn raised $12,000 from a retired clothing retailer named Lester Bernstein. The funds were exhausted immediately, and while the company finally owned its long-coveted PDP-11, it lacked the resources to move forward and market the system that the computer hosted, let alone pay anyone a meaningful wage. Matters became so desperate that Leffler recalls, "Gordon even had one of the [DEC] technicians, who was Hispanic, appointed as president so we could qualify for a minority-run business." As another moment of crisis arrived, Gunn found a new partner in Charles Hamby, the owner of a direct mail marketing company, Creative Mailing Consultants of America, who had recently relocated from Maryland.

Gordon wrote an essay three decades later describing the experience:

> Charley looked like the answer to a prayer when he agreed to get involved. This is where the [founders] began their real-world education about the "Golden Rule of Business" – i.e. "He who has the gold makes the rules." Indeed this was the beginning of a painful experience for the founders, which wouldn't reveal itself fully for several more months. But for now, there were funds to complete system development, develop marketing materials, do some actual marketing and supposedly enough capital from Charley to install revenue-producing systems in 3 or 4 communities. There was also Charley's verbal promise that there would be reasonable equity reserved for the founders group no matter how the capitalization process evolved.
>
> The infusion of Charley's capital provided meager salaries for Gordon and Albert, plus an office and computer room in Hamby's Phoenix office. He even bought out Lester Bernstein for his original net investment of $12,000. All this seemed like a "Godsend" after so many months of hard struggle to keep the idea moving forward. However, Charley apparently had ulterior motives, and had misrepresented his financial ability unbeknownst to the founders. Charley wasn't as rich as he liked people to think he was.

Leaving any heavy-handed foreshadowing aside for a moment, by July 1976 the system was ready to be demoed at its first trade show. The Auditorium Managers Association has been in existence since 1924, when seven industry professionals met in Cleveland, Ohio, to address "relevant topics such as new construction, contracts, admissions, revenue generation, creating content for their facilities and sharing their collective knowledge and experiences." The organization, which eventually changed its name to the International Association of Assembly Managers, started hosting yearly meetings, with accompanying exhibition space for vendors. On July 11 to 15, 1976, the fifty-first annual conference took place in New Orleans. Gunn rented a van and along with Leffler drove the entire system down from Phoenix, setting up a booth and handing out brochures.[2]

Ticketmaster made some connections of later significance in New Orleans and then returned home for a local push. The company's aggressive sales efforts, now buoyed by Hamby, landed two markets in short order. Albuquerque came first, holding appeal for its lack of competition and also familiarity (Gunn had grown up in the city and Leffler had attended college there). The New Mexico Symphony and Leffler's alma mater, the University of New Mexico, were among the first clients along with some area theaters.

El Paso then followed, after Gadwa determined there was sufficient computing power to utilize the existing infrastructure for that region as well.

The very first Ticketmaster event was an ELO concert at the University of New Mexico's Johnson Gymnasium on Sunday, January 23, 1977. Ticketing was handled at UNM's Popejoy Hall, where Albert had once been a student employee. Admission was $6.50 with a twenty-five cent service charge accruing to the company.

In the months to come service fees would double in many instances, a product of the company's efforts to build and maintain an outlet network, with Gunn taking the lead. "I just started making cold calls. I was raised in Albuquerque, so I had a lot of friends to network through. Originally the sales pitch was they would get the foot traffic into their store and they wouldn't get a percentage of the tickets. We had the local Dillard's [a few years before it would acquire its own in-house service] and a specialty clothing shop in one strip mall. They were spread out because we wanted sites that were equally dispersed around the community. But then we did an Eagles concert and the Dillard's was just bled. It was like a day at the state prison. Somebody broke their escalator and I think there was shoplifting. So we found out right then that if they were going to do this, then they needed to be compensated because it was more labor-intensive on their part than we thought. So I think on the next go-round we charged fifty cents, splitting it with the outlet."[3]

The original Ticketmaster business model placed a focus on "auditorium systems" as the company aimed to sell the hardware and accompanying software to individual venues and educational institutions. Peter Gadwa's principal compensation had been keyed to this, as initially he was set to receive $2,500 per installation. However, by necessity the Albuquerque and El Paso outlet equipment was owned and operated by Ticketmaster, a capital-intensive alternative that offered the greatest opportunity for long-term dividends but required up-front costs that approached $100,000.

Charles Hamby recognized that he was out of his element when it came to such capital commitment but also determined that he needed to have Albuquerque and El Paso up and running to demonstrate the system. At this point he announced the involvement of two additional partners. Jerry Nelson was a local real estate developer who had become a multimillionaire after he drilled for water and hit a major aquifer, allowing him to open a golf mecca in Scottsdale, Arizona. Cecil Crawford was the former president of Regal-Beloit, a company that produced industrial tools. As it turned out, the two had already committed resources to Ticketmaster as each, unbeknownst to the other, had loaned Hamby money for his stake.

Nelson remembers being quite skeptical when Hamby visited his home along with Albert Leffler and Peter Gadwa to make a direct appeal: "They told me about their idea, and I knocked it because at that time you already had Ticketron, which was owned by Control Data. And they said, 'Well, Mr. Nelson, Ticketron has got the wrong concept.' And I thought, 'Oh, great. Control Data is a multi-billion dollar company and they're wrong and you're graduate students at ASU and you're right. That's news.' So I said, 'Show me.'"

Not only did the pair outline the system sufficiently for Nelson to commit funds, but they also energized him sufficiently to enlist his participation, which is how the third Ticketmaster market after Albuquerque and El Paso became Oslo, Norway.

Nelson's four grandparents were Norwegian, and so he decided to bring "the boys" on a grand European sales tour. France, Switzerland and Great Britain were on an itinerary that found some genuine interest (Ticketmaster walked away from a French deal where a customer was quite frank about his interest in manipulating the system to defraud France's tax authorities). Ultimately, the company secured a new client on Nelson's ancestral soil, reaching an agreement with the Kingdom of Norway.

"What interested the government was a political motive rather than a profit motive," Nelson explains. "Norway is a socialist country and they felt this was a fair way to give everyone a chance for good tickets. The rich people in Oslo wouldn't have a greater opportunity than some little farmer out of town to get the best seats in the house."

What emerged from this initial success was a renewed push for system sales. Hamby was particularly interested in the cash flow they provided, while his investors believed that this approach offered Ticketmaster its greatest opportunity for success. Eventually, customers in such varied destinations as Cedar Rapids, Dallas and Washington, DC, signed licensing agreements.

Ticketmaster reached its next crossroads in New Orleans. Back when the firm had displayed its system at IAAM, it had caught the attention of officials from the newly opened Superdome. Hamby had courted Denzil Skinner, recently tapped as executive director of the facility by the Hyatt Management Corporation. Skinner was hired by eighty-two-year-old Abram Nicholas Pritzker, whose family owned 100 Hyatt hotels around the world, including an $80 million facility just across the street from the Superdome. The Hyatt Management Corp. had been created for the sole purpose of running the venue, after the state of Louisiana grew frustrated by the local corruption and political favoritism that led to bloated overhead costs and rising losses. Skinner was interested in Ticketmaster, albeit cautiously, predicating his involvement in the establishment of an extensive area outlet network.

Hamby made a renewed pitch to Nelson, appealing for a multimillion dollar commitment that far exceeded the developer's original six-figure investment. "They needed a major infusion. I understood that and I agreed with it," Nelson remembers. "I could have put in eleven million dollars, but then I'd be living out of a suitcase and I wouldn't see my kids. So I took the eleven million dollars and did Troon North instead [a golf community built around two courses designed by Tom Weiskopf, who had won the 1973 British Open at Royal Troon]. That way I could go home for lunch and be with my little kids after school."

Ticketmaster did ultimately secure alternative financing. However, the Superdome price tag also came at the expense of a company founder.

"This was when Cecil Crawford informed me that they couldn't afford to pay me anymore," Gunn explains. "He told me that, as it was, we did not have the means to purchase the equipment necessary for New Orleans. They offered me a chance to work on commission if I paid my own expenses, but I was then divorced and supporting a wife and four children. So after looking around for an area job, I took a position as a branch manager with Wang Laboratories in Atlanta, Georgia."

Gunn was ousted from Ticketmaster along with his friend Tom Hart, who had become a vice president and stakeholder eighteen months earlier, when his company, Plexus, began contributing circuit boards. Gunn contends that the two were promised "options on 6,000 shares of stock if and when shares were ever issued" but never collected. Meanwhile Peter Gadwa would remain director of programming through the 1990s, while as vice president of new product development Albert Leffler still takes pride in his Employee Number One badge.

As for Gordon Gunn, while financial considerations were said to be paramount, it was likely a case of one entrepreneur too many. Gunn had certainly put in sweat equity (at times quite literally, when short-staffing obliged him to pick up nearly $5,000 of ticket proceeds in cash from the Albuquerque head shop serving as a Ticketmaster outlet), but his partners may well have sought to close the circle a little tighter now that the start-up phase had passed. Looking back on his experience, he adds: "Everything turned out fine. Sure, I wish I had a small piece of Ticketmaster. That would have been great, but it didn't happen. So I say the tuition was high, but the education was marvelous."

Charles Hamby, on the other hand, never quite learned his lesson when it came to fiscal restraint (one contemporary paraphrased Will Rogers to suggest, "He never met an obligation he couldn't incur"). Bill Birsdall, Jerry Nelson's attorney, who came on as executive vice president during this era, recalls, "Charley was a flamboyant character, and when we traveled with him, we all traveled first-class. Typically we'd fly from Phoenix to New Orleans, where he'd rented an apartment down on Bourbon Street. And it wasn't unusual that we'd arrive in town and Charley would have all the stewardesses from the flight joining us. We'd arrive at six or seven in the evening and party until two or three in the morning at our apartment. Fortunately no one in New Orleans went to work before eleven."

Well, perhaps a few folks did, among them the Pritzker family and the Hyatt Management Corp., which, in exchange for lending the finances required to complete the New Orleans install, secured Ticketmaster stock warrants on very favorable terms. A quarter of a million dollars was required, which considerably diluted the original investment group. A few more warrants later, facing additional financial hardship, Charles Hamby and his backers opted to sell.

Still, it appeared that unless a drastic change took place, Ticketmaster would suffer the same fate as its fellow Arizona start-up, Select-A-Seat. The path to profit looked to be a long one.

Meanwhile the news at Ticketron was mixed.

OVER THE COURSE OF THE 1970s Ticketron's gross ticket sales had increased, hitting $25 million in 1975 and continuing to arc upward. Public awareness had reached the point where the company's name had become synonymous with computerized ticketing. However, success was not uniform, and the company was forced to pull out of failing operations in Florida and Georgia.

The Fototicket study commissioned by the team that had aspired to launch a new service shares a would-be competitor's perspective from the fall of 1978: "Ticketron is the largest of the computer services and is a subsidiary of Control Data Corporation. It sells over thirty million tickets per year out of a network of over 1,000 terminals. . . . It has had a golden opportunity for over a decade to almost create a monopoly in the market but has not apparently been successful in meeting industry needs, customer needs, or the advertising and promotion requirements of the market. . . . If Ticketron had been doing the right job over the years of its existence, it is unlikely that any other ticket selling systems would exist or that there would be an opportunity for any newcomers in the market."

Part of the problem was that Ticketron had not been designed to handle the volume of requests associated with the sale of an arena rock show. When compared with the general flow of tickets to Broadway theater or even sporting events, the demand was faster and more furious. As Ticketron's director of operations, Kurt Devlin, described in his 1978 master's thesis, *Automated Ticketing: A Case Study*: "Several times a year, ticket sales for 'hot' rock concerts would put the system under heavy stress. System response time would degrade from 15 seconds to over five minutes as every available terminal was vying for the 'hot' tickets. Disturbances occurred in the retail outlets and customer dissatisfaction grew."

In 1975, when the Rolling Stones announced six Madison Square Garden shows on the band's first U.S. tour in three years, precautions were taken not to overtax the system. As the band's tour manager, Peter Rudge, then explained, "We've pulled the New York tickets from the Ticketron computer already — if we didn't, the computer would jam with the sudden overload and we'd have a riot like they had in Boston for Led Zeppelin."[4] Ticketron locations were transformed into hard ticket outlets, which produced new concerns. As Rudge observed, "There's a greater chance for abuse, for somebody skimming them off and selling them to scalpers." In response he announced that he would be vigilant in monitoring the sales "at random Ticketron outlets."

Such a turn of events became increasingly significant for the company, as a growing percentage of its business focused on rock music. In 1976 president William Schmitt estimated that forty percent of Ticketron's sales came from concerts. At that time he also identified the four criteria he utilized in gauging whether Ticketron should enter into a new market: "The city and its surrounding area must have a dense population, a major league team, a multiple facility arena and heavy rock promotion activity." The last of these was a new consideration.

Meanwhile the company was still regularly receiving only a limited ticket allocation. In the case of the 1975 Rolling Stones Madison Square Garden dates, this meant just over forty-five percent of the house. By contrast a 1978 *New York Times* article detailing the practices of the Shubert Organization's counting rooms (which manually matched ticket stubs against box office receipts to prevent graft) revealed that a particular performance of *The Gin Game* sold 605 seats, of which a grand total of four could be attributed to Ticketron. Not only was the company's revenue stream circumscribed, but partial inventory called into question whether consumers actually received the "best available" tickets through the outlets.

Season ticketing remained another shortcoming. Although Dorothy McLaughlin had beat them to it by a few years, in 1976 Ticketron finally provided an option. However, rather than offering this as part of a standard package, Ticketron's System 2000 required a $35,000 annual lease. Beyond that expense the system necessitated extensive training as it called for a CDC 1700 minicomputer to be installed in the box office (essentially replicating Ticketron's central hardware and software on a slightly smaller scale). System operators were required to run fifty-seven separate programs, and the three-volume user manual exceeded 600 pages. An estimated sixty-five days of training were required during the first year. The Los Angeles Dodgers moved their box office onto the 2000 system, as did the Montreal Alouettes of the Canadian Football League, but market appeal proved limited.

The inability of Ticketron brass to anticipate the drawbacks of a system that called for two months of training pointed to another predicament. Particularly at the high executive level the company often seemed insensitive to its clients' practical needs in the work environment. Ticketron acquired a reputation for standoffishness, if not all-out arrogance.

This made it all the more trying for the company's field operators to handle other issues that arose. As Ticketron started to move into some of the older facilities, entrenched union workers feared the possible elimination of jobs as well as an unwelcome window into their dealings. Charlie Williams, who joined the company in 1972 as an account rep, remembers that one of his first responsibilities was working with the Philadelphia Spectrum: "Part of my assignment was to train these people how to use the system, and these were not people who wanted to be trained. I remember one Saturday morning we had five of them come up to the office, and two of these old-time unions guys spent the whole session with their backs turned to me. They wouldn't even watch. They didn't want anything to do with it."

The situation hadn't improved when he was sent up to Boston about a year later. "The Boston Garden made the same type of conversion, and in order to be more effective with the union guys in the Garden box office, someone came up with the crazy notion, 'We'll send Charlie, but we'll represent him as an employee of the Spectrum, so the union guys will pay more attention.' So I went up to Boston and I go into the box office and the second guy I meet is the shop steward in the Garden box office. I'm dressed in a white shirt and a suit, and after they introduce me, I stick out my right hand to shake hands, and in his left hand he's holding a cup of coffee which he pretended to fumble and he threw it on my shirt."

Local responsibility fell to Matt Whelan, fresh out of a management trainee program. "I can remember I was sitting at my desk in the old Ticketron office in Boston, and I got a call from the head steward at the Boston Garden saying his equipment was broken. I went over and I looked at it, and it was obvious that they had used a sledgehammer on it. So I said, 'It's not broken. You took a hammer to it.' And everybody denied, denied, denied. But part of the deal was we would service the equipment. If it was broken, we would replace it. So I said, 'Okay, I'll get you another computer.' It was a big test for me, but I told Control Data to build another one. What was I going to do?"

Ticketron backed him and delivered a replacement. Perhaps this is not so surprising because one of the ways that Control Data engineered a positive balance sheet was through steady hardware sales to its ticketing division. However, within a few short years, account reps began to face considerable resistance when they turned to the corporate office for help.

BLAME IT ON FRED.

For a period of time from the late 1980s through the mid-1990s, any number of disgruntled would-be ticketholders and publicity-courting attorneys general did just that.

Over a stretch that began shortly after he assumed the top post at Ticketmaster in 1982 and extended through his departure sixteen years later, Frederic Rosen polarized the concert industry like few others. The brash, confrontational executive earned his share of vocal detractors even as others professed their loyalty and (sometimes grudging) respect. He certainly kept things lively.

Under Rosen's watch Ticketmaster redefined the function and scope of a ticketing company. He recognized the leverage generated by a sound distribution network working with full and exclusive inventory. Rosen approached facilities with an offer that made little sense to refuse, proposing to transform what had once been a cost center into a profit center. With the luxury of hindsight Ticketmaster's rise to prominence seems inevitable, although Rosen himself acknowledges that it did not always play out that way.

The starting point was the relatively simple concept that despite Norway's noble intentions, in America's free market economy Ticketmaster was a for-profit enterprise and not a public utility. Nearly three decades after Rosen first initiated his new approach, consumers still summon indignant outrage, questioning the justification for fees above the base ticket price. Without delving into the particulars of any given situation just yet, it can safely be said that the rationale for any of these charges, quite simply, is profit. (Which, if one thinks about it, isn't so surprising since the base price itself is the product of a profit motive. It's just that the performer generally is seen to be a deserving recipient and most always receives a pass from fans.)

Public grousing about service fees is nothing new and certainly not exclusive to Ticketmaster. Back in 1969 when Peter Schniedermeier was working at TRS in Chicago, a patron came in to purchase tickets for a Ten Years After show at the International Amphitheatre and, upon learning of the twenty-five cent service charge, howled "Rip off, man! Rip off!" By the time Fred Rosen stepped into the role of Ticketmaster's CEO, those halcyon days of quarter-induced rancor were long past. He changed the metrics altogether, and ticket prices have never been the same.

Rosen first formulated his theories while serving in an advisory role eighteen months prior to his formal involvement in the company. In early 1980 Hyatt Management Corp. and the Pritzker family had come to the conclusion that Charles Hamby and Ticketmaster were a losing proposition. Not willing to sink any more money into the operation, they set out to find a buyer.

Eventually they located one in their tax adviser, Burt Kanter. The Chicago-based attorney was a nationally known figure, an editor of the *Journal of Taxation*, who graduated from Chicago Law School and later returned as an adjunct professor. Kanter maintained an interest in the entertainment business and worked with Hollywood producers to limit their tax exposure on *One Flew over the Cuckoo's Nest* and other films. (Phyllis Carlyle, who produced *The Accidental Tourist* and *Seven*, called Kanter "the mother of the tax structure deal.")[5]

While in the process of determining whether to commit himself to Ticketmaster, which would cost him a few million dollars of additional investment beyond the purchase price to remain afloat, Kanter called a lawyer friend of his in New York City. As the phone rang at 6:30 on a January evening in 1980, sitting in the friend's office back east was Fred Rosen. A few years earlier, on a referral, Rosen had briefly represented Select-A-Seat in the post-Dorothy McLaughlin era as the company negotiated with its creditors.

"Oh, you should talk to Fred Rosen. He's sitting right here."

And with that moment of serendipity the concert industry was transformed.

Rosen reflects: "If the call did not come in at that very instant, and I was not sitting in that room, none of this would have happened. He recommended me because I was there. It wouldn't have happened any other way."

After Kanter acquired the controlling interest in the company, he enlisted Rosen as special counsel to keep tabs on Ticketmaster.

Over the ensuing months Rosen traversed the country on Kanter's behalf, observing the dozen or so systems in operation. One of these was in Houston, where Ticketmaster had partnered with the Astrodome, the Summit, Angelo Drossos (owner of the San Antonio Spurs) and the PACE management group. The discussions were often contentious, as any decision required unanimity. On this occasion one of the subjects was tickets for the Houston Rockets basketball team, each of which carried a dollar service charge.

"But there are forty-dollar tickets," Rosen interjected. "Couldn't there be a two-dollar service charge on the forty-dollar tickets?"

"Yes, but we have five-dollar tickets as well."

"Well then why can't you have a two-dollar service charge on the forty-dollar ticket and a one-dollar service charge on the five-dollar ticket because it's not the same audience?"

Silence.

"No Fred, we can't do that because you can only have one service charge on the same event."

"Oh really?" an exasperated Rosen responded. "Well, that must have been the tablet Moses dropped . . . Where did that come from? Guys, why can't you have multiple service charges on the same event? Why must you have the same service charge for every event in the city? Why isn't this all based to a certain extent on ticket prices?"

THE MOMENT ROSEN STOPPED POSITING questions and started implementing policy happened in July 1982. That spring Chicago White Sox Vice President Howard Pizer had finally connected with Rosen's pitch on the virtues of Ticketmaster. Pizer and the team were willing to sign a letter of intent predicated on three conditions: (1) Ticketmaster had a system up and running in Chicago by October 1; (2) the ticket outlet network could be confirmed by the end of the summer; and (3) the company could secure additional financing as it had burned through Kanter's funds.

Then came the addendum. Pizer and the White Sox did not want to deal with the current Ticketmaster management, preferring to maintain their relationship with Rosen.

Rosen, who was then in his late thirties, had been practicing law for a decade. He harbored his own interest in the arts, peppering his conversations with film references and briefly contemplating life as a stand-up comedian. ("I did some stand-up in the mountains at the bungalow colonies at two in the morning. . . . You haven't lived until you've died onstage.") His sharp, often acerbic wit served him well in the professional context, where the graduate of Clark University and Brooklyn Law School often was called into confrontational situations. Rosen had never joined a large firm, preferring the freedom of a sole practitioner. Now he wondered whether it was time to pursue the life of an entrepreneur and go toe to toe with the entrenched Ticketron.

"My view was that anybody who's willing to give a company a shot based on its getting financed is telling you that the competitive landscape is pretty poor," he says. "That's when I started to think that there would be an opportunity to challenge Ticketron. Everybody saw them as a giant, but I started to see them as a dinosaur, and clearly you could make competitive inroads. At the beginning I never quite believed what would happen because I assumed that after a period of time they would change. The perfect analogy is from the movie *Animal House*: at some point you think the band is going to make a left turn and not keep walking into the wall."

By May Rosen's internal compass was set and he decided to raise the $4 million to purchase the company and fund its ongoing operations. A friend of his put a proposal in front of A.N. Pritzker's son, Jay, who wasn't willing to provide all of the money but was in for a million if Rosen could raise the other three. By July Rosen had done just that from a series of smaller investors and went back to Pritzker to confirm his interest. The International Association of Assembly Managers annual convention took place in Milwaukee that year from July 18 to 21, and on a Sunday afternoon following IAAM, Jay invited Fred to join him for the afternoon at his home in Winnetka, Illinois. Three hours later, Pritzker announced that he would come on board as the *lone* investor. As Jay told the *Los Angeles Times* thirteen years later, "It was a small business and it didn't make a lot of sense but he was brash and bold and he convinced me he could do something with it."[6]

The Pritzker family carried considerable clout in its native Chicago, and by the end of 1982 Ticketmaster had three major new clients. The White Sox came first, after Rosen locked in outlet agreements, choosing a balanced approach with a sporting goods retailer (Sportsmart), a department store (Carson Pierre Scott) and a record chain (Rose Records). The ChiSox were then joined by crosstown rivals the Cubs and local music promoters Jam Productions.

The pressure was now on to find success in a major market outside the Pritzkers' immediate ambit.[7] New York hadn't come together, so the first significant test of the new regime took place in Los Angeles. Fred acknowledged the precarious situation in signing two leases for an office on Wilshire Boulevard, one for six months and another set to run for five years.

The US Festival sale had proven successful (for everyone except Steve Wozniak, who found himself in exactly the same predicament, yet another $12 million in the hole, after discovering that his accountants had misled him regarding profitability because "press estimates of attendance were greatly exaggerated," and that was it for the US Festival). Ticketmaster's new vice president, Jerry Seltzer, then closed a deal to sell advance tickets in a few Southern California theaters for the much-anticipated conclusion to the *Star Wars* trilogy, *Return of the Jedi*. Other clients soon followed, including the Long Beach Arena, local concert promoter Avalon Attractions and the Los Angeles Philharmonic.

As in Chicago, one element of Ticketmaster's approach paralleled Ticketron: the emphasis was now on establishing company-owned operations rather than striking licensing deals. "When I came into this and started working with Ticketmaster in 1980 and '81, I can tell you there wasn't any model in my head," Rosen explains, "but I knew that as life evolved you could not make money selling systems because there were too many variables. It reminded me of practicing law on some level. You sold a system, you took the equipment, marked it up, created the software, marked it up and you wound up with a very small residue going forward. So every year you were starting all over again, as opposed to building a business that had a model of steady revenue stream."

To secure that steady income, Rosen diverged from the Ticketron blueprint. His new foundation was a requirement for full inventory from any facility or promoter who wished to sell tickets on the system.

The distinction was captured in a May 13, 1983 *Los Angeles Times* article, which echoed the coverage from over a decade earlier (and referenced the *Return of the Jedi* sales) in proclaiming, "Welcome to Ticket Wars." This era of Ticketmaster media coverage stands in stark contrast to what would follow only a few years later, as it tends to characterize the company as a scrappy young competitor (or in this case, "a maverick young firm, that sees itself as an agile David tackling an aging Goliath").[8] Reporter Michael London's description of the variances in inventory could have come straight out of Ticketmaster's marketing materials:

> Ticketmaster's computers will have access to the entire box-office supply of seats for every show it handles. . . . Customers will receive the best available seat at any given moment whether they buy from an outlet or the central box office. That's no small concern to rock fans who line up overnight for choice tickets to a big show.
>
> Ticketron, by contrast, often has access to a limited allotment of seats rather than the total box-office inventory for an event. And in those cases where the agency does handle the entire supply – as with the Universal Amphitheatre, the Irvine Amphitheatre and the Forum – there are occasional snags in the Ticketron computer system.
>
> "There are times when the orders come in so fast from different outlets that their computers or their operators can't handle it all," said Milt Petty, director of public relations for the Universal Amphitheatre. "You have a better chance of getting a good seat at the box office than at Ticketron."

The article also quoted Rosen with what would become a common refrain over the years to come: "We're a ticket service that makes use of computers, rather than a computer company that sells tickets." The logo was modified accordingly, eliminating the Optical Character Recognition font, because Rosen felt, "When people looked at the original logo they saw us as a computer company and not a ticket company, so we redid it. I think it cost us a grand total of $250 to create the 'Ticketmaster meatball.' [The name appears in a much sleeker typeface, with the second T in 'ticket' and the M of 'master' joined within a circle in the middle.] I thought that was a more hip thing and people would be more willing to put that in their ads."

Rosen always underscored the need for the system to be "rock solid" in terms of security and throughput, occasionally leading companywide cheers to that effect (One former employee remembers, "At the company meeting he'd call out to the employees, 'What's the most important thing?' and everyone would have to chime in, 'The system!' That became Fred's mantra.") Within the industry Ticketmaster positioned itself as a marketing partner, telling potential clients, "If we don't sell your tickets, you're leaving money on the table."

And that wasn't the half of it. As Rosen and his staff pitched it, forget about the money on the table; Ticketron clients were watching their profits draining through a sieve in the box office. Ticketmaster, however, offered a solution.

When Ticketron contracted with a facility, it billed the customer for the use of equipment along with a per-ticket inside charge for every sale. In addition Ticketron accrued revenue through the service fee added to the face of each ticket, at a rate that could be modified "by mutual consent." This consent would rarely if ever be granted by the client. One former Ticketron sales rep remembers New England promoter Don Law holding the line in the early 1980s, refusing to permit a nickel increase, seeing no benefit to himself or his Tea Party Concerts if fees moved from sixty to sixty-five cents.

Fred Rosen, however, was eager to share the wealth. Jerry Seltzer had once earned a client in Bill Graham by offering him a small piece of each service fee. Now Rosen was willing to step things up by doubling existing charges, with a portion of the hike going to the client.

As one Ticketmaster employee from this era relates, prospective clients were often wary of switching vendors. However, given Ticketmaster's alternative approach, a swift pitch would sometimes suffice:

"So with Ticketron you now have a seventy-five cent service charge."

"That's true."

"If you sign with us, it's going to be a dollar and a half."

"That's terrible. Why would I want to do that?"

"Because you're going to get a half dollar back."

"Sounds great to me. Where do I sign?"

While rarely this easy, occasionally it came close, particularly after Ticketmaster established its reputation as a stable organization that offered its clients the hardware and software needed to run the system free of charge.

Terry Wojtulewicz, who, as the ASU athletic department ticket manager, championed Dorothy McLaughlin's Select-A-Seat and over a decade later joined her at Dillard's, recalls with some bitterness the negative impact of Ticketmaster's policy on his own company: "When Fred went around hustling the big arenas, he started offering them free equipment. Then everybody had to have a terminal, and when everybody has to have a terminal that increases the connectivity costs, which was a huge expense. It just changed the whole picture of things."

This had a similar impact on Ticketron because of the way its box office terminals polled the central computer. Only two terminals could be assigned for each data circuit installed by the phone company. Michael Walthius, who worked for Ticketron in the late 1980s before joining Ticketmaster in 1991, remembers: "If you were going to computerize Oakland Coliseum, you would have to put up twenty data circuits, and depending how far they might be from the Ticketron hub, the cost really impacted on the kind of deal you could give someone [because of data line charges]. But Ticketmaster's technology was such that if there were any limitations as to the number of terminals that could be connected to a single circuit, I didn't know about them."

In exchange for the revenue share and the mechanisms to earn it, Ticketmaster required full inventory of all tickets sold to the public and an exclusive agreement to provide ticketing services for each client. Rosen instituted these policies in a direct effort to win market share from Ticketron. "Everything was exclusive from day one in every building," he confirms. "If you didn't get full inventory, you would lose. If I had half the tickets and they had half, people would go to them just because that's what they've been doing for twenty years. But if the competition didn't have any, people were going to find our distribution system real quick."

The demand for exclusivity eventually would be seen as nefarious, anti-competitive conduct, particularly after alternative rock band Pearl Jam questioned the practice in the mid-1990s. Initially, however, the industry viewed it as the aggressive tactics of an upstart company.

It's worth noting that the same model has long been implemented by food concessionaires. Deals are typically struck with facilities that grant an exclusive right to a particular vendor, who then shares a percentage of gross sales with the building (typically thirty-five to fifty percent of the proceeds). This in turn impacts the price point, which is why a microbrew purchased at an amphitheater can set one back a ten spot.

Rosen observes: "The whole premise of service providers in an arena or facility is built on third parties paying for the privilege to sell. At the end of the day the public pays the price based on the economics."

Gary Bongiovanni, founder and president of *Pollstar*, the trade magazine devoted to live performance, agrees that exclusive ticketing followed the industry-wide pattern of practice: "It's not different in my mind from going into an arena that only sells Coke. I can't buy a Pepsi in there, and Pepsi can't go in there and sell me one because that arena made an exclusive agreement to vend Coca-Cola products. It's the same thing with any restaurant. You're not going to find Coke and Pepsi in the same restaurant because that battle was fought before you walked in the door."

Where Ticketmaster broke with custom was in encouraging its clients to close their box offices on the first day of a sale. Since tickets typically were available at the box office without service charges (particularly in the 1980s and 1990s before facilities fees began creeping in), this offered the public no place to purchase seats without additional expense. In a May 1998 interview with *Amusement Business*, a few months before he left Ticketmaster, Rosen acknowledged, "If we made any mistakes in the 1980s, it was not having a place for people to buy tickets without service charges." While public advocacy groups and state attorneys general would give him grief about the policy, he deemed it good business sense and otherwise necessary to sustain the outlet network that benefited a public that was often eager to avoid the inconvenience of a trek to the box office. The facilities certainly had a hand in this as they made the final decision to close, influenced as they were by the revenues that accumulated from outlet sales.

In the mid-1990s Aerosmith manager Tim Collins would decry such arrangements: "If the only tool you have is a hammer, then anything that stands in your way just looks like a nail. Fred is a brilliant businessman who has single-handedly made ticket distribution 100 times better than it was before he arrived on the scene. But in the process he has turned from a driven businessman into an arrogant bully who has forgotten who his true customer is: the fan."

Yet to Rosen's mind such a charge is off the mark. Ticketmaster's ultimate interest was in protecting its client base, which consisted of the buildings and promoters who contracted to use the system. Rosen would continue to state for some time to come that "concert tickets are the most underpriced commodity in America." So he made a calculation that price elasticity would support the additional fees (although in the broader context of ticket costs, as booking agent Bruce Houghton comments, "It gets tiresome when price elasticity always seems to be pushing upward and never downward or side-ways").

Alan Citron, whom Rosen hired away from his post as a *Los Angeles Times* business reporter to become Ticketmaster's senior vice president for new media (and who later served as the initial general manager of TMZ), com-ments: "I think that Ticketmaster, in effect, agreed to take it on the chin in return for these contracts with venues. Part of the unspoken agreement, or maybe even spoken, was that we will be the face of ticketing. Buying a ticket is not a real enjoyable process. We'll make it as good as it can be, and we'll also take the bruises from people who don't like the process."

Jerry Seltzer breaks into laughter as he concurs: "We took all the shit for the promoters. Bill Graham and others would say, 'You know we can't do anything about the service charges. It's the ticketing company.'"

While still gaining his bearings in Los Angeles, Rosen sought to solidify his role as a champion of the buildings by tangling with the schoolyard bully. At issue were the service charges at the Long Beach Arena for the Ringling Bros. and Barnum & Bailey Circus. Feld Productions, which owned the circus, had long built a reputation among arena managers for its combativeness in exacting favorable contract terms on facility rental, service fees and the right to sell its own merchandise (which the venues otherwise did themselves on commission). While working as a Ticketron account rep, Charlie Williams recalls that a Ringling representative regularly would walk through Chicago Stadium counting the seats and comparing them with those listed on the building manifest to ensure that no potential ticket sales would be hidden from the circus.[9] In 1974 a dispute over the proceeds from skyboxes at the new Capital Centre in Washington, DC, led building owner Abe Pollin to mount a counterattack by forming an alternative, Circus America, featuring former Ringling Bros. clown Emmett Kelly (Circus America lasted for two seasons while the animus with Feld endured).

Within this context Rosen decided to battle longtime Ringling promoter Allen Bloom (described in his 2008 *Washington Post* obituary as "a hard-bargaining, cigar-chomping promoter of pomp, panache and spectacle"). It was a skirmish that Rosen had no intention of winning. He acknowledges: "I intentionally began an extremely contentious relationship with the circus. There were a couple calls I had with Allen that I guess would be in the Hall of Fame, where occasionally I would have one or two building guys on to listen because I knew it would be viral and they'd talk to the other building managers. I got to say the things to Allen that all the buildings managers wanted to say but were afraid. No one ever fought back with Allen because if you made it really difficult for the circus, he would appeal to the mayor, who would say, 'Why aren't you bringing the circus to town? This is apple pie and motherhood.' The net effect was that everybody in the industry got to know us in two years. So instead of being a little regional, lost-in-space ticket company, everybody said, 'Here's a guy taking on the circus.' Then, as we got larger, there was no reason to fight anymore, and we became good friends."

Before that moment, though, the two found themselves on the same panel at an IAAM conference. "Everybody thought there was going to be fireworks," Rosen remembers. "So I said to him, 'Why don't we confuse everybody and go out there and be nice to each other for an hour?'" The promoter was a willing accomplice, and the two recognized a common spirit

that eventually produced a friendship, with the circus even yielding a bit on
service fees (if not on merch sales, but that was out of Fred's domain).

Ticketmaster's "lose the battle, win the war" tactic was again designed with Ticketron in mind, as Rosen was confident that his rival would not involve itself in such an imbroglio. This fed into a plan of attack that Ticketmaster's former chief operating officer Gene Cobuzzi describes as "Ticketing 101." Cobuzzi, an accountant who joined Ticketmaster in 1985 as a regional controller, explains: "Control Data would rent the equipment to the box offices because, well, they were Control Data. So Fred came in and said, 'Right now you have a cost center, it's called your box office. You pay for the equipment and you have to pay for the labor to sell the tickets. I'm going to give you the equipment for free. I'm going to equip your entire box office with terminals. I'm going to teach your people how to sell tickets over those terminals, and I'm going to support those people. What I'm going to ask you to do is close down the first day of sale on concerts and let me sell those tickets through my outlets. So now you don't even have to pay the labor on the first day of sale. But if that's not enough, I'm going to give you a piece of every ticket I sell. So I've just turned your cost center into a profit center.' That was what did in Ticketron. You can say anything else you want about the stupid mistakes that were made here and there and the personalities here and there, but fundamentally that was the difference between Ticketmaster and Ticketron and why Ticketron lost the entire business."

That being said, in the summer of 1983 Ticketmaster was far from a juggernaut, so Fred Rosen tempered his optimism when the Los Angeles Forum came calling. Lou Baumeister, the president of California Sports, the entity that ran the Forum, contacted Rosen in the late spring of 1983, a few months before Ticketron's contract was set to expire, encouraging Ticketmaster to submit a bid. The Forum had been Ticketron's first arena client, and Rosen assumed he was being used solely to exert pressure on his competitor. What he didn't realize was that Baumeister was dissatisfied with Ticketron's unwillingness to integrate its system with the Forum's accounting program. Rosen said the right things and made the right offer, and on July 4 Baumeister awarded the contract to Ticketmaster.

While still celebrating his good fortune a day later, Rosen received a phone call from the office.

"We've got a problem. Ticketron just told Lou Baumeister they're not giving him sixty days. They're going to pull out right away."

Rather than wait until the end of the formal contract period, Ticketron immediately severed its fifteen-year relationship with the Forum.

"That was a straight New York play," Rosen observes. "If the Forum weakens on any level, you're in trouble."

Baumeister explained to Fred: "If I had any doubts before, I have none now. We're switching. I only have one question: can you get us up in ten days?"

Rosen agreed that he would, only to be told shortly afterward by one of his staff: "We're screwed. The phone company says they can't put in the line for three weeks."

One steaming hot call to Pac Bell later, Rosen had secured a single line into the Forum box office. It wasn't a data line, just a standard phone line, which a Ticketmaster employee scrambled to modify. Within a week the company was moving into the Forum box office, even as Rosen and Baumeister hammered out the final details in an office below.

"Lou was a total man of honor," says Rosen. "Can you imagine? They're loading the equipment in upstairs and we're negotiating downstairs. The first contract had handwritten notes all over everything. And a year later Lou calls me up and says, 'What does this note mean?' I said, 'I don't know, let's figure it out. . . .'"

The loss of the Forum still stings Ticketron alum Kurt Devlin: "The first chink in our armor was letting the Los Angeles Forum go. There were some very hefty demands because Ticketmaster was making a very lucrative offer, and rather than bite the bullet we told the Forum we wouldn't do it. That gave Ticketmaster tremendous credibility."

In exchange for their support Rosen rewarded Baumeister and Forum vice president Claire Rothman with a Ferrari and a Rolls Royce, respectively. The vehicles were slightly less than twelve inches in length and designed for children's play, but perhaps that was fitting as well, given Rosen's increasingly dismissive view of the competition.

TICKETMASTER GREASED THE SKIDS OF Ticketron's departure from the Los Angeles market two years later when Bruce Springsteen performed four dates at the 50,000 capacity Los Angeles Coliseum. Although the building was a Ticketron venue, the promoter, Avalon Attractions, was a Ticketmaster client, and the ticketing services each agreed to handle two shows apiece. Things did not go well for Ticketron, with the *Los Angeles Times* reporting on slow response time as well as outlets that had been knocked out of service. While Ticketmaster sold through its allotment on the first day, Ticketron was still holding 40,000 seats. Rosen stepped in and as a "favor" agreed to handle a considerable percentage of Ticketron's allotment and hand over the service charge to the company.

"So basically what goes around America," Rosen chortles, "was that Ticketron couldn't even sell out their two shows. I come out the good guy and ensure their burial. How could I do any better?"

Springsteen was also in the center of a significant transition from Ticketron to Ticketmaster in the New York market. In the late summer of 1985 the Jersey icon was slated to break the area attendance record he had set the previous year (ten dates at the Meadowlands' Brendan Byrne Arena) via a six show run at Giants Stadium. As initially projected, three of the dates would fall during the existing Ticketron contract and three would occur during the succeeding agreement. While still evaluating the proposals, the New Jersey Sports and Exposition Authority, the state-run entity that operated both the Byrne Arena and the Giants Stadium, asked Ticketron if it would be willing to handle the sales for all six shows to ease the potential transition in case another vendor was selected. Ticketron declined, indicating that it would commit to only three.

Mike Rowe, who served as general manager of the facility before leaving to become president of the New Jersey Nets in 1995, remembers, "Everybody thought Ticketron *was* ticketing, and so they were going to show us the foolishness of our ways if we switched to another company. We took that as a challenge, and it was one of a number of factors that weighed against Ticketron's negotiating style as opposed to something smart they did."

Sensing that the Meadowlands could become a flashpoint, Ticketron went all out and in a rare extension of its muscle (and its desperation) drew in a benefactor. The Speaker of the U.S. House of Representatives, congressman Thomas "Tip" O'Neill, chimed in with his opinion.

"O'Neill phoned us and told us that Ticketron was his favorite company and that it should be ours," recounts Rowe. "He told us that he hoped we had researched the background of Ticketron, which had been around for a long time, and Ticketmaster, which literally had just popped up. He wasn't telling us what to do, just informing us, based on his years of successful decision making in the public sector, that we'd be wise to spend a little time on this and make sure we did the right thing."

Alas, from Tip's perspective the Exposition Authority did not. Rather than re-up with Ticketron, the Authority signed a five-year pact with Ticketmaster, which was ratified by the NJSEA's sixteen member board of commissioners.

The bottom line was, in fact, the bottom line. The determining factor was money. Three years into its new regime, the business model that Ticketmaster now employed went beyond simply divvying up service charges. By now Rosen had refined his approach to provide an annual advance against proceeds and in select instances, when needed, a signing bonus. In this instance the Meadowlands received a quarter of a million dollars up front.

This particular practice raised the ire of certain industry professionals such as future Ticketron president Peter Jablow, who characterized these funds as "kickbacks."

Rosen still bristles at that term, which implies underhanded and confidential dealings where financial benefit is funneled to individuals in their private lives as a means to influence their public decisions: "When you live in Jay Pritzker's world, you have to run your business straight up. There was nothing going on, and it's not a kickback if it's a contract. If you have a contract with the Meadowlands and the Meadowlands Authority approves it and the Meadowlands is going to make a million dollars a year for five years, that's not a kickback — that's business."

These up-front funds were particularly consequential to facilities such as Byrne Arena and Giants Stadium, which were under the purview of the state government. *Pollstar*'s Bongiovanni explains: "That gave the arenas a certain amount of money they could reliably budget. If you're a public building, you've got to build out a budget projecting your income over the course of the year. Well, with a Ticketmaster contract you knew what your minimal income stream was going to be, so it was much easier to build that budget."

"Fred came in with an enormous amount of money," Rowe affirms. "It was more than a million dollars a year. It had a marketing component and a straight cash component. He was going to go out and help us market tickets with a lot of retail locations and a lot of advertising. He also made us a guarantee that our numbers would always be at least seven digits a year. Ticketron didn't do that, didn't understand that."

Although somewhat slow on the uptake, Ticketron did eventually come to understand Rosen's model; it just rubbed company executives the wrong way. Matt Whelan speaks fondly of Ticketron senior VP Bob Gorra, who ran the day-to-day operations, yet acknowledges: "One of Gorra's weaknesses was he always wanted to protect the consumer with low fees. He was very parochial. He thought, 'We can't finance this business on the backs of the consumer. It's a service and the service should be paid for.' He completely missed the boat there."

Kurt Devlin laments: "At the time we took a high road. We demonized Fred and said, 'We're not going to be like that.' We were in a life-or-death struggle, but we wouldn't utilize the same strategies. I look at it like the Revolutionary War, where the Redcoats wore their red uniforms and marched in line, while we shot at them from trees. They looked down their noses at us, but eventually we won. So we would have to adopt the same strategies or better, and people didn't really want to do it."

Still, it wasn't all sniper fire. When Ticketron dispersed the proceeds from ticket sales to its clients, these checks were drawn on a New Jersey bank. Many of the payees operated thousands of miles away, and it could take three or four days for a check to clear. Rosen made a point of establishing regional offices with local bank accounts to expedite this operation and earned some appreciative clients in the process.

Meanwhile, as Mike Rowe observed in outlining Ticketmaster's virtues, the company also placed an emphasis on marketing. Tim Wood, who began his career in the phone room and in 1999 succeeded Gene Cobuzzi as COO, explains: "We had marketing people in every city. They had minimal budgets but could create a lot of hoopla, and Ticketron wouldn't do that." *Pollstar's* Bongiovanni echoes: "Another thing Ticketmaster did that Ticketron never did was they helped promote shows. They used to buy ads in music magazines and newspapers with a strip of shows Ticketmaster was selling that was really free advertising for the promoters and the artists."

Jerry Seltzer, by now living in Los Angeles as Ticketmaster VP while licensing the company's technology to provide the back end for his Northern California service, still branded BASS, spearheaded these efforts with his own frenetic skill set. "Jerry emphasized that clients do not just want you to sell their tickets," Wood remembers. "We'd say, 'Ticketron will sell your tickets, but we will promote your event.' And he was the father of that whole concept."

Seltzer continued to dip into his guerilla marketing handbook. For instance, he originated the Ticketmaster Event Guide, which listed area shows and inspired bands to vie for the cover spot. While offered at a cost of $12 per year to consumers, it covered its costs via a push from Ticketmaster's trusty phone operators. Seltzer also targeted radio stations and sold them the ad space on the back of tickets with Ticketmaster receiving both cash and airtime, utilizing the latter to promote client events. Seltzer further advocated selling advertising on the envelope flap that held the tickets, which culminated in some angst when he finally lined up two customers, each of whom sought exclusives (to which Rosen responded dryly, "We'll see if they'll make an envelope with two flaps").

The impact of these collective efforts was quantifiable. In 1982 the company's sales hovered around $1 million, supported by twenty-five employees. Three years later that number jumped to just over $200 million, a vast improvement but still only about a third of Ticketron's efforts. Then in 1987 Ticketmaster finally eclipsed its competitor, with both selling just under $400-million worth of tickets.

Rosen closed almost all of the early deals himself, and as Tim Wood offers: "Early on Fred was unbeatable. He was Sandy Koufax in 1963. You could not a get a hit off him."

Ticketmaster's CEO earned a reputation for his combativeness and deep antipathy for the competition (although he generally maintained his humor about matters, as on one occasion when a *Wall Street Journal* reporter "complimented him on going through an entire interview without bashing his rival. 'Are they still in business?' Mr. Rosen responded"). Ticketmaster's account reps often dropped their boss's name as a bugaboo to gain leverage, threatening to involve Rosen when conflicts arose: "You don't want Fred to come down and get involved."

Meanwhile the CEO increasingly took heat in the media for rising service charges and such policies as its refusal to refund the fees from canceled events. To Rosen's mind this refusal made perfect sense because Ticketmaster incurred expenses when issuing the tickets and again when providing the face value refund. The policy would eventually be altered in the summer of 1993, however, because of the increasingly erratic behavior of Guns N' Roses vocalist Axl Rose, whose propensity to cancel gigs led Rosen to label the band "Guns N' Refunds."[10]

While Rosen was the public face of the company, he was also well-supported back at the home office. The phrase "home office" seems particularly apt as multiple employees have described the corporate culture as a family atmosphere (allowing for the fact that Fred "could be something of a demonic father"). One staffer characterized Jerry Seltzer as the "lovable, crazy uncle." A more measured avuncular presence was provided by President Robert Leonard, who held a master's in applied mathematics and computer science from MIT. Leonard had been hired as president and CEO by Burt Kanter and then supplanted in the latter role by Rosen, who nonetheless used him as a sounding board.

Fred took particular pride in the fact that most of his executives were not MBAs but rather had ascended through the ranks via long hours, street smarts and pluck. Still there was never a misunderstanding as to who was in charge.

On one instance Rosen's senior staff assembled in his office to discuss a particular matter. He decided to poll them on whether or not the company should move forward with a certain course of action. Upon hearing the results, which did not favor his position, Rosen opened his desk drawer and announced with a flourish, "I just heard from Mayor Daley. We found fourteen votes and we win."

"SELL THE SIZZLE, NOT THE STEAK!" This was the charge that Ticketron executive VP Robert Gorra made to his troops. Gorra, an industry veteran who had moved over to Ticketron when Computicket closed its doors, was quite familiar with the ticket-selling landscape, even if Ticketmaster's new approach had altered the terrain.

What, exactly, was the sizzle?

Former BASS employee Dan Deboer, who became Ticketron's area manager for Northern California and Nevada in the early 1980s, laughs as he recalls: "Well, there really wasn't any. There was a new system that came out for season ticketing, but that was something Ticketmaster could handle online instead of selling people their own private system for doing a relatively poor job of processing season ticket orders. The sizzle was that we can sell nationwide, that you can go into a record store in New York and buy a ticket for Los Angeles and vice versa. [Ticketmaster's outlets maintained a regional focus.] And it was all guaranteed. You've got a big company backing this up. We've got redundancy. All these other companies don't necessarily do that. We've got the best outlets: we've got Sears Roebuck and Macy's. So that was basically the sizzle — and it wasn't much of a sizzle."

It calls to mind the Ticketron sales brochure that promised, "In the extreme case of a power surge or complete power failure on the part of the public utility supplier, the Ticketron computer center will automatically switch to its own independent emergency diesel generator power supply." In other words, if all the lights were to go out in a Sears location, looters could line up single file at the customer service desk to purchase *Phantom of the Opera* tickets.

As for those *Phantom* ducats, they represented one of Ticketron's achievements, albeit a moderate one, in an era where successes were in short supply. After many years of giving Ticketron only limited ticket inventory — a history that went all the way back to the founding of TRS — in 1983 the seventeen Shubert theaters on Broadway finally placed all of their seats in the Ticketron system. Until that time each theater had its own individual phone room, selling tickets in a manual environment where operators would take requests from potential customers, jot down credit card information, walk over to the box office, pull hard tickets out of the rack (if available) and then charge the card. The company finally automated the process via its branded Telecharge service, but in so doing the Shubert Organization bought its own dedicated minicomputer from Ticketron (a Control Data Cyber 18, the successor to the CDC 1700s, which were replaced during this era), housed in the Hackensack facility and supported by the technical staff. Phone sales were handled exclusively through Telecharge (as opposed to Ticketron's new Teletron service); however, the inventory was released to the Ticketron system, so that its outlets had access to the same seats.

When it came to Broadway ticket sales, Ticketron had been patient and persistent, a trait that would not soon be shared by its parent company. Back in the 1960s Control Data made the decision to invest much of its resources in mainframe computers, utilizing a strategy that *Business Week* described in 1969 as "betting on bigness." Richard Beatty, whose Ticketron tenure lasted nearly two decades, asks, "How did that turn out? All you have to do is look at your desk." The rise of the personal computer devastated the company, which at any rate had long since lost its star developer, Seymour Cray, to his own Cray Research corporation. In 1985 Control Data posted losses in excess of $568 million and defaulted on a $300-million loan. Early the next year, facing increased heat from Wall Street, William Norris relinquished his post as CEO of the company he had founded nearly thirty years earlier.

As if this weren't enough, Richard Beatty, Bob Gorra and their colleagues faced a competition for resources from within Ticketron itself. After an initial flirtation with off-track betting in 1971, Ticketron had since moved aggressively into the lottery business. By the time Fred Rosen took over Ticketmaster, Ticketron had been bifurcated into an Automated Wagering division and a Sports and Entertainment division. At the time state lotteries were coming into their own, and the profit margins were relatively large. By 1986 the wagering side accounted for three fourths of Ticketron's operating profits and was thought to merit a corresponding percentage of its budget. Bob Price, then the president of Control Data, affirms, "The management of Ticketron put more resources into the Automated Wagering piece than into the Sports and Entertainment ticketing piece because they thought it was more profitable and a bigger opportunity long-term."

Ticketron's Andy Nyberg remembers: "Control Data was doing all types of things for Automated Wagering, and we lusted after that. At one point I signed a contract with the Chicago Stadium for all new high-speed termi- nals, and I got my hand slapped pretty well because they had no plan to send these terminals to the Sports and Entertainment side of the business. But we were committed, so we did it, and that helped save the account. So you'd ask forgiveness instead of permission, and there were a lot of instances like that."

"They had a way of accounting for their network costs and their data center costs that when you looked at a new market made it very prohibitive from a cost scenario to justify that you were going to sell enough tickets," Ticketron's Charlie Williams remembers. "It became very difficult to make sound business cases. I wanted to do business in St. Louis, but when I sub- mitted the numbers back to New York, I ran into my own people. They were my enemy."

Meanwhile Fred Rosen made every effort to contribute to their misery. He explains, "There were times for one reason or another when I'd tell a building, 'Let [Ticketron] know that I'll give you more, and then you'll get more and you'll owe me a lunch.' There were times that I walked them into a wall, and I did it with a big smile, and I got a lot of good lunches."

Matt Whelan says: "Rosen was an entrepreneur just like the promoters were, so he could talk their language. Plus when a promoter called you up and said, 'Can you advance me $100,000 against ticket receipts?' Fred could make a decision right then and there, where we'd have to get back to you in a week. Now we might have agreed to do it, but it would take us a week. But Rosen on the other hand had the ability to make those decisions then and there."

The situation Whelan describes increasingly became the norm by the late 1980s as music promoters were looking both for short-term and long-term financial assistance in the face of escalating performance fees demanded by top tier acts. Rosen and Bob Gorra agreed on one overriding principle regarding the computerized ticketing industry: the economics dictated that only one company could survive in a given market. However, Ticketmaster's chief went a step further in proclaiming: "The only true monopoly in the business are the acts. An act decides how much it's going to play, how much it's going to charge, and the big acts in particular have total control of what they do. So I was going to protect the buildings and I was going to protect the promoters." This was beyond Ticketron's commitment level, as Gorra's boss, William Schmitt, and the executives at Control Data viewed concert promoters as a necessary evil at best (and weren't all that convinced of their necessity).[11]

Yet this was precisely the time when promoters needed the help. The era of the flat deals that secured Bill Graham the hilltop estate he named Masada were a thing of the past. Graham said that two things remained constant year after year: "We get older and the audiences stay the same age," and "Promoters have to work more to earn less." Tom Ross, who would help to strike a new balance while booking such artists as Fleetwood Mac, Eric Clapton, Prince and Crosby, Stills & Nash, remembers, "I would say somewhere in the mid-'70s was the turning point of the agency business realizing that really there is a chance here to make a lot more money than the acts were making."

This worked in two ways. On the one hand by the late 1980s top performers were increasingly demanding and receiving eighty-five or ninety percent of the gross ticket sales (sometimes even more). On the other hand these same acts would also demand a larger gross from which to receive their percentages, driving ticket prices even higher. Ross adds, "Everybody was kind of looking to see what everybody else's pockets were filled with rather than their own."

Promoters by dint of their job profession are risk takers and at times seem to be genetically incapable of exercising self-control when it comes to pursuing high-level talent. They also are territorial, seeking to maintain their relationships with acts (often asserting "history" with a band, which equates to an exclusive first-look right to work with that group in that promoter's market). So as the price to secure superstars swelled, it wasn't long before calamity struck.

Fred Rosen was sitting in his office one afternoon when he received an angst-fueled call from the general manager of an arena in a major metropolis.

"I'm screwed."

"Why? What happened?"

"Well, to get the act, I gave away the rent."

"What do you mean you gave away the rent?"

"I didn't charge any rent so that they'll play my building instead of the other building."

Rosen turned this over a bit before asking, "How much do you need?"

"Oh, about fifteen, twenty grand."

"Okay, I'll get it for you."

"How do you propose to do that?"

"I'll raise the service charge by a couple bucks. I'll give you your rent and I'll keep the spread."

"Done."

This was another one of those brief conversations that forever altered the concert industry. Service charges were established by contract, which meant that contrary to what the public often believed, Ticketmaster could not uniformly raise the fees. However, on a case by case basis, in consultation with the other party to that contract, such modifications could be made.

Rosen acknowledges, "That's when I realized that I had a water faucet and I could turn it on and turn it off."

It's fair to say that in this metaphor, the ticket buyer was the one who ended up hosed (although Rosen felt that the public was underpaying anyhow, at least those individuals sitting in the first third of the house, closest to the stage).

The long-term significance of Rosen's offer to that flustered building manager can't be overstated. With the ability to earn extra funds from heightened service charges, promoters now had the freedom to match the ever-amplified demands made by booking agents, in a sense overpaying for the acts and then making up the difference by tacking an additional expense onto the service fee. The consumer was hit twice.

Barry Fey was one of those who cut a deal with Fred. "I ended up getting between thirty-five and forty percent of the service charge," he recounts. "I was ashamed of that. I guess I thought the fans were more powerful than they were. I said, 'My God, if the fans find out I'm getting a dollar-something, they're going to turn against me.' But they never found out, I guess, or didn't care."

Former Aerosmith manager Tim Collins remembers being confronted by a number of promoters at an industry event in New York City around this time, regarding Aerosmith's demand for a ninety–ten split. "They all got pissed at me, and I said, 'I'm not the first guy asking for it. You gave it to other people, and you can give it to us.' I remember being in grade school. You can't give ice cream only to one kid. You have to give it to all the kids. That's the way rock bands are. I said, 'You guys created this mess yourselves.' But instead of saying to me, 'No, that's crazy, I'm not going to do this,' these promoters were saying, 'Yeah, okay,' and they would get their kickbacks and they would get their profit elsewhere. Would you risk a half a million dollars for a ten percent return back then, which was a long shot? It would be stupid, but they were doing that because they knew they were going to get it other ways."

Promoters were unlikely to get it from Ticketron, which maintained a particular distaste for them. Plus, the company was not about to extend itself at a time when it was having fiscal troubles of its own. These issues finally rose to a head in mid-1989, when, as characterized by Ticketron's VP of systems and operations, Larry Litwin, "The business was sinking, and so to try to keep it afloat, they decided to sell some of the lifeboats."

This was the second time that Control Data initiated such an action. Three years earlier, as a result of its loan default, the parent company explored the possibility of selling Ticketron but found no suitors after setting the price at nearly $150 million. William Schmitt, a former NBC executive who became Ticketron's president in 1973, believes the earlier effort forever damaged the company's reputation ("From then on, people were afraid that we wouldn't be around"). It's a fair point because in 1986 Chargit, the service that focused on telephone ticketing sales, went bankrupt, taking its client funds with it.[12] *Pollstar* founder Bongiovanni offers: "The one thing the large ticketing companies did is they provided a degree of security for the artists and the fans. In the early days it was pretty common for the promoters to hold all that advance ticket money and run their own ticketing. But if you had a fly-by-night promoter or a promoter who was undercapitalized and couldn't pay the band so that the show was canceled, then the fans were out of luck. What Ticketron and Ticketmaster brought to the table is they were large, dependable companies that you knew would be there the next day."

By the fall of 1989, however, industry analysts began questioning whether Ticketron *would* be there the next day. Until someone with a deep antipathy for Fred Rosen saw a future in the company.

ABE POLLIN HAD A DECISION to make. Should he take Ticketmaster to court, or should he take on the company at its own game?

For well over a decade Pollin (who passed away in 2009), the owner of the Washington Capitals, the Washington Bullets and their home venue, the Capital Centre, had been a Ticketmaster licensee, holding the rights to ticket not only his building but the entire mid-Atlantic region. Pollin had secured a very favorable rate at a time when Charles Hamby was delighted to place any cash in the coffers, without giving much consideration to the next month, let alone the next ten years. The nature of this deal rankled Fred Rosen, who had become increasingly surly when it came to Pollin's franchise, which operated under the name Ticket Center. At first Rosen appealed to Pollin's sense of fair play by asking him to reconsider the situation and requesting a $100,000 annual fee (Pollin had been paying a mere fraction of that amount), while noting that Pollin had benefited from a variety of upgrades subsequent to the original agreement. Pollin was indignant, holding his ground on the sanctity of the original contract. Ticketmaster then attempted to put the squeeze on, and Peter Jablow, who ran Pollin's operations, contends that the company withheld its full software suite from Ticket Center. The upshot was that Pollin's lawyers ultimately filed paperwork with the intention of bringing Ticketmaster to trial. "I've been in business since I was 18 when I started building homes," Pollin told the *Washington Post*. "I've never sued anybody until Fred Rosen. I went out of my way to avoid that."

At this same time another opportunity presented itself that could keep Pollin out of the courtroom. Control Data was actively shopping Ticketron, which had lost $2.5 million in 1989. Through his friendship with David Rubenstein, the managing director of the Washington-based investment firm the Carlyle Group, Pollin became part of a team that spent $16 million for Ticketron. For someone who had founded Circus America to thumb his nose at Ringling Brothers, the decision to compete directly with Rosen rather than become embroiled in a legal matter was second nature to Pollin.

Ticketmaster had made an offer of its own to acquire Ticketron, but as Control Data president Bob Price suggests: "The Pritzkers approached me about combining Ticketmaster and Ticketron, and I actually was positively inclined toward doing something with them. But my management team at Ticketron didn't want anything to do with Rosen, so they all threatened to quit." Perhaps of greater significance, though, Pollin and his associates were willing to far outbid Ticketmaster.

At the time of sale Rosen observed, "[Pollin] is going to find competition is different where he does not own the only building in town. They cannot get most of the major markets for three or four years due to my long-term commitments. We have a much better system. All they can talk about is fixing a system that may or may not work." These comments proved prescient.

Jablow, a former executive director of a trade association, the Cultural Alliance of Greater Washington, and a future National Public Radio CEO, was installed as the new head of Ticketron. He soon announced that the company would distinguish itself from Ticketmaster through its more cordial dealing with clients. Upon learning of this tactic, Matt Whelan was incredulous: "I remember Peter Jablow telling me we'll do business like we do in Washington. We'll be nice guys and people will do business with us because we're nice guys. I can remember rolling my eyes. 'What planet are they from?'"

What Jablow failed to countenance was that, even if some building managers or promoters held a grudge against Ticketmaster, the basis of their professional relationship had little to do with personality politics. One Ticketron staffer described the ensuing conversations as follows:

"We're a new Ticketron. We're nicer than Fred, and we're going to lower service charges for your customers."

"Well, I make $500,000 with Fred. If you lower service charges, then what am I going to make?"

"Oh, you'll make less."

"Fred's fine. We don't have a problem with Fred. "

Whelan points to a related dilemma: "[Pollin's] partners completely undercapitalized the company to the tune of $7.5 million. I can remember being at the Carlyle group, doing my math in this little conference room, and I knew we needed $7.5 million for three contracts we had coming up that month [in the Northeast], never mind what other people had around the country. There was no way they could compete the way they had the thing set up. I was sitting there two weeks into the Jablow era. They're taking us through the numbers and I'm shaking my head, going, 'There's no way.' Early on they shot a bunch of people quickly, though, so I wasn't going to speak right up."

Jim O'Chery, a longtime Ticketron Southwest regional manager, soon to become vice president of sales, adds: "Because Abe Pollin owned an NHL franchise and an NBA franchise, he pretty much dominated the market in the DC area. They believed that they could take his connections, make a couple phone calls and get the New Jersey Devils to switch from Ticketmaster to the new Ticketron. But they found that it wasn't going to be that easy. When you own the major arena and the major sport franchises, you have a pretty big shadow, which made it easier to convince people in your immediate vicinity to use your services, even in other venues."

The new management team also discovered that the new software platform it believed would be ready to launch at the time of the acquisition was far from complete, in terms of both time frame and budget. O'Chery notes, "I think they realized it was like trying to turn the *Titanic*." Jablow was inspired to visit the Hackensack computing center to deliver "my best fire and brimstone speech," in which he emphasized, "People aren't necessarily buying the technology, but Ticketmaster is saying that what Ticketron has sucks, and at the moment they're right by comparison."

Devlin retorts: "We had been working seventeen-, eighteen-hour days for ninety days straight trying to get this done. We knew it was important, and everybody was incredibly motivated for many reasons: out of pride and also because 'If we don't get this done, we'll all be out of work.' So Peter Jablow's theatrics were not really needed."

Ticketmaster sensed blood in the water and ratcheted up its own efforts. As Rosen had mentioned, only a limited number of contracts were up for renewal, and each increasingly took on the tenor of a life-or-death struggle. The new Pyramid Arena in Memphis was in play, but as Jablow looks back in disgust: "We went down to Memphis, and we thought we had a deal with the guy who ran it. We basically shook hands, and then when we got back we found out no, Fred had a deal, and the guy's handshake meant nothing."

Charlie Williams winces: "I remember near the end they were building the Shedd Aquarium Oceanarium [in downtown Chicago] and we won the bid. We got the call, sent the contract down there, and about a week and a half later I was told that it was going to be rebid. As I understood it, Cindy Pritzker was on the board and had donated $7 million for a penguin exhibit. So they threw out the bid, rebid it, and guess who won?"

While it seems counterproductive for Ticketron to have vested much effort in such a context, Williams adds, "I guess we were young and naïve, so we thought we had it." The same would be said of Ticketron's last stand, which again, because of contract renewal dates, also took place in the Chicago area.

When the tiny village of Rosemont, Illinois, was founded in 1956, it began as a two-and-a-half square mile plot that consisted mostly of warehouses and industrial buildings. Fewer than 100 residents occupied the small township. However, two factors eventually elevated Rosemont and yielded a series of top-notch entertainment and lodging facilities. The first was Rosemont's proximity to Chicago's O'Hare Airport and a confluence of Illinois' major thoroughfares. The second was the purposefulness and pluck of Mayor Donald Stephens.

When Stephens told the *Chicago Tribune* in 1999, "I gave birth to this village," he was not being immodest; he was recounting historical fact. In 1956, when none of the surrounding suburbs opted to annex the area, Stephens filed the paperwork himself to incorporate Rosemont. He became an old school political boss, serving as mayor from that point until his death in April 2007 (when he was succeeded by his son, Bradley A. Stephens). During his fifty-year tenure Stephens initiated a number of public works and civic projects in an effort to raise the village's profile (and to find employ-ment for his friends and family). In the mid-1970s, during a national arena-construction boom, Stephens set his sights on a multi-use facility. Rosemont issued bonds for a building that was to initially serve as the home of the World Hockey Association's Chicago Cougars. Although the WHA fran-chise folded, Stephens opted to move forward and catch as catch can (the mayor had big, soft mitts).

Rosemont Horizon was completed in 1980 (apparently the Donald E. Stephens Arena would have been a tad *too much*) and began as a Ticketron facility with a standard five-year contract in place. It appeared that the con-tract would be renewed in 1985, yet at the twenty-fifth hour Ticketmaster was allowed to resubmit a bid and prevailed. With this agreement about to expire in late 1990, Andy Nyberg set out to reclaim it for Ticketron. In admittedly desperate straits, he structured the revenue-sharing deal of all revenue-sharing deals, proposing to make the Horizon an equal partner in ticketing revenues, an extraordinary proposition that far exceeded similar arrangements. Nyberg was told that the deal was a lock; it just had to be approved by the board of trustees that evening.

The following morning Nyberg was informed that the trustees had indeed signed a deal — a last-minute bid from Ticketmaster.

It turned out that before Mayor Stephens had coveted an arena, his pri-mary focus had been on a convention center. He targeted a warehouse that he intended to convert, but to be successful, he needed a hotel partner. In 1972 the Pritzkers stepped in and opened the Hyatt House. Other hotel chains soon followed suit, allowing for the construction of the Donald E. Stephens Convention Center three years later, an 840,000-square-foot facility that also currently hosts the Donald E. Stephens Museum of Hummels. In many respects the mayor owed his good name to the Pritzkers.

Nyberg was enraged. "The mayor had gone off to the fat farm at Duke University, so I called him there and said, 'I really want to come talk to you.' He told me, 'It's not going to do you any good,' but I said, 'That remains to be seen.' So I got in touch with my boss and said, 'We've got to go see this guy.' Well, we did, and basically Don was very friendly, but he explained, 'You can offer me whatever you want; Pritzker's going to match it. He built a big hotel in my town and that's the way it's going to be.'"

And that's the way that it was.

The new Ticketron soon crumbled, and on February 27, 1991, Ticketmaster announced that it would acquire the Ticketron assets for $11 million, $5 million less than the Carlyle Group had paid fifteen months earlier (as part of the deal, Rosen agreed to restore Pollin's license to run the mid-Atlantic region — at a fair market rate).[13] Ticketmaster earned back the purchase price within months and in 1992 boasted its first-ever billion-dollar year in total ticket sales. The government initiated a relatively cursory antitrust investigation, and in response Ticketmaster agreed to sell the Ticketron system in Hackensack to the Shubert Organization. Kurt Devlin and his colleagues finished the new platform shortly afterward and it went on to power the Telecharge service for the next decade.

Fred Rosen woke up one morning feeling slightly disoriented, without his familiar nemesis serving as a lodestar. But while he had finally eclipsed and then absorbed Ticketmaster's longtime rival, he soon would discover a whole new class of contenders out to raise his ire.

In the interim Ticketmaster began the process of converting former Ticketron clients to the new system. Among those staffers charged with this task, selected for his affable nature, training skills and company knowledge, was a tickled Employee Number One, Albert Leffler.

CHAPTER 4

"A Bunch of Wooly Freaks"

FRED ROSEN PASSED ON THE CALAMARI.

Not only did the fried appetizer fail to tempt him, but with a wave of his hand he dismissed the totality of the leather-encased room service menu held aloft by his host. John Pritzker, who had brokered the current gathering, took some pride in the selection of hors d'oeuvres at the San Francisco Hyatt Regency, one of the cornerstones of the family-owned chain. However, Rosen was in combat mode, and his bearing emphasized that he did not wish to dither.

Which is precisely why a lightly breaded nosh suited Hal Kant just fine.

Kant, attorney for the Grateful Dead, was part of a four-person contingent that had traveled to the ornately appointed suite atop Union Square to meet with Rosen and Pritzker on this early spring afternoon in April 1991. The lawyer was accompanied by periodic Grateful Dead manager Danny Rifkin, former rafting guide and current Grateful Dead tour manager Cameron Sears and Steve Marcus, the head of the Grateful Dead Ticketing Service (GDTS).

A little over a month earlier Rosen had finally vanquished his longtime foe, Ticketron. Now it was on to new challenges, in particular the audacity of a group that demanded the right to sell half the tickets to any of their concerts, in direct contravention of his existing exclusive agreements with the buildings. Beyond the monetary issue (and Rosen insists that there was "a beyond the monetary issue"), the limited inventory available for three Grateful Dead shows in Albany that had gone on sale a few weeks earlier had led fans to "trash the outlets." In an attempt to facilitate some form of reconciliation, Pritzker, a longtime Deadhead whose father, Jay, had purchased Ticketmaster in 1982, arranged for the two sides to meet and work toward a mutually beneficial solution.

Ticketmaster's CEO was eager to quash GDTS, an irregular organization staffed by individuals whom the band's own Bob Weir described as "a bunch of wooly freaks." The time had come for a righteously indignant Rosen to assert the primacy of contract.

But first he would have to wait for the squid.

THE GRATEFUL DEAD WERE RELUCTANT rock heroes, which in part is how they attained this status. The group came into its own in the mid-1960s as the house band at Ken Kesey and the Merry Pranksters' Acid Tests, where the boundaries between artist and audience were blurred (along with the vision of most acid-drenched attendees). The band passed the Tests, with its members thereafter striving to achieve the "group mind," which bassist Phil Lesh hailed as "the pipeline for that eternal music that we're all trying to channel and funnel through ourselves so that it can exist in our plane." Given such an emphasis, the Dead came to perform with minimal pomp and circumstance, typically delivering two extended sets devoid of stage shtick. What the group offered, however, was a tacit invitation to join a collective improvisational journey, as the Grateful Dead eschewed a setlist and spent upward of three hours a night striving to ensure that "the nodes of that eternal consciousness link together and become one consciousness" (while aspiring to remember their lyrics, which became something of a challenge for its principal songwriters and vocalists, Jerry Garcia and Bob Weir — the acid may have played a role there).

Since the band members envisioned themselves as conduits, they held a particular respect for those individuals who wished to share the experience, often viewing them as fellow travelers (in "Dark Star," the Holy Grail of Grateful Dead compositions, Jerry Garcia sings somewhat elliptically, "Shall we go, you and I while we can?/Through the transitive nightfall of diamonds"). This outlook extended to the group's support staff, where a loose collective of crew members and cronies often shared management duties. In 1971, when the Dead informed Warner Brothers Records that its forthcoming live album would be titled *Skullfuck*, no fewer than fifty-five of the band's associates flew from San Francisco to Los Angeles for the meeting with the label (an entourage that exceeded the capacity of the conference room, requiring Warner to move the meeting to the Continental Hyatt House, the "Riot House" depicted in Cameron Crowe's *Almost Famous*).

When Warner eventually released the album — the band had agreed to the title *Grateful Dead* — the back cover proclaimed:

DEAD FREAKS UNITE:
Who are you? Where are you? How are you? Send us your name and address and we'll keep you informed.

Dead Heads
P.O. Box 1065
San Rafael, California
94901

The list reached 25,000 names by the late 1970s as the Dead fulfilled its promise of distributing occasional newsletters a few times each year — antecedents to the band websites of today — filled with tour dates, commentary and artwork.

While the Grateful Dead received occasional media attention and a modicum of radio airplay in the early 1970s, its fan base tended to define itself against mainstream culture. This is not to say that the group lacked popularity. On July 28, 1973, the Dead were on a three-act bill with the Allman Brothers Band and The Band at the Watkins Glen Raceway in Watkins Glen, New York, that drew more than 600,000 fans, long credited by the *Guinness Book of World Records* as the largest attendance ever for a musical event. However, the "Dead Heads" typically viewed themselves as something of a secret society, and the band's intermittent newsletters helped to foster a sense of inclusiveness and self-selectivity (even if Deadheads occasionally became objects of derision, as when detractors joked, "What did the Grateful Dead fan say when the drugs wore off? Dude, this music SUCKS!").

As the 1970s gave way to an increasingly socially and culturally conservative new decade, the Grateful Dead fan base continued to grow, seen by many as one of the last bastions of 1960s idealism. One significant event took place on December 26, 1979, after the first of the band's five performances at the Oakland Auditorium. A small park adjoined the venue, and on that evening Bill Graham's staff spontaneously permitted a few concertgoers to sleep on the grass following the show. As the group's longtime publicist and biographer Dennis McNally recalls: "The first night there were, like, twenty people. By the end of the week there were a couple hundred. By the next year there were a lot of hundreds." The 1979 Oakland shows ushered in an era of sanctioned camping that the band's management preserved whenever possible. Deadheads could now travel with the group from show to show with some confidence regarding fallback accommodations in each city on the tour.[1]

In an effort to assist these itinerant fans, co-manager Danny Rifkin mulled over the idea of creating "tour books," which would include tickets to a complete run of shows. In June 1976, after the group returned from a twenty-month hiatus for a theater tour, New Jersey promoter John Scher had helped ease the band back into the business by organizing a one-off mail order out of his office at the Capitol Theatre. Still, Rifkin wasn't committed to launching an ongoing initiative of any sort from the Dead's home office until a charity event presented the ideal opportunity to test the waters.

After closing out 1982 with a five-night sold-out run at the Oakland Auditorium Arena, the Grateful Dead regrouped in March for three Bay Area shows at the relatively intimate Warfield Theater. In conjunction with these dates the band announced that it would institute an internally managed mail order out of the group's office in San Rafael. The impact of this decision would reverberate through the management offices of arena-level acts (U2, Pearl Jam, Dave Matthews Band), echo within the headquarters of national promoters and later resound in Ticketmaster's executive offices.

It is fair to say the Grateful Dead did not anticipate this legacy. Nor would it be the first time that what amounted to a default policy by the band yielded such unforeseen results. The group has long been hailed for the savvy, community-building impact of its decision to allow audience members to tape and trade live performances. However, it had never been the group's intent to create a taping section as a means to nurture and sustain a grassroots following. Instead the taping culture was already underway when the Dead sanctioned the practice (with audience members implementing stealth measures, hiding gear inside specially designed briefcases, fake casts and one storied, hollowed-out medical journal). The band members simply had knuckled under when placed in the uncomfortable roles of authority figures.

The establishment of the Grateful Dead Ticketing Service proved similarly serendipitous.

"The general drift of what I laughingly call Grateful Dead management theory was, 'If you want it done right, do it yourself,'" explains McNally. "In the very early '80s there were a couple of benefit concerts that left a bad taste in people's mouths. One was at the Moscone Center in San Francisco. It was a benefit for Vietnam vets, and there were competing groups of Vietnam vets and it became unpleasant. We had done the gig as a favor because somebody at the city had asked us. It was a convention center, an odd place, an underground space, acoustically bad and generally dubious. Benefits typically were fraught with problems because the beneficiaries frequently were involved with the production of the show and they were amateurs."

The Rex Foundation was created to address this predicament. Named after former Grateful Dead crew member Rex Jackson, who had died in a car accident, Rex became an independently staffed, non-profit organization where the band members occupied key seats on the board of directors to help select beneficiaries. "The idea then was to do some shows for the Foundation, separating the making of the money from the giving of the money," McNally adds. "It began with a series of benefits at the Warfield, and because we knew that everyone wanted to go to a small theater show, we did a mail order."

Rolled into this decision, beyond sheer ticket demand, were a number of other considerations. Since the Dead's fan base had grown older with children and (contrary to stereotype) gainful employment, it became increasingly inconvenient for Deadheads to wait in line for tickets, which was still the standard manner to secure prime seats, as phone charge was not yet fully implemented in most markets. In addition there was the musicians' internal, seemingly eternal, suspicion that some promoters were playing fast and loose when accounting for ticket sales. The band's direct involvement would allow for greater oversight.

The subject of a ticketing initiative came up at one of the group's free-wheeling, anarchic monthly "company meetings," typically presided over by crew members. Although the concept initially elicited some enthusiasm, when the call followed for a volunteer to administer the system, all zeal subsided. Eventually Eddie Washington, who had entered the fold after producing the *Grateful Dead Movie*, expressed some moderate interest and found himself conscripted.

Nearly two weeks after taking on the ticketing project, Washington reached a significant conclusion: he was a filmmaker by trade who just didn't know all that much about ticketing. So he put out a call to his cousin Steve Marcus, a semi-employed former BASS employee, offering him a "part-time job for five or six weeks" in early 1983. The gig lasted through the band's final performance in 1995, with Marcus swiftly taking charge of an organization that would come to sell more than 600,000 tickets a year.

STEVE MARCUS GREW UP IN the Bay Area during the 1960s with a unique perspective on the emerging business and culture of rock and roll. In 1968 his brother Greil wrote a letter to *Rolling Stone*, which had debuted the previous year, criticizing Decca Records and its release of The Who's compilation album *Magic Bus* (the letter opened, "This is not so much a review as a complaint . . ."). Rather than print it on the Correspondence page, however, Jann Wenner opted to run it as a review, sent the elder Marcus a check for $25 and soon hired him as the magazine's first record review editor.

Steve, then a high school student, looked on with envy as his brother received free albums and concert tickets. So he joined his student newspaper, began writing reviews and contacted the various labels, looking for comps. ("They told me, 'Sorry, we don't put high school newspapers on the mailing list. But if there's an album you want to review, just tell us and we'll send it to you.'") Marcus then decided to expand into the live setting, calling Bill Graham's office in search of guest list privileges for upcoming concerts. "I was told they could get me free tickets to general admission shows," he recalls. "And if a reserved seat show wasn't selling well, they could get me free tickets, but otherwise they could get me good tickets. So I started getting to know people."

These people were some of the most significant figures in the San Francisco music scene. Marcus parlayed a job doing window displays at the local Discount Records into a gig as a box office manager at the BASS office in Oakland (one of Marcus's co-workers at Discount Records was Jerry Seltzer's son Steve). In the mid-1970s Marcus also began working for Bill Graham Presents as a stagehand and a "blue coat" (the BGP in-house name and attire for security personnel).

His departure from Bill Graham Presents later served as an icebreaker during the initial interview with Grateful Dead management for the GDTS job. "I went in for my interview at their office at 1016 Lincoln Avenue, and I'm walking up to Danny Rifkin and Rock Scully's office, and as I'm halfway up the stairs, I said, 'I think you should know that I was fired by Bill Graham Presents.' And they said, 'Why?' And I said 'Because I complained about them overselling Grateful Dead shows.' And in unison they said, 'You're hired.'"

Bob Barsotti, who, unlike others at BGP, often was responsible for one band (the Dead) rather than a particular music venue, counters: "I liked Steve, but he wasn't really cut out to work at BGP. We had a certain kind of drive that was present in everyone who worked there, and he didn't quite have that drive. But he fit in really well at Grateful Dead; they had a different way they worked. It wasn't really set up for efficiency; it was really set up to have a relationship with the fans."

The mail order for the Grateful Dead's March 1983 Warfield Theater run proved a success in terms of solicitation and distribution with only the slightest of wrinkles. One of Bill Graham's hallmarks, particularly in the Fillmore days, was the creation of full-color tickets to his shows, which in most instances were scaled-down versions of the concert posters that he commissioned for each performance. GDTS would perpetuate the tradition of vibrant design, ultimately sprucing up all of its mail-order tickets with a variety of band logos and insignias, including skulls, roses and skeletons involved in all manner of activities (line dancing, lounging in a pool, playing baseball and, for one rare Minnesota gig, modeling a Viking helmet). However, for the first go-round, it opted for a relatively simple approach, conveying the basic information on different colored stock each night (the variance made it easier on ticket takers).

The one exception was the third and final show, in which Eddie Washington, on something of a whim, had added a blue star to the design. By show time on March 31, a small but vocal percentage of the Grateful Dead audience had interpreted the image as a coded message that the band would be reviving its cherished, open-ended, psychedelic exploration "Dark Star," which it had only performed once in the preceding four years. The sole crimp in this theory was the fact that band members had not even seen the tickets and were not about to fulfill a promise they never made. As Bob Weir reflects, "Those were just flights of fancy. All along, the ones that have been way deep into the acid and that side of the Dead fandom tried to read stuff in that we had just not laid in."

Prior to the formation of GDTS, the practice of mail-order ticketing for rock concerts was uncommon but not altogether unknown. A number of events in the late 1960s and early 1970s opted for this distribution method, from the Woodstock Music and Art Fair on through the Erie Canal Soda Pop Festival. However, the solicitation of orders and distribution of tickets was handled by concert promoters, radio sponsors or music facilities rather than the artists themselves, who lacked the infrastructure and inclination to handle the load. As things turned out, it fell to the most unconventional of the arena-level acts to do just that.

FOLLOWING THE WARFIELD SHOWS, Steve Marcus assumed design responsibilities along with all else, as he became general manager of the Grateful Dead Ticketing Service. Eddie Washington, the filmmaker who had never quite taken to life in the ticket office, departed the scene for Canada, where he had become a citizen a decade earlier to avoid the draft. The Dead envisioned GDTS as a relatively modest ongoing venture, with an initial focus on the tour books that Rifkin had once contemplated, offering wayfaring Deadheads the opportunity to purchase all of their tickets in advance.

As a concession to local promoters, the band agreed that GDTS would not advertise its services. Information regarding upcoming on-sale dates could only be gleaned from calling in to the official Grateful Dead Hotline. Responsibility for recording the messages fell to longtime staffer Eileen Law, becoming something of a comic ordeal. As Marcus recalls, "She had ten Code-A-Phone answering machines, each one hooked up to a different phone line that rotated. So if you dialed the hotline and it was busy, it would rotate to the next line. She had a shelf put on her desk with the ten Code-A-Phones, and when she would make the hotline messages, she would try to record all of them at one time by having the machines right in front of her and turning them all on at once. These were three-minute messages because that was the longest tape that they made, and it was hysterical because she had to talk so fucking fast to get all the information in."

Still, the hotline was not the principal means of transmitting ticketing information to Deadheads; that task fell to Deadheads themselves, who utilized what increasingly have become archaic means of exchange: verbal communication and the written word. The group's fans took pride in their collective identity as a community, promulgating their own values and sharing any news of import (even as others joked, "How many Deadheads does it take to change a lightbulb? None, they follow around a burned out one.")

GDTS ticket sales rose from 24,000 in 1983 to 115,000 in 1984, and the Code-A-Phones in Eileen Law's office started creating such cacophony that they were relocated to Marcus's work space, since he was identified as the proximate cause of the din. By the end of year two, an increased demand led the band to move beyond tour books and offer general mail-order ticketing to all of its performances. Then, following the group's improbable Top 10 single "Touch of Grey" in 1987 (it was the first Top 40 song of the group's career, and the Dead hadn't released a studio recording in seven years) and attendant media coverage (including an equally stupefying "Day of the Dead" special on MTV), the band was soon selling fifty percent of the tickets to all of its performances with collective sales cresting at 600,000. The staff swelled to eight full-time employees and thirty part-timers to implement the labor-intensive method of processing orders.

Filling out a GDTS ticket order often felt like completing a scavenger hunt. Customers were required to collect a white three by five index card, two No. 10 envelopes, two postal money orders and a pair of stamps for each tour stop. On the card ("Not paper! Any other size will not fit in our files and may get lost") patrons were required to provide their contact information and identify how many tickets they requested for the specific dates at a single venue, with a four-ticket maximum typically in effect. Depending on the nature of the show, Deadheads also needed to designate whether they wanted taper tickets, general admission, reserved seating or "anything available." The first money order covered the full requested ticket amount, while the optional second one represented the cost of registered mail. "One of the main reasons why we didn't accept credit cards," Marcus contends, in a stereotype-validating admission, "was that we felt there were too many Deadheads who didn't have credit cards, especially not the majority who had been following them for years." The index card, the money order(s) and a No. 10 self-addressed, stamped envelope with proper return postage for the maximum number of tickets would then be placed in the other No. 10 envelope (a standard legal-size business envelope, although the GDTS specificity for a No. 10 occasionally became the catalyst for a last-minute freak-out, particularly for mail-order rookies). On the designated mail-in date identified on the hotline, all of these materials would then be sent to the GDTS post office box with the name of the requested venue also listed on the envelope, which required a postmark, since postage meters were not permissible. (In 1974 Marcus had tilted the scales of a local mail order for the Bob Dylan/The Band tour by manipulating the dates on more than a dozen envelopes with a postage meter machine.)

Former manager Cameron Sears acknowledges, "You had to jump through some hoops. It was intended for single users trying to get tickets to their favorite show. It wasn't intended to aide ease of transmission, necessarily." The mail-in day often became an impromptu meeting of the tribe at the local post office, with Deadheads waiting in line to secure money orders and then returning to ensure that their envelopes were hand cancelled with the proper date.

It then fell to the ticket office to receive and fill the orders before the general on-sale of each performance, which generally loomed two or three weeks later. This self-imposed deadline allowed anyone who did not receive tickets to pursue them via traditional means. At times this could be a challenge, as high-demand events like the band's annual New Year's run would yield 300 postal bins, each three feet long and crammed to the brim with No. 10 envelopes. On very rare occasions the task became insurmountable, and an update would appear on the hotline relating the odds of ticket fulfillment, but typically, with the office devoting ten-hour days, six days a week, to the task, it was completed prior to outlet sales. Well over a decade after ticketing the final Grateful Dead show, longtime employee Frankie Accardi still gushes over a 1988 *New York Times* article that described GDTS as "ruthlessly efficient."

There was a common thread in the GDTS staffing decisions. Steve Marcus had been tapped by his cousin Eddie Washington. Accardi, who started in November 1984, was drawn in by her friend Carrie Rifkin, the wife of manager Danny Rifkin ("I was just being laid off from my seasonal ambulance position and needed a job"). As GDTS employee Carol Latvala, whose husband, Dick, had become the band's archivist in 1985 after years of friendship with the group, explains: "A lot of people got [GDTS jobs] through family connections. They weren't qualified for anything in particular, but they were members of the extended family, and part of the Grateful Dead approach was to include everybody. I wouldn't say it was an exclusive club; it was an inclusive club." Joanne Wishnoff, like Carol a longtime sala-ried staffer, adds: "I always said, 'Thank God for nepotism,' because that's what it was — as high as you could get — nepotism. But everybody loved it, and everybody was happy that their family members could work there."

Because of these hiring practices, the GDTS employee roster spanned generations. During school vacations the children of band and crew mem-bers mingled with the parents of band and crew members, as well as the coterie of individuals that Bob Weir likely had in mind when he character-ized the staff as "a bunch of wooly freaks put to work doing our ticketing for us." Given their colorful upbringings, the offspring of Ken Kesey (Sunshine), Dead soundman Dan Healy (Ambrosia) and acid evangelist Owsley "Bear" Stanley (Redbird) were not likely fazed by their tie-dyed-in-the-wool co-workers. (Laughing, Wishnoff comments, "This is Bear's daughter we're talking about. What could we show her that she hadn't already seen?")

One of the oldest employees, well into her seventies, was Maria Gerenek, the mother of Maruska Nelson, a secretary in the management office (as these things tended to go, Nelson was also the wife of Jerry Garcia's New Riders of the Purple Sage bandmate David Nelson). As Wishnoff, who still carries vivid memories and ongoing associations with many of her former co-workers, remembers: "Maria had something happen to her during [World War II] or after the war, where she was constantly being interro-gated in her own mind. She'd be sitting there answering the questions to whoever she imagined was talking to her. And sometimes — well, lots of times — if somebody new started working, we'd put them in the room with her. We'd be wondering all day, 'What are they going to say, what are they going to do when they come out?' Because she'd have a whole conversation, and if you didn't know, you'd think it was pretty weird because she'd say, 'No, I will not tell you this. No, I will not do that,' all day long. Yet she'd be doing registration and, if something were a penny off, she'd notice it. She was brilliant in math."

The work often could be monotonous, such as counting the 70,000 tickets allocated for a pair of Giants Stadium performances or sorting tray after tray of envelopes by the requested venue. "Your mind would start melting around the handwriting and words would stop making sense," Latvala reflects. "Like Philadelphia. For a while I remember thinking, 'Philadelphia. What a strange word that is.'"

When handling such tasks, the staff devised various means to keep them-selves entertained, such as a popular ritual that took place on Fridays at five o'clock, when local radio station KFOG aired the Toyes' "Smoke Two Joints." GDTS staffers typically cranked up the volume and then doubled their plea-sure by smoking four, before returning to the task at hand (this is not to suggest that everyone participated, as a few staffers were recovering addicts). The co-workers also participated in softball games and football pools, although, given the deeply entwined relationships in the office, gossip often became the sport of choice. Another memorable event was a surreptitious "hot dog party" for Jerry Garcia. The guitarist had been denied frankfurters by his wife and doctor, yet the GDTS staff fired up a grill one afternoon and allowed him to indulge in an outlaw wiener or three behind the building.

A more common way to blow off steam was through the processing of orders. "If we didn't have fun, it wouldn't work right," Latvala explains. "Sometimes it was a real grind to get it all done, and we had these little things that we could play with now and then." The objects of diversion were often the seating assignments, as Latvala and her pals amused themselves by creating a row of concertgoers named Brian or filling an entire section with Deadheads from the same city who had requested tickets to a show on the opposite coast. There was an internal logic to this, as longtime staffer Forest Schofield offers: "It was all kind of the Grateful Dead thing, which wasn't, 'Here's a ticket, don't talk to the person next to you.' That was not what it was all about. So what we were able to do via the mail order made a lot of sense to us."

The most common practice of this nature took place via requests for single tickets because as Frankie Accardi remembers, "The yentas in the office always tried to be matchmakers." Staffers would seat two Deadheads of the opposite sex together for an extended run of shows, "and every now and then we'd get the letter . . . 'Hi, this is Mary. I met John on spring tour and we're getting married.'" The wall of baby photos that Joanne Wishnoff maintained from such Deadheads only reinforced such efforts.

A July 1987 *Rolling Stone* article offered a glimpse of another wall in the GDTS office. The cover story on the Grateful Dead contained an image of a bearded, bespectacled Steve Marcus, cradling an armful of tickets while standing before a display of decorated envelopes. Savvy Deadheads with an artistic flair had discovered one way to distinguish their orders from the white noise that often numbed the staff. These were not mere doodles but typically covered the entire envelope, at times folding in elements of the group's iconography and in other instances offering original works of psychedelic art. A few patrons even made a point of extending their canvas to multiple envelopes, so that orders for various stops on a particular tour could be fitted together to form a larger piece. Schofield remembers, "Steve impressed upon us you can't give seats to people because they're great artists . . . but how you could not?"

Carol Latvala recalls one such envelope. In 1995 GDTS had been allowed to participate in the band's annual Mardi Gras parade, creating its own float for the spectacle that opened the second set of the Oakland Coliseum performance on February 26. A few months later, while processing orders for the summer tour, Latvala pulled out an envelope embellished with a drawing of herself atop the GDTS float on Fat Tuesday. "I still have it today because it completely knocked my socks off. It was one of the thrilling moments of my life to be on that float in the last parade, feeling like I was part of the bigger energy that put this whole thing on. We threw out necklaces and tickets, but I didn't know anyone had taken a photo. And then to not only have someone photograph a moment that I thought I would never see, but then to draw it on an envelope and find it in front of me . . ." It is fair to assume that this mail-order customer was not relegated to the rear balcony.

Still, most outright appeals to the order processors went unheeded as the salaried employees viewed their responsibilities with a moral imperative. Shortly after GDTS began operations, Garcia offered a charge to the initial staff: "I want you to keep it clean and I want you to keep it honest." The ticketing office threw itself into these efforts in part because the home team didn't want to disappoint.[2] GDTS was happy to support the band as it took a more aggressive approach than any of its peers to thwart counterfeiting and ticket scalping.

The first-line efforts began with the ordering of the tickets. During its twelve years of existence, Grateful Dead Ticket Sales employed two principal ticketing companies: Texas-based Quick Tick and Arkansas's Weldon, Williams & Lick. Two to three months before a given show, Marcus typically would secure the seating manifest from a venue, allocate the ticketing inventory and then solicit mail-order requests. As the orders began flowing into the office, he would work with artist Randy Tuten to select ticket designs and then submit the specs and images. Quick Tick and Weldon each had their signature styles, with the former company known for its glitter tickets, while the latter incorporated foil.

Like most of their competitors, Quick Tick and Weldon, Williams & Lick are privately held companies that guard their identities and manufacturing processes with equal fervor. While they aim to promote themselves within industry circles, both prefer to maintain anonymous public faces since tickets are such liquid commodities. As Jim Walcott, president of WW&L, explains: "We're basically handling Uncle Sam's greenbacks. So the Secret Service, FBI and private security firms have all advised us that the fewer people in the general public who know what we do, the better off we are. We do not like our name in print. We take out some ads in trade mags, but we try to avoid general circulation media to reduce the possibility of somebody trying to bribe an employee or break into the facility. The local radio station used to read the obituaries on Saturday morning, and a number of years ago our night watchman expired on Friday night. On Saturday morning the local AM radio station reported that 'So and so passed away from Weldon, Williams & Lick' and that night someone tried to break into the plant."[3]

The Grateful Dead was the first rock band to become an ongoing Weldon customer. Walcott suggests that while some of the printer's employees may have initially approached the job with apprehension, these sentiments were swiftly jettisoned. "Whatever negative connotation you want to put on the Grateful Dead, that they were a bunch of cranked up, long-hair hippie freaks, they were the first band in the rock business to go out and recognize their fan base and support their fan base and make sure their fans got treated as fairly as possible," he emphasizes. "The Grateful Dead was an account who bought a ticket that, if you looked at it, was very similar in size and shape to a rodeo ticket or ballet ticket. But they took it upon themselves to take it to the next level. They made the decision to invest in their fans and do as much as they could to defer fraud. So they called us up and said, 'What can you do?' Every time we had a chance, we'd give them something different. They were always asking, 'What else can we do?' and we'd say, 'We can do this. It might cost more money or take more time . . .' But they'd say, 'Fine.' They wanted to protect their fans."

They also were good to their partners as well, and when a Weldon manager was in the hospital following an accident, GDTS sent along a flower arrangement, which caused a stir, as Walcott explains, because "every administrator, nurse and doctor had to come in and see the flowers from the Grateful Dead."

Over the years, while working with Weldon and Quick Tick, GDTS added a variety of security elements to their tickets. At the outset the unique graphic designs provided some protection. However, as Steve Marcus notes, "Pretty much as soon as you came up with something, there was somebody out there who could counterfeit it." So GDTS sought to create moving targets, switching back and forth between its two printers, while incorporating additional features. Eventually, mail-order tickets came to be printed on a stock that utilized variegated threading in a manner similar to U.S. currency, with a center that differed in color from the face of the ticket, all of which was embellished by a holographic foil strip.

Starting in the summer of 1989, Marcus accompanied the band on the road for reinforcement, setting up a table outside the venues and offering to validate tickets for fans who may have purchased them from a secondary source. (One might argue that this initiative carried the unintended effect of promoting such sales by offering a safety net to those who purchased from resellers, as anyone who knew the provenance of their seats would have no need for confirmation. Still, no other group, either before or since, ever went so far to offer such a service.) While Marcus saw his share of GDTS knockoffs, he also grew frustrated with the "received wisdom" that circulated regarding Ticketmaster's new thermal ticket stock: "People said, 'If you light a match underneath it and it turns black, then you know it's real.' Well, any printer anywhere in the U.S. could buy rolls of thermal paper, so it was a crock. Plus, if you leave your wallet in the car or your tickets in the car and it's hot, then they turn black and they're unreadable. I absolutely hated them."

John Rhamstine, the box office manager of RFK Stadium in Washington, DC, affirms: "If someone left those tickets out in the sun, they would become unreadable. People would come to the window and say, 'I bought these, they're real tickets and I don't know where I'm sitting.' We'd have to decide how much pity to take on this person. It's all spur of the moment and how convincing people were with their stories. You might go to the promoter and say, 'I've got a couple guys here. Can I find them some seats? They seem legit.'"

In terms of taking pity on the Grateful Dead's fervid fans, BASS's Doug Levinson remembers one occasion when he stepped in. "The classic part of the Dead was all the counterfeit tickets that showed up. We let one guy in out of sheer creativity alone. He had half a Grateful Dead ticket from three years prior Scotch taped to the other half of an Oakland A's ticket, and he swore up and down it was a legitimate ticket. So we went to Robin Alexander at BGP and said we should let this guy in on creativity alone, and she allowed us to do it for this one ticket."

While Levinson had called an audible for amusement's sake, GDTS was typically more draconian when it came to the legitimacy of ticket requests. The office went so far as to enlist someone to spread out thousands of envelopes on the floor of their offices, looking for duplicate handwriting.

They found their answer in Calico, a Dutch-born member of Wavy Gravy's Hog Farm, who, like the other members of the collective, had often assisted the Dead with tasks such as babysitting and maintaining the band-sanctioned campgrounds. So when the fledgling office realized it needed another set of hands to help process the initial wave of orders, she volunteered.[4]

Calico led the charge to ensure that GDTS customers did not submit multiple orders. Before any of the staff members opened envelopes, she would spend a few days examining each of them with Steve Marcus or another senior staffer. Marcus explains: "Calico and I were really good about checking for matching handwriting. But it was also like she had a sixth sense. She would go through these envelopes, look at one and say, "This doesn't feel right," and put it aside. Now sometimes it turned out to be nothing, but other times, sure enough, there would be twenty or thirty envelopes that looked similar, and something would be consistent. So we'd open them up and see that the money orders were all consecutive numbers, and it was clear that one person was buying forty money orders, that these tickets weren't going to Deadheads; they were going to scalpers."

At times the challenge of getting tickets to Deadheads long preceded the actual mail order. One of Steve Marcus's responsibilities at GDTS was coordinating the ticket splits with the individual buildings. After receiving the seating manifest, he would determine how many seats would be allotted to both the promoter and the venue, and would then take the band's share, which typically amounted to fifty percent of the house. "You have to understand: you're the box office manager at the Hartford Civic Center or the Spectrum in Philadelphia, and all of a sudden this band is saying, 'Send us 10,000 tickets and we'll pay you the night before the show.' There was a huge amount of trust. We weren't even [financially] bonded, but the bottom line is, if we lost the tickets, it came out of the Grateful Dead's pocket. I think between 1983 and 1995 we had twenty-four tickets missing total. We had that many missing in one weekend at the BASS box office."

The Dead organization also recognized that some fans appreciated the relative ease of a Ticketmaster transaction (even if its service fees could be slightly higher, as GDTS ultimately set its ceiling at $2.50, with the exception of the New Year's Eve concert, which went to $3 to cover the costs of a special ticket). "You could pick up the phone and get a ticket or you could go to an outlet and get a ticket or you could use your credit card and get a ticket, none of which we offered," Cameron Sears comments. "We supported the technology, but there was a point in the business where people thought, 'Isn't it great that you can sell out a show in five minutes?' Well, it doesn't really matter to us that you could sell a show out in five minutes. If the show sold out in a day, that's fine. If the show sold out in a week, that's fine, too."

As for the allocation of the specific seats, the goal was an equitable split. "So what we would do at first was take every other row or, in a lot of buildings, draw a line down the middle and take one side," Marcus remembers. "Then I decided that every other row would be better. So that we wouldn't fight about who would get the front row, I divided the first four rows in half, where we'd get the left side of the front row, then the right side of the second row and so on. That way, if you went to Ticketmaster, you had a chance at front row seats, and if you went to GDTS, you had a chance at front row seats."

On one occasion early on, Madison Square Garden arrived at its own notion of a fair division. The arena, which the band would play at a total of fifty-two times over the course of its career, acknowledged GDTS's request for half the tickets in the building. However, the Madison Square Garden box office administrators examined the seating map, drew a line at center court and gave the band the rear half of the building.

Manager Danny Rifkin was livid.

An expletive-laced phone call went out to promoter John Scher, who successfully interceded on behalf of the group.

IN THE MID-1970S JOHN SCHER had become the Grateful Dead's "tour coordinator" for the eastern two thirds of the country. This was a unique role that in many respects encompassed the responsibilities of booking agent, promoter and even, on occasion, manager. Scher confirms, "I filled a lot of needs since none of the management people wanted to deal with the outside world because it would bum them out."

One might well contend that the role of a manager is precisely to deal with the outside world, but the Grateful Dead organism applied its own logic to each situation and, both by design and temperament, renounced centralized power. Personal relationships became paramount, which is how Scher came into the fold, as Garcia would tell him, "You might not be our brother, but you're our cousin."

Cousin John was born in 1950, making him a few years younger than all of the band members, including baby-faced Bobby Weir, who was three years his elder. Scher grew up on the outskirts of New York City in a lower middle-class New Jersey household, where he acquired a fascination with live music as a preteen. "My parents were not very hip people," he recalls, "but they sort of had this guilt thing about making sure my brother and I got to experience what was going on in the world. I have very vivid memories of being brought to Murray the K and Alan Freed rock and roll shows at the Brooklyn Paramount and the Brooklyn Fox. I have recollections of seeing these shows, of seeing Fats Domino, the Drifters and Jerry Lee Lewis, when I was seven, eight, nine years old."

As a sophomore college student at Long Island University, Brooklyn, he produced his first concert, a folk show that featured Jerry Jeff Walker, Tim Hardin and Melanie. He put this together with the help of a middle agent, someone who serves as an intermediary between college talent buyers and an artist's full-time booking agent, insulating the booking agent from the whims of the neophytes who work their way onto the college concert committees each year. The middle agent, who had first helped Scher secure the Chiffons for his high school prom, told him, "Hey, I don't know anything about this stuff. If you can book these shows, I'll split my commission with you." So Scher booked the acts, pocketed $375 and then encouraged his friends at other schools to join their concert committees, offering to share *his* piece of the commission with his pals.

Scher swiftly acquired a taste for the business, and although the major East Coast markets were already locked up by "promoters of record" who had established relationships with many of the major acts (Larry Magid and Allen Spivak in Philadelphia, Don Law in Boston, Bill Graham in New York), Scher saw that the "secondary markets" were still fair game. So he began promoting shows in Rochester, Buffalo and Syracuse. Scher's major coup came after Graham shut down the Fillmore East in June 1971.

Graham had placed a very restrictive exclusivity clause on any group that performed at the Fillmore, limiting their ability to perform in North Jersey within a few months of a Fillmore gig. Graham's departure enabled Scher to open the Capitol Theatre in Passaic on December 16, 1971, with music from J. Geils and Humble Pie. Scher kept ticket prices low and often rolled the proceeds from one show into the next, but the 3,000 capacity venue remained active for nearly eighteen years, with Scher screening X-rated films on off nights to help subsidize costs.

Meanwhile Scher's relationship with the Grateful Dead was advanced by a road manager's poor sense of geography. On March 27, 1973, a New Jersey State Trooper popped Jerry Garcia for marijuana possession in Mount Holly, New Jersey. Garcia was pulled over for driving seventy-one miles per hour on a highway with a sixty miles per hour speed limit, and when he opened his briefcase to grab his driver's license, the trooper spied Garcia's stash. From jail the guitarist called road manager Sam Cutler, who then called Scher. Mount Holly actually was far closer to Larry Magid and Allen Spivak in Philadelphia than Scher in northern Jersey, but Cutler associated New Jersey with John Scher. The young promoter posted bail and bonded with Garcia as they beat a retreat.

So when the Grateful Dead decided to resume active touring in 1976 following twenty months off the road, Bob Weir invited Scher to a band meeting at his house. Because of a limited supply of chairs, Scher sat on the floor for the daylong confab, which focused on the general question, "Who has any ideas about how we can do this and keep it under control?" What ultimately ensued was that Scher became the tour coordinator for all shows east of the Rockies, while Bill Graham would handle the west. (The elder promoter was not pleased with this arrangement and in 1987 staged a series of Jerry Garcia dates on Scher's turf at Broadway's Lunt-Fontanne Theatre, which led the two men to snipe at each other in the pages of *Performance* magazine. However, Scher is quick to acknowledge, "The modern art of concert producing really began with Bill Graham in the late '60s.")[5]

In designating the tour coordinators, the band made a point not to cut ties with the promoters who had supported the group over the years. This was not solely a reward for their early faith but also a conscious decision not to consolidate power, a lesson Weir indicates that the Dead gleaned from the demise of the Family Dog's Avalon Ballroom, which once served as an alternative to Graham's Fillmore Auditorium.

It fell to Graham and Scher to negotiate ticketing issues. Scher remembers: "Every once in a while my staff and I would have to go have a meeting with the muckety-mucks of Ticketron or Ticketmaster and explain that they could have half the tickets or they could have none of the tickets because we didn't have to come to their town. And everybody understood that, when it was a band *this consistent*, that was touring *this much*, that was selling *these many tickets*, it was only good for everybody. If they had said to me, 'Well, we can't do that because so-and-so act will want the same thing,' I could only say, 'It's not my problem. Does so-and-so come *every* year to the major twenty arenas in the country?'"

Scher intervened with those few venues that initially refused to cooperate. In the case of Madison Square Garden, he deputized staffer Shelly Diamond to present a briefing on the fine art of sharing. The lesson took (generally) and the intransigent venue assigned GDTS an equitable share of the tickets (nearly).

Although the band never overanalyzed it, what the Grateful Dead sought to implement flew in the face of concert industry practice (none too surprising since, as Bill Graham once famously described the group, "They're not the best at what they do; they're the only ones who do what they do"). A debate that has come to take on additional urgency today, with multi-rights deals and VIP packages, is the question of who actually "owns" the ticket. The promoter is the risk-taker, purchasing the act and renting the building where the show will take place (in many cases the promoter and the facility are one and the same). The ticketing company distributes the seats and handles the proceeds. Lost in all of this at times is the artist, the raison d'être for the entire process.

One person keenly aware of the performers' potential sway was Fred Rosen. As he had said: "The only true monopoly in the business are the acts. An act decides how much it's going to play, how much it's going to charge, and the big acts in particular have total control of what they do." Albany's Knickerbocker Arena had been open for little more than a year, and Rosen recognized that allowing the Dead to run roughshod over a new contract, where the band did not have an extended history with the facility, would make for poor precedent (and on top of this he was perturbed by the treatment of his outlets, resulting from the quick sellouts caused by the limited available inventory). These instincts led Ticketmaster's CEO to conclude that he had to move against the band. He issued a mandate limiting the group to ten percent of the tickets to an upcoming Giants Stadium show. The Grateful Dead did not respond warmly to this fiat. And so it fell to billionaire Deadhead John Pritzker to bring the two defiant parties together in his San Francisco hotel suite.

GRATEFUL DEAD ATTORNEY HAL KANT possessed a skill set that rendered him well suited for a tussle with Rosen. Prior to graduating from Harvard Law School in 1958, Kant had received a master's degree from Penn State and then spent a few years as an army psychologist. Yet beyond any insights he may have gleaned from his educational and clinical experiences, Kant also was a formidable adversary because he could play his hand exceptionally well. The attorney's World Series of Poker bracelet was a testament to that fact.

Kant first indulged his "yen for the felt" in the mid-1940s as an occasional student at DeWitt Clinton High School in the Bronx. There he spent nearly half his days playing penny ante poker in the basement of an adjacent tenement. His passion for the game extended into his adult life, and after some successful finishes in local casino tournaments, he entered his initial World Series of Poker event in 1986. Kant found himself at the final table on a few occasions before earning his bracelet (and $174,000) a year later with a victory at the Omaha Pot Limit event. Kidd Candelario, the head of Grateful Dead Merchandising, commemorated Kant's ongoing success, which included a first place finish at Donald Trump's U.S. Poker Championships, with a T-shirt that featured a skeleton card dealer with Kant's "nom de poker," Deadman.

Kant had come to work with the Dead through happenstance. In the 1960s the lawyer began a music practice and represented such groups as the Association ("Along Comes Mary," "Cherish" and "Windy") because the boutique Beverly Hills law firm he had joined was next door to the William Morris Agency, and Doug Weston, owner of Los Angeles folk club the Troubadour, had ambled over searching for someone to assist the Good Time Singers (who were then backing Andy Williams on his television show).

By 1971 Kant had moved on to TV and film law, when a friend of his from grad school introduced him to the Grateful Dead, who, for accountability's sake, requested his services to the exclusion of any other music clients (the group's previous manager had just emptied the coffers and lit out for Mexico, and he was the *father* of Grateful Dead drummer Mickey Hart, no less). Given the direction of his practice and the nature of the personalities involved, Kant assented, thinking that the results would be "at the very least, entertaining." To his mind the gig proved to be just that, involving such tasks as convincing Jerry Garcia to pursue a legal remedy after Ben & Jerry's began marketing their new flavor of ice cream, Cherry Garcia, without his consent or concern (the guitarist told the lawyer, "At least they're not naming motor oil after me," before eventually receiving a sizable stipend) on through negotiating the briefest recording contract of the era, a four-page deal with Arista Records in 1988 at a time when most agreements topped seventy pages.

It was a cavalier attitude buttressed by a sense of righteousness and a penchant for the absurd that Kant, who passed away in 2008 from pancreatic cancer, brought to the Hyatt that day.

The calamari finally arrived, signifying that the meeting proper could begin. While Kant focused on the appetizer, Cameron Sears opened the proceedings, affably if awkwardly, by making unnecessary introductions. He began, "John, you know us, but for Fred's edification let me explain who we are. We're a family. . . ." Sears then offered an overview of the Grateful Dead organization, detailing the connections between band, staff and fans.

John Pritzker saw some symmetry and chimed in next: "Cameron, Steve, you know us, but for Danny and Hal's edification let me explain who we are. We're a family. . . ." Pritzker then delivered a quasi-serious riff on the fact that his side of table also represented family, which was not to be discounted and would not yield any moral high ground.

Sears quickly countered, "John, you know when you need tickets to shows or your brothers need tickets to shows how we accommodate you?"

Pritzker, who was in his late thirties at the time, acknowledged: "Yeah, you guys have always been great. I appreciate it."

"Well, we have a lot of friends like you guys. We have people that are steelworkers that are our friends. We have people who are business people who are our friends. We even have lawyers at the Justice Department who are our friends."

This was Fred Rosen's cue. He grabbed the reins and set off on a lengthy diatribe that began with the outlet damage in Albany, emphasizing that while the Dead only came through once a year to play three shows, he was attempting to preserve his reputation for the other 362 days. From there he related the history of Ticketmaster and its recent success in liberating concert facilities from the stiff, lifeless Ticketron operating system. Rosen puffed out his chest and turned up the volume a notch as he explained that such advancements rested on the fundamental principal of exclusivity. He harped on this theme, insisting that the Grateful Dead was attempting to undermine Ticketmaster's signed, enforceable agreements to secure the totality of a given venue's ticket inventory, which it had acquired through fair bidding on the open market.

Looking back, Sears reflects with some understatement: "I would say that Fred Rosen is a very combative personality. He digs in and he knows what he wants, and he didn't want to give it up. He felt he was giving and we were taking. That was the premise he came into it with. From his point of view he was right. I mean, he was paying money to the buildings to be able to sell these tickets, and here's a hot act coming in that's saying, 'We're taking fifty percent.' He's going, 'But I know those tickets would sell instantly on my system, and I would be deriving the revenue.' It's not that dissimilar from the vendor who sells Coca-Cola, the vendor who sells beer, the vendor who handles the parking. Those guys have a contract. It's not as if you can come in and say, 'Hey, we got our own parking guy.' There's a contract. And that's what Fred did shrewdly. He offered people a lot of money to give him exclusive rights."

Though the ultimate outcome is of no dispute, there is a difference of opinion as to what happened next. Rosen recalls: "When I told them what happened at the outlets, they weren't happy. I looked them in the eye and asked, 'Why is your fan club better than the people standing in line?' And they said, 'Well, they're not,' and I said, 'Well, you have to have balance.' I knew I'd make a deal. There was never an issue that I wouldn't make a deal, but the only way to make a deal is to sit in a room and get to a place where people will compromise, and they'll compromise because they know you're tough and you will take the most extreme stand." Still, Rosen asserts, "I had great admiration for how they treated their fans and was willing to work with them."

The Dead contingent remembers it slightly differently. To their recollection, as the Ticketmaster CEO began building up momentum on particular points, Kant started interrupting him with seemingly innocuous questions about Rosen's personal life or work habits and then appeared to jot down the answers. Rosen abided this for a short while, but after the seventh or eighth time the agitated executive stopped his monologue altogether and demanded, "Why are you doing this?" In fact, Kant was coffee housing, a common poker tactic to render an opponent unsettled. However, the lawyer answered, "I just want to see what kind of witness you're going to make."

Rosen sputtered to a complete stop.

Kant laughs. "I was just scribbling. I was surprised by his reaction. He was really taken aback."

The Grateful Dead attorney then took the offensive. After Rosen attempted to build up steam once again, Kant interrupted: "First of all what you're doing presents antitrust problems. As you know, the antitrust division is looking into this, and we've hired counsel to assist them."

Rosen retorted, "Forget about antitrust. Have you ever heard of interfering with a business relationship? You're interfering with my business relationships."

Kant went all in: "It's interesting you mention that because just this morning I told our lawyers to forget about antitrust, to go after you for interfering with a business relationship. How long have you been in business?"

As the band recalls, Fred Rosen then fell silent. His line of argument had been predicated on the changes he had wrought since taking over Ticketmaster in 1982. However, he recognized that the Grateful Dead had been in business with many of the same promoters and facilities for upward of twenty years. Then the CEO blurted out, "Who are your lawyers?" suspecting that perhaps Kant was bluffing.

"Morrison & Foerster."

Once again Rosen found himself at a loss. He, too, had contacted the same firm, known within the profession as MoFo for its tenacity and aggression. Ticketmaster had enlisted the San Francisco office while Kant had hired the New York and Washington office.

In looking back, Pritzker shares Rosen's account of the meeting at the Hyatt, which runs counter to the brief overview presented in Dennis McNally's official biography of the Grateful Dead, *A Long Strange Trip*: "In McNally's book, he said something about how we were using the same law firm and they out-clevered us. That isn't at all what happened."

At this point Kant decided to pile it on a bit, asking their host whether he really wanted to unleash thousands of angry Deadheads on the Hyatt hotel chain. Pritzker answered, "As long as they pay the going rate, that's okay." But sharp responses aside, to the band's mind at least, the momentum had shifted.

The meeting wrapped up shortly thereafter, as the parties arrived at what the Grateful Dead would deem "The Fifty Percent Solution." This nearly ratified the status quo, as the band was permitted fifty percent of the tickets to arena shows, thirty-five percent to amphitheaters and twenty-five percent to stadiums. Steve Marcus interjected himself at this point, expressing reservations regarding the stadium figure, as it represented half of what GDTS had been selling. However, he was hushed and now recalls, "We ended up being able to do almost fifty percent of the stadiums anyway."

No written agreement was ever tendered. However, this course was acceptable to Kant because, "We got everything we wanted. As long as they didn't annoy us, there was no need to do anything else. It never was a problem again, and I didn't see any reason for us to be pushing it or spending any money on it."

OVER THE MONTHS THAT FOLLOWED, while Ticketmaster continued to consolidate its power, a number of bands began asking GDTS for advice. Metallica approached the group regarding the tapers section that the Dead had carved out for each show. Marcus brought this request to the band members, who encouraged him to "tell them everything." So he handed over all the materials GDTS had created for the venues, promoters and fans, explaining, "You're welcome to use it all, word for word." And so the biggest metal band in the world did just that, utilizing precisely the same language in establishing and promoting their own dedicated taping realm. A Deadhead from Vermont named Shelly Culbertson also contacted Marcus and received similar support as she developed a mail-order ticket service for the band Phish.

Two arena-level acts then initiated discussions about the possibility of outsourcing their own ticketing efforts to GDTS. U2 inquired as to whether GDTS would be willing to take on responsibility for what was projected to be a two-year international tour, but ultimately the office concluded that the Irish group would not be a perfect fit because, as Frankie Accardi states rather plainly, "None of us were U2 fans. We were all Deadheads."

Pearl Jam manager Kelly Curtis then visited and, after he watched the staff in action, raised the possibility of hiring GDTS to handle the group's ticket fulfillment. Ultimately both sides decided this wasn't feasible either, as Pearl Jam was searching for methods to keep its ticket prices at a bare minimum and indicated that GDTS needed to establish a lower service charge for Pearl Jam fans than for Deadheads (the $2.50 fee was still above Pearl Jam's target price).

Still, the legacy of that meeting at the Hyatt Regency would resonate with the Dave Matthews Band (who would become the largest touring artist of the 2000s) and their manager Coran Capshaw, himself the veteran of 400 Dead shows, who later tweaked the GDTS model and established the ticketing and merchandise fulfillment center MusicToday. The String Cheese Incident, who would wage their own battle with Ticketmaster a decade later, used the Dead's precedent as the main platform for their argument.

In the near future the Grateful Dead's successful stand against Ticketmaster would embolden Curtis and Pearl Jam to launch a crusade of their own.

CHAPTER 5

Rumble in the Jungle

WEDNESDAY, JULY 5, 1995, WAS a muggy day in Washington, DC. With temperatures in the eighties and humidity high, it was typically oppressive weather in the U.S. capital. As Robin Williams' radio DJ character in the film *Good Morning, Vietnam* once offered, "It's hot and wet. Nice if you're with a lady. Ain't no good if you're in the jungle."

The political landscape in Washington has always been something of a jungle. Vast, dense and unforgiving, its hierarchal web of players and policies constantly changes and regenerates like a natural ecosystem.

Given the seemingly infinite activity of Washington politics, the decisions, legislation or activity of any given day in its history require some amount of gravitas to be remembered. The passage of the Child Protection and Obscenity Enforcement Act by Congress that day — requiring that producers of pornography keep records of all models who are filmed or photographed, and that all models be at least eighteen years of age — perhaps sticks out given the multibillion dollar industry it affected. There was another multibillion dollar segment of the entertainment industry that received notice that day, too. However, it didn't receive any legislation or lengthy critique — just two sentences from the Department of Justice's antitrust division.

"The Department of Justice announced today that it has informed Ticketmaster Holdings Group, Inc., that it is closing its antitrust investigation into that firm's contracting purposes. The Department will continue to monitor competitive developments in the ticketing industry."

The story behind those two sentences involves the first public battle the concert industry had faced since its humble beginning three decades earlier.

THE MUSICAL GENRE KNOWN AS grunge that developed in the Pacific Northwest in the late 1980s and early 1990s was an art form reacting, in part, to what it perceived as the country's apathy-inducing commercialism. The Reagan years in particular seemed unnecessarily greedy, personified by Michael Douglas's character in the film *Wall Street*, who famously boasted, "Greed, for lack of a better word, is good."

Much like the punk music that preceded it, grunge was very much a DIY movement that was happy to fly under the radar of the mainstream. It relied upon itself for support — not on the institutions that had become music's salesmen. Still, any band's dream is to be able to ply its craft for a living. If that opportunity happens to come from a major label, so be it. Grunge presented a raw and brooding sound but one that, like punk, became commercially viable.

The Seattle-based band Pearl Jam released its debut album, *Ten*, in August 1991. Nirvana's *Nevermind* followed in September and then Soundgarden's *Badmotorfinger*. Each album rocketed into the charts, all eventually going platinum. Suddenly these grunge bands were on national radio, cutting videos for MTV, appearing on magazine covers and playing to a lot more people than they had just a few months earlier. What was once alternative was now, suddenly, the mainstream.

In May 1992, having already toured extensively throughout the United States and Europe — *Ten* was a worldwide success by no small measure — Pearl Jam wanted to do a free outdoor concert in its hometown of Seattle. Though the band had spent five months getting the necessary permits and paperwork for Gas Works Park, city officials pulled the plug three days before the event, citing crowd concerns: the 5,000 people initially expected had swelled to 20,000 to 30,000. The show was eventually rescheduled for September in Magnuson Park.

While the rescheduled show was still free, the city required tickets to help deal with crowd issues. Pearl Jam contacted Ticketmaster to inquire about its ticketing services for the show. The company asked for $1 to $1.50 per ticket, asserting the need to cover its costs. The thought of shelling out $45,000 so 30,000 fans could see the show for free didn't agree with the band. Dissatisfied, the group found other solutions, utilizing local radio to spread word that tickets were being distributed at the Seattle Center Coliseum. While the show was a success, little did the band know that it was only the beginning of its troubles with Ticketmaster.

That December Pearl Jam culminated its tour with three shows at the Seattle Center Arena. The band had earmarked $20,000 of its projected profit as a charitable donation to the Seattle Center Arts and Sciences Academy. According to Kelly Curtis, the group's manager, he had gotten a local Ticketmaster representative to agree to match the amount two months earlier.

The day the tickets were to go on sale, says Curtis, the band received a call from the rep informing them the donation had not been authorized. Ticketmaster, the band said, wanted to increase the service charge by a dollar to cover its donation.

Curtis said he ordered Ticketmaster to cancel the shows. He contends that after a lengthy discussion Ticketmaster consented to a donation without a rise in service fee, though only $14,000 went to charity — one dollar per ticket sold.

Conversely, as Chuck Philips reported in the *Los Angeles Times*, anonymous Ticketmaster officials said it was Pearl Jam who caused the problem — the band wanted to raise the service fee by fifty cents to cover its portion of the donation. As Ticketmaster spokesman Larry Solters would later tell Philips, "When Pearl Jam needed to raise money for their charity, they didn't seem to have any difficulty with raising the service fee to accomplish it. It kind of makes you wonder what this whole dispute is about."

From its beginning Pearl Jam tried to be price sensitive to its fans. The band's modus operandi was that if they were willing to take less money, then so should those that they were doing business with (or, from their point of view, were *giving* business to).[1] It was a contentious conceit but one Pearl Jam could theoretically toe the line on, given its popularity.

As it began planning for its summer 1994 tour, after the conclusion of the winter 1993 tour — it already had its spring 1994 tour in place — Pearl Jam told promoters that it would again be keeping its ticket prices low: an $18 base price with no more than a ten percent service fee on top. In addition the band had two other provisions: the service fee had to be printed on the ticket separately from the base price, and the ticket stock could not have any advertising.

These conditions put promoters in a precarious position. Pearl Jam was one of the hottest acts performing — any show was likely a sellout — and promoters competitively bid for the show. However, the per-ticket service charge and the particulars of what appeared on the face of the ticket were not things that promoters unilaterally controlled. The demands struck at one of the concert industry's main pressure points.

Ticketmaster negotiated its contracts with venues (and promoters) on a case-by-case basis. As previously discussed, the company would incentivize buildings to sign exclusive, multiyear contracts with monetary compensation. Depending on the size, location and history of the venue, the building would get an advance on future sales (as a record company gives an artist) and, occasionally, a signing bonus. Once the advance was recouped, the buildings and promoters would get annual rebates as part of a revenue share of the service fees with Ticketmaster.

Within each contract specific terms as to what service fee caps could be for various events (concerts, sports, circuses, etc.) were laid out. From those benchmarks Ticketmaster, the venue and the promoter would then determine the service fee for a specific event. Sometimes the promoter, having paid too much for an act, would need to recoup some of its money with an increased service charge. Other times, if the band was big enough, they would request part of the service charges. Or perhaps the building, having paid for extensive renovation, wanted to add a facility fee, too. The point being: if a band makes a unilateral demand about the service fee, all of those elements are potentially affected.

Ticketmaster was not inclined to take less money just because Pearl Jam saw fit to do so. It had paid handsomely for its exclusive contracts with many of the country's premier venues and would not allow the band to dictate policy. It operated on negotiations, not demands.

For its spring 1994 tour Pearl Jam made efforts to keep prices down and service charges identified on tickets. For the two Chicago dates Ticketmaster wanted to levy a $3.75 service charge to the $18 ticket. While the band consented, it made arrangements with the company's Chicago general manager to separately identify the fees. Shortly before the tickets went on sale, the group says the company reneged.

"It was necessary for us to threaten to perform at another venue before Ticketmaster backed down and agreed to sell tickets that separately disclosed its service charge," the band would later write. "Even then, Ticketmaster told us that its concession only extended to our Chicago shows and we should not expect them to be willing to do it elsewhere."

For the March 19 show at the Masonic Temple Theater in Detroit, the group made approximately 300 tickets available via mail order to its fan club. Receiving a letter in the mail, Ten Club fans were informed "the band will be playing a small venue in Detroit and we are offering you the chance to buy tickets before they go on sale to the general public." The other 2,900 tickets were distributed to the public via a mail-in lottery promoted through newspapers. Fans mailed in a coupon from one of the local newspapers with their social security number; later the papers printed the winners' names (several hundred thousand requests are said to have been received).

The show's promoter, the Nederlander Organization, had an exclusive deal with Ticketmaster. The ticketing agent threatened to sue for breach of contract if the venue used another ticketing service. Taking a precautionary step, Ticketmaster shut off the company's machines, disabling them from printing tickets that were needed to fulfill the orders. Once again, after heated discussions, Ticketmaster allowed the shows to move forward only after being allowed to take a portion of the $1.75 service charge.

After selling out two shows at Boston Garden, Pearl Jam decided to add a third at the city's significantly smaller Orpheum Theater. When discussing ticketing options with the band's management, Ticketmaster CEO Fred Rosen suggested a phone lottery, just as Sting had done when he did an underplay at the Wiltern Theater. It would also help prevent scalping.

Ticketmaster initially wanted a $3 or $4 service charge on top of the $18 ticket price — in part because of the increased credit card transaction fees that came with all purchases made over the phone. The band balked and threatened to sell tickets via coupons in *The Boston Globe* and *The Boston Phoenix* as it had in Detroit. The ticketer soon agreed not only to a $1.80 charge — making the total ticket price $20 — but it also agreed to chip in twenty cents per ticket for charity. Kelly Curtis told the *Globe*, "Ticketmaster fought us in Detroit but they came to the party in Boston."

For its New York City gig on Sunday, April 17, at the Paramount Theater below Madison Square Garden — once known as the Felt Forum and now known as the Theater at MSG — the band again bypassed Ticketmaster, making an initial mail-order offer to its Ten Club members and then utilizing local radio stations to give away the rest two days before the concert. Ticketmaster threatened the Paramount with legal action but ultimately did not pursue it.

Pearl Jam's team had carefully scrutinized Ticketmaster's contracts and found three loopholes, never publicly discussed, that they could exploit. Detroit and New York were test runs. Having stood up to Ticketmaster successfully on both occasions while smoothly delivering tickets, Pearl Jam felt it had temporary ticketing options while it figured out longer-term solutions.

THE PREVIOUS YEAR THE BAND had met David Cooper at one of its shows in Boulder, Colorado. Cooper, an accountant and a computer whiz, had gotten his start developing concert accounting software in the early 1980s. His first piece of software allowed venues and promoters to get accurate counts of their ticket allotments from their regional outlets in a timely fashion. Accurate ticket counts were a typical problem as tickets sold differently in different locations and made decisions like where, or whether, to advertise haphazard (although some systems, such as Jerry Seltzer's BASS software, were up to the task). Now each day there was an accurate count of inventory. His next advancement was in tour accounting for bands. Whereas managers would often have to wait days to get updates on a given show or tour's finances, they could now receive precise daily updates via an acoustic coupler modem that

could be printed out from a computer. This proved to be particularly handy
for international artists — The Who, David Bowie and U2, among others, were clients. Cooper would go on to help build what was essentially a private internet for managers in the mid-1980s called International Managers Communications that would allow them to communicate with their bands while they were on the road. At the time his promoter accounting software was being used by most of the industry's biggest names.

Cooper eventually got involved with ticketing technology, approaching its functionality from an accountant's point of view while always keeping the music fan at the forefront of the transactional experience. He had done work for Ticketron and Ticketmaster, started his own ticketing company and has subsequently dabbled in numerous other ticketing technologies.

He had met Pearl Jam's manager, Kelly Curtis, when Curtis was a tour accountant for the Japanese band Loudness. Curtis had used Cooper's accounting software and was now encouraging Pearl Jam's tour accountant, Mike "Goon" McGinley, to adopt it, leaving behind his old-school, pencil-and-paper approach.

When the band expressed frustration in Boulder about Ticketmaster in November 1993, Cooper piped up. "We could ticket ourselves," he said. How, the band asked, when Ticketmaster had exclusives? Cooper told them about three loopholes in Ticketmaster's standard contract: promotional shows could be ticketed any way you wanted, benefit shows could be ticketed any way you wanted and private shows could be ticketed any way you wanted.

It was Cooper who orchestrated the Paramount show. "I went to ten rock radio stations in the New York area and sold them each 500 tickets for face value plus my $2.10 service charge," he recalls. "They were allowed to dispense the tickets only in the following way: you had to play a Pearl Jam song — if your station was 91.6, you had to take the ninety-first caller; if you were 106.8, you had to take the one hundred and sixth caller — winners couldn't be in any way affiliated with the radio station, and they had to give you their driver's license number to pick up the tickets."

Cooper and the band had gotten away with ticketing their own show in a Ticketmaster venue — no small feat.

Simultaneously, it turned out, Ticketmaster was stepping up its efforts to quell Pearl Jam's efforts to use alternative ticketing methods. The first step was making sure promoters knew where the company stood.

The North American Concert Promoters Association (NACPA) was formed in the mid-1980s to function as a trade organization with the aim to create better communication among promoters. NACPA CEO Ben Liss sent a letter to all members on March 24, 1994. "Dear Friends," it began.

"Obviously, spring training has begun and it's going to be a long season."
The topic of the letter was Pearl Jam, in capital letters:

> PEARL JAM is putting out feelers once again to require promoters to bypass
> Ticketmaster on their dates later this summer. TM has indicated to me
> they will aggressively enforce their contracts with promoters and facilities.
> Ticketmaster's stance is that they have been loyal to their partners in this
> business and they hope & expect their partners will reciprocate. I do not need
> to remind you that loyalty in our industry is a valuable asset and that long-
> term relationships depend on it.

A day later, Liss sent another letter entitled "Pearl Jam Ticketing," which
began, "This is an update on the Pearl Jam/Ticketmaster controversy."
What had transpired in a day to prompt such a stern letter on the heels of
the previous message is unclear, but whatever the case, within the industry
it was now officially a "controversy." Ticketmaster CEO Fred Rosen was
drawing a hard line in preparation for a foreseeable battle:

> Fred has indicated that he intends to take a very strong stand on this issue to
> protect Ticketmaster's existing contracts with promoters and facilities and,
> further, TM will use all available remedies to protect itself from outside third
> parties that attempt to interfere with those existing contracts. TM views the
> Pearl Jam issue as an all or nothing proposition, meaning they will not agree
> to handle half the available inventory on a show in any situation where a
> contract exists.
>
> If asked, you may wish to consider and cite this fact: you and/or your venue
> have an existing contract with TM which precludes you from contracting with
> others to distribute tickets. I urge you to be very careful about entering into
> a conflicting agreement which could expose you to a lawsuit.
>
> I know all of you hope this matter is resolved amicably to everyone's
> satisfaction. In the interim, you may want to review your situation in preparation
> for an important decision that you may be asked to make next week.

When Liss notes that Ticketmaster "will not agree to handle half the
available inventory on a show," he was referring to the Grateful Dead. The
Dead, who had formed their own ticketing service in 1983, controlled up to
fifty percent of the ticket inventory for every show it played, regardless of
Ticketmaster's contracts. After much consternation Rosen stood down on
the matter in April 1991. The Grateful Dead would be the exception — no
one else.

One promoter, still wishing to remain anonymous, offers his assessment of the situation: "Let's say the ticket is $30 total, and Ticketmaster's portion of that was $5. [Pearl Jam] said, 'We want yours to be $2.50 so we can make $27.50 instead of $25 a ticket.' Ticketmaster said, 'Fuck you,' and they said, 'Well, then we're going to tell everyone you're making all this money, and we're going to get everyone hating you.' When it was really Pearl Jam's greed, they wanted to make a greater portion of the gross ticket — that's what it was all about. All they had to do to keep ticket prices down was charge less for the base price. It wasn't about how much the consumer was paying; they wanted to charge more for a ticket and have everyone else make less. When they couldn't do that, they tried to get the public on their side to force Ticketmaster to charge less so that they could charge more and get a greater share of the ticket. They were full of shit."

Another promoter, less strident in his criticism, said, "The minute they became a headliner, this band refused to compromise with anybody. Unlike a lot of other acts, Pearl Jam is not greedy. But they could care less about the middlemen in the business, and anytime you disagree with them during a negotiation, they just tell you, 'Hey, man, it's either my way or the highway.'"

During the spring of 1993 Rosen made it clear that he *would* intercede in certain circumstances, as he did with the group Fugazi, when that band found itself frustrated by the $3 service fees attached to a base ticket price that it held at $5. The issue rose to a head when the group's fiercely independent leader, Ian Mackaye, decided he would cancel a three-night stand at the Palladium in Los Angeles rather than endorse a charge that added sixty percent to the ticket price. At the suggestion of the promoter, Mackaye called the corporate office and found a self-described "Dutch Uncle" in Fred Rosen.

Mackaye affirms: "I don't think Fred's a bad guy. I think it's a bad system. It's sort of like nerds with guns. So I spoke with him and we agreed it would be a $1 service charge and $2 if you used a credit card. In L.A. people can drive two hours for a gig, so they'd gladly pay a dollar for a more central location and buy a ticket for it. I told Fred I'd like to use this as [the band's] template for the whole country, and he was true to his word."

And Tre Cool, drummer for Green Day, offered his pragmatic take at the time: "We take a lower cut than Pearl Jam. I'm not picking on them — I'm just saying that to anyone in general who's complaining about it. You don't want tickets being $27 and shit? Take a lower cut, guys."

AMID ALL THE BEHIND-THE-SCENES JOCKEYING that Pearl Jam had faced with Ticketmaster on its tour which ended at the Paramount on April 14, the band was still reeling from Nirvana front man Kurt Cobain's suicide nine days earlier on April 5, 1994.

Pearl Jam's lead singer, Eddie Vedder, and Cobain had reluctantly been held up as musical spokesmen for Generation X. While the two were by various accounts friendly, whatever relationship existed had become strained with their mounting popularities: quotes to the press were misconstrued, reasons for canceled co-bill gigs were questioned and fan assumptions about the perceived tensions grew louder.

Pearl Jam was on tour in Washington, DC, when Vedder learned of Cobain's death. He swiftly destroyed the hotel room he was staying in. The band had seven more shows booked plus an appearance on *Saturday Night Live*. The members considered canceling but pressed on. In Boston two days later, Vedder told the crowd, "It is tough to play. I personally felt we shouldn't play at all. It is really very odd; it's just like that empty feeling."

According to then-drummer Dave Abbruzzese, at a tense band meeting prior to the Murfreesboro, Tennessee show a few weeks prior to Cobain's death, Vedder said he didn't want to tour that summer, though no official decision had been reached. Now, after the band's sound check at the Orpheum in Boston, the singer made it official: the summer tour was canceled.

Adding to the situation was guitarist Mike McCready's alcohol and cocaine abuse. He had been "semi-clean" for about a month before Cobain's death sent him off the edge. (He would finally get sober that summer after going to rehab at the Hazelden Clinic.)

By the time the band arrived at the Paramount Theater on April 17, it was ready to come off the road. "This could be our last show in fuckin' forever as far as I'm concerned," Vedder told *Melody Maker*'s Allan Jones backstage. "Kurt's death has changed everything. I don't know if I can do it anymore."

Pearl Jam would not perform again for nearly nine months (it would do a few songs at Neil Young's Bridge School Benefit that October). Committed to taking time off and having faced considerable obstacles from Ticketmaster in booking a summer tour that was now canceled, the band received an unexpected phone call before it left New York: the Justice Department wanted to talk about the band's experiences with Ticketmaster.

A popular misconception is that Pearl Jam contacted the Justice Department. On the contrary, having continued to keep tabs on the company since the 1991 merger with Ticketron, Justice had been taking note of the band's recent battles and encouraged them to take action to help spur a wider investigation.

Before the group returned home to Seattle, it hired the prominent law firm Sullivan & Cromwell. It's unclear if the Justice Department suggested a specific course of action, but it was determined the band would file a complaint — not a suit — that asked for an antitrust investigation into Ticketmaster.

On May 6 Sullivan & Cromwell filed the complaint in a memorandum sent to the Justice Department outlining Pearl Jam's grievances with Ticketmaster: the company was exercising a monopoly over the country's concert ticketing and, through its exclusive relationships, had made it impossible for the band to effectively tour major markets without using them.

Also at issue were Ticketmaster's service charges. Ranging anywhere from $2 to $8, the varied amounts — in Pearl Jam's view — bore no relationship to the actual cost of the service provided. "It doesn't cost them any more to print a concert ticket than a circus ticket," band manager Kelly Curtis said. "We thought four bucks was too much for an $18 ticket." By May 24 the Justice Department had sent three officials from Washington to Los Angeles to begin an investigation.

Investigative journalist Chuck Philips broke the story that month in the *Seattle Times*, the *Chicago Sun-Times* and the *Los Angeles Times*, portraying the band's fight favorably. For the *Chicago Sun-Times* piece Philips quoted country superstar Garth Brooks' manager, Pam Lewis: "What Pearl Jam is doing is precedent-setting. Garth and I support the band, and we'll help in any way we can. We think greed is ruining the business and encourage others in the industry to rally to Pearl Jam's defense." (Lewis would retract the portion of the statement that applied to Brooks, writing a letter to Rosen later entered into the congressional record that clarified: "Garth Brooks does not have a quarrel with your organization, and I hope my comments did not make it appear as though that was the case. He was not in touch with the press at all on this issue nor did he speak to anyone or give a quote to any media on this matter.")

Philips also quoted Claire Rothman, general manager of the Los Angeles Forum: "I admire any young band who tries to reduce ticket prices but the service fee just can't be brought down to the price Pearl Jam is asking. It's an unrealistic demand."

So too said oft-quoted editor Gary Bongiovanni of the concert industry trade publication *Pollstar*: "Venue owners and promoters aren't just going to turn their backs on the revenue stream that Ticketmaster provides simply because Pearl Jam want them to. And, besides, these surcharges stem from legal contracts."

It was an op-ed piece in the *New York Times* by Bob Herbert on Sunday, June 5, that catalyzed the next turn of events. Herbert's piece, one of his "In America" columns for the paper, was entitled "Ticket Trust Busters." Pearl Jam were fighting the good fight, he wrote, and could, if they succeeded, "change the way tickets to major events are priced and sold."

John Edgell, a congressional staffer for the Information, Justice, Transportation and Agriculture Subcommittee at the time, was late reading his Sunday edition of the *Times* that week. The subcommittee for which he worked, part of the House of Representatives' Committee on Government Operations, oversaw the antitrust division.

"I read it on Friday [June 11] and said, 'Holy cow, that would make a good hearing,'" Edgell recalls of Herbert's column. "I ran it through the traps and everyone said, 'Sure, if we can get good witnesses, including Pearl Jam, let's make it happen.'"

Edgell called Pearl Jam that morning and was told they would need to think it over. "Lo and behold, by the middle of the afternoon I started getting calls from reporters saying, 'Is it true you guys are doing a hearing?'" recalls Edgell. "Obviously Pearl Jam had agreed to do the hearing and was putting it into the press."

WITH A HEARING SET FOR June 30, less than three weeks away, witnesses were gathered quickly. Testifying against Ticketmaster would be Pearl Jam guitarist Stone Gossard and bassist Jeff Ament, Pearl Jam manager Kelly Curtis, Pearl Jam business manager Mike McGinley, Aerosmith manager Tim Collins, R.E.M. attorney Bertis Downs, journalist Dave Marsh and Nitty Gritty Dirt Band manager Chuck Morris. On behalf of Ticketmaster were RZO managing director Joe Rascoff, Ticketmaster CEO Fred Rosen and Los Angeles Forum general manager Claire Rothman.

Collins and Curtis had met as part of an informal group of managers that would occasionally get together and talk about the business. "Kelly and the band wanted to take this thing on and called me up," recalls Collins. "I said, 'Let me know what we can do.'" Curtis asked if members of Aerosmith could testify. Unfortunately, the band was touring Europe at the time and couldn't do it, so its members asked Collins to testify on their behalf.

"I think I knew it was going to be an exercise in futility because you can't change the course of the river, you can't change the tides, but the band and I felt at the time we needed to make a stab to stand up for the fan," says Collins.

Bertis Downs, having been with R.E.M. since the Athens-based band began in 1980, was its closest adviser. Interestingly, R.E.M. had not toured behind its highly popular *Out of Time* (1991) or *Automatic for the People* (1992) records. Now the band was beginning to make plans for its first tour in six years to support the forthcoming album, *Monster*. In that time service fees had crept up steadily. "I think the Pearl Jam thing did it," Downs says of the escalating ticket fees finally being red-flagged. "They were trying to do the $18 tour — were trying to keep it really reasonable, a band of the fans, a band of the people — and clearly that was hard to do with the service charges. They were inflexible, so it made it in stark relief what would have otherwise been more of a creeping, incremental phenomenon."

Edgell had asked journalist Dave Marsh to testify. Marsh had been writing critically of the concert industry for some time, largely through his own *Rock and Rap Confidential* newsletter. "I don't think it was a hard event to put together from his point of view," Marsh says of Edgell's task. "He worked pretty hard to get it as right as he could from his distinctly partisan position. It was his hearing in the end." And Marsh notes, "Gary Condit was the kind of a guy who liked a headline."

Californian voters elected Gary Condit to the U.S. House of Representatives in 1989. Condit had made his name as a conservative Democrat and served as chairman for the subcommittee that would oversee the hearing. Condit concurs with Marsh in acknowledging who was really behind the hearing: "If it hadn't been for Edgell, I would not have been turned on to this issue. He knew the issues [with Ticketmaster], did all the research and set the stage for us to be able to air them in a public way."

Ticketmaster CEO Fred Rosen had already been through a Justice Department investigation for potential antitrust violations during the company's acquisition of Ticketron in 1991. Rosen, to a large degree, knew what to expect and how to prepare defensively. It also helped that he was a lawyer and knew how to judiciously couch his arguments for maximum effect. Nonetheless, a member of the team recalls that, despite his outward bravado, Rosen was a bundle of nerves the night before his testimony.

"Any time you get called in front of Congress, it's not a good thing," Rosen now acknowledges. "You'd be a fool not to be concerned."

Even President Bill Clinton weighed in: "The White House is impressed by Pearl Jam's commitment to its fans," said Clinton senior adviser George Stephanopoulos. "We want to make it very clear that we can't judge the merits of the band's allegations against Ticketmaster or prejudge the Justice Department action in any way. But that said, we think the goal of making concert ticket prices affordable is a laudable one. It's something we believe in."

That spring Pearl Jam bassist Jeff Ament told writer Kim Neely, "This summer, if Ticketmaster's gonna do something with us, they're going to have to come around, or we're gonna deal with this tour ourselves." He went on to talk about concert industry dynamics and how bands were typically on the losing end of the stick when it came to dealing with promoters or record companies. "The one thing that's really, really great about being in the position we're in," he concluded of the band's popularity, "is having the power to go in there and fuck with these people. It's a beautiful thing."

Shortly before the hearing Pearl Jam guitarist Stone Gossard told journalist Chuck Philips: "This thing has been building up for a long time. And deep down, it's really not about money. It's about music. It's about fairness. It's about a band who believes good intentions can translate into sound business practices and a giant corporation that's completely out of touch."

For three weeks the stage had been built. It was time for the show.

THE HEARING BEGAN AT NINE o'clock on the morning of Thursday, June 30, in room 2154 of the Rayburn House Office building in Washington, DC's Capitol Complex.

"They had to rotate the audience every fifteen or twenty minutes," remembers Condit. "Once people found out that Pearl Jam was in the building, staffers — young people that worked for the government — they lined up and down the halls, encircled the Rayburn Building to get in just to see these guys."

Walking in, the table to the left facing the subcommittee was Pearl Jam's side; the table to the right, Ticketmaster's. The eight representatives of the subcommittee consisted of Condit, Major Owens (D–NY), Karen Thurman (D–FL), Lynn Woolsey (D–CA), Bart Stupak (D–MI), Craig Thomas (R–WY) and Stephen Horn (R–CA). Subcommittee member Ileana Ros-Lehtinen (R–FL) was not present, though Collin Peterson (D–MN), "the subcommittee's musician" according to Condit, and the chairman of the Government Operations Committee, John Conyers (D–MI), were both added. Edgell and other support staff watched. Democrats outnumbered Republicans on the subcommittee two to one.

"Is there a monopoly in the ticket distribution industry?" asked Condit in his opening remarks. "In short, who is there to protect the consumers? Is the ticket distribution company industry for the consumer's convenience or is it a cartel? We need to investigate the serious allegations made against Ticketmaster. And we intend to have a full and fair review of the charges." Condit noted that the Justice Department had announced a formal investigation, though, given its early stages, it would not appear that day.

"We are honored to have a number of witnesses willing to tell it like it is from their perspective," he said. "Some of them have put their careers at some level of risk testifying today. We are grateful for their cooperation."

When asked what he meant by "some level of risk," Condit suggests the claim came out of his own experiences — that if the hearing had generated unexpected pressure on him, then surely those testifying were at risk for some form of retaliation. "Before the hearing, I got a call from a very reliable source in California who told me they got a call from someone at Ticketmaster and said that if I proceeded with the hearings, they were going to make life miserable for me as well as Pearl Jam." The source told Condit that "Ticketmaster did not want Pearl Jam to give this kind of exposure to this issue."

By contrast, someone on the Ticketmaster side remembers this moment as "a bit of sensationalist posturing for dramatic effect."

Next to speak was Representative Conyers, who congratulated "these artists who have dared to come forward" and believed that "this is an issue that is of great interest to the American people." He concluded with an observation: "When art is successful, it unavoidably becomes a business. The question, then, is whether artists have an inherent right to control the limits of their business and how it relates to the growth of their art. The answer, I'm convinced, is that artists have a right to that control."

Ranking Republican Craig Thomas followed, noting that, "At the outset I believe as a general proposition that the market is an effective regulator for determining prices to selling one's product efficiently." While in favor of a laissez-faire approach, he did feel that, "There are instances, however, where a minimal competition exists and we should take a closer look at how to foster it, not just in the music industry but in other areas as well."

Pearl Jam bass guitarist Jeff Ament and rhythm guitarist Stone Gossard were then sworn in. Condit, in a rather hokey, groan-inducing manner, noted, "Before we start, no bottles, no cans, no Frisbees or beach balls are allowed at this hearing. Lighters are okay though." (Woolsey's comment later, "We all know that the music won't rock if the consumer gets rolled," was a similar misfire.)

"You have been courageous in bringing your complaints forward and dealing with an issue that is important to the American people," said Condit as he gave way to the hearing's opening testimony. "I don't know the full extent you may have put your own careers at risk, and I think it is a very courageous thing for you to do. Hopefully this will help consumers across the country."

THOUGH CONDIT AND CONYERS' TONE suggested they were addressing an imperiled whistle-blower, the band's career was never in any danger. At the heart of the complaint and the hearing were consumer issues — which Condit tried to focus on — and yet the press, Pearl Jam and, most strategically, Fred Rosen, would paint it as a Pearl Jam versus Ticketmaster fight.

"Realizing that the consumer was actually a younger person," suggests Condit, "and that in our society and political structure young people sometimes don't have the power or authority because they don't have the money or the vote, I was pushing it from that angle, and that was the angle I'd heard from the band. They were interested in making sure that young people were able to afford tickets, and they thought they were being gouged by fees and by a monopoly."

Gossard's statement on behalf of the band struck a balance between the group's plight and that of consumers: "Although given our popularity, we could undoubtedly continue to sell out our concerts with ticket prices at a premium level, we have made a conscious decision that we do not want to put the price of our concerts out of the reach of our fans," he began. The band's interest, he said, was quite narrow. They simply had a philosophy of how tickets to their concerts should be sold that differed from Ticketmaster's. "We can't insist that Ticketmaster do business on our terms," he continued, "but we do believe we should have the freedom to go elsewhere if Ticketmaster is not prepared to negotiate terms that are acceptable to us."

The band's underlining grievance: "Something is vastly wrong with a system under which a ticket distribution company can dictate the markup on a price of a concert ticket, can prevent a band from using another less expensive approach to distributing tickets and even effectively preclude a band from performing at a particular arena if does not want to use Ticketmaster."

Concluding, Gossard declared, "We feel Ticketmaster has in essence dug its own grave on this issue." Pearl Jam also submitted a statement that outlined its struggles with Ticketmaster and used Liss's memos to NACPA as validation of its claims.

"Do you readjust your fee to get that $20 or is your expectation for the stadium and Ticketmaster to readjust their profit margin to get to that total?" asked Condit as the questions began.

"Well, I think we were willing to talk about that," responded Ament. "Essentially what we did, how we came up with it, with the $18 was that we figured out what our expenses were."

The guitarist talked about the band's expense of putting on a tour, how it had lost money the previous three years and how it needed to make *some* money so it could pay for things like the free show in Seattle. Ament never answered the question, though. Yes, the band expected venues and Ticketmaster to readjust their profit margin to meet the $20 ticket price. Pearl Jam, however, was not willing to readjust its fee. This exchange followed next:

Condit: Why was your summer tour canceled?
Ament: I don't know what the exact date was. Probably two and a half months ago.
Gossard: Did you say why?
Condit: Yes, why.

Gossard: We didn't feel like we could coordinate – because of our dispute with Ticketmaster and feeling really the only way we could tour was to sort of go outside and try it on our own, given the amount of time we had and our feelings about security and whether we could actually put on a safe show consistently in these sort of – we would be in outdoor venues probably in fields and stuff. We just felt it wasn't appropriate and we should deal with this issue first and focus on recording music.

Condit: So your dispute with Ticketmaster is the reason you canceled the tour?

Gossard: Yes.

Stone Gossard was fudging the truth. His bandmate's timeline was right — two and a half months earlier was the Paramount show — but it was Vedder who canceled the summer tour in the wake of Cobain's death and strained band relations.

The day before Sullivan & Cromwell delivered its complaint to the Justice Department on behalf of the band, *Billboard* ran a story about the canceled summer tour. Curtis said the band was taking time off to rest and deal with Cobain's passing but also, for the first time, said the group would not tour until it found a viable alternative to Ticketmaster.

"Kurt died right at the point when Pearl Jam was encountering all these complications with putting together the tour," Curtis said shortly before the hearing. "Coupled with everything else that was going on, it just about knocked the wind out of the band." However, now during the hearing and subsequent months, he put the tour's cancellation squarely on Ticketmaster's shoulders: "What if we had spent two months assembling the show and Ticketmaster threatened the promoter with a lawsuit before we were set to hit the stage? What if a show got canceled at the last second and (a fan) got hurt? We just couldn't risk it."

David Cooper, the concert accounting and ticketing guru who helped execute the Paramount show and would be instrumental in helping the band tour without Ticketmaster in the future, had the sense that "the lawyers who were preparing for the antitrust complaint were more creating excuses of why the band couldn't tour economically than the agents who were actually booking dates."

As former Pearl Jam drummer Dave Abbruzzese would tell Kim Neely for her band biography, *Five Against One*, "We'd spent so much time getting alternative venues going. People were working so that we could do tickets through the mail and 800 numbers, and anything else. Then all of a sudden [Eddie says], 'I don't want to tour this summer.'"

Gossard, years later, admitted, "The Ticketmaster thing came at a perfect time for us to say you know what? We can't tour. It was perfect for us to wallow around in some controversy with Ticketmaster."

CALIFORNIA REPUBLICAN STEPHEN HORN, perhaps the least sympathetic member of the subcommittee, quickly rankled Gossard with a series of questions that saw him soon defer to the band's business manager, Mike "Goon" McGinley.

> Horn: Now from listening to the testimony it is the band leadership itself, the group's leadership, that sets the ticket prices.
> McGinley: In the case of this band, the band sets the ticket prices.
> Horn: Now, is there any service charge ever added when you do these outside of a Ticketmaster venue? I mean, do you have an additional service charge or is it just a flat fee they decide on and that covers all of your expenses, what they are?
> McGinley: There is a cost of selling tickets, and no matter who sells the tickets, yes, there is a fee to sell tickets no matter how you do it. Somebody has got to pay to sell the tickets.
> Horn: As I understand it, then, the basis of your dispute seems down to about fifty cents between what you want Ticketmaster to charge versus what they claim their basic service charge is. Are we talking about a fifty cent difference here?
> McGinley: I don't know how you arrived at that figure.

McGinley knew exactly how Horn arrived at the figure. Pearl Jam had demanded that tickets for its summer 1994 tour, with service fees, not exceed $20. It had set its base price at $18, leaving $2 allocated for the service fee. Ticketmaster requested $2.50 for its fee but the band refused.

Band manager Kelly Curtis would later recall, "We would have settled for $2.25," but by the time Ticketmaster agreed "it was too late." Rosen's testimony would offer a different take: it was Pearl Jam who refused to budge over the twenty-five cent incremental difference.

Horn continued to grill McGinley, bringing up the Seattle Arena shows, on whether Ticketmaster's service to the band could be monetarily quantified and whether Ticketmaster had taken legal action against the band. Condit stepped in and asked Horn to "wrap it up" as there was still much testimony to be heard and ninety minutes had already transpired.

Pearl Jam bassist Jeff Ament cut in, letting Horn know, "We still want to make sure that the other panel members get a chance to talk about this stuff."

Horn responded curtly: "We are here all day."

Ament snapped.

"They told us we were going to be here for an hour," he shot back. "Actually, I have to go to the bathroom, so I will be right back." Ament stood up and walked out of the room.

"To me, that was the highlight," says journalist Dave Marsh, who testified a short while later. "Nobody else really picked up on [Ament's sudden exit] for what it was, which was a real act of defiance. It was a guy genuinely feeling like, 'You think you're better than me, don't you? You think you're smarter 'cause you've got different clothes on or because somebody was stupid enough to vote for you. *Fuck you.*' He didn't say 'fuck you,' but it was a giant fuck you for all time."

Edgell, Marsh recalls, "turned white" because Ament *could* have theoretically been found in contempt of Congress. Though it's unlikely members on the subcommittee would have motioned for it, it's a federal misdemeanor, punishable by a maximum $100,000 fine and a maximum one-year sentence in federal prison.

"We were going on with the hearing," Condit reflects now, "and I knew that if he didn't come back after that exchange with Steve, someone in the press would say that they got angry or frustrated with the questioning and so on. Somebody would couch it as contentious and that Pearl Jam couldn't hold their own."

Condit found Ament and asked that he walk back in and sit down for the remainder of the panel. "I was impressed that he came back," says Condit. "Not every young person listens to an old guy sometimes."

WHAT MADE AEROSMITH MANAGER TIM COLLINS' testimony powerful was that his band had sold more than fifty million records, played live to nearly twenty million people and regularly worked with Ticketmaster. So while Collins acknowledged the company's high level of service, he expressed his grievances over some of its conduct.

In 1989, for example, Aerosmith approached Ticketmaster prior to its highly anticipated *Pump* world tour, for which it would sell millions of seats, and inquired about a volume rebate. "We either wanted Ticketmaster to lower its service charge or pay some of kind of rebate to the band so that Aerosmith could in turn lower the ticket charge to fans," Collins testified. Rosen, Collins said, was unwilling to support either option.

Then, on January 5, 1993, he met with Rosen prior to the band's world tour for *Get a Grip* to seek similar options. The CEO again refused, although he offered a different option: if the band agreed to advertise an all-in ticket price that included the service fee, he would raise Ticketmaster's charge by a dollar and split the profit with the group.

"I told Mr. Rosen that his offer was like offering a cold man ice cream in winter," Collins relayed to the subcommittee. "Admittedly, his solution would make us and him more money, but at the expense of an already overburdened young fan. The moral of this story is that monopolies like Ticketmaster tend to raise prices and rarely, if ever, lower them, even for their best customers."

Rosen remembers the conversation slightly differently. "The dollar I offered him was hypothetical because he kept saying he wanted to do something and I kept saying, 'What do you want? If you want something, have the promoters do it.' I said, 'Hypothetically I could give you one dollar, but that would set a bad precedent because I don't deal with the acts. If you want more money, get it through the ticket price.'"

Today, Collins' assessment remains the same: "It wasn't like he was [just] going to raise [the service fee] for the kickback — he was going to raise it so he made money as well. It was counterproductive — it was driving [the overall ticket price] up. These guys are all free market guys and we were down there [testifying to Congress] saying, 'This needs to be regulated because, left to its own devices, look what happens. It's just greed; they're going to do what they can get away with.'"

SOME OF THE HEARING'S MOST articulate testimony came from R.E.M. attorney (and later manager) Bertis Downs. Downs, who also taught courses in entertainment and sports law at the University of Georgia School of Law, was acute in his analysis of the concert industry, even providing a chart entitled "Anatomy of a Concert Deal."

For the first time during the hearing, all the moving pieces of how a concert comes to fruition were clearly explained. All of the components — promoter, venue, agent, manager — had competition, Downs argued, save for one: ticketing. He lauded Ticketmaster for its efficiency and effectiveness and made clear that his comments should not be taken as anti-Ticketmaster but rather as "pro-competition, and more specifically pro-price-competition."

His assessment of the landscape was simple: "At this point in 1994, for at least the last few years, there really isn't any choice. If you want to do a major tour, a major arena level tour in major markets, you have no choice. [Ticketmaster] comes along with the building. It comes with the building the same way concessionaires do."

WHILE DOWNS' ASSERTIONS WERE RELATIVELY accurate, it's important to note that a series of alternative ticketing companies had cropped up over the prior few years, often supported by promoters and facilities eager to give their business to a competing service.

Portland promoter David Leiken first entered the concert industry in 1972, producing three B.J. Thomas dates in the Pacific Northwest. He lost money on two of the shows, which nearly torpedoed his career. However, when Oregon State University called him before the third date, asking if they could co-promote a Thomas show over parents' weekend with the school taking all the risk, Leiken said to himself, "Well, gee, maybe we can get this done."

Sixteen years later he was still doing it when Bill Graham brokered a meeting between Leiken and Fred Rosen to discuss the possibility of Leiken's Double Tee Concerts receiving some form of a rebate akin to what Washington-based promoters John Bauer and Ken Kinnear accrued from their Ticketmaster sales.

"I was selling about 300,000 to 400,000 tickets a year. Bauer-Kinnear I think were getting seventy-five cents at the time, so I felt I should be getting fifty cents. That was my theory. It didn't go very far," Leiken laughs. "Then I brought up the idea that for $200,000 I could do my own computer ticketing company, and [Rosen's] comments were not very nice. Not only were they not very nice, they were probably the worst anybody's ever spoken to me in my entire business life."

At this time Rosen certainly had a reputation for his brusque persona, although he contends that much of this was posturing. During this same era Jane Kleinberger, cofounder of Paciolan, a ticketing software company that would be purchased by Ticketmaster twenty years later but was then mostly servicing colleges, approached Ticketmaster's CEO at an International Ticketing Association conference to discuss working together. "I went up to him and my first mistake was I said, 'Excuse me, Mr. Rosen?' And of course his dad wasn't there. He turned around, gave me a glare and then I started explaining who we were, and I said, 'The reason I'm coming to talk to you is I have some clients that I know would love to use your distribution services.' And Fred looked at me and he not only increased my vocabulary using words I had never heard before, but he said, 'We are going to crush you.' Then he turned and walked away. I felt like Shrinking Violet. This little girl from Ohio had just learned some new California language."[2]

As for Leiken, immediately after his meeting with Rosen, "I called Bill Graham and said, 'What the hell did you get me into?'"

As it turned out, what he got him into was the ticketing business. "I didn't even want to start a ticketing company. We started it because Fred Rosen stonewalled me." Leiken soon partnered with Tom Keenan, the founder of a local record chain, Everybody's Records, who had handled hard tickets in the area since 1971. Keenan began researching software providers, and the two eventually signed a deal with Softix, the system designed by BASS developer Bruce Baumgart. Leiken and Keenan's new company, Fastixx, made a commitment to low service charges, holding them to less than $2 until the late 1990s, when, to offer competitive packages to such major performers as Jimmy Buffett, Leiken began giving himself rebates. ("All of a sudden our service charge, which was reasonable, now was not so reasonable because our competition was using their ability to manipulate the service charges to take shows away from me.")

Fastixx also is a testament to tenacity, political savvy and the threat of legal recourse. In 1987 a Federal Court of Appeals upheld a lower court decision in which Atlanta-based Tic-X-Press, a hard ticketing company, successfully sued the Omni Arena for violation of the Sherman Antitrust Act because the Omni had mandated the use of the SEATS computerized ticketing service for any event.[3] Leiken clung to this decision, eventually ensuring that all of Portland's public venues installed Fastixx terminals alongside the existing Ticketmaster systems, so that one or the other could easily be utilized for any given show (the competitors never shared inventory). This was quite a coup, if a logistical nightmare for the outlets that had to maintain two systems for selling tickets.

Meanwhile in mid-February 1991, when Ticketron's New England regional Vice President, Matt Whelan, learned that the company was soon to be sold, he beat it out the door and up the street to the Boston Garden, where he was encouraged to take on Ticketmaster. "They really thought there needed to be some competition, so they encouraged me to get into the business, and they gave me an opportunity and I took advantage of it." This encouragement soon amounted to a ten-year contract at a time when "I had no hardware, I had no software, I had no employees and no ability to sell tickets." Whelan soon rectified all of the above, licensing the equipment and ticketing program, outsourcing his phone room sales and securing limited outlets. "Our plan wasn't to be in the outlet business; our plan was to be in the phone business. I thought the business was changing, and so I wasn't going to put as much emphasis on outlets as I was going to put on the phone room."

The new company, TicketPro, had a tremendous run through 1993, adding the Providence Civic Center and most facilities in Boston's Theater district, proving that Ticketmaster was not invincible. On the other hand Ticketmaster wasn't penurious either, as the company eventually contacted Whelan's principal investors and, to his dismay, purchased the upstart. So while TicketPro had been successful, it joined a long line of companies that had been absorbed by Ticketmaster, such as Ticket World USA (New York, 1985), Capital Automated Ticketing (Kansas City, 1989), Dayton's Ticketing (Minneapolis, 1989) and SEATS (1990). Leiken's Fastixx would not join this list, although the burgeoning TicketsWest would acquire it in 1999 as the rising cost of business led Leiken to focus on his concert promotion company, Double Tee.

DAVE MARSH, MUSIC HISTORIAN and journalist, followed Downs at the hearing. His testimony had a salient observation: "Ticketron had a similar stranglehold on the off-site ticket market through the early '80s, and industry dissatisfaction led to the development of its rival. But from the consumer point of view, Ticketmaster has resolved few of the problems Ticketron presented." Thus, Marsh argued, "I don't think it is any longer reasonable to assume the concert industry is going to self-regulate."

As for who testified that day, as Marsh looks back, he's equally unimpressed. "Were the people that had the most complicated relationships with Ticketmaster, were they there?" he asks rhetorically. "No. Were the people that had the most to gain or lose there? Not really, except for Pearl Jam. Did anybody stick their neck out? No, not that I'm aware of. Look, they had to do business with these guys, and from that day to this." After a pause Marsh adds, "Look at Barry Diller trying to bully Jon Landau in the press now," he notes of the Springsteen ticketing fiasco in which Ticketmaster found itself embroiled in February 2009, when some customers looking to purchase tickets were redirected to the company's TicketsNow secondary ticketing site. "They were thuggish then and they're thuggish now."

TICKETMASTER CEO FRED ROSEN THEN had a chance to present his side of the story. "He was probably more animated and more agitated by the hearing than anyone," recalls Condit. By the time Rosen and Rothman finally testified, only four subcommittee Representatives remained of the original nine (the other five had left over the course of the hearing to attend to other commitments).

Rosen quickly set the tone of a company whose merited success was being unfairly attacked for actions that it was not responsible for. He clarified that any parking fees or facility charges belong to the buildings, not Ticketmaster. And, as a timely example, he responded to Representative Conyers' concern from earlier in the hearing as to why consumers in his district paid service charges to Ticketmaster when buying tickets at the box office. Knowing that he was the last to testify, Rosen had sent out a colleague to confirm that the fee described by Conyers was a facility charge, not a service charge. It was yet another persistent misunderstanding by the public according to Rosen.

He went on to note that all of Ticketmaster's contracts with venues expired. "Contracts have durations of three to five years," he said. "There are probably 30, 40, even 50 companies out there today that are bidding against Ticketmaster for ticketing concessions across the country." Rosen concluded, "In the universe of tickets sold in America today, there are approximately 1.5 billion tickets sold for live events per year, and we only sell approximately 51 million of those tickets."

This may well have been the case, although Rosen's statistics were based on the broadest of definitions, encompassing every live event that required a ticket. The billion-ticket figure was derived from research conducted by a company out of Valley Stream, Long Island, called Marketdata Enterprises Inc., which Ticketmaster had commissioned for the report. Nearly seventy percent of the 1.5 billion came from museums, amusement parks, state parks and county fairs.

Although, at the time of the congressional hearing, he had yet to meet with the Department of Justice, Ticketmaster's CEO was already anticipating its antitrust investigation. The Sherman Act, which prohibits monopolies, requires two elements to be proven to establish a violation. First, a court must find "the possession of monopoly power in a properly defined relevant market." Once that determination is made, a company can be deemed an illegal monopoly if a preponderance of the evidence demonstrates "the willful acquisition or maintenance of that power by means of anticompetitive, predatory conduct, as distinguished from growth or development as a consequence of a superior product, business acumen, or historical accident."

So the Justice Department's initial hurdle was to establish the "relevant market" that it believed Ticketmaster was operating in illegally. If the market were defined broadly, for instance as all live event ticketing in the United States, then Ticketmaster certainly did not possess monopoly power, given that the company sold only three percent of the total available inventory.

By contrast, if the relevant market were defined more narrowly, the government would have a better chance of success. While 1.5 billion tickets were sold the previous year, if one looked only at professional sports (minus season tickets) and events that took place at arenas, auditoriums and theaters, the number dwindled to approximately 178 million. What's more, if the relevant market were further circumscribed, and a court examined the company's position in the live concert space, then Ticketmaster just might be vulnerable.

Pollstar, the concert industry's respected trade publication, estimated that a total of 9.9 million concert tickets existed in the United States in 1994. Ticketmaster, it reported, had exclusive contracts with 63.2 percent of the halls and arenas that were part of the 9.9 million total. It also, on a non-exclusive basis, handled part of the remaining 36.8 percent.

Rosen testified that Ticketmaster sold about twenty percent of the tickets in any major arena where it held an exclusive contract. However, the company typically handled 100 percent of an arena's concert ticketing (it did a far lesser percentage of its sporting events, which make up the majority of any arena's event calendar).

When one looked at the major concert markets in North America — New York, Los Angeles, Chicago, Boston, Philadelphia and Detroit — Ticketmaster unquestionably had exclusive contracts with the majority of venues that hosted large-scale concerts by such artists as Pearl Jam, U2, the Grateful Dead, Bruce Springsteen, Madonna and the Rolling Stones. Take New York and Los Angeles alone: Ticketmaster controlled all of the arenas in both cities. Did they control all the stadiums and theaters in those markets? No, but stadium plays for a single band were relatively uncommon, and theaters were far too small for bands like those listed above. It was arenas and amphitheaters that were the sweet spot for big rock or pop acts, and Ticketmaster had a firm grasp on the most coveted ones.

The very title of the hearing identified an intent to explore "questions about concert, sports, and theater handling charges." However, as Rosen and his legal team began their dialogue with congressional aides in anticipation of the proceedings, it became clear that the forum would focus almost exclusively on live music. If the Department of Justice were to take a similar position and define the relevant market solely as rock concert ticketing, then there was a chance that Ticketmaster could find itself on the losing end of an antitrust prosecution.

REPRESENTATIVE HORN THEN HAD A few questions about service fees. "How does it work" — he asked in response to Rosen's acknowledgement that all service fees are discussed — that Ticketmaster was never in a position to unilaterally decide the amounts levied?

"You define contracts by the type of event," replied Rosen. "Different events have different service charges that are negotiated, and revenue streams are determined based on the service charge."

Still, Horn asked, "Aren't you performing the same task for every type of ticket that crosses your box office, whatever it is?"

No," said Rosen evenly. "This business was built on choice. If you don't want to pay a service charge, you go to the box office. If you want a lesser service charge, you drive to an outlet. And if you don't want to leave your home, you can pick up the phone and call."

Representative Woolsey still wanted to know how service fees, in general, had gotten so high. "Service charges have risen to the level that they have because there is competition," relayed Rosen. "Because the buildings require you as concessionaire to pay them for the rights to sell the tickets, competition among concessionaires leads to higher concession fees, which leads to higher service charges."

It was one of the industry's unique dynamics that was counterintuitive: competition drove ticket prices up, not down. There, in a nutshell, was one of the key principles that nobody outside the industry seemed to understand. In turning ticketing into a concession — into a highly profitable Pandora's box — Rosen proved the theorem time and again.

Four hours after it began, the hearing came to a close at one o'clock.

"Testifying was the greatest disappointment of my life," laments former Los Angeles Forum general manager Claire Rothman. "I thought, 'I'm going to see my government at work. I am going to be part of something that is history.' The congressmen only stayed when the stars were testifying because that's when they got photographed. As soon as we lay people testified, even though our testimony was in many respects more important to the outcome of the case, they left their staff to listen and make notes." Indeed, by the hearing's end only three congressmen remained.

"It was very clear to me walking out that day that this thing was over from the point of view of further hearings or anything because it didn't do what it was supposed to do," says Dave Marsh. "It didn't either excite the pundits or galvanize the public."

PEARL JAM'S VITALOGY WENT INTO wide release on December 6, 1994. Once again the response was overwhelming: in its first week the album sold more than 877,000 copies. At the time it became the second fastest selling CD in history behind the group's previous record, Vs.

The Justice Department continued with its investigation that month, speaking to representatives for Soundgarden, Alice in Chains, Phish and the Indigo Girls, among others. It had already conducted interviews with promoters, venue operators and managers from several states. As Pearl Jam began plotting its 1995 summer tour that would circumvent Ticketmaster, the ticketing agent supported the move as it "validates the idea that Pearl Jam has always had, and will always have, the ability to tour whenever they want."

As the year came to a close, the band announced two benefit shows in Washington, DC, that January to support the abortion rights group Voters for Choice. They would be held at historic Constitution Hall — built in 1929 by the Daughters of the American Revolution — a Ticketmaster venue in the heart of the nation's capital, equidistant between the White House and the Washington Monument. "Pearl Jam doesn't just sing about issues they care about," said Voters for Choice cofounder and president Gloria Steinem. "These guys walk it like they talk it."

The band had again called upon David Cooper to orchestrate a means of working around Ticketmaster, this time utilizing the second loophole in the company's exclusive contracts: benefits can be ticketed in any way the promoter or venue wants. The 3,700-odd tickets for each night would be sold via a mail-order lottery system. Tickets were $25 each and had no surcharge. Estimates for the number of requests received ranged from 167,000 to 175,000.

Despite being off the road for nearly a year, the band was in top form. The shows confirmed that the benefit loophole within Ticketmaster's contracts could be effectively exploited. Cooper acknowledges the idea of a national benefit tour was discussed — "I could do Madison Square Garden, the Spectrum in Philly or the Centrum in Boston. I can go anywhere I want" — but that ultimately the band's "lawyers weren't quite ready yet to do a national benefit tour and really take on what it would have meant. I think if they wanted to they could have carried on that way, but the cost of the litigation of doing this kind of shit was humungous. This was all about politics."

That spring a group calling itself Consumers Against Unfair Ticketing (CAUT) formed in Seattle. Made up of student groups and members of the entertainment industry, it struck an alliance with the U.S. Public Interest Research Group and the Consumer Interest Research Group to help advocate ticketing reform.

Seattle PR executive John Hoyt was one of CAUT's founders and his company, Pyramid Communications, had worked with Pearl Jam on several occasions — notably Nicole Vandenberg, who oversaw the company's arts and entertainment division. (Vandenberg would start her own PR firm in 1998 and remains the band's publicist today.) Hoyt, who acknowledged that there was a "certain Pearl Jam impetus to starting the organization," also rented CAUT space at the company's offices.

One of CAUT's first actions was to send a public service announcement about its concerns to fifty-seven radio stations around the country. In addition, Hoyt was able to get the group's ticketing reform initiatives in front of his brother, New York assemblyman Sam Hoyt, who sponsored a bill in his state. (In February Representative John Dingell (D–MI) along with Condit and two others introduced the "Ticket Fee Disclosure Act of 1995" to the House of Representatives, to little avail.)

The three-group CAUT alliance officially kicked off their joint campaign on March 21, 1995, at the National Press Club in Washington, DC. Executive director Maura Brueger declared, "The entertainment ticketing industry is one of the least consumer-friendly industries in the country, providing consumers with no choice, no information and unreasonable charges." Mary Ellen Fise of the Consumer Federation of America was even more succinct in her attack against Ticketmaster: "The ticketing situation can be summed up in just four words: Monopoly power hurts consumers."

Yet when asked about Pearl Jam and John Hoyt's involvement in the group, Brueger deflected questions, stating that CAUT is not "in any way connected" with Pearl Jam.

The same day, Ticketmaster issued a press release entitled "Let's Let the Facts Catch Up with CAUT."

In it Ticketmaster vice president Alan Citron — once a business editor at the *Los Angeles Times* — chastised the group for "disseminating false and misleading information about Ticketmaster and the ticket service industry. Employing half-truths and innuendo, the group seeks to blame Ticketmaster for everything from high ticket prices to bad seat locations.

"If tickets cost a lot of money, it is because some performers like to earn a lot of money," wrote Citron. "You don't need an advanced degree in economics to recognize the reality of the marketplace. To pretend otherwise, as CAUT does, is to stand the truth on its head."

For all of Ticketmaster's outrage, there seemed to be little sympathy. The Consumer Federation of America's spokesman, Bradley Stillman, saw no issue with CAUT or wrongdoing with John Hoyt asking his brother to support a ticketing reform bill.

"The principle is right, and it really doesn't matter whose brother or sister is involved," he offered. "You think the other side wouldn't have pursued access to a lawmaker? That's why Ticketmaster has hired all those lobbyists — to gain access."

Indeed, in response to the various consumer groups rallying against Ticketmaster and what he felt was a general misunderstanding of the company's practices by the government and the press, Ticketmaster CEO Fred Rosen fortified the company's defenses by hiring some of best lobbyists in the business.

Judy Black was hired by Ticketmaster as senior vice president, governmental affairs, on March 1, 1995, for an annual salary of $250,000. Black was the wife of Charlie Black, whom Edgell describes as "the preeminent Republican corporate lobbyist" and someone whom Rosen had previously worked with.

"Most industries have associations that deal with lobbyists, and there was legislation introduced in a lot of states about us, so ultimately you needed to get lobbyists in those states, and you became more sophisticated over time," Rosen relays now. "Charlie Black's firm was one of the firms we used in the early '90s, and then ultimately I hired Judy. She was our lobbyist because until you had someone as an advocate, you had young [congressional] staffers sitting there saying service charges were high and it looked like a great consumer issue — but it wasn't. When you sat and explained what you did to most congressmen and congresswomen, they agreed."

At the time, Charlie Black was the chairman of BKSH & Associates (he left in 2008 to help run John McCain's presidential campaign). He had served as a senior adviser to presidents Ronald Reagan and George H.W. Bush in addition to serving as a political director for the Republican National Committee.[4]

Judy was no slouch herself. From 1978 to 1986 she served as the vice president of the Tobacco Institute. The following two years she served as special assistant to Ronald Reagan for Intergovernmental Affairs. And from 1989 until she joined Ticketmaster in 1995, she was the lobbyist for the International Council of Shopping Centers, a global industry trade association, with more than twenty-five national and regional shopping center councils in more than eighty countries.

Today Citron says, "The only thing that was crystal clear was that defending Ticketmaster was virtually impossible." He pauses. "The more accurate way to say it is that it wasn't easy, and the likelihood of success was pretty low, just because there was no obvious constituency for Ticketmaster in this battle. Anyone who paid a service charge had some sympathy about the high price of service charges, or the perceived high price. It wasn't easy to find that constituency that was going to be on our side, so my main point of view was that the best we could do was tell our story as effectively as possible and just hope for the best."

ON APRIL 10, 1995, AFTER approximately nine months of planning, Pearl Jam announced its U.S. summer tour dates. "Pearl Jam is back and we're trying something brand new," announced the band's manager, Kelly Curtis. "I hope the fans will be patient, because we're bound to have a few hiccups with this new ticketing system as the tour unfolds. But if things work out the way we plan, we'll probably announce more shows before the summer is over."

ETM ticketing principal Peter Schniedermeier, the very same Peter Schniedermeier who had moved from TRS to Select-A-Seat to BASS before leaving the business in the 1980s to provide in-house inventory systems for auto dealers, had been drawn back in by an investor seeking to fund a new start-up. Soon afterward, Schniedermeier met with Pearl Jam accountant Mike McGinley in ETM's new Irvine, California office.

"I have a band who wants to try to tour without Ticketmaster," said McGinley.

"Who?" asked Schniedermeier out of curiosity.

"I can't tell you," he responded. "But there's another guy back in Philly I want you to meet — you two should work together on this — David Cooper."

Cooper led the system design, overhauling an inventory control system that he had created in 1985 that was designed to run venue box offices and outlets utilizing a manned phone room, and customized it to the band's needs.

After extensive work on it, McGinley brought Vedder out to meet the ETM team and hear the plan. "We laid it out for him, and I remember Eddie got up and started jumping around and getting excited that it would work," Schniedermeier recalls. "[Vedder] had been trying to figure out if we could compete with all of Ticketmaster's outlets and call centers. He said, 'Let's do this,' and that was his stamp of approval."

Among the band's needs were equal access for its fans when it came time for ticket on-sales, payment options that included checks or money orders, anti-scalping measures and the assurance that the system could handle significant queue volume in short periods of time. Cooper also gave fans the ability to buy tickets over the Internet via the band's website.

Pearl Jam's fan club members were offered tickets first, which were typically $18 with a $2 service charge plus an additional forty-five cent handling fee (a mere nickel less than Ticketmaster's rebuffed offer).

"The band has fought long and hard to come up with an alternative to the existing system — and in the process, I believe we've succeeded in changing some things for the better," said Curtis at the time. "Pearl Jam is finally ready to get this tour out and get back up onstage where they belong." However, he noted somewhat prophetically, "because of [Ticketmaster's] exclusive contracts, we are going to have to play at weird places like a ski resort in Lake Tahoe and a fairground in San Diego." As time would tell, the band would not perform at either venue. In fact, nine out of the fourteen dates initially announced were either canceled or moved locations. And the biggest show of the tour, it turned out, was hardly even a Pearl Jam show.

In mid-April the band canceled its first gig on June 16 at the Boise State Pavilion. Curtis, citing that ETM could not get local government approval before the needed on-sale, moved the performance to the Event Center in Casper, Wyoming. In actuality, the Boise State Pavilion had an exclusive contract with Select-A-Seat and therefore could not accommodate ETM. They were happy to ticket the show — and in fact were only charging $1.50, nearly a $1 cheaper than ETM — but the band was not willing to work with them. (A similar situation arose for the band's New Mexico date at the Pan American Center, though the building's exclusive ticketer, Dillard's, was willing to allow the band to use ETM, albeit at a higher service fee.)

"We're frustrated and disappointed," said Pavilion assistant director Charlie Spencer. "Long before Pearl Jam made affordable tickets fashionable, we've worked hard to bring [concertgoers] the lowest ticket price possible. I'm surprised that [Pearl Jam] professed a certain ideology and then veered off that stance."

More accurately, as one promoter pointed out at the time, "I don't think Pearl Jam anticipated some of the ramifications that would occur when it decided to use ETM. I don't think the band wanted to start making exceptions out of the box, so it moved to a more amenable facility." Once it got the green light, however, ETM lived up to its promises.

In its first on-sale for the show in Casper, Wyoming, it sold all 7,500 tickets in twenty-four hours. For the second on-sale, the 13,000-seat Wolf Mountain amphitheater in Salt Lake City, it took only seven minutes to sell out. Next up, two nights at Colorado's famed Red Rocks: 19,000 tickets in thirteen minutes. The system — selling all tickets via phone — was firing on all pistons without a hiccup. It was ready for its ultimate test: the June 24 show at Golden Gate Park.

"Well that was stupidity," David Cooper proudly says now. "We rented 2,000 phone lines on a Saturday morning from the biggest owner of phones in the United States. We crushed phone systems all over the United States because they just didn't understand — they never had a place where they could push 2,000 phone calls simultaneously."

Sure enough, ETM sold 48,000 tickets — two tickets per call — in twenty-one minutes. It was a feat certified by the *Guinness Book of World Records*. And for all of these on-sales ETM was capturing customers' phone numbers for future use. Cooper was also particularly proud that within two minutes after the sellout, an extra 10,000 phone numbers had been captured for those still hoping to buy. Now, having upstaged Ticketmaster, the band just needed to play the shows.

On June 13, three days before the band would play the first date of its highly publicized non-Ticketmaster U.S. summer tour, it announced the cancellation over safety concerns of its two dates in San Diego — the only southern Californian stop and Vedder's hometown. Curtis told reporter Chuck Philips that, "After this tour, we are going to reassess everything. It took us a whole year to plan [these summer dates], and we're not going to go through that again." He made it explicitly clear: "We did want to make a point of how difficult it is to tour without Ticketmaster, and we made the point. I think you'll find the band is just going to do whatever it takes to just play. And if that means they're going to have to play some Ticketmaster shows, they're going to play Ticketmaster shows."

On June 15, a day before the tour started, the *Los Angeles Times* and the *Washington Post* published the same piece by Philips, though each outlet augmented it with additional reporting. "I regret to say that it's impossible for a major rock group to put on a national tour under the current circumstances without Ticketmaster," Curtis relayed. "They've got a monopoly. We did everything we could over the past 14 months to get around them and put this tour together, but we failed. It's up to the Justice Department now."

Curtis compared the fight to David and Goliath with the giant winning: "In the end, you just have to face the fact that Ticketmaster calls the shots and give in to it. Pearl Jam is living proof that Ticketmaster can't be beat. If the government doesn't want to see the problem or take action at this point, I don't know what else a rock band can do to change it."

The band announced later that day that the canceled shows had been rescheduled for the San Diego Sports Arena. Though the arena was a Ticketmaster client, Ticketmaster agreed to a contractual waiver that allowed the Del Mar tickets to be honored. (It was an easy transfer, given that all the shows were general admission.) Ticketmaster would receive an undisclosed fee that it would donate to charity.

With the Justice Department's investigative findings expected shortly and the tour about to begin, it was high stakes drama. Though the concerts were canceled over safety concerns at the behest of the band, the public perception — thanks to Curtis's comments to the newspapers — was that Ticketmaster had won the war with a strategic blow.

Two days after Pearl Jam had supposedly hoisted the white flag to Ticketmaster, the band took to the stage for its much anticipated tour. Before playing any music, Vedder addressed the sellout crowd. "I don't know if you've heard, but in New York and Los Angeles there're papers sayin' we surrendered to Ticketmaster and all those kind of things, but it didn't happen . . . take my word, it's a lie," he told the crowd. "So that's New York and Los Angeles, but I'm in Casper and I don't give a fuck anyway."

Veteran *Los Angeles Times* music critic Robert Hilburn flew to Casper to talk to Curtis in person about the sudden turn of events. According to Hilburn, Curtis said his comments to the press were made out of frustration and that he only mentioned using Ticketmaster as a means to quickly reschedule the San Diego shows.

"Jeff and Eddie were furious after reading the reports that we had changed our policy, because that was not their intention at all, and we are in agreement that is not what we're going to do," said Curtis.

No manager, particularly of a world-famous rock group as socially and politically conscious as Pearl Jam, would make comments of Curtis's nature to the national press without being absolutely in step with their band — let alone on an issue the band had spent over a year battling publicly that involved Congress, the Justice Department, countless hours of work and a significant amount of money. These were not comments made in the heat of a moment as Curtis suggested but rather given during a strategic interview

scheduled with Philips, a sympathetic reporter who had been covering the
band's crusade since its beginning.

In all likelihood two decisions had been reached by the group and its organization that led to Curtis's comments to Philips. First, the band felt that its continued commitment to non-Ticketmaster venues was becoming excessively expensive and kept them away from major markets. Second, its tour was supporting Ticketmaster's argument that viable alternatives existed.

Though Pearl Jam had to play in less-than-ideal venues in less-than-ideal markets, the ETM ticketing system it utilized was highly successful. For Ticketmaster this was proof it didn't have a monopoly on ticketing. However, as band publicist Nicole Vandenberg argued, in retrenching the band's position after Curtis's comments, "The difficulty the band has faced [in booking venues for its summer tour] only reinforces the position that Ticketmaster has a monopoly. It's not a fight [the band] are going to quit."

In a six-page memo to venues and promoters on March 9, Ticketmaster Vice President and General Counsel Ned Goldstein discussed the company's recent meetings with the Department of Justice that had left it feeling less than confident. "We nonetheless remain troubled by indications that at least some DOJ staff members believe that there is a 'market' or 'market segment' of the live-entertainment business that is comprised of live music concerts, and that ticketing for those events should be handled differently than ticketing for other events," it read in part. "To put it succinctly, DOJ staff members have expressed the view that rock bands should be given more control over ticketing for their performances."

Goldstein went on to write, "We frankly cannot understand what makes the DOJ staff believe that it is a good idea to engage in social engineering on the live entertainment business, rather than leaving the participants in that business to sort out their relationships in accordance with their perceptions of what is in their best interest and the forces of the free market."

On June 19, four days after newspapers said the band was throwing in the towel against Ticketmaster, Vedder took the stage for the band's two-night stand at Colorado's majestic Red Rocks amphitheater riding in on an old bicycle. "This place fucking sucks," he said facetiously. "It's obviously the farthest thing from the truth — just like us going back to Ticketmaster is the farthest thing from the truth."

Halfway through the show Vedder began reflecting on the notion of Generation X and how he believed the media propagated it. "It's obvious that every person in this audience is an individual and has their own choice and can do whatever he fucking wants," he charged before debuting a song that would eventually appear on the band's following album, *No Code*. "This is a new song about choice — it's called 'Habit.'" Less than a week later in San Francisco, the band would face its own tough choices.

The band's historic gig for 55,000 at Golden Gate Park turned out to be memorable for an unforeseeable reason: Vedder, stricken by what was reported as a case of severe food poisoning, left the stage after only seven songs. The audience was outraged. Neil Young quickly subbed for Vedder as the band worked through the collaborative *Mirror Ball* material which it had recorded with Young earlier in the year alongside some of his classics like "The Needle and the Damage Done," "Hey Hey My My," "Down by the River" and "Cortez the Killer."

The next day Pearl Jam canceled the remaining nine dates of its tour, including the two San Diego shows it had moved to the Sports Arena that were to begin the following day. The band's publicist, Nicole Vandenberg, stated, "The cancellation was brought on by the business problems and controversies surrounding the band's attempt to schedule an alternative tour."

Looking back on the Golden Gate show, Curtis says: "We were afraid there'd be a riot. Neil just went down and wore 'em out. After that show Neil said, 'You know what? If it doesn't feel right, go home.' And the band looked at each other and said, 'You know what? We feel like going home.' So we called it quits and went home."

Pearl Jam guitarist Stone Gossard says much the same of what became a turning point for the band. "That was a day we acted as a band," he would later posit. "In the past, we had kind of allowed Eddie to steer the ship in some ways, and it's still that way. You want him to feel good about the situation, because when he's feeling good about it, it makes the whole thing work. But that day you could see he was totally sick but still trying to push himself. When we saw what was happening, the band finally said, 'This is insane. We've got to stop.' We couldn't let him feel like he's got to tour because we're expecting it from him."

As was the case for the canceled 1994 summer tour, the band's real reason for the latest cancellation was artfully obscured. While physical and mental health were completely valid reasons to postpone a tour, the press would undoubtedly ask questions about what was wrong. It was the last thing the band wanted to deal with.

It was easier to blame Ticketmaster.

ON WEDNESDAY, JULY 5, the Department of Justice made its long awaited announcement on its antitrust investigation of Ticketmaster: "The Department of Justice announced today that it has informed Ticketmaster Holdings Group, Inc., that it is closing its antitrust investigation into that firm's contracting practices. The Department will continue to monitor competitive developments in the ticketing industry."

The following day, July 6, at a regular press briefing, Attorney General Janet Reno said, "It did not seem an appropriate time to continue to pursue the investigation. . . . My understanding is that the division found there were new enterprises coming into the arena and based on that evidence . . . we do not have a basis for proceeding."

Pearl Jam issued a press release that day at 5:30 p.m.:

> Pearl Jam is disappointed with the Department of Justice's decision to drop the investigation of Ticketmaster's monopoly of the entertainment ticketing industry. Unfortunately those who will be most hurt by the Justice Department's cave-in are the consumers of live entertainment. They are the ones who ultimately pay for the lack of choice in the marketplace. What we've accomplished over the past year was to raise awareness of Ticketmaster's anti-consumer practices. And what we've learned is that touring without Ticketmaster is a difficult and tiresome process. Nevertheless, we have no plans at this time to use Ticketmaster, and will continue to work on behalf of our fans to keep our tickets affordable and accessible to everyone.

Ticketmaster, having fought and won the toughest public battle it had ever faced, felt vindicated. The company issued its own statement, which read in part, "Ticketmaster is pleased that, after an intense, year-long investigation, the Justice Department has concurred that we are conducting business within the bounds of the antitrust laws."

During the months and years following the DOJ ruling, some parties, frustrated by the decision (and disappointed by the brevity of the department's statement) suggested that perhaps undue influence was brought to bear. Rosen dismisses such murmurings out of hand: "We beat them fair and square. All the rest of this is sour grapes. The case was dismissed on the merits. Anything else is nonsense and untrue."

Indeed, multiple lawyers who worked for Justice on the investigation have confirmed that despite an initial zeal to mount a case against Ticketmaster, the department eventually concluded it could not find sufficient evidence and a proper legal theory to move forward and file an antitrust complaint.

"The one thing I can say with complete confidence," says one of the attorneys assigned to the matter, "is there wasn't any outside or political influence on the investigation. The people who work at the agencies are basically there to stop antitrust violations, not to give people a green light. But the fact of the matter is that, if the Justice Department is going to take an antitrust action against a company, it needs to have confidence that it will stand up in court under the antitrust law, and in this case the conclusion was that there was not enough evidence."

"Technically it wasn't even dismissed," a colleague adds. "It was dropped after the investigation phase because the government wasn't able to present a legal basis to win in court."

Ultimately, after assessing the ticketing landscape over the course of a year, the Justice Department concluded that the two theories it had floated internally over the preceding months would not suffice. Initially the antitrust division had considered the notion that the ticket-buying consumer was the ultimate aggrieved party. However, upon learning more about how the ticketing industry functioned, the department came to understand that Ticketmaster's customers for the sake of Sherman Act enforcement were technically the venues and the promoters who had entered into contracts with the company.

As the department began conversations with Ticketmaster's client base (and potential client base), it discovered that these businesses were quite content with the status quo. These customers emphasized that all of their contracts were put out to bid and that they did not wish to challenge the paradigm of revenue sharing, signing bonuses and service fee advances that had become the norm.

Nearly a decade later a federal district court in California would dismiss an antitrust action brought by Ticketmaster's competitor, Tickets.com, issuing an opinion that reached the same conclusions as the DOJ did in 1994 (a decision later upheld by the United States Court of Appeals for the 9th Circuit).

In that case the court granted Ticketmaster's motion to dismiss on summary judgment, which meant that the case would not go before a jury and that the facts as presented by Tickets.com's expert economist would be the source of analysis. The court thus took a view of the facts unsympathetic to Ticketmaster, granting that company "has by far the dominant share of the business. In 31 of the 41 regional areas, of the larger arenas, TM has exclusive contracts which cover 75% of the tickets sold. In 25 of the regional areas, TM's market share was about 90%."

Nonetheless, the judge ruled for Ticketmaster:

> The evidence points very strongly to the conclusion that the venues themselves prefer long term exclusive contracts for their own reasons, that they have the economic power to resist long term contracts if it were in their interests to do so, and overwhelmingly, they prefer the long term contracts and prefer them to include the retail outlets, the telephone centers, and the internet connections. This can be for a number of reasons. Where the venues run their own box office

at the venue site, the computers need to be compatible with the computers at the other sites, which means that changing ticket servicers every few years means retraining staff on new computers and software. Changing servicers often also means changing retail outlets (with which their customers become accustomed to) and also changing telephone and (perhaps) internet addresses. If the ticket servicer has reasonable performance and price, continuity leads to customer usage and satisfaction. Costs can be fixed for a longer, more predictable future. But by far the most important reason why venues prefer long term contracts is that this is the method by which they can obtain cash upfront from the ticket servicer, but at the cost of a long term contract, so that the ticket servicer may amortize the cost with the expected income over the years of the contract. Often, the large up-front payment is obtained to build the venue or to remodel it, to the mutual benefit of the ticketing service and the venue, but a long term contract is then needed to support the cash payment demanded by the venue. Some venues prefer exclusive contracts because it simplifies their bookkeeping and reduces the cost of renegotiating the contracts every few years. Virtually no venues have complained about long term contracts or felt forced into them against their desires.

Just as this court concluded in 2003, a primary reason for the Justice Department's decision to drop its investigation in 1995 was that venues and promoters willingly entered into contracts with Ticketmaster.

The other hurdle facing the Justice Department in 1994–95 was establishing the "relevant market." Although some DOJ lawyers had hoped to evaluate Ticketmaster's actions and impact solely on the live music front, the department ultimately determined that this theory would not hold up in court. Ticketmaster would have challenged this definition because, aside from amphitheaters, the company did not enter into contracts that focused exclusively on concerts. In addition rock music represented only a small portion of the business that the company conducted with arenas and theaters as its contracts addressed the many forms of entertainment that would take place in these facilities.

So even though casual observers of the industry (and some insiders) felt that Ticketmaster enjoyed a monopoly status, the existing legal framework did not allow for a formal charge.

What's more, while no other ticketing service came close to approaching Ticketmaster in size, Pearl Jam was in the midst of demonstrating that it could tour without having to work with them.

Fastixx cofounder and longtime Oregon-based promoter Dave Leiken thought the band could have instead highlighted service fees. "I told them they should use all the independent ticket companies that were out there where they could and use Ticketmaster where they had to," he says. "Then, at the end of the tour, they should take out an ad and show the differences in the service charges if nothing else."

To that end, what made it additionally difficult to argue for antitrust was that tickets had a huge range of prices, as did their accompanying service fees. If the broader goal of antitrust legislation is to protect the consumer, it was hard to argue that a $2.50 service charge, as Ticketmaster wanted to assess for Pearl Jam shows, was too high when the band itself was charging $2.45.

Still, there seemed to be enough artist and consumer outrage about Ticketmaster's anti-competitive nature to merit potential governmental intervention or, at the very least, an explanation of what the Justice Department found.

"From my opinion, and it's just my own opinion," says Gary Condit, "[the decision] clearly deserved more than two sentences. If that was the ruling they were going to make — because I do believe it was a questionable decision and, at best, if they ruled in that favor, it had to be a close call — tell us why you found to give the edge to Ticketmaster that it's not a monopoly."

However, as a former DOJ antitrust lawyer explains: "One thing that has changed in the Department of Justice from then to now is there is somewhat more transparency now, at least to a limited extent. If the department doesn't bring a case in a highly publicized deal, they will issue some sort of explanation of their reasoning, more than a sentence or two. For instance, in the XM/Sirius merger, the department issued a statement of a few pages that explained the reasoning, and one could evaluate whether one agreed or not."

Regardless of the Justice Department's decision, it appears that it did conduct a fairly thorough investigation in interviewing artists, managers, venues, various ticketing agencies and subpoenaing documents from promoters, venues and Ticketmaster that showed the true nature of the concert industry and its many players.

Cooper says he alone was called sixteen times as "an expert witness by either congressmen and senators though mostly by the Justice Department lawyers who were trying to learn all this shit." They paid multiple visits to his house and he went to Washington, DC, on multiple occasions.

Not surprisingly, Pearl Jam's Jeff Ament came away from the process disenchanted. "The whole thing was a joke," he says, looking back. "The Department of Justice used us to look hip. Stone and I spent a week with this guy John Hoyt; he was drilling us with serious questions that we were [supposedly] going to get asked, and then it didn't feel like we got to utilize any of it. It made me a lot more cynical about what goes on with the government."

WHEN THE HEARING TOOK PLACE in June 1994, the midterm congressional elections loomed large. Though Clinton had been elected president, Republicans were on the offensive, led by Newt Gingrich and the "Contract with America," a neo-conservative document they released that September that promised immediate action should they gain control of the House of Representatives.

"Democrats were floundering in terms of message and in terms of constituencies," says Condit, who's since left public office. "Not to say that I'm some kind of visionary, but I was thinking these people [who care about Pearl Jam] are going to be twenty-one before too long. We should be the ones out there saying, 'Look, we care about the stuff you guys care about.' [Ticketmaster] was a galvanizing issue, and it was one that we could make a statement about."

Condit approached the Speaker of the House, Tom Foley: "I told him we ought to jump on this as a political issue in terms of responding to an issue that's important to kids who will be voting in seven or eight years. . . . He listened to me, and I tried to get them to embrace this as maybe we could push it with the Justice Department or we could capture the issue, and of course in 1994 we lost the majority and it was for naught."

For the first time since 1954 Democrats lost the majority of the House in a fifty-four seat swing. It was a devastating loss.[5] Republicans reconfigured committees, prioritizing their own agendas. Needless to say, ticketing was barely a blip on the radar. Condit for his part wishes he had put forth more of an effort in pressing for answers. "I should have been more tenacious and more challenging of the Justice Department on their explanation," he admits. "But I think we got to the point where we were all sort of frustrated that you had a Democratic administration that gave us this response, and you probably had Pearl Jam saying, 'What's the use?'"

Edgell confirms that, in light of how the first hearing had gone, he tried to schedule a second hearing for September 1994. "[Congress] was rushing in to do the budget, and we couldn't get a date for the hearing," he recounts. "We put it off until after the November election, the Republicans took over and at that point there was no reason to do a hearing.

"In theory [the second hearing] would have been to bring in the Grateful Dead and focus on their successful business model," Edgell reveals. "That's been my big regret over the last fifteen years, that I did not pursue that second hearing."

Pearl Jam headlined one show in the U.S. in 1997. The band released its sixth album, *Yield*, in early February 1998. The same month it announced a comprehensive thirty-three date national tour, one that it acknowledged would see the band playing Ticketmaster venues in certain markets. The fight was officially over.

"I think bands pick their battles as to what they're going to get involved in, and I think for a while Pearl Jam didn't tour because of [its stance on ticketing] — they stayed home," offers R.E.M. general counsel Bertis Downs. "At some point you have to say, 'We're a band, we tour, this is what we do,' and there's a certain amount of resolve to just play the cards you're dealt. You try to have an impact and say your piece, but you can't sit at home and change the world."

Cooper saw Pearl Jam's decision to use Ticketmaster again as quite simple. "It's real easy," he says now. "They were used to making $10 or $15 million a year. [*No Code*] sold less, and the concert tours didn't gross as much because they were playing stupid venues. It was a financial decision, clearly. There's no art to that.

"Pearl Jam spent a lot of money on principle and earned far less money on principle," he continues. "You have to realize that playing at a ski slope and having it rain on us was not nearly as profitable as playing down the street in a nice fucking arena." For markets like New York, the appeal of playing the country's renowned venues — many of which the band never played until the 1998 summer tour began — was tough to deny. "You want to play Madison Square Garden, or are we going to play another fucking Randall Island's dump gig?" asks Cooper rhetorically as an example. "Costs are high, revenues are low because they wanted to do a $20 ticket, and then they turned around and said, 'Fuck it.'" (And, as it turned out, after repeated breakdowns, ETM ran out of financing and handed many of its contracts over to Ticketmaster in June 2000, although Cooper had long since left the company in a disagreement with Schniedermeier and ran the final two Pearl Jam ticketing efforts as Fillmore Tour & Ticket.)

In the face of questions regarding what many perceived as Pearl Jam's defeat by Ticketmaster, the band made a concerted effort to remind the public how it got embroiled in the battle in the first place. "We weren't trying to break their monopoly," emphasized Stone Gossard. "The United States government was investigating Ticketmaster to see whether they were, in fact, a monopoly. They asked us to come testify, based on our experiences. So we turned into the poster boys for this struggle, because the media said: Pearl Jam has this fight with Ticketmaster. We never had any lawsuit or took any legal action against Ticketmaster as Pearl Jam. The U.S. government did; we just testified."

Vedder feels the same way about the band's crusade against Ticketmaster: "We thought there was a bunch of people behind us; then we looked around and it was just us [laughs] — hanging there. Then the people who led us down that way [in the Justice Department] bailed, too. But it was still the right thing to do."

Former Ticketmaster CEO Fred Rosen spins the Pearl Jam years rather positively. "This is the part that made no sense," he offers. "Our business got stronger during all this, not weaker. We were lit up in the press, we got horrendous press on a regular basis and much of it was personal. And when Pearl Jam went away, they looked like kids who were on a crusade that no one understood."

One Ticketmaster insider believes that the whole investigation and hearing was about publicity and retribution, as much for Pearl Jam as the Department of Justice. "What [the DOJ] was upset about goes back to the purchase of Ticketron. I think there was an antagonism because of that transition." This view is seconded, at least in part, by a former member of the Justice Department who worked on the case and confirms: "We got into this through the Ticketmaster–Ticketron merger. That was the initial focal point for the investigation, but Ticketmaster certainly remained on our radar."

Despite now regularly working with Ticketmaster, Pearl Jam is remarkably upbeat about the whole process. "We haven't lost anything because we've learned from the experience," says Vedder. "There's no way that we, personally, could have lost. It wasn't a chess game. It was basically a case of our trying to be responsible to the people who come to see the shows, in the same spirit as us making sure that we have a good barricade, to seeing to it that the T-shirts are sold at reasonable prices. Basically, it's showing respect to the fans. And it's safe to say, a lot of these people — those who either run Ticketmaster or the arenas, or the promoters — haven't attended a show as a regular concertgoer in years."

Says one promoter who has worked with the group over the years: "Pearl Jam were schoolyard bullies. They got big and they started telling everyone how it had to be. That whole thing was about them wanting to win and be the bully and do it their way; it had nothing to do with the consumers and the public."

The band ultimately seemed, more or less, unfazed by the whole experience. "As a teenager and through your twenties, you're still wrestling with things around you, things you can't change — hence, frustration and punk rock," says Vedder, likening creating music to touring. "It's not that I find it boring; it's just frustrating: bang your head against the wall, scream in pain, record it. Okay, great, there's a song. Now I'm much more interested in taking the closest off-ramp to some kind of solution."

The off-ramp that Pearl Jam and many other bands took in the coming years would be marked clearly with three letters: SFX.

CHAPTER 6

Rock and Roll's New Bottom Line

FOR APPROXIMATELY FORTY YEARS, THE business of presenting live rock and roll remained fundamentally unchanged. While Ticketmaster had altered the role ticket distribution played, the rest of the business was the same as it ever was: a national network of fiefdoms run by regional promoters that, when taken collectively, made it viable for artists to mount national tours that covered all corners of the country.

Like a cluster of overlapping circles in a vast Venn diagram, the promoters had their core regions while overlapping on peripheral regions with other promoters. This competition helped regulate artist guarantees, venue rental costs and service charges. Although the industry as a whole was trending upward — higher artist guarantees forcing higher ticket prices, resulting in narrowing profit margins for promoters — the industry's "eco(nomic) system" was still healthy. As fiercely as promoters competed with one another, there was still a general code of conduct. All that began to rapidly change in the fall of 1996.

By the new millennium — four short years — the modern concert industry would change more than it had since its inception in the 1960s. And it was all the result of the actions of one man: Bob Sillerman.

ROBERT F.X. SILLERMAN WAS BORN April 12, 1948, in the upscale Bronx neighborhood of Riverdale. "I grew up in a very typical, liberal, educated Jewish household," he says matter-of-factly of his childhood with his older brother, Michael. Their father, also Michael, was an advertising entrepreneur who founded the Keystone Radio Network when the boys were young (he was also responsible for syndicating television shows like *Lassie*).

While the brothers were attending New York City's top private schools, their father went bankrupt. It was a pivotal moment for Robert, who was thirteen years old at the time. "If this was an Orson Welles movie, you'd cut right to 'Rosebud' with the snow falling on the sled," he reflects. Kids at his middle school teased him about it. The young Sillerman responded by taking matters into his own hands — he started his first business.

He had been selling greeting cards door-to-door prior to his father's financial woes and thought it was too much work for too little return. Faced with a new fiscal reality, he started his own greeting card company, buying the cards in bulk and hiring his own commissioned sales team of young teenagers.

Sillerman's father, "the consummate salesman," says Sillerman, passed away in 1980 before he could see his son achieve monumental financial success. "Good salespeople are optimistic. That's what I got from [my father's career experience]. When you're in your sixties and you go bankrupt, it can be debilitating. But my father, the very next day, had an idea on how he was going to make his next million. He never did. But he never lost his optimism."

After high school Sillerman arrived at Brandeis University in 1965 to major in political science, while his brother had left for Cornell a year earlier. By the time he was a sophomore, the young Sillerman had formed another company — Youth Market Consultants — a "multidimensional youth-marketing business." It sold magazines to students and offered a dating service but, more shrewdly, advised companies *how to market* to teens and youth culture.

"There were enough kids there so you could combine the desire or need to make a living with thinking you were being consistent with a counter-culture attitude," he says of his college days. "I knew I was going to be in business when nobody [else] was thinking about it." While an injury made Sillerman ineligible for the Vietnam draft, many of his peers were being sent to fight, which made it "impossible [for them] to plan for the future."

Absolutely "a product of the '60s," he credits the university for his formation of a "strong sense of social consciousness" for which he feels "immensely fortunate." Indeed Sillerman was a product — a born businessman. He sold Youth Marketing Consultants in 1972, three years after he graduated magna cum laude, to the Boston-based ad firm Ingalls for an amount he has yet to disclose. Two years later he started another marketing company, National Discount Marketers, Inc., which he based in Great Neck, Long Island.

By 1978 Sillerman had cobbled together $300,000 to help buy radio station 92.7 WALL-FM in Middletown, New York, with famed DJ Bruce "Cousin Brucie" Morrow for $1.875 million. (It was in essence two stations as it was simulcast on 96.9 FM in Arlington, New York.) "I suppose if you were a psychiatrist you could say I wanted to do well where my father had a lack of success," suggests Sillerman. The two men's partnership as the Sillerman-Morrow Group was a fruitful one from the start.

"Bob can sell igloos," says Morrow, who is ten years his senior. "Bob can sell anything — it doesn't matter — he has that kind of head." The two would charter a small plane to fly them from town to town as they began scooping up radio stations. "You and I buy a couple loaves of bread," says Morrow, analogizing their deal making. "Bob buys the bakery." Simply put, says Morrow, "I taught him broadcasting and he taught me business."

By 1985 the two had acquired eight radio stations and a television station that they liquidated for a cool $30 million. "He's not afraid to take tremendous chances, and can sleep with them," Morrow said at the time. "But me, I lost seven years of sleep in business with him." On the amicable split as business partners, Morrow says that he just "couldn't handle it anymore."

By 1988 Sillerman's latest company, Sillerman-Magee Communications, valued its assets between $750 million and $1 billion. Sillerman's success was a direct result of his business savvy. That year, for instance, as the *Wall Street Journal* would report, Sillerman bought the New York-based Metropolitan Broadcasting from investment bank Morgan Stanley. Taking a bank loan to pay Morgan Stanley, he quickly flipped one of Metropolitan's four stations and sold it to another company he had a stake in, Command Communications, and used the revenue to pay off the loan. He flipped Metropolitan the next year to Westinghouse Broadcasting Co. for $400 million. As one longtime radio insider put it, "After you shake hands with Bob you always count your fingers — he has a reputation as an extremely sharp operator."

By the early 1990s, with government regulation beginning to wane even more, Sillerman was ready to up the ante. In 1992 with radio bigwig Steven Hicks, Sillerman launched SFX Broadcasting, which combined Command Communications and CapStar Communications into one. The name came from the entrepreneur's last name and his middle initials. This was truly his company. The following year he and Hicks took it public with an initial public offering of $15 a share.

That same year Sillerman also took public another broadcasting company that he had founded — Multi-Market Radio (MMR). However, as part of the Federal Communications Commission's regulations, he wasn't allowed to head both of them. His solution to be in compliance was to simply own the majority of MMR through non-voting stock.

Of wider impact on the broadcasting industry was a new tool that he and Hicks created — local marketing agreements. An LMA allowed a broadcaster to essentially buy a station without owning it, thus increasing its

roster while circumventing federal regulation caps (that changed in 1999
when LMAs were included within market caps).

While federal regulations on media ownership had SFX and Multi-Market Radio in a constant creative shuffle of their properties, the game got a whole lot easier in February 1996.

FOR SIXTY-TWO YEARS THE COMMUNICATIONS Act of 1934 had guided the policies and regulations governing media in the United States. Politicians, at the behest of lobbyists, were convinced it was time for a change, a big change. When it was over, nearly all forms of communication in the United States — telephones, television, radio, newspapers and the Internet — would be affected.

Nearly four years in the making, the Telecommunications Act of 1996 was vigorously debated from all sides — the private sector and the public sector, Democrats and Republicans, and anybody in between. Nearly everyone agreed that the regulations in question needed updating and changing; they just couldn't agree on how.

The Telecommunications Act had bipartisan support but the political landscape within Congress had dramatically changed since the bill's birth in 1992. While some reform suggestions had been added to it since its initial introduction, none included the sweeping deregulation that came in the 1996 version. Those changes were catalyzed by the midterm elections of 1994, which saw Democrats lose their majority in the House of Representatives for the first time in forty years to the Newt Gingrich–led Republicans. Suddenly the bill began to take on a much different shape. Deregulation, at the urging of News Corp., ABC, CBS, NBC, Verizon and others, was suddenly the guiding principle. "Losing the House in 1994 was without question a seminal moment in the political history of the media," says Reed Hundt, who served as FCC chairman at the time.

Of the new landscape the *New York Times* wrote in early 1995 that "lobbyists have seldom met more receptive lawmakers. Committee Republicans have held numerous meetings with industry executives since January, at which they implored companies to offer suggestions about the ways that Congress could help them."

The 1995 version of the act, as proposed by Republicans, eliminated the ban on newspapers owning TV stations in the same market, immediately lifted price regulations for cable systems with fewer than 600,000 subscribers and, most notably, permitted one company to own two TV stations and an *unlimited number of radio stations in the same market*. The previous cap for one company had been a total of forty commercial radio stations with a limit of four per market.

In regard to radio, the act that was finally passed and signed by President Clinton in February 1996 was modified from the previous year's version but not by much. It eliminated the ownership cap on commercial radio stations while allowing one company to own up to eight radio stations in one market. President Clinton, the day of the bill's passage, told the press, "As a result of this action today, consumers will receive the benefits of lower prices, better quality and greater choices in their telephone and cable services, and they will continue to benefit from a diversity of voices and viewpoints in radio, television and the print media." A week later, when he signed it into law, he declared: "This law also recognizes that with freedom comes responsibility. Any truly competitive market requires rules. This bill protects consumers against monopolies. It guarantees the diversity of voices our democracy depends upon."

For many, nothing could have been further from the truth; diversity shrank, prices went up and near-monopolies flourished. As Eric Boehlert noted in one of his many pieces on the topic for *Salon* at the time, the act was "the kind of sweeping deregulation that most broadcasters hadn't even fantasized about two years earlier."

Prior to the telecom bill's deregulation, SFX and other major broadcasters had entered into massive acquisition deals that they couldn't, legally, be allowed to complete. Best of all, the valuations of the radio stations were set at artificially low, pre-deregulation prices. The deals were typically set up thusly: if SFX wanted stations in X market but couldn't buy them because of the existing regulations, they would have another broadcaster buy the stations they wanted and SFX in turn would buy the stations that that broadcaster wanted but couldn't buy. (Cherry picking wasn't allowed, so it was always groups of stations — a big one with a few smaller, less desirable ones.) The purchases were parked while the broadcast companies' lobbyists pounded Congress to push through the legislation on what essentially amounted to a huge gamble. With the deals in place, broadcasting groups like SFX simply had to wait for the bill to be passed before they could start swapping their desired stations to one another tax-free.

No surprise that the first issue of the trade publication *Radio & Records* after the bill's passage included headlines like "Let the deals begin!" and "It's buy, sell or get out of the way." The week after its passage — *the first week* — $700 million worth of radio-based transactions occurred.

As *Congressional Quarterly* noted shortly after the bill's passage, "There are numerous provisions that the Democratic-controlled 103rd Congress never would have countenanced, such as the ones lifting price controls on cable television systems and allowing radio broadcasters to own an unlimited number of radio stations across the country."

While SFX Broadcasting CEO and president Steven Hicks left in the spring of 1996 to form CapStar Broadcasting with his brother Tom — the previous company had been CapStar Communications — he would return in a few short years to fully enable Sillerman's latest fancy: live entertainment.

IN THE FALL OF 1996 SFX Broadcasting acquired New York–based concert producer and promoter Delsener/Slater Enterprises. The purchase, while unexpected, wasn't ultimately that surprising. Other large companies, such as Seagram, Polygram and Viacom, had already invested in the concert industry, so to the outside observer it didn't appear to portend anything more than a one-off business deal.

Four years earlier, Sillerman had met Ron Delsener and Mitch Slater at the inaugural All for the Sea benefit for Southhampton College's marine biology program. Sillerman and his wife, Laura, were co-chairs of the event and had gotten Crosby, Stills and Nash to perform. Sillerman would become the college's chancellor the next year and would come to throw many multi-million-dollar All for the Sea benefits over the next decade that included talent like Bob Dylan, Tom Petty, the Allman Brothers Band and Paul Simon, until the undergraduate campus closed in 2004.

Sillerman's broad thinking in interfacing the two types of properties was rather simple — radio operators always wanted to do concert promotions and concert promoters always needed radio to promote their concerts. There was surely something valuable if you could own both.

"While this acquisition is immediately attractive on its own, it has the added dimension of benefiting all of our radio stations with a direct association with leading concert tours and shows," Sillerman said of Delsener/Slater at the time. He also noted the "great opportunities for promotional tie-ins" between one of the country's top concert promoters and SFX's eighty-six radio stations in twenty-four cities. "This acquisition represents new and creative challenges for SFX and Delsener/Slater, and a synergistic first for our industry."

The concert industry was the last entertainment and media-based industry to be consolidated. Most of the major players in film, television, radio and recorded music had already been vertically integrated into a few massive companies. Moreover, Sillerman, as Cousin Brucie noted, wasn't the type to buy just one loaf of bread — he bought the bakery.

"When we bought Ron Delsener," says former SFX president and CEO Mike Ferrel, "what began was a dialogue with every major concert promoter in the United States. We had an opportunity to see [the concert] business from the inside and from the perspective of an operator. It gave us insight as to the opportunities there."

SFX learned two important lessons from the Delsener/Slater "laboratory," as they thought of it. The first was that the concert business had incredible cash flow. The takeaway was that while the margins were relatively thin, with the proper research the risks were minimal. If concert promotion could be done on a greater scale, with all those relatively thin margins combined into one, it could be a great business.

The second lesson, in connection to the first, was that there were artificial barriers preventing promoters from expanding. The reason Delsener/Slater didn't promote in Boston was that agents gave those shows to Don Law; the reason Don Law didn't promote in Washington, DC, was that those shows went to Jack Boyle or Seth Hurwitz. While those respected boundaries made sense to promoters from a historical viewpoint, they didn't make sense to a businessman like Sillerman.

Ferrel, in an interview at the time, threw out the idea of a national U2 tour that following spring under the guidance of Delsener/Slater that was tied to SFX-owned radio stations. "If we can control these events, if we bring U2 into Indianapolis [for example], it's absolutely our event," he argued. It wasn't by chance that Ferrel had used Indianapolis as an example. It was next on the acquisition list.

FOUNDED IN 1971 BY DAVE LUCAS, Indianapolis-based Sunshine Promotions was the leading promoter in Indiana, Kentucky, Ohio and Tennessee. In 1974 Lucas partnered with rival promoter Steve Sybesma, who had been doing well with shows in cities like Fort Wayne and South Bend, in an attempt to firmly control the region, which was seeing competition from Bruce Kapp out of Chicago and Jules Belkin from Cleveland. The duo's first real test came in late 1974 with a series of Bachman Turner Overdrive dates throughout their markets.

"Instead of making $1,000 a night, we were making $20,000," recalls Sybesma, who is now based in China. Sunshine's success continued with the Rolling Stones, KISS, Aerosmith and countless others. It began to diversify its business, launching TourDesign Creative Service (at the time the leading provider of concert advertisements for radio, television and print) and Suntex Acquisition LP (screen-printing, embroidery and tour merch) as separate companies to serve its core business.

It was in the mid-1980s that Sunshine began actively trying to build its own amphitheater. The 21,000-seat Deer Creek amphitheater in Noblesville, Indiana, was completed in 1989, followed by the 20,000-seat Polaris Amphitheater in Columbus, Ohio, in 1994. Sunshine also operated Louisville's Palace Theater and Indianapolis's Murat Centre. Owning property, particularly two amphitheaters, along with the ancillary businesses put Sunshine in a much different league than Delsener/Slater.

Sybesma had met Sillerman about a decade earlier as the two happened to regularly vacation at the same resort in Anguilla every year. "For about three years he was just some guy sitting across the pool," Sybesma recalls.

When Sillerman bought the Indianapolis-based radio stations WFBQ (FM), WRZX (FM) and WNDE (AM) that year from Secret Communications, Sybesma gave him a call to suggest they get together for a drink the next time he was in town. Unbeknownst to Sybesma, Sillerman had, just hours earlier, announced his Delsener/Slater purchase and asked if Sunshine would be interested in selling. The timing was fortuitous.

The previous year Sunshine had tried to go public in an effort to secure more financing as it paid down the debt from its amphitheater properties. "It was a grueling nine months of our lives," says Sybesma of the company's efforts to go public. "It was very expensive — it cost $1.8 million — and it failed. I told Bob [Sillerman], 'Yeah, anything I've got has a price and I'd be interested. But if you're not serious, I don't want to go through the motions.'" Negotiations began almost immediately.

"When we went into the public offering [process] before, Wall Street just didn't get it; they didn't understand our business and I can see why," Sybesma offers. "They just didn't buy it. So Bob was able to make it happen in a different way." Though Sunshine was grossing $15 million a year, it was still spending a lot on paying down its debts. The idea of receiving a huge cash infusion that would alleviate those debts and allow it more flexibility was very appealing.

In analyzing Sunshine's portfolio of businesses, SFX had a lightbulb moment when it got to TourDesign, the advertising arm. They immediately noticed the television spots the company was producing for concert promotion — something that rarely, if ever, happened in the radio- and print-heavy New York market. Backed up by substantial research, Sunshine relayed how television was the most effectual form of concert advertising, followed by radio then print. Coupled with their Suntex merchandising division, SFX saw the possibilities of taking the full-service suite of businesses Sunshine had created for itself and ramping it up to be nationally based in serving numerous promoters it could theoretically acquire.

In addition SFX was in discussions with TCI Music, a diversified music entertainment company that delivered content via satellite, television and the Internet. It had dabbled in the live Internet streaming of the Tibetan Freedom Concerts and owned the website SonicNet, among other assets. TCI Music combined with Sunshine's assets could provide the tools to create an incredibly robust company. (TCI was not ultimately purchased.)

In March of 1997 SFX announced its acquisition of Sunshine Promotions for $64 million plus its debt. For a company that was annually grossing $15 million, the price seemed surprisingly high. "It was his company, but we still had our company name and still felt a pride of ownership," says Sybesma.

Shortly before announcing the Sunshine acquisition, SFX had also purchased the Meadows Music Theater in Hartford, Connecticut, which had opened two years earlier in 1995 under the direction of Jim Koplik and Shelly Finkel in partnership with Robert Nederlander. With a $32-million price tag, the 24,000-capacity indoor-outdoor amphitheater was the most expensive amphitheater in the United States. What particularly excited Sillerman about both Sunshine and the Meadows was the radio tie-in. (In Hartford, SFX owned five FM stations and one AM.) "We anticipate realizing the immediate benefits of cross promotional opportunities," he said unabashedly.

Sillerman and Ferrel never hid their ambition for leveraging radio and concerts; the practice made good business sense. While it made some competing radio stations nervous when they foresaw the potential loss of revenue from Sunshine's advertising dollars for promoting its concerts, SFX Broadcasting wasn't seen as unruly, with just under eighty stations in their portfolio. (SFX Broadcasting was the seventh-largest radio company at the time.) Nor were there ever any accusations of using airplay as a means to secure an artist's appearance at a particular venue (that would come a few years later).

"The industry in general is trying to figure out the implications of a radio corporation investing in this business," said *Pollstar*'s editor, Gary Bongiovanni. "My guess is concert promoters around the country are a bit nervous." Those concerns were heightened with the launch of SFX Concerts, a new division of the broadcasting parent company.

Tim Klahs, director of investor relations for SFX Broadcasting, assured the press after the Sunshine announcement, "We have no grandiose ideas. If anything, the idea of the transaction is not to see any visible changes. It's more like they have a wealthy parent if you will."

BY AUGUST 1997, FIVE MONTHS later, rumors began to fly about SFX Broadcasting going up on the sales block. In the aftermath of the Telecommunications Act, there were now only a few companies that could afford to acquire SFX's 71 stations, which had generated $143 million in sales the previous year: CBS Radio Group (76 stations), CapStar Broadcasting (241 stations) and Jacor Communications (154 stations). At the time Clear Channel Communications wasn't deemed a viable purchaser. Whoever purchased SFX would be the leader of the pack (though, in regard to sales, CBS was heftily outperforming all of them with more than a billion dollars in annual sales).

SFX had gone public in 1993 at $15 a share. Since then, the stock had sky-rocketed as high as $75 per share that August. It fielded offers from all the major players — CBS offered its buyout at $76 per share, CapStar at $69 per share and Jacor at $67, though sources indicate Jacor was never in the running. Sillerman wanted cash, not stock, which Clear Channel had offered with the help of another buyer. The other caveat to the SFX purchase was the assumption of nearly a billion dollars of debt.

On Saturday, August 23, CapStar agreed to a $2.1 billion acquisition of SFX Broadcasting at $75 per share. It would pay $1.2 billion in cash while assuming $900 million in debt. While the price was estimated to be fifteen times SFX's anticipated annual cash flow, given that it was one of the few radio conglomerates that could be bought and leveraged, it was considered a fair price. The deal also turned out to be something of a family affair.

CapStar was run by Sillerman's former partner and SFX co-founder, Steven Hicks, who had left a year earlier. CapStar's parent company, Hicks, Muse, Tate & Furst, was chaired by Hicks' brother Tom, who would now oversee the 300-plus stations which had, when combined, generated a combined $1.38 billion in revenue the year before.

"I'm particularly pleased to be associated once again with SFX, a company I helped to create," said Steven Hicks immediately following the announcement. Sillerman himself had to be pleased, too; he personally netted well over $200 million from the deal. Not everyone was thrilled, though.

"I wonder if Congress knew when it passed the telecom bill that people are pigs," says Goff Lebhar, at the time president and general manager of Washington, DC's WWDC-AM and FM. "Did they realize that half a dozen people, all males, would someday control what goes on the radio, who have no obligation to satisfy anyone but Wall Street? I don't think they had any idea what would happen in the field of radio." Those same concerns would soon become increasingly focused on what was happening to the concert industry.

In the purchasing process SFX had offered CBS and CapStar its three entertainment assets for an extra two dollars a share. Both companies declined, but CapStar, in winning the bid, did so with a rather generous offer: SFX Broadcasting could use its existing cash flow from the radio business to finance the acquisition of its concert business as long as the debt was repaid upon the closing of the broadcast deal after it had cleared governmental review. The window was approximately six months, and it facilitated (what would become) SFX Entertainment in the brokering of a staggering number of deals in a very short amount of time. And in doing so — and this is part of Sillerman's genius — SFX Entertainment gained enough leverage in that window to become a publicly traded company and raise the money to repay its debt to CapStar with an IPO in February 1998.

With the Justice Department taking a look at the CapStar acquisition, Sillerman and his principals at SFX plotted their next moves. Over dinner in New York a group of five looked over a memo that listed every major promoter in the country.

"We can't own them all. The DOJ won't let us."

"So where do we put on the brakes?"

They had unanimously agreed to acquire Bill Graham Presents in San Francisco, Contemporary Productions in St. Louis and Concerts/Southern Promotions in Atlanta by the end of 1997. The only question was whether to buy Houston-based PACE Entertainment or Virginia/DC–based Cellar Door Productions.

"Let's put the brakes on Jack Boyle's business."

Cellar Door would have to wait.

ALEX COOLEY AND A FEW friends had opened up a pizza joint in Atlanta during the 1960s and found themselves failing at it rather well. While the place was, as Cooley says, "horribly unsuccessful making and selling pizzas," it did have one thing going for it: square footage.

Taking his cues from the local Top 40 station WQXI, Cooley began booking doo-wop groups into the huge space. For all-you-can-drink beer and a show, the deal was $5 for a single ticket, $8 if you brought a girl. In contrast to their their pizza proceeds, Cooley and his partners began making some real money from the informal concerts.

What interested Cooley far more at the time, musically speaking, was what WQXI would play after two o'clock in the morning. This was when the DJ would spin artists like Procol Harum, Jefferson Airplane, the Grateful Dead and others. And it was here that Cooley heard about the 1968 Miami Pop Festival.

He and four buddies had already scheduled a scuba diving trip to John Pennekamp State Park in the Florida Keys for the same time, so it felt mildly serendipitous. After attending the first night, scuba diving was suddenly secondary — in fact everything else in life seemed secondary. "I remember sitting on the concrete, thinking, 'This is what I want to do,'" recalls Cooley now from his home on Lookout Mountain, which straddles the Georgia–Tennessee border. "I came back to Atlanta and put together seventeen partners to get enough money, and we put on the first Atlanta Pop Festival."

The festival, held on the Fourth of July weekend of 1969, made $6,000. Hippies that they were, Cooley and company felt bad about taking such a profit. They decided to hire the Grateful Dead and Delaney & Bonnie and Friends to play a free afternoon concert in Piedmont Park that Monday. The success of his first festival steered him away from the University of

Georgia and Georgia State University as neither had yet to turn on any lightbulbs the way his experiences in Miami and Atlanta had. "I knew that rock and roll was what I wanted to be in," says Cooley in a smooth, steady Southern cadence. He would throw the Texas Pop Festival two weeks after Woodstock over Labor Day weekend later that year.

Cooley was responsible for making Atlanta a viable market for nationally touring rock bands. "There were two promoters in Atlanta [in the '60s], but neither one of them had a clue as to what rock and roll was," he says. They were, according to Cooley, entirely focused on acts like Red Skelton and Lawrence Welk.

"There's a lot to be said for the theory of being in the right place at the right time," he acknowledges. "I was at the right place at the right time, and I understood that there were a lot of people like me that were tired of listening to doo-wop and weren't really into it. There's no substitute for that."

Cooley opened the Electric Ballroom in 1974, his answer to the Fillmore East, the Tea Party and the Cellar Door. The rock business proved a profitable one for him, and in 1980 he partnered on a handshake with Peter Conlon, a former Jimmy Carter aide, to launch Concerts/Southern Promotions. The company revived the Chastain Park Amphitheater, built the Roxy, the Tabernacle and the Cotton Club and saved the Fox Theatre from being torn down.

By the late 1990s Concerts/Southern Promotions had fended off formidable adversaries in holding its ground. "There's an old joke that if you die in the South somewhere, you have to go through Atlanta to get to heaven," tells Cooley. "All the dividing lines started to shift. Jack Boyle did Washington, DC, and the surrounding area. When he moved part of his operation to Florida, he wanted everything from Washington to Miami. [Houston-based] PACE wanted everything from Texas to Atlanta and further north."

Concerts/Southern Promotions competed with PACE but also on occasion partnered with them. Around 1993 PACE made an offer to buy them outright, shortly after Cooley was recovering from the first of two heart attacks. "It was terrible," says Cooley of the negotiations. "I felt like, after it was all over and I went my separate way un-bought, that they never dealt in good faith [with me again]." Cooley pauses. "You're digging up some old animosities when you bring up PACE."

One of the points that Cooley, now in his early 70s, is emphatic about is the industry's move away from the long-entrenched regionalism to more nationally based tours and the constant encroachment from other promoters. Cooley's region included Florida, Tennessee and Kentucky, and in each of those markets he feels he knew what worked and what didn't better than any other promoter, whether it was in regard to venue, ticket price or radio advertising. "Acts and more national promoters were trying to take all those powers away," he says. "One of the things that led to SFX was because we promoters were getting to be marginalized."

Sunshine principals Dave Lucas and Steve Sybesma arranged a lunch for themselves and Sillerman when Cooley and Conlin were up in New York on business. "He was a likable guy," recalls Cooley of Sillerman. "It was a fun lunch. I remember asking him why he bought Sunshine, and he said, 'Because I like to go to shows and I want to go backstage.' Some answer like that, but then we started a dialogue."

Part of Sillerman's pitch, says Cooley, was to suggest that as one big company, SFX could bring stability to an industry that was finding itself to be increasingly chaotic. Promoters would once again have clearly defined regional lines and wouldn't have to exhaust time and money battling competition. "That was the thing, at least for me, that resonated," says Cooley of the potential calming effect SFX could have. "I saw my power slipping away — my power to decide ticket price, my power to decide what radio stations we were going with." Concerts/Southern Promotions was eventually sold to SFX for $17 million.

ANOTHER DIALOGUE LUCAS HAD INITIATED for Sillerman at the same time as Concerts/Southern Promotions was with Contemporary Productions founders Irv Zuckerman and Steve Schankman. The story of the St. Louis–based company's success echoed that of Sunshine, both in its humble origins and eventual business diversification.

"I was going to be a lawyer, and instead of going to St. Louis University Law School I went two blocks down the street and did the Grateful Dead at the Fox Theater in 1969," says Schankman today, sitting in his St. Louis office. "From that point on I knew what I wanted to do was be in the entertainment business, so I could care less about being a lawyer."

In 1968 the twenty-year-old Schankman was selling drugs at Walgreens, playing trumpet in a big band and booking bands while his grade school friend Zuckerman was selling shoes. Schankman couldn't do all the booking and asked his old friend if he would help. Zuckerman agreed and developed a roster of groups that would play for a flat rate of $100. For each $100 band booked, Zuckerman got $10. In short order the duo became the largest booking agency in America, booking 1,400 bands in ten states. If someone called from Bird City, Kansas, and needed a band for $300, they could accommodate as they had developed a comprehensive list of all the band unions in a ten- to twelve-state radius. The decision to get into the promotion business, however, came as an epiphany to Schankman.

"I'm standing onstage playing my trumpet with my band as the opening act for the Temptations," he remembers. "I'm looking around — 10,000 people, three dollars a ticket, $30,000 — why am I playing in the band? I want to be the promoter."

Contemporary Productions rapidly grew into one of the country's top promoters, covering a core area of Missouri, Kansas and Oklahoma and parts of Illinois. Eventually it opened offices in Atlanta, Kansas City, New York and New Jersey. By the time Dave Lucas invited them to lunch with Sillerman in 1997, Contemporary had several hundred employees working for twenty-two businesses whose divisions included a ticketing agent, management, record label, venue marketing, motor sports and corporate marketing. Their venue portfolio included two amphitheaters: Riverport just outside of St. Louis, which opened in 1991, and Sandstone in Bonner Springs, Kansas, which they took over and refurbished in 1992.

"Sunshine is 300 miles east of here, and once we heard the story from Steve and Dave, it made sense for us to get into the ring," says Schankman of the first meeting with Sillerman. "[Delsener/Slater in New York] is one thing, but when you see guys in the Midwest selling, you have to start thinking about what's going on. I don't want SFX in Indianapolis because then I know one thing: they're coming to St. Louis."

Zuckerman and Schankman met Sillerman in New York to present Contemporary's portfolio. "I presented the company because I ran all the divisions," says Schankman. "I was always president of everything, and I knew afterward, when I called my wife, I said, 'He's going to buy us.' Because we were everything he wanted: a marketing company, a concert producer and a ticketing company. PACE didn't do that." (PACE was focused on promoting music, theater and motorsports along with amphitheater ownership.)

Schankman remembers negotiating the entire deal in about an hour on the telephone with Sillerman. "I knew exactly what I wanted," he says. Playing to the trumpeter's favor was the fact that Contemporary had already entertained several buyout offers and therefore had a very good idea of their real worth — $25 million to be precise.

The first offer came from an unlikely bidder: Michael Milken. Yes, the same financier who was indicted on ninety-eight counts of racketeering and securities fraud in 1989 for what became known as "junk bonds." Milken pleaded guilty to six counts, received a ten-year prison sentence and got out after two years in 1993, thanks to a good lawyer (Alan Dershowitz) and good behavior.

Schankman says the phone call he received in 1996 was completely out of the blue. "They said, 'I work with Mike Milken, I'd like to talk to you about your company,'" he recounts. The idea was to take Contemporary public.

While Milken would assume the risk and Contemporary would get a large amount of money, Schankman just wasn't interested.

The following year, as Sillerman began making his initial forays into the business, Contemporary received at least two other offers — one from TBA Entertainment and another from Ogden.

TBA Entertainment, which had recently changed its name from Nashville Country Club (and is now known as TBA Global), defined itself as a "diversified entertainment company" with a variety of assets and investments in resorts, venues and restaurant properties. Its CEO was Thomas J. Weaver III, who had previously served as president of Hard Rock International.

"They offered us more money [than SFX]," recalls Schankman. "They had the banker on the phone, who said he would match Sillerman and pay us $10 million more. We had to make a decision, and the decision was Sillerman's buying the right companies. He's already bought them or they're on the block to buy. I don't want to be with who [TBA] buys; they may fail. And they did fail — their stocks were worth nothing and the company was going out of business until [Irving] Azoff saved and bought them." (Azoff, who had partnered with the publicly traded company in amphitheater investments in Southern California like Irvine Meadows and Glenn Helen with Robert Geddes, bought the company in 2004 for just over $6 million with Geddes and JHW Greentree Capital, bringing it private.)

Ogden at the time was the world's largest venue management and concessionaire company with 110 buildings around the globe ranging in size from theaters to stadiums. In September 1995 Ogden purchased a fifty percent stake in New York-based promoter Metropolitan Entertainment, which was headed by John Scher. While the stake was a nominal amount of money for the company, it intended to invest $40 to $50 million to expand Metropolitan's business. And by 1997 that expansion was seen in the form of strategic partnerships with some of the same promoters Sillerman was going after.

"We had our own ideas," says John Scher, now sitting in his New York City office surrounded by some of the rock and roll memorabilia he's amassed since starting out in the 1970s. Ogden's plan was to partner with companies in buying a fifty percent stake rather than purchasing them outright.

"We did a lot of number crunching on what we thought these companies were worth," says Scher, who got his start running the Capitol Theater in New Jersey. "I remember the first three promoters we approached: Irv Zuckerman, Dave Lucas and Jack Boyle. Only Jack would even take a meeting. Irv and Lucas both said the same thing — 'We don't even want to take a meeting.' 'Don't you want to hear what we have to say?' 'John, the offer that's on the table from SFX is so ridiculous that there isn't a chance that you possibly will come close to it, and we're afraid if Sillerman heard us even talking to you, he'd pull the offer.'"

Scher pauses for a moment to underscore the dichotomy. "From that moment on I couldn't see the model that was being developed by Bob Sillerman working for anybody other than the original guys who sold out to him."

Contemporary Productions was sold to SFX for $91 million. However, as Schankman points out, the selling price was in fact much higher given that twenty percent of it was in SFX stock. He recalls the company getting 1,400,000 shares at the issue price of $13.33. The stock shot up to just over $60. Had they sold at its height, Contemporary could have netted somewhere in the vicinity of an additional $70 million. It was a deal worth four times the company's self-valuation.

Says former Bill Graham Presents CEO Greg Perloff: "They overpaid for us and they overpaid for everybody. I'll tell you flat out I sold for the money. When was I ever going to get this golden opportunity again?"

Couched similarly was *Pollstar*'s Gary Bongiovanni's response: "I think part of it may be that the people who run these companies have been doing it for 20 years, and now is a time when they can realize some significant return for all their work."

"I was just horrified," recalls Tracy Buie, who had worked for Bill Graham Presents on and off for over a decade when she heard of its pending sale to SFX. "People were freaking out. 'Bill's rolling in his grave. How can you even have this conversation?' All the principals at BGP made a lot of money. I think people said, 'This is my retirement, I have $6 million, $10 million in the bank.'"

The assessment Scher gives as to whether Graham would have sold to SFX had he not tragically died in a helicopter accident in 1991 echoes that of other promoters: "I think there's only one circumstance that Bill might have sold, and that was if he had an absolute, unequivocal, non-breakable guarantee that he would run the whole thing. I think Bill had aspirations to be that guy."

On Monday, December 15, 1997, SFX publicly announced its four new acquisitions. In addition to Contemporary and Concert/Southern Promotions, it had acquired Bill Graham for $65 million and the Network Magazine Group/SJS Entertainment for $70 million. Less than two weeks later, on Christmas Eve, SFX announced its acquisition of PACE for $130 million. It was a staggering feat, like nothing the concert industry had ever seen. The game had officially changed.

Delsener had tried to unite promoters years earlier but could not ultimately get them to cooperate with one another. "These guys hated each other," he quips. "They didn't want to give up their secrets. And no one had the type of money Bob had to just buy them out." Sillerman agrees: "I was sort of astounded at the old-line acerbic nature of some of the relationships. It did keep us away from the business for a while."

As much as the PACE acquisition was about the company's theatrical, concert, touring and motorsports divisions, it was the facilities portion that was particularly attractive. PACE Facilities Group owned a one third stake in Pavilion Partners and oversaw the thirteen amphitheaters it controlled. When SFX bought PACE and its interest, it also quietly bought out Pavilion's other two partners, Sony Music and Viacom.[1] On top of the $130 million for PACE, SFX forked over another $100 million for Pavilion.

"If you look around, the concert promoters who have really prospered have been the ones that stepped out and got involved in facilities," said PACE founder Allen Becker. "You need those other revenue streams, like food, beverage and parking. You don't get them when you're renting Madison Square Garden."

THE NEXT TIME YOU'RE SITTING at your local amphitheater, drinking a beer and listening to one of your favorite bands, take a moment to thank the Greeks. You owe it to them.

The first outdoor theater was constructed in Athens around 325 BCE and was named after the Greek god of wine and fertility, Dionysus. Dug into a hillside of the Acropolis, it was made out of stone with ascending seating from the stage arranged in fifty-five semi-circular rows. It sat anywhere from 14,000 to 17,000 people. The acoustics were such that even those in the back row could hear the actors onstage during the plays.

The Romans built their own version of an outdoor theater in Pompeii around 80 BCE. In contrast to the Greek version, it was circular — looking like two semicircular Greek theaters pushed together — and therefore called an amphitheater, the Latin word *amphi* meaning "around" or "on both sides." So today, what we think of as an "amphitheater" is actually modeled on the Greek theater, whereas what we think of as an "arena" is modeled on the Roman amphitheater.

The first seated amphitheaters in the United States were developed shortly after the turn of the twentieth century from existing natural amphitheaters. The first to be built was the aptly named Greek Theater in Berkeley, California, which officially opened in 1904. The location, on the grounds of the University of California, had been previously used for occasions like football rallies and beginning in 1894 was informally known as "Ben Weed's Amphitheater" after one of the university's students. While Ben Weed hosted events, it was quite Spartan, with no seats or physical infrastructure. The new amphitheater, designed by John Galen Howard and funded by newspaper magnate William Randolph Hearst, was based directly on the famed Greek amphitheater Epidaurus and seated 10,000.[2]

Red Rocks amphitheater, located outside Denver in Morrison, Colorado, and set between two 300-foot sandstone slabs, began building its permanent seated structure in 1906. Once known as the Garden of Angels, the natural amphitheater had attracted regular visitors since the 1880s. It took on its current form after the Civilian Conservation Corps finished full construction in 1941.

Across the country Luther Ely Smith began staging pageant-masques on Art Hill in St. Louis, Missouri's Forest Park in 1914. Situated on a grassy area between two oak trees, the spot was developed as the Muny in 1917 and became the first municipally owned outdoor theater in the country.

Nearly a decade later, back in California, Los Angeles got its first seated outdoor venue. Built on the site of a natural amphitheater known as "Daisy Dell" near the Cahuenga Pass, the Hollywood Bowl opened in July 1922 with only makeshift wooden benches and an awning over the simple stage.

These venues and others developed through the late 1960s — the Greek Theatre in Los Angeles (1929), the Santa Barbara Bowl (1936), the Blossom Music Center outside Cleveland (1936), the Carter Barron (1950) and the Wolf Trap (1971) in Washington, DC, the Jones Beach Marine Theater in Long Island (1952), the Saratoga Performing Arts Center (1966) in New York, the Merriweather Post Pavilion (1967) in Maryland and the Garden State Arts Center (1968) in New Jersey — were predominantly designed to be used for symphonies, opera, theater and jazz big bands during the summer months.

If the state or federal government did not operate the venues, the Nederlanders likely owned them. Best known for its development of Broadway theater, the Nederlander Organization was founded in 1912 by David T. Nederlander with the purchase of a ninety-nine year lease on the old Detroit Opera House. As the company's website suggests, it is "generally credited with creating the outdoor amphitheater concept as it is known today" in developing a "unique ability to maintain a variety booking approach that responded to varied community interests."

"When I first got into the business in the early '70s, they actually used to call the amphitheaters Nederlanders," says John Scher. At that time Nederlander owned the Merriweather, the Greek in Los Angeles, the Garden State Art Center and Pine Knob outside Detroit in Clarkston. As rock's burgeoning popularity began outgrowing rooms like the Fillmore East and the Cellar Door, indoor arenas that were normally used for sporting events were selling out for acts like the Rolling Stones, Cream and Led Zeppelin.

While the increased capacity provided by arenas helped artists and promoters eke out more profit, the venues were extremely expensive to rent. First, they were costly for the owners to build, which meant they needed to charge a significant rental fee. Second, many of the sports-affiliated venues were union controlled, which typically meant steep labor charges. And third, sports scheduling always trumped music scheduling — playoffs could throw off a potential show quite easily.

Amphitheaters on the other hand were far less expensive to build, didn't necessarily use union labor, didn't have sports teams and could often hold more people. Moreover, they were designed for live entertainment, which meant that key elements like sight lines and sound amplification were far better than those in arenas. The only downside was that most couldn't be used year-round because of weather restrictions.

During the mid- and late 1970s, an increasing number of concerts were held at outdoor venues. And to no one's surprise, fans of rock music tended to consume more alcohol and concessions than those of classical music or theater. As a premium concession, alcohol sales generated venues significant amounts of money. So an obvious question for the owner of an older performance-based venue like the Merriweather became: What's going to make more money in 1975 — a sold-out night for *La Bohème* or Fleetwood Mac?

Amphitheaters specifically designed for rock music began cropping up in the 1970s — among them the Universal in Los Angeles (1972), Pine Knob (1972) outside Detroit and Alpine Valley in East Troy, Wisconsin (1977) — and continued to appear on into the 1980s and 1990s. One of their distinct features was a large, general admission lawn that typically represented about two thirds of the venue's total capacity. The lawn tickets were one price while the reserved seats were another price, perhaps two.

Given that amphitheaters were cheaper to build and maintain, it meant that the rental fee charged to promoters was significantly less than for an arena. At Madison Square Garden, for instance, artists often have a hard time making money because of the rental fee.

While promoters were happy with the increased margins of amphitheaters, artists began asking for more money, knowing that more was available. Promoters in turn began looking for ways to make up for their ever-diminishing returns.

For any successful promoter that had been around for ten to fifteen years (since rock and roll had become a big business), there was a clear but expensive option to ultimately make more money: build an amphitheater.

Sunshine's Steve Sybesma and Dave Lucas paid a visit to Nederlander's Pine Knob amphitheater outside Detroit in the late 1970s to see what it offered. "What I saw in an amphitheater was something that was for music," says Sybesma. "It wasn't a basketball arena that we go use if there wasn't basketball. It was something we could use any time, and it was designed for people to come and have fun."

Just over a decade later in 1989, after many hard-fought battles with city officials and community boards, Sunshine opened its first amphitheater in Indiana: Deer Creek Music Center. A friend of Sybesma's in the insurance business gave Sunshine a sweet funding deal. He put up the majority of the money for the amphitheater's construction, Sunshine put in $100,000 and both parties had fifty percent ownership.

"Nobody knew we could do it," Sybesma enthuses now. "Go to an arena and you pay rent while somebody else makes all the parking and food revenue. We're taking all the risk. They have the risk of the building of course, but I didn't see it that way. I saw [an amphitheater] as an opportunity for me to be able to do more shows and a bigger variety of shows — shows that in an amphitheater we could break even on instead of losing $20,000 because it was just another night and we didn't have to pay ourselves rent."

Sybesma recalls Lucas pushing Irv Zuckerman and Contemporary in St. Louis to build their own amphitheater. "He said, 'Irv, you need to build an amphitheater. You really do. It's the thing of the future. You should do it now and not wait."

Contemporary opened Riverport two years later in 1991. Co-owner Steve Schankman concurs with Sybesma on the position promoters found themselves in prior to owning a large venue: "I'm taking all the risk and [venues] have all the advantage, so that's why you build your own. The difference of doing a show in your own venue could be 400 percent because if you do Jimmy Buffett in an arena, you make $100,000; at your own venue you make $400,000. Amphitheaters are cheap to build, too. We built Riverport for $12 million and sold it for double eight years later."

John Scher, as head of Metropolitan Entertainment, built two amphitheaters in the Northeast: Montage Mountain in Scranton, Pennsylvania, and Darien Lake outside Buffalo. "The reason they started to get built was because artists could drive harder deals and there was a lot of money to be made in ancillaries, the same thing as the movie business," he says. "Anyone you know who owns an independent movie theater or runs big chains, they'll tell you — they're in the popcorn business."

"The weather has a lot to do with it but [the other reason] is the economics," says seventy-six-year-old Jack Boyle, who now lives in Fort Lauderdale. Boyle, the single biggest promoter before the SFX rollup, was the man behind Cellar Door Productions. "In those days, when we were first starting all this stuff, the buildings wouldn't give you a break. Some of the rents were very ridiculous, and when the amphitheaters started getting to where they could make more money, we as amphitheater owners got a little greedy." Simply put, owning a large venue like an amphitheater meant greater revenue streams for promoters from concessions, parking and ticket rebates, given the significantly lower cost of construction and maintenence. This in turn meant more was on the table for artists.

"As a guy who represents performers, when I look at what you can make working out of an amphitheater environment, it costs a lot less to pay the bills when you play Jones Beach than Madison Square Garden because it's a lot cheaper to put concrete on grass in the middle of a field and put a roof over it," says Jim Guiernot, who manages acts such as No Doubt, the Offspring and Nine Inch Nails. "Performers had great incentive [to play amphitheaters] before the promoters got into the mix and suggested that they had a corresponding incentive." Coupled with the difficulty in booking an arena tour between sports schedules, he believes "amphitheaters had a natural ramp-up."

Between 1980 and 1998, the year SFX completed the majority of its promoter acquisitions, approximately twenty-nine amphitheaters were opened in the United States with an average capacity of 21,000 people. Combined with the country's ten to fifteen existing large outdoor venues, amphitheater proliferation had a significant impact on the industry.

Barry Fey, who put Denver on the national tour route in the late 1960s and was the first to do rock shows at Red Rocks amphitheater, was appalled at the spread of what he saw as cookie cutter amphitheaters around the country.

"The amphitheater gave way to giving away tickets because they could make more money on popcorn, parking, hot dogs and beer, and they didn't care how much they made at the door — which is completely opposite of what it's supposed to be," he laments. "You've got to make money on the door. This is a music business, not a popcorn business, but that's what it turned into. It's disgusting."

Driving it all, he argues, were ever-increasing artist fees: "It went to $10,000 plus fifty percent over a certain figure. Then sixty percent. Then it progressed to seventy percent. Then it went to eighty-five–fifteen net. What the fuck is that? Then ninety–ten net. They made promoters do things like phony ticket commissions, phony insurance and phony this because they made us into thieves."

No doubt Fey would indict famed artist manager Irving Azoff as one of those who pushed promoters to such lengths. Azoff made his name early on representing acts like the Eagles, Steely Dan and Boston. Azoff, much like the agent Tom Ross, who headed ICM and CAA, took a holistic approach in assessing how much money a promoter stood to make from a concert. It wasn't just the ticket; it was the parking and the concessions, too. So taken as a whole, Azoff struck a harder line for a percentage — ninety percent, to be exact. As the *New York Times* suggested in 2010, this became known as "the Irving deal."

Tracy Buie, who worked for Avalon Attractions, Bill Graham Presents and Clear Channel Entertainment before leaving the concert business in 2000, saw a similar artist-promoter tug-of-war. "[Promoters] could get more because they could also get the parking revenue, the greatest Ticketmaster kickback, the beer, the popcorn, the whole enchilada," she says a bit incredulously. "And what's interesting is that they really screwed themselves over because of their greed, because you have this glut of tours in the summer. There's a limit to how many shows a true fan can see."

As Scher, one of the biggest critics of SFX and its subsequent consolidation, readily points out, "By the proliferation of these amphitheaters and the drive to get acts to play in them, the amphitheater owners, even before SFX, would pay acts more money." He offers a typical scenario in which a promoter offers an artist, say, $125,000 instead of $100,000 per night to push their tour back a couple of months until it could play in amphitheaters the promoter owned or worked with versus indoor venues that it would have to rent at a higher price.

"So you got driven to many amphitheaters between mid-June and Labor Day, doing shows as often as six or seven times a week, and you'd have a fall, winter and spring with far fewer shows of that size," describes Scher. "All of these things have conspired, in my view, against the consumer."

The addition of Pavilion Partners brought SFX's amphitheater portfolio to twenty-five, which now included New Jersey's PNC Art Center, Irvine Meadows in southern California, Starplex in Dallas, Desert Sky in Phoenix, Coral Sky in West Palm Beach, Florida, Starwood in Nashville and a massive amphitheater serving the Philadelphia market. Pavilion's amphitheaters were operated via long-term leases or partial ownership coupled with long-term leases whose duration ran anywhere from twenty to sixty years.

By the beginning of 1998 SFX controlled forty-two venues in twenty-two markets, forty of which were in the top fifty markets, nine of which were in six of the top ten markets. Now that the company effectively controlled national touring in the United States, it was time to leverage its position.

IN SECURITIES AND EXCHANGE COMMISSION filings for taking SFX Entertainment public in April 1998, Sillerman looked to his previous endeavors as inspiration for his foray into live entertainment: "The concert industry [is] similar to radio ten years ago, populated by some great people who have never tried to maximize advertising and sponsorship opportunities."

Part of Sillerman's vision was spurred by a family trip he had taken to Disney World with his young daughter, McKinley. While, principally, visitors went there to experience Disney's many entertainment attractions, that's not where amusement parks made their money. Their real profits came from concessions, parking and corporate sponsorship. With decades of branding in the public consciousness, advertising inside an amusement park like Disney World was highly coveted. Moreover, Disney thoroughly vetted each advertiser to make sure it fit with its values and image and then sold the advertising and marketing packages at premium prices. If patrons were already prepared to pay the price of entrance for the experience they knew was ahead, what would a few advertisements hurt?

"Disney's relationships with corporate sponsors are a good model for what we want to do in the concert-promotion business," said Sillerman. "It's extremely difficult to make money just selling tickets [to concerts]. We want to make money both by selling tickets and by putting a live audience in front of Madison Avenue."

The basic vision was that if Sillerman could unite promoters and their venues, particularly the amphitheaters, on a national level, then he could create a new market for advertisers and sponsors that was largely unavailable to them in leveraging the acquisition of national concert tours.

The company's epiphany was in realizing that Madison Avenue spent its massive advertising budget in four key areas: outdoor signage, print, radio and television. Nobody to date was able to offer them a consistent live audience. In becoming the "fifth finger" that tapped into that budget, even if it was only ten percent, SFX would be the recipient of hundreds of millions of dollars.

Knowing that companies allocated their advertising budgets a year in advance and that it would take another year to garner interest, SFX slated two years for the plan's implementation. SFX's primary focus — its acknowledged endgame — became aggregating a massive, demographically broad audience that they could sell in very specific slivers to advertisers. In mining audience data, SFX could offer what they thought of as a "rifle approach" to advertisers versus what they saw as the "shotgun approach" of television and other traditional forms of advertising.

Yes, the Rolling Stones and a few others had toured with sponsors, but this was the first time advertising could be offered on a national, targeted level from a steadfast promoter that owned or leased a large venue portfolio versus an artist that toured every few years. No one, for instance, could guarantee a company that it could place a million pieces of product in the hands of females aged thirteen to twenty-four over a summer. SFX would be able to do so. Money spent now on acquisitions for market share would come back around in a few years when Sillerman had what he called a "live, interactive advertising network."

"These are people voting with their feet and their wallets," he declared. "If you go to see Tom Petty or the Spice Girls, you've chosen to do it. You're excited. You're not doing this passively — like watching TV at home." Sillerman's methodology was that with an expansive national platform, particularly massive amphitheaters in major markets, the possibilities were endless. His basic point: "You're spending the money and you're very receptive to hear direct or subliminal messages."

Jay Coleman, founder and CEO of EMCI, which specializes in bringing live entertainment and corporate sponsors together — he's the man responsible for Michael Jackson's "Choice of a New Generation" Pepsi campaign in 1983 and multiple sponsor-driven Rolling Stones tours — wasn't entirely sold on the idea: "What they are attempting to do in this agglomeration of assets is to have one-stop shopping," he said at the time. "On the surface, that makes sense. In practice, it's not an easy task. First of all, there are a very limited number of advertisers who will do music. And only a tiny handful of tours are of interest to corporate advertisers. It's an interesting marketing idea, but very difficult."

Schankman feels Sillerman was quite clear about his modus operandi. "He didn't care about the [concert] business; he cared about the marketing advantage," he says. "If he owned this stuff and all these acts, he could market to the sponsors. His market was going to be created with the Coca-Colas of the world. That was his vehicle and that's why he bought my company."

The content of SFX's trade advertisements at the time came as no surprise. "Remember that magical moment when your daughter's eyes widened to meet her favorite characters live onstage?" it read. "It's exciting, it's magical, it's completely engrossing. And we found a way to package it."

Though the previous year SFX companies had generated $40 million in sponsorship revenue, "100 percent of it was regional and local dollars" according to company president Ferrel. With its advertising network SFX had "an opportunity to strike alliances with financial service and apparel companies, technology and communication services and offer the opportunity that is implicit in the size audience that we have."

It remained to be seen if SFX could, with any great frequency, capitalize on a promoter level in ways that Coleman's company had on the artist level. This type of overt commodification seemed at odds with concertgoers' typical ethos.

"There was an outcry when sports started to get over commercialized," contested Sillerman, "and people don't even think about it now." However, live sporting events were largely successful on local levels. It wasn't like a baseball game would ever be held in Yankee Stadium that didn't have the Yankees. Concerts were often one-night affairs in any given market in any given venue.

The difference was that if an advertiser thought the Rolling Stones' audience was an ideal demographic, it had to travel with the tour. Sporting events attracted the same people to the same building for multiple games a season, year after year. Concert-based amphitheaters were uncharted waters.

Sillerman, however, was convinced there was real money to be made. "There's no question that the excitement and energy of live entertainment has not been available for sponsorship and advertising, and we will continue to take advantage of that," he said. "[But] what advertisers and sponsors are looking for is the association with the energy of the event. They are not looking for interruption."

For managers like Scott Welch, who represented Alanis Morissette and bypassed SFX promotion at the time, "It's all we can do to keep sponsorship *off* the stage. It's a corporate mentality. The act becomes the reason to sell beer, the reason to sell parking."

No question that the push for advertising and sponsorship was the latest movement in the ongoing chess game of rising artist guarantees and promoters' scramble for better profit margins. And caught in the middle, it seemed, were agents.

THE CONCERT INDUSTRY HAD LONG operated on a specific set of dynamics. Artists hired managers who in turn hired agents to negotiate deals with promoters. Promoters, on their side, negotiated with venues; the ticketing agent was typically determined by the venue. But the focal point, the middle of the overall equation, was the agent who "sold" the act to the promoter — a guarantee, a percentage of the ticket sales or a combination of the two. Suddenly with SFX's rollup there were far fewer promoters to bid on regional shows or, for that matter, a national tour. Now there was one company that controlled not only the majority of the country's promoters but also the majority of the country's premier venues. What would prevent SFX from dealing directly with artists and managers?

"I think they're the enemy," said Tom Ross at the time, who was head of Creative Artists Agency's music division and one of the industry's more powerful players in representing artists like Eric Clapton and KISS. "An act that does 200 club dates at $500 a night does not pay the bills for CAA. We lose until they're at least $3,500 a night, and sometimes they never get there. We identify the new acts, take them on and develop them, and at the point they're worth money, [SFX] are going to give them an offer and take them off the table."

Ross talked with Sillerman, who assured him that SFX wanted relationships with everybody. "He was almost romancing me to be the commissioner," says Ross today. "'With all these little pirates [being] rolled up, I need someone they respect.' I said, 'We can talk, but my responsibility is to the acts I represent, and I need to know you're going to play by the rules.'" While he was looking to save some money for the promoters, it would still be business as normal, Sillerman assured him.

Today Ross recalls the tipping point between CAA and SFX, when it no longer became "business as normal." When Clapton, an English resident, toured the States, he had to make a formal IRS withholding agreement because he didn't pay U.S. taxes. CAA, for Clapton, was the signatory of the holding agreements that were based on a tour's estimated gross income. For bigger artists a promoter would typically pay a deposit — and in Clapton's case that deposit typically backed CAA's holding agreements for him. Ross hadn't received the deposit for the guitarist's SFX dates for his *Pilgrim* tour and rang Contemporary's Irv Zuckerman that September.

"Irv, we haven't gotten your deposit on Clapton," said Ross.

"You're not getting a deposit on Clapton," Zuckerman relayed back. "We're SFX — you don't need a deposit."

"Irv, business as usual, you always paid a deposit on Clapton. We don't pressure you or anybody else, but with Clapton we need the money to withhold."

CAA obtained an internal SFX memo from Sillerman that said agencies were no longer getting deposits.

"That's when I switched on the lights," says Ross. "It was like, 'Wow, these guys are going to fuck with us without the deposits.' The leverage suddenly went out the window for an agency, and I was convinced we were in jeopardy."

Ross pulled a handful of dates from Zuckerman and gave them to New Orleans-based promoter Don Fox. (More recently, Fox has been the promoter behind Michael Bublé's success on the road.) "That started the showdown," confirms Ross. "Zuckerman never forgave me — 'How could you do this?' I didn't do anything. He switched the rules."

As tensions began mounting — it wasn't good that someone like Ross was routinely and publicly rebuking them — SFX tried to assuage agents' fears. "We are committed to maintaining the agency system," SFX president Mike Ferrel insisted. "There is a level of concern out there, but that is the position of SFX. We believe it is a crucial alliance." The company backed down from its stance on no deposits.

Tim Klahs, ostensibly the company's mouthpiece to the public as "investor relations director," began toeing a similar line. "We will serve different functions at different times," Klahs told reporters. "There's no intention to bypass the industry structure that's already in place. We regard what we've created here as an easing of the somewhat trying and often difficult process of having to book an act into a number of locations. We regard our ability to provide one-stop shopping as a plus to the industry as a whole."

As a business built on competition, one-stop shopping didn't necessarily sit well with many of its players. One of live entertainment's unique qualities is that compared with most other businesses, competition typically drives prices up. Artists, along with their managers and agents, always want promoters to bid them up. Now, suddenly faced with one massive promoter that controlled many of the country's primary amphitheaters in most key markets, the longstanding power dynamic was unstable. SFX could — in one theory — shut out a top-level artist like Tom Petty or Jimmy Buffett from a summer tour if the asking price was too steep.

"It is virtually impossible for an artist to tour the United States without an SFX venue," a report generated by Goldman Sachs & Company noted at the time. "SFX has, in essence, become the gatekeeper for outdoor music concerts." The report saw the company's growing dominance as a positive in its financial projections, estimating that SFX would double its revenue to $60 million from sponsorship and advertising for 1999.

Some felt that SFX was abusing its power. "They'll say, 'We'll give you about 90 percent of what you want; in return, you have to give us the entire tour, all our venues,'" said one manager. "Then they come back and say, 'We talked to all our promoters, and we have to reduce the offer.' By then, your band's already rehearsing, you've done your marketing plan with the label based on the money you think you're getting, and you have no alternative — I know a lot of managers that's happened to." Doobie Brothers manager Bruce Cohn could, as he said, "see where the jury's still out on national tours. It gives SFX power. There's not a lot of back-and-forth with just one promoter. It's take it or leave it, pretty much."

Conversely, one manager suggests, SFX opened up opportunities for bands: "The funny part about the independent promoter network as it existed prior to Sillerman consolidating [was that] these fucking guys ran their local markets like Attila the Hun. You talk about monopolistic and predatory practices. You couldn't do business in Boston around Don [Law] if the channels didn't exist. Thank God the channel was there [as] it gave you one place where you didn't have to deal with those guys. Bill Graham ran San Francisco like a tyrant. Arnie [Granat] and Jerry [Mickelson] in Chicago, you'd get fucked every time you'd go there. As soon as competition appeared, it was like, 'Phew! Finally I have an alternative in those places.' And suddenly those guys became realists."

In addition, Jack Boyle says, "By going around and grabbing all the venues, everyone thought SFX would get a break because people couldn't afford not to play them. As it turned out, the trio, as I call them — Howard

Kaufman, Irving Azoff and Howard Rose — realized [the SFX rolled-up promoters would] have to pay more money because they *had* to put artists into these amphitheaters. Whatever they thought was the strength of these big companies turned out not to be so much a strength as a weakness."

Indeed for the trio, the new paradigm simply meant more money for them and their artists. "I said, 'Of course you're going to give me 90 percent of the money [generated from ancillary or sponsorship revenue], Bob,'" Azoff recalls of a typical conversation. "'That's our standard split or we're not going to play. How many people do you think will pay to see Robert Sillerman at the Boston Garden?'"

Kaufman and Rose, Jimmy Buffett's manager and agent respectively, took the holistic approach to artist fees to legendary new heights. Knowing that Buffett's rabid, hard-drinking fans, affectionately known as "Parrot Heads," would do an order of magnitude more of alcohol sales than nearly any other act, they asked — and still routinely receive — 105 percent of the net. When a band has a proven track record of significant alcohol sales — the Allman Brothers Band, Lynyrd Skynyrd and Tom Petty, for instance — it can have an impact on the end deal.

That said, SFX felt confident in having leverage over an artist in matters such as a tour sponsor. If, for instance, Buffett was being given $750,000 by Corona beer for a tour sponsorship and SFX was striking a deal with Budweiser, the $20 million SFX was paying Buffett for the tour easily trumped any other conflicting offers.

SFX contended that if it could make artists more money, then it should get help from an artist to enable it to do so. Whether it was agreeing to a sponsorship deal or getting patrons into the building earlier so they could buy more beer, SFX's general aim was to make more money, not at the expense of anyone else making less but rather by everybody involved making more.

"It's very, very tasty," said Rod Stewart's manager, Arnold Stiefel, of SFX's artist guarantees. Stewart was one of the prime examples SFX critics cited in which artists were being unnecessarily overpaid. In the mid-1990s Stewart was typically getting a $175,000 to $250,000 guarantee per show. Now, in return for letting SFX book the entire tour with its promoters using its venues, he was getting $350,000 to $400,000. (Not surprisingly, Stewart was happy to play one of Sillerman's All for the Seas benefits that July.) The trickle down economics of these new deals was immediately apparent: consumers were now paying on average nearly fifty percent more than they had been just a few years earlier.

Still, not all artists went for the money grab. Tom Petty tried to keep his tickets to $65. "I make millions on the road," he said. "I see no reason to bring the price up, even though I have heard many an anxious promoter say,

'We could charge 150 bucks for this.' . . . It's so wrong to say, 'Okay, we've got them on the ticket and we've got them on the beer and we've got them on everything else, let's get them on the damn parking. You got to care about the person you're dealing with."

The Ross-led CAA fight, now fully public, needed resolution. SFX met with Ross's boss, Rich Lovett, and, while assuring him the agency system would be fully respected, also threatened that if Ross didn't back down, then, yes, Ross's fears would come true. Says one former SFX employee of the situation at the time: "We were about to go to war with them. The alternative, if they had said no to that, [was] we *were* going to call all the managers directly and say, 'You know what? They're right. Fuck 'em. If you want a tour this summer, here's our head of booking. We're not going to take any orders from CAA.' We told CAA we were going to do that. They were negotiating from a point of weakness, which is never a smart thing to do."

"The other agencies were rallying behind me, but my own partners didn't like it, and that led to me being pushed out," says Ross of his exit from CAA at the behest of its young, ruthless clan of executives known as the Young Turks. "I believe Brian Murphy from Avalon went as [SFX's] ambassador to meet with [the Young Turks] and say, 'This guy is rocking the boat and we don't like it. We're not going to put up with it.'"

Ross exited CAA that November and ultimately left the music business altogether in a few short years because of the changes catalyzed by SFX. "The whistleblower gets shot," the former agent says. "I was compensated — I was paid to leave — but I miss the business."

To his credit Ross was the most prescient in his assessment of the company's future. "SFX's long-term interests have nothing to do with building careers or protecting artists," he railed earlier that year in March (just a month earlier he was named agent of the year at the annual *Pollstar* Awards). "They are going to strip mine the industry, move on in three years to airplane parts and maybe some of us will still be around to put the industry back together again."

He was more or less right, save for the airplane parts. Two years to the month after this prediction, SFX would announce its sale.

BY AUGUST 1998 SILLERMAN HAD ACHIEVED another phenomenal round of promoter purchases: Don Law Presents ($71 million), Cellar Door Productions ($106 million) and Avalon Entertainment ($27 million). Michael Cohl, a Canadian-based promoter of some of world's most lucrative tours including the Rolling Stones, U2 and Pink Floyd, sold his company The Next Adventure for an undisclosed amount in April of the following year. "This is lightning in a bottle," said Sillerman of his rapidly growing promoter portfolio. "It's clear that because of what we're doing, the playing field is not what it was."

Boyle was one of the last major promoters to sell to SFX. While he had entertained various offers for Cellar Door over the years, he always ended up turning them down. When he was approached by Ogden and John Scher in 1997, he considered their proposal. Ogden had been financing Boyle's amphitheaters and had treated him well. "They made me a very nice deal, except the majority of it was in stock," he recounts now. "We never got far enough along. We had a falling out of who would be in charge. I wasn't ready to have somebody else run my company. In later times we even met with John's people to buy his company." As time would prove, Boyle's decision was a wise one. Ogden, which would be bought out by the energy company Covanta, would see its stock fall apart in a few short years.

Boyle also met with Universal Concerts, which would eventually be sold by its parent company, Seagram, to House of Blues in July 1999. At the time Universal was run by Jay Marciano, though the proposed deal with Cellar Door was led by a key player within the industry who was looking for his next big gig: Fred Rosen. Having transitioned out of Ticketmaster in 1998 (more on that later), Rosen, according to Boyle, was trying to start a promoter-based company.

"It was one of those things that if it worked, it [would have] worked really well," says the veteran promoter. "The fact is, we were out at [Rosen's] house when we were talking and we were looking at different things that could happen, so we never really made any deal. I like Jay Marciano, but the money difference was uniquely different between what one company offered us and what the other company was going to offer us."

His relationships with both Scher and Rosen, which he described as once being close, were both largely destroyed after he sold to SFX. "John hates me because I went with them," he says. "Now John doesn't even go to one of my restaurants, which is four or five miles from his home in Florida."

Seth Hurwitz, a longtime Washington, DC area promoter whose company, IMP, had competed with Cellar Door since the 1980s, recalls a lunch he had with Boyle shortly before Cellar Door sold to SFX. The two were meeting once again to talk about a strategic partnership that would essentially control concerts in the DC area. The previous meetings over the years, from Hurwitz's recollection, had gone something like this:

Cellar Door: "We'll give you a quarter of the business."
Hurwitz: "But I'm doing more than that. I want a third."
Cellar Door: "That ridiculous."

Talks would stop until a year or two later when Cellar Door would say, "We'll give you a third now," and Hurwitz would respond, "But now I'm doing half." And so forth.

Boyle and Hurwitz scheduled a final lunch to see if, one last time, they could make something work. After general pleasantries the conversation got down to brass tacks.

"Let's split everything, half and half," said Boyle.

"Jack, that was two years ago," said Hurwitz of the previous conversation. "I have more than half now."

Boyle let out a long sigh as he looked off into the distance. "Maybe I'll just sell to Sillerman," he said to himself. "Everyone else has."

It seemed, to Hurwitz at least, that it was a turning point for the veteran promoter.

Born in Youngstown, Ohio, Boyle began working at the steel mill in nearby Gerard at the age of sixteen to support the family after his father, an attorney who had graduated from Georgetown Law, died. He remembers the routine precisely. Each morning he would get up and go to school, come home at two o'clock in the afternoon, sleep until five-fifteen and catch the five-thirty bus to town, where he would work at the mill from six in the evening till four in the morning. He'd get a ride part of the way home after work and then walk the remaining two miles.

The mill then laid workers off from the night shift, forcing Boyle to drop out of high school his senior year so he could work during the day. Two weeks prior to graduation, the plant closed entirely and Boyle was allowed to reenter school and complete his final exams to graduate.

Boyle enlisted in the Air Force and was in pilot training during the Korean War when he broke his leg. While at home on leave, his mother facilitated a meeting that led to his admittance to the Georgetown School of Foreign Service on a scholarship. Once in Washington, DC, at Georgetown, his father's alma mater, Boyle began bartending to make money while in school, which ultimately led to his buying a quarter of a bar in 1962 with money he'd won in a poker game. He eventually owned all of it, changed the name to the Cellar Door and started putting on concerts in 1971.

By the time Boyle sold Cellar Door to SFX for $106 million, he was the single largest promoter in the country. He owned, leased or booked eleven amphitheaters along with a string of venues on the Eastern Seaboard. Besides, Boyle was nearing the prime retirement age of sixty-five. Had he not broken his leg, Boyle believes he would be a retired Air Force major in some California city — "probably dead."

IN SEPTEMBER, A MONTH AFTER the Cellar Door deal was announced, the Justice Department began what Ferrel described as an "informal inquiry" into SFX Entertainment and its acquisitions in regard to antitrust violations.

"It flatters me that they think I might be a Bill Gates," said Sillerman, referring to Microsoft's well-publicized antitrust investigation that was in full swing at the time. "But what we do hardly approaches that scale. It's not our plan to own everything. Nor would we want to." SFX was more interested in owning the key parts of various businesses that made up the concert industry.

With its massive venue portfolio, SFX had taken a hard look at whether it should get involved in the concession and ticketing business as those contracts came up for renewal. With the help of PACE the company crunched the numbers on worldwide concessionaire Ogden, which handled most of its venues' food and beverage services. Leveraging its sheer size, SFX cut what it thought of as a rather "crazy deal" with Ogden that saw the concessionaire getting five to six percent profit margins while assuming all the responsibility and inventory risk.

A similar conversation about Ticketmaster occurred within SFX prior to contract renewals in 1998: if SFX did ticketing themselves, what could they make incrementally? More importantly, because of SFX's advertising-based model, consumer data collected in the purchasing process was extremely important. If SFX could control ticketing for all of its concerts, theater and motor sports, it would be in an extremely powerful position. With that in mind, one of the primary reasons SFX acquired Don Law was for his Next Ticketing system. While Next Ticketing was a viable platform for a limited number of venues in the Northeast, it was unclear what kind of volume and demand it could handle on a national level compared with Ticketmaster. Moreover, the details were such that Next Ticketing was actually leasing its system from another company, Hill Arts and Entertainment Systems, which would come to do battle with Ticketmaster in a few years as part of ticketing conglomerate Tickets.com.

"There was a point in time where we could have gone into ticketing on our own or we could have made a deal with Ticketmaster," confirms Brian Becker, who joined SFX from PACE and served as part of its upper management before eventually taking over as CEO once SFX was sold to a new parent company. "Whether it was Next Ticketing, Tickets.com or whatever, there was no question that Bob was absolutely committed to maximizing the revenues from ticketing. If doing it on our own was the best way to do that, taking into consideration all the risk and costs, I think we would have done it," says Becker. "SFX and Bob were ready to go as far as it took" to get the best deal.

Ticketmaster was in transition with Rosen's departure and the beginning of media mogul Barry Diller's tenure. The relationship between SFX and Ticketmaster had increasingly soured as the exclusive contract they had struck years earlier inched toward expiration. "Barry reached out to Sillerman, but that wasn't really working because, if I remember correctly, Barry said something in the press that pissed off Bob and they started fighting in the press," recalls Gene Cobuzzi, Ticketmaster's CFO at the time. "[Longtime Ticketmaster executive] Terry [Barnes], the phenomenal relationship guy that he is, got us a meeting in New York."

Ticketmaster was committed to making it work. The two companies met at the Plaza Hotel in New York to hammer out the deal, ensconced in a conference room. Present from SFX were Becker, president Mike Ferrel and, periodically, Sillerman. From Ticketmaster were Cobuzzi, CEO Terry Barnes and CFO Stuart DePina.

"We said, 'This is silly. We shouldn't be fighting,'" says Cobuzzi. "'We can do a deal that can be good for both companies and it'll achieve what you want to achieve, which is having a guaranteed revenue stream which you can go out to the public with and it's going to make your stock price go up. And at the same time you'll be with a company that you know can sell your tickets. You won't be taking a chance like with Tickets.com. We're prepared to stay in this conference room until we get that deal done.'"

Ticketmaster was aware that it was likely coming to the game late and was aggressive in accepting highly favorable terms for SFX. "We got the whole deal done, and there were a lot of facilities that we had to negotiate service charges going out for a long time and royalties and percentages and all that stuff," recounts Cobuzzi.

Becker describes the Ticketmaster deal as a classic one that only had a temporal window of opportunity to happen. "It wasn't going to be open for very long. Everyone had to stretch a little bit, and there was some common good that could be accomplished by working together," he says. "We didn't leave that room until we had it done."

Becker describes the general experience thusly:

Sillerman screams at him yet again to get a better deal.

Becker and SFX go back to the conference room and reemerge hours later.

"Bob, we really think we have a great deal this time."

"What is it?"

Sillerman listens.

"You idiots! That's not what I told you to do."

"Okay, Bob, we'll go back."

"Before we finalized the deal, we had a *great* deal," says Becker, laughing. "We made a real tough deal." Various sources have indicated that part of the deal was largely predicated on SFX receiving fifty percent of the service fees levied by Ticketmaster. It was an extraordinarily high percentage for Ticketmaster to allow, but given the sheer volume of business SFX was now responsible for — Cobuzzi's rough estimate is that SFX represented up to thirty percent of Ticketmaster's 100 million tickets sold at the time — it ultimately made sense.

To that end Becker gives a rather pragmatic assessment of the deal: "Even though we had a common interest, there was always a tension between the service fee that was being charged and what its impact would be on the ability to sell tickets to a consumer. On the one hand we promoters were participating in the fee, and Ticketmaster, it was their primary source of revenues, so in a sense we had the same interest. If we could maximize that, great, but on the other hand if we sold less tickets, it was a much bigger impact on us than it was on Ticketmaster because of all that ticket revenue."

What was initially envisioned as a one-day deal that began on a Monday spilled into as many as five for some involved, with negotiations ending on Friday. The original contract was for a total of fourteen years, but the companies' antitrust lawyers advised against it. (The longer, the better for Ticketmaster, as company wisdom said that it took at least a five-year deal to amortize the advances they were paying buildings.) In the end a ten-year contract — seven years with a three year extension — was signed. Sillerman and Diller made up, and once again, for many, it was business as usual.

In two years SFX had spent more than $1 billion in its buying spree. It now controlled sixty-nine concert venues in twenty-eight of the top fifty markets. Central to its holdings were fourteen amphitheaters in nine of the top ten markets. It would produce approximately 5,000 concerts and an equal number of theatrical shows in 1998. Collectively, along with its specialized motor sports divisions, more than thirty million people attended SFX events. The concert industry as a whole topped $1 billion in revenue for the second year in a row.

Underscoring all of this was the fact that SFX Entertainment was a public company. At the end of the day its obligation wasn't to the fans, the acts or the agents; it was to the public shareholders of the company and maximizing value, period. The same goes for Ticketmaster, which was, and is, part of a public company. Priority number one is stock value. What's good for a company's stock value isn't necessarily always good for the consumer.

Critical in understanding SFX's methodology is that it did not view itself as a concert promoter; that was simply an end to a means. Given the advertising/sponsorship-based model, securing audiences became essential. That's why SFX was routinely willing to overpay artists by five to fifteen percent more than they were asking to secure as many dates on a national tour as possible. It needed those captive audiences. If they had to overpay to get forty-two out of forty-five dates for a tour, so be it.

"Here's what we created at the heart of this new business," said SFX CEO and president Mike Ferrel. "We brought together people who were entrepreneurs who have been very successful with their lives and said to them, 'Run your businesses with the same autonomy, fervor and passion you always have.'" What SFX offered was, according to Ferrel, a "blended economic opportunity" that allowed their promoters unprecedented leverage.

Tracy Buie, at the time heading Bill Graham Presents in the Pacific Northwest, suggests the new dynamic stifled promoters' ability to effectively do their jobs. "SFX was coming and telling us, 'Okay, every promoter needs to contribute $45,000 of your ad budget to a *USA Today* ad.' We're going, 'That sucks. Who reads this? Nobody — people at hotels and airports. Oh no, this is no good.' You start to wonder if the lunatics are running the asylum or if there's some horrendous kickback going on. You were no longer allowed to be the creative promoter, taking care of artists in your market, doing the right thing for their career."

Contemporary's Steve Schankman, while quite thankful for and supportive of SFX's investments, also saw inherent flaws. "You take a promoter that's making a million dollars a year, owns his own company and he sells it for a lot of money. Now he makes $300,000 and he's got to answer to Bob Sillerman at his beck and call? A promoter never had to do that in his life because he owned the company." Internally, SFX was concerned about the same thing: as they gave life-altering, generational money to people, how did they get them to come in to work the next day?

"Now you've got to do things [Sillerman's] way, and he didn't give you any incentive. 'Why do I want to work hard to do what he wants me to do?'" Schankman continues. "I think that was a mistake he made. You just can't take these entrepreneurs and give them jobs."

Concerts/Southern Promotions' Alex Cooley feels much the same: "You could even say that the whole Sillerman idea, if it was truly his idea to create a synergistic group of promoters that could control the situation better — if that was truly his vision — maybe it was founded on a false supposition."

IN NOVEMBER 1998 SILLERMAN GATHERED all his promoters at a hotel in Nashville over two days to assess their potential. It was the first time the once-rival promoters had sat in a room together.

"Before I got in the lobby, I was having arguments with other promoters," recalls Cooley. "It seemed like everybody was mad at somebody. I remember different promoters taking potshots at others over past grievances, trying to get more territory and trying to push somebody out of this place so they could take it over. It was the same old thing. Maybe it was a natural process because here were a bunch . . ." His voice trails off into a pause. "To think that we were going to cooperate with anything, maybe, was a pipe dream."

Crystal clear in Cooley's memory is the elevator ride up to the banquet room where everyone was assembling. "Sillerman was on there with another promoter who will remain nameless (one would guess Boyle or someone from PACE), and the promoter and I were going at each other's throats. I remember looking in Sillerman's eyes and him just shaking his head and saying, 'I'll never be able to do this.' I think, at the time, he really did mean to consolidate it in a good way, and I think that maybe he changed his mind at that national meeting because we were all furious with each other." Cooley again pauses. "It was a turning point. But maybe I'm totally wrong about that. That's my supposition."

On the first day each company was told to make a ten- to fifteen-minute presentation about its business and strategies they found successful in maximizing revenue. It was the little things that were memorable. One example Bill Graham Presents talked about was how they rented chairs to patrons for the massive lawn at Shoreline amphitheater for $5 but required a $15 dollar deposit. Ten people would be renting them out, and when the show was over, only two people would be collecting. They found plenty of patrons were willing to forfeit their deposit to avoid the long return line.

Don Law talked about the need for cup holders. Their existence had less to do with convenience than it did with spurring fans to buy two drinks because they had the ability to put one down while they were drinking the other.

The second day all the promoters were arranged around a huge square table. Sillerman wanted the group to talk as it was clear that many had retained reservations about being entirely open and honest with one another (thirty years of rivalry and competition can do that). He was interested in their psychology, how they made decisions, how deals were struck. This wasn't his world, and he wanted to see how its longtime architects would operate and behave if there was complete transparency with one another.

One of the hypothetical questions Sillerman threw out to the group: if a high-level artist did a show with them for $150,000 versus ten percent of the gross, and the next time the artist asked for $220,000 versus twelve percent of the gross, would they take it? Beginning counterclockwise from his right, the group began answering: Sybesma, "No"; Law, "No"; and so forth until it got all the way around to Slater, who was seated immediately to Sillerman's left. "They all said no?" Slater asked rhetorically. "I say *yes*." Sillerman turned to Sybesma. "Yes," he said. "Yes," Law said and so forth. It was a team-building epiphany on the character of promoters — that one zealous promoter could create an overpriced domino effect.

Reflecting on SFX's internal communication at the time, Jack Boyle, who had been installed as the company's chairman, says it was indeed a big problem. "[The promoters] were still trying to guard their secrets from everybody else," he says. "The interesting thing you found about promoters was they could get in a room and talk down an act very simply, and at the same time they could get in a room and talk themselves into buying something that made absolutely no sense whatsoever. I've watched that many times. Promoters start to believe the crap they tell other people. I hate to use the term, but it sounded like con men doing it. The easiest person to con is a con man. One of my greatest abilities in that business was the ability to say no. I think that helped me more than any other thing in that business."

Whatever turbulence may have been felt in Nashville, those close to Sillerman say he left Nashville inspired and excited.

SILLERMAN NOW PREPARED TO FACE the industry as a whole with the keynote speech at the annual Concert Industry Consortium in February 1999. Attended by all of the key players, the event in its fifth year had become something of the concert industry's state of the union. Sillerman would be addressing the industry for the first time since his foray into it began.

"In the words of Godzilla," said Sillerman, trying to play to the crowd, "size is good. Size matters." It echoed Michael Douglas's famous Gordon Gekko character in Oliver Stone's film *Wall Street*: "Greed . . . is good."

"There has to be a market leader in every business segment," he continued. "And how you handle being the market leader — you either make things better for all your constituencies or you are abusive, or some combination — there's no question in my mind and in the minds of 99 percent of the people that we're making things better. I respect the fact that other people will be concerned about it. We have plenty of competition."

Sillerman's speech was by all accounts long on rhetoric and short on substance. Promoters who'd been in the business their whole careers didn't need to hear someone with little practical experience in the field talk about ideas like the communal value of the concert-going experience.

"It was like Moses coming down from the mountain revealing the tablets," recalls Great Northeast Productions owner Dave Werlin of the audience's expectation. "Here's a man who has so much influence, and it was astonishing he would impart so little useful information about his intentions or whatever his dream is — good, bad, or indifferent. It's what he didn't say — like in jazz, the space between the notes is resonant."

Says another promoter: "It was amazing. He's in a roomful of promoters explaining why it's important to do live shows. They already know. He's obviously a smart guy, but everyone was waiting to hear what the point was, and he was trying to be one of the boys, but it backfired."

Despite his history and continued spending spree, Sillerman routinely dismissed the common assumption that he was going to flip SFX Entertainment. "I never founded a company for the purpose of selling it," he contested. "I happen to be the largest shareholder in this company [with fifteen percent]. If somebody came in and said, 'Here's $200 a share,' if I didn't agree to that I'd be sued and maybe killed. (SFX, in 1999, was trading at around $60 a share.) We're operating the company as if it's going to be here forever."

Promoters within the SFX family didn't believe him. "The people in our industry know he's wasting millions of dollars that he doesn't need to," said one. "They throw ridiculous amounts of money away. His only concern is driving up stock prices with a new press release every day."

Harry DeMott, an analyst at Credit Suisse First Boston who followed Sillerman's business moves over the years, asked, "Do leopards change their spots? No. It's a time in the economic cycle when people are feeling good and they're willing to spend more money on live entertainment. Bob is taking advantage of that, and I expect that when he produces something of great value he could well sell it."

"The leopard doesn't change his spots," echoed Alanis Morissette's manager, Scott Welch. "Look at this guy's history. Look at what he does. They keep trying to color it something else. Let's just cut the bullshit and call it what it is: A stock play." Welch's main criticism was that it took the focus off the artist as it aimed to increase revenue streams like concessions, parking and advertising.

Pollstar's Gary Bongiovanni, always one to strike a fairly objective tone, conceded: "A lot of people expect that [selling out] is his real endgame. Time will tell. He's had great taste in the assets he's bought. But he's carrying a huge debt load and I'm not sure they can challenge that with concert business. The rule of thumb is most of the money goes to the artist and representative and the risk goes to the promoter. You may make 5 or 10 percent on a sellout."

With a debt of approximately $742 million — nearing the debt mark of his previous company before he sold it — there was sufficient reason to question Sillerman's strategy of deficit spending.

AS 1999 CAME TO A CLOSE, SFX Entertainment's receipt of purchases exceeded $2 billion since it entered the live entertainment business in 1996. It owned or operated 120 venues throughout the country in addition to assets in sports and entertainment management.

Generating $1.5 billion in revenue for the year, SFX reported operation earnings of $209 million — more than quadruple what they had reported in 1998. Consolidating its debt in August, the company closed on a $1.1 billion senior credit facility.

Since SFX Entertainment entered the live entertainment business in 1996, ticket prices had gone up nearly fifty percent, from an average of $25.82 to $38.56 (the latter is from the first half of 1999). While prices had undoubtedly been increasing incrementally, there's no question SFX's entry to the market dramatically raised them.

"People are charging what they think it's worth," said Boyle, who now oversaw SFX's music empire, of escalating ticket prices. There was a philosophy that had long held true in the industry that Boyle reiterated: "Every time someone buys a ticket, they're saying it's a fair price." In that regard, ticket prices are ultimately a consumer issue.

"I want people to think that our generation, and me as an example of it, changed the world," said Sillerman at the time in an unusually reflective moment. "Because we did, make no mistake about it. We did change the world, and those of us that went into commerce recognized that we had a continuing responsibility to perpetuate that methodology."

Schankman is as pragmatic as he is candid in his assessment of Sillerman. "Will Bob go down in history like Michael [Cohl], Irv [Azoff] and Barry [Diller]?" he asks somewhat rhetorically. "I don't think so. Ask Britney Spears when she did that video with him — she didn't know who he was. It was a flash in the pan. He may have changed the horizon, but he'll never go down in the history books."

Sillerman passed the torch sooner than even his biggest skeptics predicted. On February 29, 2000 — just over three years from when it got into the concert business — SFX Entertainment announced its sale to Clear Channel Communications for $4.4 billion.

Nobody could say they were surprised.

CHAPTER 7

Bigger Bangs for Your Bucks

LOWRY MAYS SAID HE NEVER intended to get into the radio business. And yet by the turn of the millennium his seemingly happenchance career found him at the head of the world's largest radio broadcaster, Clear Channel Communications.

In 1972 Mays was made an offer by Tom Moran, a local businessman. Moran wanted to buy San Antonio, Texas radio station KEEZ-FM. Mays, an investment banker at the time, politely declined but said he would be willing to cosign a bank loan for him, an offer Moran happily accepted. Ninety days later the bank called Mays to inform him that — surprise — Moran didn't have the money. Lowry Mays, against his initial wishes, had just purchased a radio station for $125,000. He was now in the broadcasting business.

To help salvage the situation, Mays partnered with local car dealership owner Red McCombs, whose businesses had been well served by radio advertisements. The duo soon began buying other radio stations in the south before branching out to the rest of the country. The company took its name from a standard industry term for an AM station operating on a specific frequency that could not be shared by any other station.

By 1984 the company had acquired enough holdings to go public. By the time the new millennium began, Clear Channel owned or controlled more than 1,000 radio stations, 550,000 outdoor billboards and nineteen television stations. Its reported net revenue was $5.345 billion.

Mays had turned his perceived misfortune into an unparalleled media powerhouse.

THE MILLION DOLLAR QUESTION — or rather, the $4.4 billion question, based on what Clear Channel Communications paid for SFX Entertainment in 2000 — is whether SFX CEO Bob Sillerman created SFX to flip it. Ask most anybody in the concert business and they'll tell you, "Of course he did." And, as rather valid evidence, they'll point to Sillerman's history in the radio business, which saw him flip various broadcasting groups back and forth before eventually exiting the business with a $2.1 billion sale of SFX Broadcasting to CapStar Broadcasting in 1997.

But ask anybody who worked closely with Bob Sillerman and they'll tell you, "Absolutely not." It's a fine but critical line of distinction between the "dids" and the "did nots." Ask the question a different way — did Sillerman do whatever he could to increase shareholder value? — and both sides will agree: yes.

Brian Becker, who was tapped to be the CEO and chairman of SFX Entertainment after the sale to Clear Channel, had joined SFX from Houston-based PACE Entertainment and served as part of Sillerman's upper management team. "To me, this is not a serious question," he says today of whether or not Sillerman rolled up concert promoters to flip them. "Bob is always very clear: he builds shareholder value, period. If he could build it and turn it into a substantial publicly traded company — if that was the best way to build shareholder value — great. If the best way to build shareholder value was to sell it because an offer came along that was the kind of value he couldn't create, guarantee or was going to take too long to create, he'd sell it."

Another colleague affirms of Sillerman: "He never entered into a business with a perspective on how he's going to get out or when he's going to get out. He appreciates the fact that as a public company, there is currency he can use — and it's easier to use public currency when you're buying businesses than not — but it was never with a perspective of, 'How do we get out?'"

A Sillerman confidant says much the same: "Bob Sillerman never shopped a company he's ever owned. Anyone who really knows Bob would know that's not what Bob Sillerman does. He is the master — he is not going to shop something. Shopping is a sign of vulnerability. It doesn't mean he's not going to entertain phone calls when they come to him — but his is not an outbound-based shopping ship. That's point blank."

"People like to pick on him because they like to pick on people that have done what he did," says Steve Sybesma of Sillerman. Sybesma and his partner, Dave Lucas, sold their Indianapolis-based Sunshine Promotions to SFX for $64 million. "A lot of people blame the concert business troubles on what he did. He may have helped speed it up a little bit — things change in the world."

One of the things that had changed in the world was that the business of rock and roll was now openly valuated and one that now largely operated on bottom lines and shareholder value. Not only was the largest promoter in the world publicly traded, so too was the world's largest ticketer, Ticketmaster. With the two companies' exclusive deals — between them and their respective clients — what was good for their shareholders was not necessarily good for consumers.

Between 1996 and 2003 the average price for a concert ticket rose eighty-two percent. By comparison, tickets for sporting events, theater and movies during the same period rose twenty-one percent, with the overall Consumer Price Index rising seventeen percent.

By rolling up the number of promoters it did, SFX fundamentally changed the business model and pricing of live concerts — whether the remaining independent promoters wanted to change or not.

Former SFX employees readily acknowledge that the company knew it was overpaying acts, often giving them five to fifteen percent more than they were even asking for. The higher artist guarantees flowed directly down to fans as higher ticket prices, but they allowed SFX to secure a tour (or nearly all of it) and, for the first time, to deliver sponsorship from the promoter level versus the artist level.

Attendance was key, not only for developing and analyzing demographic groups for sponsorship opportunities, but also for ancillary revenue streams like food, beverage and parking. This, for a time, took pressure off the slimming margins of the traditional promoter/artist split, but in doing so created a dynamic where SFX was roundly criticized for overpaying popular artists because once they got that amount of money from one promoter, they expected it from all promoters.

"I've always been in favor of lower prices, trying to get more people in [venues]," says Boyle. "You've got to give credit to the [promoters and managers] who want to take the risk — the Michael Cohls and Irving Azoffs of this world — that have raised the prices. In raising prices I may have been following the leader, but I certainly wasn't *the leader*, that's for damn sure."

However, as SFX and its subsequent incarnations argue, it's really the artists who are responsible for the high ticket prices. It's the centerpiece to an argument that the general public is likely unfamiliar with but one that Ticketmaster architect Fred Rosen and others have made on multiple occasions: artists are the ones with the true monopoly.

While it sounds outlandish to most consumers, its reasoning is helpful in better understanding the complicated dance that is the live music business: there is only one of every artist. There is only one Dave Matthews Band; there is only one Madonna — meaning that a promoter doesn't have the option between this Rolling Stones and that Rolling Stones. If they want to promote a Stones concert, they have to deal with the one and only Rolling Stones. The reality is not several Rolling Stones bidding against each other to secure a promoter. As such, the artist, based on their guarantee and deal with the promoter, wields tremendous power over the ticket price.

One former SFX employee argues that the increase in ticket prices was a natural market adjustment to the prices being fetched on the secondary market: "They would say we overpaid the artists and that filtered down to the consumer. The reality is that you could pay the artists anything; it doesn't matter — the ticket price is what's set by the broker community, which is set by the people buying it. So ticket prices may have gone up, but what people actually paid to a see a concert did not go up."

So while other companies like PACE and Cellar Door pursued various forms of consolidation, none was envisioned on SFX's model-changing size. Moreover, as Sillerman's proponents point out, at the time it was unclear what, if any, company would buy this type of debt-laden business portfolio. Who would be interested in an over-leveraged rollup of self-made entrepreneurs who had battled each other for thirty years? It's easy with twenty-twenty hindsight to say Clear Channel, but at the time it wasn't apparent, and in fact several radio conglomerates passed on it.

John Scher says he was asked to consult for several potential SFX suitors. "I had meetings with Citadel, Intercom and CBS," says the veteran promoter, who still runs Metropolitan Entertainment. "They were all sitting back and didn't see that it would work — and were proven right."

Herein lies part of Clear Channel's failure to ever turn a profit — what the "it" was had changed from what SFX originally envisioned "it" would be.

SFX ENTERTAINMENT FORECAST REVENUE FROM three key areas: ticket sales, ancillary revenues from venue ownership and, perhaps most importantly, advertising and sponsorship. Selling the "fifth finger" of a live, demographically specific audience to Madison Avenue advertisers would take a few years to come to fruition, but once it did — even to the tune of ten percent of advertisers' budgets — SFX projected hundreds of millions dollars to come rolling in.

When Clear Channel purchased SFX, the plan was in mid-execution. Sillerman's team had not yet secured big, national advertisers, just local ones, but was very committed. The company had accrued nearly a billion dollars of debt based on the potential profitability from the synergy of the three revenue streams and in fact was ready to spend even more on a number of international acquisitions to expand into Europe, Asia and South America (which Clear Channel eventually did). In a nutshell, SFX was rapidly morphing itself into a global marketing company.

When Clear Channel Communications purchased SFX, it was positioned — on paper — to leverage and synergize its holding of 550,000 outdoor billboards, 1,000-plus radio stations and nineteen television stations with the concert promoter's control of 130-plus venues.

"We consider this acquisition and our entry into live entertainment to be a natural extension of our existing radio operations and a critical part of our long-term strategy," said Lowry Mays at the time. "Ultimately this will allow us to leverage our combined marketing and promotional strength to help our customers sell their products and services."

His son Randall, who along with his older brother Mark ran the company with their father, concurred: "The acquisition of SFX Entertainment allows us to take further advantage of the natural synergy between radio and live music events. We believe the SFX acquisition brings valuable entertainment assets to our company that, when combined with our other media assets, creates a powerful platform of products to help our clients more effectively and efficiently reach their customers."

There were two significant deals on the table, relatively close to completion, that the Mays family and Clear Channel had approval rights over when they bought SFX. They passed on both, deeming them cost-prohibitive.

The first was the purchase of Feld Entertainment, the company behind the Ringling Bros. and Barnum & Bailey circus as well as family-friendly events like the Ice Follies and Walt Disney's World on Ice.

The second deal was one whose like the industry had never seen. It was to become the flagship of a new division within SFX called Grand Entertainment that Michael Cohl, the man responsible for record-setting tours by the Rolling Stones, U2 and Pink Floyd, would lead. After months of negotiation the details of the deal had been hammered out and an agreement seemed near: SFX would buy eighty percent of the Rolling Stones for $345 million.

The breakdown was $280 million for assets that would include everything from publishing to touring revenue to album sales, $50 million for the first tour and $15 million for services for ten years. All involved agree that it was the prototype of what the industry now knows as a 360 deal or unified rights deal.

"When I first sold the company to Bob [Sillerman, in the summer of 1998], we had the idea," confirms Cohl. "Grand Entertainment was just an idea of saying, 'Okay, if [as a promoter we effectively already did this] with the Rolling Stones and it worked, and we did it with U2, what would happen if you added the rest of the rights?' Because it worked: we were increasing gross revenue, we were increasing margins — instead of making ten percent were making twenty percent, twenty-five percent. You had to sit there and go, 'I wonder if we put it all together in one barrel, what would happen?' In theory it was like, 'Everyone should do better. What a grand idea!'"

"Grand Entertainment's ambition was much broader than only the Rolling Stones," recalls Clear Channel's CEO at the time, Brian Becker. "If I remember correctly, the size of the financial commitment that would have been necessary, versus the merits of the investment, were the issue for us." He underscores the company's economics at the time. Not only had Clear Channel just spent more than $20 billion on SFX and radio broadcaster AMFM, but the economy was suddenly in a tailspin. "Our perspective was, 'Let's see how we do with what we just bought.'"

"When all was said and done, as we got closer, the band wasn't comfortable with it," says Cohl of the revolutionary deal. "They just weren't comfortable making that kind of commitment and putting themselves in that kind of position."

Cohl's auspicious ascendancy in the concert world over the previous decade, in assuming leadership of some of the world's most lucrative tours, struck many as a beguiling combination of luck, foreignness and pluck. Just how did this scruffy Canadian become involved with such striking business ventures as Grand Entertainment?

As the saying goes, there's no such thing as luck; it's opportunity meeting preparation. While Cohl is someone who prefers to operate behind the scenes, pull back his life's curtain and you'll find a clear-cut path forged from a persistent methodology and a dogged determination to succeed.

THEY'RE THE SEEDS OF AN unlikely success story: a dope-smoking Canadian teenager drops out of college and decides to go into the adult entertainment business. Not every parent's dream — and certainly not those of a nice Jewish boy from Toronto who went to Hebrew school — but Michael Cohl showed a tenacity for business from an early age.[1]

"I took a hit on my first five shows," Cohl says today with a chuckle, thinking back to his first year as a concert promoter in 1970, as he wound down his foray into the strip club business. "I'd lost all my money and some of my aunt and uncle's money." Within the first six to eight months he owed every family member money. "Every friend, associate and casual acquaintance too," he says. His first show — Buck Owens and the Buckeroos at Maple Leaf Gardens — went so badly he didn't have enough money to pay for Owens to go onstage. Cohl trudged upstairs and asked the venue's owner, Harold Ballard, if he could borrow $12,500.

"I don't know why I'm doing this," responded Ballard to the forlorn promoter. "You look like a nice man, but I lend strangers like you money all the time, and no one ever pays me back."

"I'll pay you back," promised Cohl.

True to his word, Cohl paid Ballard back that New Year's Eve, along with a bottle of champagne and a watch as gentleman's interest. It would prove to be a wise move.

A YEAR LATER, HAVING FOUND at least limited success, Cohl saw an opportunity when Maple Leaf Gardens, home to the National Hockey League team the Maple Leafs, made the decision to align itself with a concert promoter as its counterparts in New York, Philadelphia and Chicago had done, to increase business. Chances were Ballard would partner with either Jerry Weintraub and Concerts West, who were responsible for booking the biggest rock and roll acts across North America, or the number one local promoter, Marty Onrot. Cohl, having made good on his promise to Ballard and done shows periodically at the venue ever since, was able to toss his hat in the ring. Ballard told all would-be candidates that he'd evaluate what they brought to the venue in the coming year and make his decision based on that.

Cohl asked himself a basic question: why would Ballard choose him when there are all these other, seemingly better, more established options? It occurred to Cohl that artists like the Moody Blues and Creedence Clearwater Revival would continue to play Maple Leaf Gardens regardless of who the promoter was. What if he could bring in business that was uniquely his?

Convincing his partners that they needed to spend and potentially lose money now to win the bid and make money later, Cohl created multi-act shows billed under famous album titles like *Cheap Thrills* or *Beggars Banquet*. The shows, which cost $5, included free health food dinners and featured up to nine bands, most of which Weintraub and Onrot would never have heard of, let alone booked. Sure enough, after a year it was clear that if Cohl went away, so too did the brisk business from the shows that no one else was putting on. Cohl won the bid and became the in-house promoter for Maple Leaf Gardens, Toronto's premier venue. The strategic victory didn't take rocket science to accomplish, but its simple but erudite analysis of basic business dynamics — asking fundamental questions that were at the root of a situation versus the ground level — would become the hallmark of his career.

After winning the bid Cohl was hired by Concert Promotions, a company owned by Maple Leaf Gardens Ltd., and worked for them, receiving a salary and fifteen percent of the company. In 1973 Ballard sold Concert

Promotions to his son Bill, Cohl and a few others for $105,000 (the name was then changed to Concert Productions International).

With the cornerstone of exclusively booking the 18,500-seat Maple Leaf Gardens in place — something he would have until 1989 — Cohl grew his business across Canada through a series of strategic alliances and acquisitions. In 1975 he informally partnered with Donald Tarlton's Montreal-based Donald K. Donald Productions, with the acknowledgment that the two promoters would stick to their respective cities and surrounding territories and by working together could entice bigger acts to tour Canada to mutually beneficial ends. In 1977 the two companies invested in the Vancouver-based Perryscope Productions, founded by former Pink Floyd and Who tour manager Norman Perry along with Riley O'Connor. Cohl and company now effectively controlled Canada's concert market.

Mounting a large tour in Canada was significantly more challenging than doing so in the United States. While a band could do big numbers in Toronto and Vancouver, the driving distance between those cities was massive, and the markets in between them were rather small by comparison. At a cursory glance it often didn't make sense to a band's manager or agent to tour Canada.

"The agents we were trying to impress and convince in the States about Canada couldn't name six cities in those days," says Cohl of his efforts in the mid-1970s. "Not that they were dumb, but it's just the way the world was. So we had to learn to scrape, scrimp and promote on less money and learn how to do forty-city tours across Canada."

Once again Cohl did a simple Q&A with himself: "Why don't artists want to tour Canada?" The answer: because they think they can only draw big crowds in a few cities that are far apart, and all the cities in between won't draw enough for them to make money, let alone cover travel expenses across the massive country.

"What if they were told they'd still make money playing to a small crowd?" They would play. But how can that happen?

"So we developed this idea that a forty-show tour of Canada was one show," says Cohl. "We cross-collateralized everything."

If cross-collateralization on a promoter level sounds obvious — assessing the P&L over a number of concerts versus one — it wasn't. Number one, even if a promoter had a few venues or was responsible for a handful of shows, each concert was still typically treated as a discrete deal with a flat fee or revenue split. Number two, cross-collateralization only really works when there's enough volume. In the 1970s and 1980s very few promoters ever had an artist for a significant number of concerts. There were, however, some notable exceptions that ultimately paved the way for Cohl and SFX.

CONCERTS WEST, RUN BY JERRY Weintraub and Tom Hulett, was the first to do national tours of big rock artists like Led Zeppelin from the late 1960s through the 1970s. Its model was based on either paying local promoters a flat fee ($2,500 was the going rate for years) after expenses or bypassing local promoters entirely and striking deals directly with venues. As for the artists' profits, the agreements were on a case-by-case basis, as some got flat fees while others got a share of the profits based on attendance, while still others got one-time signing fees with a combination of all of it.

Weintraub had already changed the concert business with one deal: Elvis Presley. In 1970 he paid Elvis and his manager, Colonel Tom Parker, $1 million for the right to book a national tour — something that had never been done.

"It was a groundbreaking tour," recalls Weintraub, who would go on to have a prestigious film career as a producer (*Karate Kid*, *Ocean's Eleven*) and head of United Artists. "It changed the nature of the business. Before that, the concert business had been broken into territories, each region of the country controlled by a local promoter. . . . [An] artist moved from fiefdom to fiefdom, and the manager cut deals with the local power brokers — the man who 'owned' Philadelphia, the man who 'owned' Buffalo — who made subsidiary deals with local police, local unions, local arena operators. This system was Byzantine and wasteful."

So Weintraub cut out the various middlemen and struck deals on his own. While normally that would be an unlikely scenario — trying to do so would cause a promoter or manager to be frozen out of particular markets on all levels since the respective businesses fed off each other — it all changed with Elvis. "He was simply too big," confirms Weintraub. "If you said no, someone else would say yes, meaning you would miss out on the biggest pay day ever."

"Many of us did not necessarily agree with what he did, but I'd have to say we owe Tom and people like him a debt of gratitude," says promoter Larry Magid, who still owns the Electric Factory and was likely the one Weintraub was referring to in "owning" Philadelphia, along with his former partner, Herb Spivak. "Without him laying the groundwork, the concert business might not be as we know it."

Indeed many local promoters were angered by Concerts West's circumvention — it went against the understood terms of agreement within the live music business.

"Basically we did [the national tours] ourselves," confirms Weintraub. "We were kids and we didn't know any better. We went and got smarter and continued doing it anyway. We got sued and people were irate that we were changing the concert industry. But we did it anyway. Just because someone said they owned Denver didn't mean we couldn't go in. We were strong-headed and strong-willed."

It's not surprising that Cohl welcomed Concerts West's business in Canada. "They were the devil before I became the devil," he says, smiling, of his later industry-changing endeavors. "I became the all-time devil, but they were the first devil to promoters and agents."

By a similar token Weintraub says, "I became the most hated man in the industry. But as Don Corleone said, 'It's better to be feared than loved.'"

Cohl saw their efforts in trying to create consistent tours — both in terms of production and profit — akin to his own in many ways. "Concerts West were my heroes in this respect," he says.

As American promoters' ire increased over Concerts West's national tours, many began calling for what amounted to a boycott. Cohl, in turn, would phone Tom Hulett and offer as much of Canada as he wanted to make up for any lost dates in the States. "Some years we had thirty-five to fifty shows from Concerts West," Cohl recalls. The Concerts West model, applied to a consolidated Canada, was profitable for Cohl in a way it wasn't for his American counterparts: the expenses Concerts West was willing to pay for in addition to its flat fee of $2,500 to promoters — largely those of employee and advertising costs — were already part of Concert Productions International's operating budget. This meant that CPI and its partners could make anywhere from $5,000 to $7,000 a show. "I wasn't the Jack Boyles of the world," Cohl says of the Cellar Door founder, who would have likely passed on shows with such relatively small margins. "To me that was $250,000 that we wouldn't have had [at the end of the year]."

It was, by Weintraub's account, a tough but successful go for Concerts West. "Every local promoter wanted me destroyed," he says. "I was ending their reign. It was a tremendous fight but I knew if I came out intact I would have a new livelihood."

In response to Concerts West some promoters encouraged Bill Graham to start his own model of national touring, one that would use local promoters for their marketing skills and cut them in on more of the deal. In 1974 Graham did just that, taking out Bob Dylan with The Band, CSNY and George Harrison for national tours.

Graham was the tour promoter for each and then subcontracted the dates to local promoters. Any promoter, even at reduced margins, wanted these shows, given each of the artists' star power at the time. Such was CSNY's popularity that it mounted the first-ever all-stadium tour — thirty-five dates. "It was the largest-grossing tour ever to that point," says then-manager Eliot Roberts. "But it was a very low *netting* tour because the expenses were *astronomical*. Because of the mistakes made, we ended up having to hire double crews. We had extra people in every hall to set up. Extra union people. So the expenses got outrageous."

To that end Roberts says: "We realized that what we should have done was use a number of promoters, each responsible for their own city. What Bill ended up doing was getting a subcontractor in each city for a low figure. Bill was making five-percent deals with them, and they had so little money that they had to cut everything to try and save here and there so they could pad their bills."

"It took me and the company into a very different realm, creating what eventually became a very problematic situation," recalled Graham in *Bill Graham Presents*, his autobiography written with Robert Greenfield.

This time the criticisms, unlike those with Concerts West, were coming from agents, who were concerned about their well-being, given that Graham bypassed all of them for national tours, seemingly disregarding their services. "[Agents] were angry with me for cutting tough deals and coming into their cities with the acts I had taken on national tours," Graham said. "The major agencies thought this could be the start of a trend. Major artists bypassing the agency system. All I kept saying to them was, 'This was a one-of-a-kind situation. I felt like doing this, and that's the way it's going to be.'" (That Graham saw four tours as "one-of-a-kind" was part of the potential problem.)

A meeting was called at a Long Island estate between many of industry's top agents, promoters and managers, with Graham to discuss matters following the Harrison tour. After various amounts of back and forth and even some theatrics — Graham had hired a group of actors to storm the room dressed like 1920s gangsters wearing Bill Graham Presents emblazoned shirts — the promoter backed down. "I agreed to forego national touring in the best interests of the industry," he later recalled. "Not that I was that generous. I knew full well that the major agencies, at their whim, could freeze me out of business in the Bay Area by not selling me talent. So much for national touring."

While Graham had ruffled the industry's feathers with national touring, none of them had been cross-collateralized. With Concerts West and Bill Graham's national tours in mind and his continued success in cross-collateralizing Canada, Cohl saw the seeds of opportunity to do the same in the United States.

IN THE EARLY 1980S COHL'S CPI bought the Brockum merchandising company from Peter Lubin for $2 million. At the time, Cohl estimates, it was probably the eighth biggest music merchandising company in North America. Far out in front was Bill Graham's Winterland Productions.

CPI made the acquisition for three reasons. The first was that it provided a direct line into a band's inner business circle. "If I'm the band's merchandiser, I get to go to every show," says Cohl. "I get one of my reps, me or one of my partners into the dressing room with the management or agency every night [for settlement]."

Second, it was a defensive move. "If I'm the band's merchandiser 365 days a year and someone takes a run at us in Vancouver or Toronto, I presume the meeting in the office goes something like, 'Why wouldn't we play for Cohl in Toronto, when we have to see him the other 363 days a year? We're going to play for this other guy in Toronto to embarrass the crap out of him?'" While business usually didn't work that way, Cohl thought it wise to fortify his position just in case. "It worked," he says.

Third, it was an offensive move. Given that he and Tarlton controlled Canada's live music scene, they needed an outlet to grow to the degree that if they got any bigger, the Canadian government would come after them for antitrust (or as it's known in Canada, competition). The purchase of Brockum provided them with the ability to get a foothold in the United States from which to further expand.

Their operational plan for Brockum was simple: they were going to leverage their existing relationships with bands like AC/DC, Genesis and Pink Floyd and sign them as clients. Still they needed more of a competitive edge.

"Where are we going to make our difference?" Cohl asked Norman Perry, whom he'd assigned to run the new venture.

"I don't know what we can do," Perry responded.

"Bring me the roster. Show me every act Winterland has," Cohl said, feeling mildly flummoxed.

Perry handed him the list, and Cohl began looking at it, eyes scanning each line, taking mental inventory.

"They don't have Diana Ross and the Supremes. Let's go get them. They don't have Stevie Wonder. They don't have Prince." Cohl paused. "Wait a second. I'm Canadian, they're American. I don't want to say the thought that just crossed my brain, but why is it . . ." He quickly scanned the client list of Bravado, another major merchandiser. "Why is nobody signing black acts?"

"Because their per capitas aren't very good, and people have had a lot of difficulty with those particular acts," Perry replied.

"Norman, it's going to work! Go sign every black artist on earth!"

Brockum quickly became home to a number of black artists.

When Michael Jackson announced the Jacksons' *Victory* tour for 1984, a fifty-five date stadium run that would go from July to December and was to be their final tour, Cohl won the bid as the exclusive merchandiser for $3 million (that Brockum supported black artists wasn't lost on the band's representative, Don King). Coming on the heels of the worldwide success of Michael Jackson's album *Thriller*, which had been released just months earlier, the tour was destined to be one of the biggest of all time.

Three weeks into the tour, reports started surfacing that the tour's promoter, Chuck Sullivan, the New England Patriots football team owner, was in dire financial shape. "We knew if the tour went down — and it started to look like it might — there's no way we're getting our money back," says Cohl. "We're out of business, we are bankrupt, we are gone-zo."

Cohl joined the tour a month in and began to observe the situation. It took a few weeks, but he quickly realized that the tour, with its massive overhead and precariously struck deals, had put Sullivan against the ropes with little hope of keeping *Victory* afloat unless drastic measures were immediately taken.

"First I had to get inside," says Cohl. "I go, 'Chuck, what's wrong with your deal? Everybody says you're losing money. You're telling me you're not, but you are. I've got to find out why.' I found out — he trusted me to tell me the deal."

According to reports, the initial agreement was as follows: the Jacksons would receive 84.44 percent of the concert proceeds, and Sullivan would get 16.56 percent; money owed to the Jacksons was due twenty-four hours after each concert; and, the most precarious aspect, there was a provision that required Sullivan to pay the Jacksons $21 for every ticket, whether it was sold or unsold. (As collateral for a $12.5 million loan to make the down payment on the contract, Sullivan had put up the Patriots, Sullivan Stadium and a family-owned racetrack.)

A critical problem was that, in doing ticket projections for the concert bid, Sullivan based the counts on full use of a stadium's concert capacity. It turned out that the eight-story, 365-ton stage that was built in secret took up approximately a third of a stadium's field. So, for instance, at the tour opener at Arrowhead Stadium in Kansas City, there were only 45,000 tickets available versus the expected 60,000.

"I said, 'Look, I can fix it. I know how to make this tour make money. You've made certain mistakes," recounts Cohl. "You know how to run a football team, but . . ." Sullivan wouldn't listen to him.

Cohl looked at the schedule, saw an open weekend and offered Sullivan a deal he knew the struggling promoter couldn't refuse: "Come play three nights at a stadium in Toronto. Because I know your deal, here's what I'll do — I will stand in your shoes and guarantee what it is I know you owe Michael for those three nights, and I'll give *you* a guaranteed $100,000." After Sullivan agreed, Cohl gave him a proverbial wink before exiting and said, "Then, after the shows, you're going to hire me to run the tour for you."

Walking into settlement after the three sold-out Toronto shows, Cohl proudly paid Sullivan his $100,000. "Congratulations, Chuck. You did really well for a one third partner." Cohl remembers underscoring Sullivan's complicit understanding of what he meant. "From then until breakfast the lawyers negotiated, and by breakfast he hired me to run the tour for him."

Over the next twenty shows Cohl shifted the monetary scale more favorably in the beleaguered promoter's direction. The revenue share was adjusted to approximately seventy-two percent for the Jacksons, twenty-eight percent for Sullivan; the per-ticket guarantee and the twenty-four hour payment requirement were also cut. "I thought of five or six ways to help him make money," says Cohl, "but not the ticket because he'd given it all away." Those ways included a better merch deal, travel packages, ticket rebate deals, hotel deals and limited sponsorships.

"I saw all those P&Ls and I saw what could happen because nobody thought you could do giant, stadium-only tours," says Cohl of the experience. "Number one, the *Victory* tour was an invaluable lesson, to be able to walk home and go, 'Wow, I didn't think anybody could make that much in three shows, never mind one show,' and just filed it."

While CSNY had done a stadium-only tour with Graham a decade earlier, it was twenty dates shorter. Moreover, both the *Victory* tour and CSNY were strictly domestic — none had attempted to go international. The numbers and contracts Cohl had been privy to were at that point for the biggest tour *ever*. It didn't get any bigger, and Cohl had not only managed to get access to the numbers but in fact was allowed to come in and adjust them. It was a career-changing coup.

"Number two," continues Cohl, "for the first time I'd met all these names that I'd been reading about in *Amusement Business* and *Billboard* all my life, whether it was Larry Magid or Jack Boyle, all of them. The only one I really knew was Bill Graham because he'd been coming to Toronto. I came home and I said to my staff, 'We do it at least as well, if not better, than all of these people we read and hear about, see pictures of, and they get trophies and awards. All the acts say we look after them as well or better than anyone and we're doing a great job. I now know it's true."

The *Victory* tour is where the college dropout finally received his diploma. "It was like going to school and getting my Ph.D. and being paid for it," says Cohl. "And it was on Chuck's tab."

In the years to come Cohl's visions of the future lay well beyond Canada and the United States.[2] He would periodically pull the *Victory* tour file out of his desk drawer and, as he says, "doodle numbers." "This was really powerful information," Cohl would tell himself. "I should go after the Rolling Stones. I should go after Pink Floyd. I should do something with this information." He would stare at the file and his hypothetical doodles and think, "I will, one day."

THE SECOND AMNESTY INTERNATIONAL TOUR, Human Rights Now!, a multi-artist benefit show featuring Bruce Springsteen, Sting, Peter Gabriel and others, came to Toronto's Maple Leaf Gardens on September 15, 1988.

Bill Graham was the tour's promoter. As show preparations were being made, Graham, known for his explosive personality, was tearing into Cohl's employees as he would any production staff. "A couple of my people called and quit," recounts Cohl, who was up in his office at the time. "'We're going home. This guy just told me I'm a piece of shit.'" He persuaded them to stay and told them he was en route to deal with the situation.

He immediately found Graham backstage: "'Bill, stop. For the rest of the day talk to me. You cannot talk to my people — that's literally it.' Whatever you need, let's work it out."

He then gathered his staff and made another declaration: "I promise you we'll never have to work with Bill Graham again. This is it."

After the necessary soundchecks were completed and all seemed in order, Cohl found Graham, who was taking a break. "By the way, we're never going to work together again — ever, ever," he told the veteran promoter. "We don't need you coming in and abusing everybody, so thank you, this is it."

Cohl walked over to the hot stove lounge and sat down for some steak and mushrooms with his longtime partner, Lori McGoran. After a few bites he started to feel ill, thinking that it was perhaps the food. He opened his belt and unzipped his fly halfway to try and relieve the increasing pain. No luck. Minutes later he turned to McGoran: "Take me to the hospital. Something is terribly wrong."

The doctor quickly diagnosed the problem: kidney stones. He passed them quickly. "The next morning I'm calling the doctor to see if stress can cause kidney stones," retells Cohl. "It's Graham's fault I have kidney stones. He caused me to have such a stressful day. It wasn't the mushrooms. I'm driving to the office going, 'That's it.'" When Cohl arrived at work, his staff of sixteen greeted him.

"Boss, we need to talk to you."

"I know exactly what you're going to say," Cohl said, cutting them short. "I gave you my word and I'm keeping it. We're never working with Bill Graham again."

"No, we're going to give you your word back on this one. It's okay."

"Why?" Cohl asked incredulously.

"Because you realize that if we don't ever work with Bill Graham again, we'll never get to work with the Rolling Stones again, and that's clearly a highlight of why we're all in the business."

"Just go back and start working again," said Cohl, waving them off. "I promise you we're never going to work with him again, and don't bet that we're not going to work with the Rolling Stones."

When all the employees had left the room and closed the door, Cohl opened his desk drawer and pulled out the *Victory* tour folder.

The day had come.

THERE ARE FEW THINGS THAT veterans of the live music business agree on. If common parlance suggests there are two sides to every story, the concert business typically has four or five perspectives for any given tale. There are two moments that the industry collectively agrees were a watershed: SFX's promoter rollup in the late 1990s and Michael Cohl winning the Rolling Stones' 1989 *Steel Wheels* tour.

Everything in Cohl's career had led up to this point: the constant questioning of the business's fundamentals, the cross-collateralized touring of Canada, the strategic partnerships with Canadian and American promoters, the development of the Brockum merchandising arm, finding a deep-pocketed parent company and, finally, the insight from the *Victory* tour deals.

"I saw hall deals that I didn't think were possible," Cohl says of the *Victory* tour's contracts. "Getting halls for free, halls for $50,000 when everyone thought they were $150,000, expenses that halls were paying that promoters normally paid."

Cohl had been sitting on the information for four years. "It was more that I was afraid of not getting it than I was of anything because no one likes to fail," he confides. He had often asked himself, as he mocked up hypothetical schemes based on the *Victory* tour, who would be the best act to help give this new platform life? And the answer, for him, was always easy: the Rolling Stones — arguably the most popular band in the world. It was his answer to Weintraub's Elvis. He just had to be patient.

At the time the Stones hadn't toured since 1982 with *Tattoo You*. Cohl went to Peter Bronfman, the owner of Labatt's, to ask for his financial support.[3]

"I'm going to do this, but I need your backing," Cohl told Bronfman. "This is big money — I don't have this kind of money. This is going to be tens of millions of dollars. Will you back me?"

"Yes."

"Good. I'm going to go get the Rolling Stones. We're going to put them back together and we're going to do the tour."

Given Bronfman's wide network of connections in the entertainment world, particularly with its majority stake acquisition of CPI the year before, he asked around to gauge what others thought of the plan. According to Cohl, everybody told Bronfman that there was no chance on earth he was ever going to get the Rolling Stones and no chance that Bill Graham was not going to have them, and that they were all wasting their time. Bronfman, feeling a bit embarrassed with what he perceived to be his sudden lack of business acumen, called Cohl for a meeting.

"Everybody thinks you're nuts," said Bronfman.

"Who's everybody?" asked Cohl. "What do you guys know? You know about beer."

"We talked to all your partners, and they think you're nuts, too."

Cohl persuaded Bronfman to trust him and to believe that all the people Bronfman had talked to had an almost xenophobic image of themselves — that CPI and the Canadian concert business was always going to be "the other guy" in the view of American promoters.

With Bronfman's support secured, Cohl phoned a mutual friend of the Stones' financial adviser, Prince Rupert Loewenstein, to get introduced. He told them that he was going to pitch a new kind of business model for large scale touring.

Ten minutes later the phone rang.

"Excuse me, young man," said the Prince in a formal British accent. "I understand you have something to say to me."

"$40 million for forty shows," Cohl initially offered for a Stones tour.

"Very interesting," replied the Prince succinctly.

As luck would have it, in January, shortly after Cohl received Loewenstein's call, the Stones entered the studio to record *Steel Wheels*, the beginning of their commercial comeback. As always, it was the tour that made the band its real money, not the album sales.

Graham had successfully helped produce the last several Stones tours — 1972, 1975, 1978 and 1981. So when he received a call in early 1989 from one of the band's business managers, Joe Rascoff, the tone of the conversation was disarming. "'They're going to go on tour,'" Graham recalled Rascoff saying. "'Bill, the situation is that there's another organization bidding to do it. . . . You should consider whether or not you want to make a bid to *buy* the tour. Because we already have an offer.'"

"I didn't really know what he was talking about," Graham later reflected. "I have never *bought* a tour." He asked what exactly he meant.

"'You have ten days to get a bid together,'" Rascoff responded. "'We'll have a sponsor. I don't think you'll be able to beat these numbers, and I'm not telling you what they are. If you buy the tour, you'll need to guarantee ticket sales and merchandise and so on.'"

"During my first conversations with Joe, I began to get an inkling that something was wrong here," said Graham. "He kept saying, 'We didn't approach these people. They came out of nowhere, Bill.' I said, 'Joe, but you *accepted*. When they came to you, why didn't you say, 'You want to bid on our tour? *This* is our team. The Rolling Stones, Rupert, Rascoff *and* Bill Graham.'"

Over the course of several meetings with the band, Rascoff and Loewenstein, Graham felt like he was treading water as time and again he was told, "The numbers are just too big," "The numbers are so incredible" and "You can't possibly match the numbers." The "number," as Graham would eventually find out, was an approximately $65 million guarantee for fifty dates. Word had reached him that it was Cohl and CPI leading the bid.

Prior to calling the Stones with his offer, Cohl had gone through various scenarios of how Graham would react to the bid — knowing that Graham was the incumbent promoter — which, based on the *Victory* tour model, had the band only playing stadiums. After running through them in his head, Cohl was struck with an epiphany: Graham was in a no-win situation.

"I'm going to walk in and I'm going to bid an amount of money that people think I'm nuts," he says of the first scenario. "Graham's going to absolutely never come close because he's going to think I'm out of my tree." The alternative, Cohl realized, was just as bad for Graham: "He's just not going to share [this type of model and its profits] with people anyway because he's known this all along and he's never had to share it."

Meaning that if he shared it now, the Stones and other acts would know he'd made more money off previous stadium shows than they'd realized.

Compounding the problem for Graham was his belief that, "If [CPI] owned the tour and cut all the local guys into their deal, each promoter would make less than in the past because the pie was being cut another time."

While Graham had taken the Stones out on their previous, mostly stadium run in 1981–82, his role was as tour director, not tour promoter. He still utilized local promoters in their respective cities, often giving them the standard ten or fifteen percent of profit after expenses.

After a long conversation with Mick Jagger about the *Steel Wheels* tour deal, Graham felt confident that he'd be able to win the bid back or at least involve himself to a large degree in the tour. The singer had agreed to let him get the numbers from Rascoff. Yet no sooner had the spring returned to his step than Rascoff was telling him that the deal with CPI was done. Graham's right hand at BGP, Gregg Perloff, was getting calls about CPI calling stadiums for availabilities.

Furious, frustrated and confused, Graham called Rascoff. "You tell me the money is too big but it's not really done yet, and yet they're already calling stadiums. This is an example where by not having me involved, you and I already disagree in how this should be done. Call the *promoters*, not the stadiums, to get the local avails. Let *them* do their jobs. Let them keep their part."

Rascoff's response said it all: "Bill, you see, here's the first example already of the problems we're going to have."

Graham's loss to CPI stunned the industry. "When we got the contract, I don't think anybody could believe it," says Cohl. "They just went, 'Who is this guy?'"

THE BUSINESS MODEL FOR NATIONAL — and international — touring that Michael Cohl created had two key differences from those developed by previous promoters. The first was that, like his earlier Canadian shows, the entire tour was cross-collateralized. It wasn't viewed as fifty separate business deals but rather one massive one. To that end it was predicated on local promoters getting flat fees after costs and expenses — just as Concerts West had arranged in the 1970s. Cohl contends it was never positioned as a take it or leave it type offer, despite relaying how a typical conversation with a local promoter would begin: "We'd like you involved. We'd love to have you be a part of it. We don't want to offend you and make you not part of it in your own market. But there's a certain value for services, and we have our business to conduct." If a local promoter opted out — as some did — Cohl struck a deal directly with the venue.

The second key difference was that CPI's rights as a promoter were expanded to include as much as possible. "You might be losing money as a promoter, but there's this other merchandiser who's come in and is making money," Cohl remembers. "It didn't seem right. Then you would see different promotions — the record company over there trying to do this, as if the show didn't mean anything; the merchandiser would be off with some local store; and it seemed very disjointed. What we decided, very simply put, was there had to be a way to get a bigger bang for your buck, a more effective way of pooling all this."

If they could package it all, control all the various elements and enable them to cross-promote and feed off each other, the returns could be much greater. "Most important," says Cohl, "is you're going to get inside people's heads and you're going to make it a bigger thing, a bigger event, a bigger stature for the bands." As he'd put it to prospective clients, he wanted to give them a reason to work more and therefore make more money.

He also created new revenue streams for the band such as travel packages for fans, TV deals and VIP seating.

Local promoters from around the country were up in arms. "I've never seen greed at this level — ever," said longtime New England promoter Don Law. "It's insulting. The Who cut a tight deal that everybody complained about but they didn't insult people like this." The revenue share, according to Law, equated to ninety-nine percent for the band, one percent for the promoter. "You can't pay people's salaries on that. We're enormously disappointed. We've done the Stones every time in Boston since 1972, but we're out of it completely on this one. We're not going to do it just for the prestige."

Today Atlanta-based promoter Alex Cooley still recalls his dislike of CPI: "I was never in favor of the Michael Cohl school of national promoting," he says, noting that he did work well with Concerts West's national model, which saw adjusted rates and pricing in different markets. "I can't put words in a dead man's mouth, but I think if you interviewed people that were close to Bill Graham, they had pretty much had the same feeling, too. One thing Bill felt like he brought to the table, and promoters like us brought to the table, was that we understood our markets; we understood what went on in those markets. The Cohls and [Arthur] Fogels of the world, they started painting the whole United States with one brush. It was then, and it still is to this day, very much a regional country. Lyon in France is not Paris. Atlanta is not New York. It used to be terrible when somebody would say, 'No, you have to price tickets like this; it's the same as in New York.' But people in New York pay double what an apartment in Atlanta costs, so why should the ticket price be the same?"

Cohl confirms local promoters' displeasure. "I think it angered most of them," he says rather matter-of-factly. "Some of them were furious. John Scher was furious and made no bones about telling the press. Bill Graham's best quote was in *Rolling Stone*, where he said, 'My lover's done a deal with the devil.' And I don't think I was the lover."

Graham, for his part, wanted desperately to work with the Stones purely for the prestige. The money, he said, was secondary for him. Several days after Graham's final phone call with Rascoff, the band faxed him an apology letter that they had all signed. It read, in part: "We're sorry it's not going to be the way you would have wanted to do this tour but we have decided to go about our business in a different way."

By tour's end their new way of business with Cohl — greater ticket scaling with higher priced premium tickets, lucrative merchandising and licensing deals, and sponsorship (this time from Anheuser-Busch) — netted them more than $260 million, a record for a concert tour at the time.

One of the drivers, as Cohl notes, was venue deals that he didn't previously know existed until the *Victory* tour. There were instances, sources indicate, where he got 100 percent of the ticket revenue and others still where he perhaps got even more. (Indeed, for Pink Floyd's *Division Bell* tour in 1994, there were dates at college stadiums where he garnered as much as 110 percent because the frequently empty venues could make considerable money from the concessions of a packed show.)

Not that it was all easy. Several months into the tour, for instance, Cohl crunched the numbers and realized significant adjustments had to be made. His experience from the *Victory* tour had honed his decision making when it came to tours of this scale.

Years later, Jagger says, "I think Michael would admit that it was a huge learning curve for him doing *Steel Wheels*. He had never done it before really, so it was a bit of a gamble."

"It was a deal where I said they could make a whole lot of money, and I would guarantee it 'subject to,' and the 'subject to's' made us partners at the end of the day," says Cohl. "So we all had to learn how to do it."

Graham's world, meanwhile, had completely stopped. He went into an emotional and psychological tailspin. As he shares in his autobiography: "During the months after I lost the Stones tour, I thought about suicide many times. For the first time in my life, it seemed like a choice."

"For the first time in twenty-four years, the world was being told that in the business sense, I was a loser," he continued. "My definition of madness is those months. I was ready to be committed to full-time care." The entire industry took notice of its most public figure's downward spiral.

"I was sad," says Cohl of Graham's reaction. "When I started out as a promoter, he was my hero. I wanted to be the next Bill Graham; I wanted to replace him; I wanted to be the king promoter, and I admired him. It was tough on me, but I had decisions to make: 'All right, I can feel bad to a point and do the Rolling Stones and embark on this new adventure in my life, or I can go home and be the Canadian promoter.' It was never an issue to me. I was going to do it. I felt bad, and it was unfortunate that Bill had such a horrible reaction."

A year after he lost the Stones, Graham happily told his autobiography co-author Greenfield: "I am over the pain. I feel so good now that I really don't want to say how much I grieved. But they changed my life. That's the irony. Now I *love* the fact I'm alive. A year ago, I didn't know if I was going to live." Still, some of his fellow promoters thought Graham never fully recovered from the Stones ordeal.

Graham died in a tragic helicopter crash in October 1991, a year after he'd shared with Greenfield how healthy he felt again. While Cohl had won the Stones bid for *Steel Wheels*, it seems likely Graham would have challenged him for future tours.

"Nobody could have come close to the number I was going to offer them then," Graham boasted of his newfangled plan in the aftermath of the *Steel Wheels* deal. "They're being offered $65 million? I was going to give them *$125 million. Twice* as much, *guaranteed*."

WITH THE SUCCESS OF *STEEL WHEELS* the Stones were back. Whatever acrimony or infighting there might have been — even that which continued — was dealt with in whatever ways were necessary to make sure the show went on. For the forty-five dates in North America alone in 1989, the band grossed $90 million. (Cohl would later acknowledge that he had "worked out that they could make way more than $1 million" per show).

The next decade, beginning with the next forty-five international dates for *Steel Wheels*, followed by the *Voodoo Lounge*, *Bridges to Babylon* and *No Security* tours, saw the Rolling Stones gross more than $750 million from 333 shows to claim the decade's top touring spot (all but twenty-six were reported as sellouts).

Cohl's new model gained traction with several other global superstars. U2, after a bidding war involving CPI, CAA and BGP, hired Cohl and company for its 1992 ZooTV tour, which saw the band getting a $115 million guarantee (CPI, which would morph into The Next Adventure [TNA] in the mid-1990s, would go on to do the PopMart tour as well). The aforementioned Pink Floyd hired Cohl for its 1994 *Division Bell* stadium tour, from which the band grossed $152.5 million. In addition artists such as CSNY, David Bowie and others used TNA to reap previously unimagined profits.

Each time TNA took out a tour, particularly for a returning client, it looked for ways to increase revenue. Maybe it was more fluid stage production. Perhaps it was more sponsorship. Or maybe, as the Stones camp found, it was about securing your fans' information in the burgeoning age of technology.

AS TICKET DISTRIBUTION WAS REVOLUTIONIZED with the rapid growth of the Internet, the ensuing ticket demand, fueled by the ease of the purchasing process, meant that premium tickets were harder than ever to get. As tickets became harder to control — both in terms of how quickly a show could sell out and the ever-growing secondary market — artists began looking for ways to harness the unbridled power of the Internet to greater benefit.

Once again it was the Rolling Stones who developed a new business model for the industry. David Bowie, Bob Goodale and Bowie's business managers Joe Rascoff and Bill Zysblat — the same duo the Rolling Stones used along with Prince Rupert — launched UltraStar in 1998. While Cohl and the

Stones didn't utilize the company right away, it soon became an integral part of the band's touring cycles.

UltraStar was originally designed to be a "management, technology partnership that specializes in the arena of Internet services, bringing major entertainment, sports and fashion clients to the world in a community-based forum delivered over the Web." In short that meant providing someone like Bowie with a comprehensive, interactive website where fans paid for exclusive access to gated content in addition to offering a private label Internet service provider (ISP) for fans. Longtime Bowie fan Jane Smith could now get an email address like jsmith@davidbowie.com for $19.95 per month.

The late 1990s was a time when companies were giving consumers opportunities to customize previously generic items for the first time. If you were a fan of a particular sports team or a supporter of, say, the World Wildlife Federation, you could reflect that in your credit card or checkbook design. UltraStar saw its private label ISP offerings as a natural extension of that ethos. Its first big clients after Bowie were sports teams: the Baltimore Orioles, followed by the New York Yankees. The websites offered free content and online stores for casual users, with exclusive content and access to ticket purchasing for paid users. Perhaps most importantly the websites offered a place for fans to congregate online and presented artists and sports teams with a new medium for a direct relationship to them.

"It was clear that there was this tremendous appetite for fan connection and for artist interaction," recalls Larry Peryer, who began consulting with the company from its launch, came on full-time in early 2001 and eventually became president in 2005. "In retrospect you're like 'duh,' but back then the only way I could connect with a fellow music fan was by picking up a copy of *Relix* and finding somebody in the back I could trade tapes with. I did that and made lifelong friends, but the model was only so satisfying with one person at a time. When we saw what happened when we opened up a portal into people, it was really powerful."

It was powerful enough that in 2000 SFX bought a ten percent stake in UltraStar for $10 million, with hope of capturing unrealized revenue from their massive tour investments (the $100 million valuation was entirely speculative at that point). While the profits of a company like UltraStar could never be as high for a promoter as a tour would be, the margins were significantly better.

The pitch to SFX was, according to Peryer, "You're going to go write a big check to acquire the rights to this tour. Write an incrementally larger check or no larger check — make your large check dependent on acquiring the web rights — and we'll implement and execute those rights for you, and you can make the extra profit as well."

UltraStar largely got out of the private ISP business and began to focus on those rights — particularly content development and e-commerce opportunities — as it was clear they were being underutilized by both artists and promoters. Add to that access to tickets, and it was an expensive proposition for an artist to fund on their own. With the SFX deal UltraStar was able to develop meaningful relationships with artists because SFX was buying entire tours.

"At the early turn of the century, there really weren't any other companies doing it as a product or a service," recounts Peryer. "A lot of artists had them — I think Bon Jovi has always had one, Whitney Houston had one, Red Hot Chili Peppers — but it could have been like, 'Mail a check for $25 to my brother-in-law's basement.'" UltraStar saw a need for a meaningful, hands-on platform provider. How exactly it was going to run, they weren't sure. "We didn't have all the fine points figured out," says Peryer, "but we knew that that was really the proposition."

UltraStar's first artist signings after Bowie to include a ticketing component were the young pop rock act Hanson and the Christian artist Bill Gaither. While access to good tickets was certainly an appeal of paid membership, it wasn't necessarily the driving force for any of them. And while the exclusive content for members was good, it wasn't, for lack of a better term, sexy. All that rapidly changed thanks to the Rolling Stones.

In late 2001 the Stones began exploring how to fully build out revenue opportunities for their *40 Licks* tour the following year. The band had found some success with ARTISTdirect-led Stonesbazaar.com, which was tied to the 1997–98 *Bridges to Babylon* tour, but was now, with the rapid improvement in Internet technology, looking for their website to have a more meaningful role in their next touring cycle. With RZO behind UltraStar — a company that had long worked with the Stones on the business side — it allowed the band and its camp to be completely hands on. "Michael Cohl, and really the Stones, came in and to a large extent brought the vision," says Peryer. "They told us what we were going to do and we listened. We kicked and screamed a little bit, but we did what we were told. And it was phenomenally successful." It was quickly realized that dealing with a band the size of the Rolling Stones — size largely defined by ticket demand — changed the drivers of UltraStar's business in a way that allowed for robust, self-sustained growth.

Fans, it turned out, were willing to pay a substantial amount of money for a better chance to get good seats. It is commonplace now, but at the time getting consumers to pay $95 a year just to have a chance — a chance, not a guarantee — for better tickets was unheard of. And for the *40 Licks* tour, most fans who joined the subscription service did get good seats. What they also got with their membership was what UltraStar called Virtual Ticket. This was premium content available on the Stones' website that included video of rehearsals and soundchecks, chats with the band and crew and periodic tour updates, along with the occasional video and audio feed from a show. This content wasn't an afterthought; it was high-quality and something the band believed in. The website also offered a barrage of merchandise, some of it exclusive.

Every single ticket purchased for the world tour included a $1 service fee that was designated for UltraStar, to the degree that in the settlement each night there would be a line item for UltraStar. Say the Veterans Stadium show in Philadelphia had 55,000 paid tickets; $55,000 would be wired to UltraStar. The band played 117 shows that tour (not all were stadiums; a number were indoor arenas and large theaters). UltraStar would cover its expenses for Virtual Ticket (which often saw a one or two-man video production team on the road) and the website service and then do a revenue share of the remaining profit with the band.

More importantly Virtual Ticket became UltraStar's Trojan horse in the battle for access to customer information (the same battle would come to divide Ticketmaster and its biggest promoter client). As odd as it may sound, artists were rarely given access to their fans' information — ticketing agents largely won the battle in not sharing it. Now, by entitling *every* customer who bought a ticket during the general on-sale to a Virtual Ticket membership via an opt-in at checkout, UltraStar effectively argued that it needed customers' information to deliver on services they had specifically requested. And just in case a customer missed the opportunity or was unaware they were entitled to access Virtual Ticket, as soon as they walked into the show, signage in the venue and from the stage told them: "Your ticket includes a membership into the fan club, go to Rollingstones.com for details." Once there, they had to create an account that required them to give their email. Now, the next time the Stones toured, they could notify anybody who had accessed Virtual Ticket about the $95 subscription service that entitled them to participate in a presale (along with regular emails about merchandise sales).

"Every subsequent cycle, the Stones do an order of magnitude bigger business, because now you've trained the fans to go to the artist's website," underscores Peryer. "They have some sense of the quality of the tickets they're going to get. It's a known quantity. They've learned new behavior."

As the *40 Licks* tour wound down in 2003, Cohl was so enthused with UltraStar's results — it having created a wide net to effectively capture fans' data while simultaneously driving website traffic — that he bought a majority stake in the company and brought it into his family of businesses.

UltraStar developed a suite of services and products it could roll out in repeated scale. Within the next two years it counted Madonna, Mariah Carey, Sting, Genesis, Gloria Estefan, the Red Hot Chili Peppers, Tim McGraw, Destiny's Child and The Who among its clients. As its synergistic model began to ramp up, particularly for the Stones, the ever-growing fan subscription list created a higher demand for tickets. When the artist came back around after an initial UltraStar rollout, an eight to ten percent presale ticket allotment would only meet a fraction of subscriber requests.

From the time it started until about 2002, UltraStar offered to handle presale/fan club ticketing for clients. It would turn the transaction, pay the promoter and take physical possession of the tickets to mail out or distribute at the venue. When the company wasn't handling the ticketing transaction itself — many of UltraStar's clients handled their own ticketing — it would work with several ticketing companies like MusicToday, Next Ticketing and eTix.

Peryer says that eventually companies like MusicToday, echo, SparkArt and Artist Arena became competition. "At some point we started to look at the food on each other's plates," he says. "They said, 'Why should [UltraStar] be doing fan clubs when we have all this great infrastructure and technology?' And we said, 'We can put fifteen hippies around a card table and mail tickets just as well as they can' — and we started to."

However, time and again ticketing proved to be a headache. "The whole thing about receiving tickets and then mailing them back out was really a drag," recalls Peryer. "Wiring money to promoters and chasing down invoices, that was just not fun, and there are companies that I think have gotten really good at it, God bless them, but that was really never our core business."

Simply put, UltraStar did not like dealing with ticketing. "While we knew it was important to our business," Peryer says, "we always operated under this idea [that] as long as the fan clubs are dependent on ticketing, we don't control our own destiny."

UltraStar in turn tried to create a more valuable fan club and subscription service experiences for users, primarily focusing on original content and exclusive merchandise. The company needed a reason for people to keep coming back, even if tickets weren't being offered. "I live in reality — I know it was about the tickets — but we really tried to build toward this future where it would be about content and about artist subscription services," says Peryer.

As the Stones began to ramp up for the *Bigger Bang* tour that would begin in August 2005, Cohl tasked UltraStar with two simple directives: significantly grow the business from the *40 Licks* tour and do not have a U2-like ticketing snafu.

In late January U2 had done an Internet presale for its forthcoming Vertigo tour. The band's longtime fan club, Propaganda, had recently merged with U2.com, and now all members, who paid an annual $40 subscription fee, got early access to tickets.

U2.com, which was run by Signatures Network, randomly issued codes for the presale instead of ranking fan club members' access to tickets based on length of membership. So now for $40 anybody — including what turned out to be a large amount of scalpers who registered a number of times with a variety of names and credit cards — had an early shot at good tickets. When the sale went live on January 25, many longtime fans were shut out and loudly complained when they saw tickets being sold for many times over face value on eBay shortly after.

The band's drummer, Larry Mullen Jr., posted an open letter to fans on the website a week later, admitting that "some of it was beyond our control, but some of it wasn't." "Many people who joined U2.com and didn't get tickets are understandably angry," he went on. "They now have the option to get a full refund of their subscription fee. The idea that our long-time U2 fans and scalpers competed for U2 tickets through our own website is appalling to me. I want to apologize to you who have suffered that. If your U2.com presale experience has left you disappointed, I hope this will go some way towards reassuring you of our total commitment to our audience." He apologized again later that month on national television during the Grammy Awards.

In short Cohl's request amounted to finding a way to effectively deliver a higher volume of presale tickets to subscribers. Whatever happened, the Rolling Stones certainly did not need a PR fiasco like U2. Peryer recalls putting Cohl's directives on a white board in UltraStar's office and the team ruminating about how to accomplish them. When the basic answers presented themselves — "Let's stay as far away from the ticket transaction as possible [to avoid a U2-like situation], and let's get access to as much inventory as possible" — one clear solution presented itself: strike a deal with Ticketmaster and other ticketers to keep all of the presale tickets on their platforms.

"We had a meeting out at Ticketmaster," recounts Peryer, "and they painted this picture for us about how they could help us with the ticketing and help us sell fan club memberships. Part of the offer was, 'Go to RollingStones.com, pay your membership fee, get your ticket link and code, and go to Ticketmaster.' Conversely, you could go to Ticketmaster.com, search for Rolling Stones, and you'd see that there was a fan club–only presale. Instead of sending you back to us to join and then have us send you back to them, they would say, 'You can come into this presale and we're going to stick this membership fee onto your ticket price. Then in a day or two or three, you're going to get an email about how to enter the website and take advantage of your fan club.' It exploded the business. The Stones did an order of magnitude over what they did the first time around, and that really became UltraStar's model."

Specifically, Ticketmaster developed functionality for the *Bigger Bang* tour that allowed anyone to participate in the presale by allowing prospective fan club members to see the actual seats they were going to get as part of the fan club prior to purchasing. So Joe Smith logs on to Ticketmaster for the "presale," sees that he can get two tickets in Section 123, Row E, which is pretty close to the stage with a good view, and then buys the tickets for face value plus the $95 subscription fee.

"Ticketmaster really started to provide tangible services to us: email marketing about the fan club presales, banner ads on the Ticketmaster website, places to put our copy about our offers," adds Peryer of the more comprehensive ticketing and marketing deal UltraStar struck with the company in 2006, following the *Bigger Bang* deal. "That stuff was substantial, and it grew the business, so once we got out of that mindset of a couple of dollars per ticket and ticket fee and thought about, 'We need early access to tickets; the more tickets we can sell, the better,' it was really an inflection point for our business."

UltraStar clients, such as The Who, Sting, Counting Crows and the Red Hot Chili Peppers, were being allocated anywhere from fifteen to thirty percent of the house if they agreed to keep the tickets on the primary platform, whether it be Ticketmaster or another company like Tickets.com. Meanwhile, most artists who sold tickets directly to fans were allocated ten percent or less of the total allotment from Ticketmaster.

Peryer acknowledges that UltraStar gained a reputation in the artist community for being somewhat corporate, that the rap against them was, "We love you guys, but you're kind of the man." His response is pragmatic: "When you sit on the business side and you get the results and you see, 'Oh, a fan club might sell this many memberships when we do ticketing ourselves,' and it sells an order of magnitude higher [with a company like Ticketmaster], you have to really be attached to your worldview to not try it." Or, put in more blunt terms, says Peryer, "I don't want to have to call up any artist and say, 'For an ideological reason, we chose to make you less money.'"

This is where bands like the String Cheese Incident, Dave Matthews Band or any number of popular country artists differ from the likes of the Rolling Stones, Madonna or The Who. For largely ideological reasons they have chosen to keep ticket prices comparatively low, whether by asking for less of a guarantee from the promoter or by leveraging mass popularity to cap service fees at a lower price than average.

Artists help determine their ticket price based on the guarantee they're asking for; service fees are directly scaled to ticket price. While no artist can do away with service fees — those that disappear, as with some Eagles shows, are simply charged on the "inside" of the overall ticket — artists can absolutely affect what a service fee will be. Moreover, some of the most popular artists will often tack on additional money to the service fees so as to lower the promoter's guarantee while keeping their desired take at a premium.

As for UltraStar's impact — Peryer is reluctant to use the term "legacy" for fear of coming across self-important — he says that the company tried to make its services about more than just tickets. "I would like to think — and let other people tell me I'm full of shit — that we worked hard to expand the idea of what the artist subscription club could be," he says, reflecting on his decade-long tenure with the company, which he left in 2008.

Perhaps of more significance was how UltraStar helped position Ticketmaster for the future. "I think we played a big role in Ticketmaster being embraced as an artist services platform," suggests Peryer. "They would have gotten there but as the largest artist website company — that had the roster we had — we embraced their model. I think that was helpful."

Just what a ticketing agent and a promoter did had been shifting since the late 1990s. Their traditional roles had been expanding into each other's as each sought to increase artist awareness with the hopes of driving ticket sales. This happened at the same time as revenue streams from record labels began to quickly dry up in the face of Internet-driven music piracy.

When Clear Channel Communications entered the game, its diversified media platforms held the potential of bringing in a new era of how music could be consumed and promoted. But achieving that, as the multi-billion dollar company would soon find, was going to prove easier said than done.

WHEN CLEAR CHANNEL CLOSED ON the all-stock SFX deal on August 1, 2000, SFX's stock was valued at $45.11 per share, nearly twenty percent higher than what it had been trading at. The previous year SFX had generated $1.7 billion in revenues, an eighty-nine percent increase from the previous year, but still lost $69 million.

Brian Becker's marching orders as CEO were rather daunting. "We were expected to operate profitably as opposed to when SFX was really in building mode," he says. "We were part of a larger company as opposed to a stand-alone, so we had a whole different set of criteria related to the use of capital and the margins that we were expected to generate because we had to compete effectively with the other divisions within [Clear Channel] for the whole company to benefit." Carrying more than a billion dollars in debt made profitability a tall order; the economic crash that occurred in the fall of 2000 made it an impossible order.

At the time of the purchase announcement Clear Channel's stock was trading at all-time highs, at one point hitting $95.50 per share in January (it had opened at $4.60 per share in 1993). As chairman and CEO, Lowry Mays had provided his stockholders with an annual average return of sixty-four percent over the previous decade. Clear Channel also completed its acquisition of broadcaster AMFM Inc. on August 30 for approximately $23.5 billion.[4]

Almost immediately the following month, Clear Channel's stock took a massive hit, dropping from $83 per share to $63. The stock, along with nearly every other radio and media company, continued to plummet as the market reacted to fears of a steep advertising downturn. By September 2001, in the weeks following the September 11 terrorist attacks, the stock fell to $35. Even as it began to climb back in 2002, trading at just over $50 in the first quarter, Clear Channel was hit with a one-time charge of $17 billion to comply with an accounting rules change. To say the company was hemorrhaging money is an understatement; that it survived at all is rather remarkable.

In December 2000, six months into his tenure as CEO of SFX — the company would change the name to Clear Channel Entertainment in 2001 — Becker reflected on how the company was adjusting. "SFX was formed by aggregating a number of different businesses around certain key strategies, and to that extent we are the same company," he offered. "The difference is now we are very focused on taking the assets we have accumulated and organizing them in a way to yield the profits we expect."

Becker and Clear Channel found themselves stymied in their ability to execute on some of their synergistic goals. "We never really generated as efficient a use of media as I hoped we would have," he confesses now. "I think the reason was because the company had to be very clear that we were minding our manners when it came to that. People would accuse us of acting inappropriately because of our size, and we'd think to ourselves, 'God, if they only knew [how conservative we've actually been].'"

In theory some of the synergy would work like this: Billy Joel is coming to a town where Clear Channel owns half the billboards and radio stations (the situation in nearly all major cities in the country). For no incremental cost it can spread the word to the general public about the concert via billboards and radio, which, in theory, attracts more people and results in a higher percentage of tickets being sold, which results in cash flowing to the bottom line without the company having spent anything. On top of that, if, as with the SFX model, Clear Channel aggregates Billy Joel's audience across the country as he plays all their venues, it could then sell his audience to a potential sponsor and include within the package radio and billboard advertising, never mind the ancillary revenues from concessions.

"I think the thing they failed most at wasn't so much the core business," says New York–based promoter John Scher. "Like Bob [Sillerman] they kept overpaying and overpaying, but they failed to really create any real synergy between [the entertainment division] and the radio side or, for that matter, their outdoor side."

Steve Martin, North American president of The Agency Group, which represents 700-plus bands, got into the business in 1979 and has worked for a variety of agencies over the years. He saw one of Clear Channel's "massive failures" was its inability to put together any marketing plans involving radio, even on the simplest of levels. "We had this artist called the Funk Brothers," he offers as an example. "I went to Rick Franks, who was the head of Clear Channel [Midwest] at the time, and said, 'Listen, this is great. You own a bunch of classic soul stations. Let's make this your classic soul summer show.' He said, 'This makes perfect sense. We should be able to do fifteen of these around the country.' They couldn't deliver one and were incredibly frustrated. They had no influence of connectivity to the radio side."

Despite its (seeming) lack of execution, Clear Channel was still pilloried by the press with its scathing coverage of the company, primarily attacking its radio division for what it said was abusive and homogenizing behavior. In a high-profile series of articles penned by Eric Boehlert for *Salon*, beginning in the spring of 2001, the company was accused of cutting DJ staff in favor of cost-saving automation, shrinking playlists and bullying smaller competitors, among other actions.

One of the most damning charges — and one that the company was never found guilty of — was its leveraging of radio airplay to force artists into Clear Channel-owned tours and venues. (It successfully settled out of court with Colorado-based promoter Nobody In Particular Presents in 2003 over abuse stemming from its vertical concentration of assets.)

After eight long months, the Future of Music Coalition, a governmental lobbying group, submitted a 150-page report during congressional hearings over rising concerns of radio consolidation in 2003. (The hearings were spearheaded by Senator John McCain.)

A 2003 *Fortune* profile of Clear Channel didn't help matters, though the notoriously press-adverse company agreed to interviews with the specific aim of bettering its image.

In the feature's opening paragraph, Lowry Mays is quoted as saying: "If anyone said we were in the radio business, it wouldn't be someone from our company. We're not in the business of providing news and information.

We're not in the business of providing well-researched music. We're simply in the business of selling our customers products." He was quoted elsewhere at the time as saying, "Clear Channel is in the business of selling Fords, burgers and toothpaste."

While they made for seemingly shocking sound bites that were held up by critics as proof of the company's evil ways, they ultimately weren't all that out of step with what SFX Entertainment had planned to do since its inception. Live concerts were ends to the means of creating a new, viable medium for advertisers. Mays was just being blunt. It was no mystery that the majority of media survived off advertising revenue.

"There were a lot of efforts at synergy, a lot of which were successful, some of which were not, primarily because the environment got to be very difficult," says Becker, who served as CEO of Clear Channel's entertainment division from 2000 to 2005. "Environmental difficulties" is his polite way of acknowledging the anti–Clear Channel backlash that the company had to navigate, whether it was congressional inquiries into media consolidation, damaging press, inner industry fights or consumer frustration at higher ticket prices.

When Becker began his tenure with Clear Channel, he was confident that the company could overcome the "noisy environment" and succeed. "I didn't mind being unabashed about saying, 'We're here to grow and to make a profit,'" he says. "And it was always, 'You're monopolistic, you're pushing your weight around, you're harmful to the environment.' Those were the things we had to address, and I never felt uncomfortable doing it."

To that end, "because of the noise of the industry," Becker says the company couldn't do some of the things he thought they should have, despite being perfectly legal. "We just had to be too sensitive of those things." Asked for specifics, he cites national advertising rate deals as one example.

In 2004 the company's entertainment division posted revenues of $2.75 billion but was making no money because of its debt. Shortly after posting a fifty-nine percent companywide drop in earnings during the first quarter of 2005, Clear Channel Communications announced it was spinning off its entertainment division into a separately traded company.

While its outdoor, radio and television divisions were embattled, its entertainment division remained the redheaded stepchild of the portfolio. The concert business's nature — quarterly earnings varying greatly as artist guarantees were often paid far in advance of the actual concerts, when the promoter would recoup its money; projections thrown off by delayed tours; weather-based factors; the perpetually high cash flow with perpetually low margins — didn't sit well with a company that was economically conservative.

"I believe the thinking was that the entertainment business was really distinctive from the advertising-driven media business of Clear Channel Communications — radio, outdoor, television," says Becker, who stepped down as CEO with the transition. "Live entertainment was different — not better, not worse — but different than the nature of the business of the media properties. Nonetheless one had to understand that Clear Channel Communications was overwhelmingly an advertising-driven media business, so I think it was eventually determined that there was just not enough synergy there, or there was financial conflict."

Even Cohl distanced himself once the company seemed to lose its course. "I love Brian, but I didn't visit with him very much," he says. "We were on different paths, even if it was within the same company."

Clear Channel Entertainment was now estimated to be worth $1.5 to $2 billion, half of what it had been sold for five years earlier. The conversation within the industry about Clear Channel had become riddled with skepticism that it would ever turn a profit. If it was using its size and power to secure tours, where were the ancillary revenues and sponsorship dollars? If it was bleeding money, then why was it still overpaying artists?

As the decade grew older, questions of the kind only grew louder. In response, how Clear Channel Entertainment and its exclusive ticketing partner, Ticketmaster, did business — with and without each other — was about to change.

The concert-going experience, with increased ticket prices and ever-growing service fees, needed help with its image. Ticketing — at the core of it all — was about to get a facelift.

e-Ticket

TICKETMASTER CEO FRED ROSEN WAS itchy to unlock the company's net worth. In the late summer to early fall of 1992, he approached Jay Pritzker and suggested two options to him: take the company public or sell it. Pritzker, Rosen says, was against taking it public but was open to selling it. They hired an investment banker to assess the company's value and shop it. Within thirty days there were three bids for $200 million cash. Pritzker had a stipulation — he wanted a price that was the equivalent of tax-free.

"It became an odyssey of trying to get an equity deal with a company," recalls Rosen. "There was never a question of *if* we were going to sell it; it was a function of price. Jay asked me to let him negotiate the price. This was the one thing in eleven years he wanted to do, and considering that he was the best on the planet to do it — and my interest was the same as his — whatever he got was to the benefit of all us."

The process turned out to be a protracted one. Ten months in and entertaining offers from Time Warner, QVC and Kohlberg Kravis Roberts, Microsoft cofounder Paul Allen entered the conversation around June 1993.

Tom Lasley was a Ticketmaster licensee in Oregon who handled, among other things, ticketing for the Portland Trailblazers NBA basketball team, which Allen owned. When Lasley heard through the grapevine that Ticketmaster was potentially up for sale, he got in touch with Trailblazers president Marshall Glickman to see if Allen might be interested. Glickman called him back and said Allen wanted to buy it.

"Fred came to me and said, 'Who's Paul Allen?'" says Lasley now with a laugh. "The next thing he said to me was, 'It's not going to go to Paul Allen because it's going to Time Warner.' I said, 'I think it's going to Paul Allen.'"

Since Rosen had taken the reins in 1982, Ticketmaster had grown tenfold. By 1993 it was moving sixty-one million tickets annually for 2,500 clients in forty states, plus Canada, Europe and Australia, generating $1.3 billion in revenue. Outlets were moving tickets more efficiently and accurately than ever before, while call centers had revolutionized ticket distribution. Ticketing had come a long way from the days when hard tickets were dropped at various record shops or department stores. And driving it all, of course, was a network of rapidly advancing computer technology.

At the time Allen was worth more than $3 billion in Microsoft stock alone. He was also invested in America Online and Egghead Inc. and owned the Trailblazers. While the Hyatt-owning Pritzkers had enjoyed watching Ticketmaster grow to dominate the ticketing industry, they had nowhere near the technological prowess of someone like Allen.

Negotiations with Allen went on for several months until an agreement was reached wherein he would pay approximately $240 million for eighty percent of the company. "Ticketmaster is an important vehicle for the informational and technological highway of the future, and complements my existing suite of technology companies," Allen said after the acquisition.

It's easy to understand Ticketmaster's skeptics, who had a tough time accepting that the company only netted about $9 million in profit for 1992 and 1993 combined, according to its congressional testimony at the Pearl Jam hearing, when someone with the business acumen of Allen was willing to make that substantial an investment.

Rosen, for his part, thought it was perhaps time to move on, despite the fact he would be given the same authority as he had under the Pritzkers. Allen made him an offer that Rosen resoundingly rejected and countered with an offer that even Pritzker characterized as "crazy." Time passed before Pritzker told Allen, "I wouldn't pay it, but the only one who knows where everything is in this business is Fred, so I don't know what to tell you." Rosen eventually signed a five-year, $20-million contract.

"The contract itself gave me total freedom to run the business, and that was key to me," says Rosen. "Paul ultimately had just one thing, which was selling tickets online and using the Web more often." That one thing would ultimately come to drive eighty percent of the company's business.

"Nothing happened to cause people to sit up and say, 'Oh my God, we've got to jump into this business,'" recalls Alan Citron of Ticketmaster's slow entrance onto the Internet. "My main role there was pushing like a crazy person — and I mean that literally — to get this thing started, to convince people it was a good idea and that we had a reasonable chance of getting it right."

In early 1995 Rosen hired Citron as Ticketmaster's vice president of media ventures. At the time Citron was a business editor for the *Los Angeles Times*, where he'd worked since 1982. The son of a journalist, he'd moved from New Orleans to California and worked his way through the ranks, starting as an entertainment writer and then working as an entertainment editor before sliding over to the business section. He credits a young business reporter named Amy Harmon for turning him on to the Internet.

"She started talking about the Internet before it had really become something everyone was reading about, and because of her stressing what a big deal it was going to be, I started paying attention to it," says Citron, who went on to work for Real Networks and TMZ.com and is currently president of online social media portal Buzz Media. "It was the first thing since journalism that really appealed to me."

Out of the blue, Citron says, Rosen called him one day looking for someone to help with Ticketmaster's public relations as the Pearl Jam–Justice Department investigation was reaching its pinnacle. Citron told Rosen he wasn't interested; he was looking to break into the Internet. Rosen made him a deal: if Citron helped with the PR, he could start Ticketmaster's Internet site.

Ticketmaster launched its website in two phases. The first premiered in June 1995 and was simply a searchable database of events that the company was responsible for selling tickets to. The second phase, launched September 11, 1996, was transactional.

"In those days no one had any real Internet credentials," offers Citron. "So the single biggest benefit to us was Paul Allen owned Ticketmaster, and he happened to have a technology group that was able to help us figure this out. He basically had to connect the Ticketmaster system to the Internet in such a way that would work for an interface."

While Rosen was, by several accounts, somewhere between indifferent and nervous regarding Ticketmaster's efforts to launch a transactional website, he allowed it to follow course.

"I don't think Fred hesitated over anything other than it wasn't his world," suggests Citron. "He wasn't someone who was spending a great deal of time on the Internet — like most people [at the time] — and his business was perfectly fine. He had no real compelling reason to jump on it and, inarguably, he had a reason not to because of the security concerns." Again, remember, this is 1996. The Internet was still the Wild West.

Rosen defends his hesitancy similarly: "My level of concern was cleaning up the mess if there was one. I was concerned about being hacked. I was careful about recognizing the role Ticketmaster played with its clients and that you had to protect their interests. None of them wanted to be a guinea pig. That was the feeling underneath all of this and was the reason for my conservatism. I knew that once we turned the switches we would be profitable from day one."

"We tried to be extremely cautious with regard to ensuring that whatever we launched worked," Citron continues. "There was this joke that would go around the office that you don't want to find out that, for the first on-sale that occurs on the Internet, some kid named Skippy has gotten hold of all the tickets. That was always the threat hanging in the air. So we had to make sure this thing could not be hacked."

Ticketmaster soft-launched its transactional site in two cities, Seattle and Portland, Allen's hometowns. On the day the site went live, Allen, Rosen, Citron and others gathered to watch the first purchase. And then it appeared: one ticket to a Seattle Mariners game. The group decided to place a call to its first online purchaser.

"We hope you don't mind us calling, but you're our first buyer."

Silence.

"We would just like to know why you chose the Internet site."

The group waited with bated breath.

"Because I don't like talking to people, and I don't like talking to you."

Click.

Despite this lukewarm reception to its e-commerce debut, Allen's investment, along with Time Warner and QVC's interest, signaled a shift in how the market was valuating and, more importantly, thinking about Ticketmaster. While QVC lost this round, the man behind the effort would be back with a renewed sense of vigor four years later. And this time he would get what he was after.

BARRY DILLER BEGAN HIS PROFESSIONAL career, as many have, in the mailroom at the William Morris Agency in the early 1960s, having dropped out of UCLA after one semester. His fellow mailmen at the time included David Geffen, who would go on to form Asylum Records and eventually Geffen Records before partnering in DreamWorks, and Elliot Roberts, who would manage Neil Young and others. While Geffen had to forge proof that he was a college graduate, one of the company's requirements, Diller got in through a family connection. The two became lifelong friends.

In 1968, at the age of twenty-six, Diller had become the ABC network's programming chief. He was promoted to vice president of development the next year and pioneered the made-for-television movie model.

At thirty-two he became chairman and CEO of Paramount Pictures Corporation, where he would remain for the next decade. During his tenure the company was responsible for such hit television shows as *Laverne & Shirley*, *Taxi* and *Cheers*. Its movies were some of the biggest of the 1970s and 1980s: *Saturday Night Fever*, *Grease*, *Raiders of the Lost Ark*, *Terms of Endearment* and *Beverly Hills Cop*.

At Paramount he relied on a team nicknamed the Killer Dillers, all of whom would go on to become powerful players: Michael Eisner (eventual chairman and CEO of the Walt Disney Company), Jeffrey Katzenberg (principal of DreamWorks SKG with Geffen), Dawn Steel (head of Columbia Pictures) and Garth Ancier (president of BBC America), among others.

Steel, who tragically passed away from a brain tumor at the age of fifty-one, said of Diller in her book *They Can Kill You but They Can't Eat You*: "In the flesh, he was power incarnate. . . . He handled power differently than anybody I'd ever known, in this very complex, sexual way."

Diller left Paramount in 1984 to become chairman and CEO of Fox, the parent company of 20th Century Fox and Fox Broadcasting, and created television's fourth major network alongside NBC, ABC and CBS. It was under Diller that shows like *The Simpsons* and *Married... with Children* began their meteoric rise. He left in 1992. Having been number two his whole life to moguls like Martin Davis and Rupert Murdoch, Diller wanted to be his own boss.

Diller had dated fashion designer Diane von Furstenberg in the mid-1970s, when he was in Los Angeles. "I was twenty-eight and he was thirty-three," she recalls. "We were both kind of famous. He was a tycoon and I was a little tycooness." They broke up after six years but remained close friends, never more, it seems, than after he left Fox. "I thought, 'This is the dumbest thing I've ever done in my life,'" says Diller now of his decision to leave the company. "It was, like, what the hell am I going to do? Because I didn't have an idea in my head."

So it was in 1992 that Diller, searching for his next venture, found himself in a car with von Furstenberg heading to Westchester, Pennsylvania, having agreed to accompany her to the television home-shopping network QVC (one may recall Albert Leffler and his wife finding inspiration as a result of a ride in an automobile as well). She was there to sell women's tops that were wraps, fashion items that eventually morphed into her now-famous wrap dress design. Diller watched as von Furstenberg sold 29,000 items to 19,000 customers in less than two hours for $1.2 million.

While the wraps were a hit, it was what Diller saw in QVC's overall operations that proved most rewarding (not unlike Sillerman's epiphany at Disney World). "I was struck," he says simply. "I'd never seen a television set used that way. All I'd known from television screens is telling stories."

Specifically, he "saw this interactivity, this primitive interactivity, and this mix of computers and televisions and phones. . . . This seized my curiosity."

The two headed back to the city with new visions. "We got lost because we were, like, so excited, talking about this entire new world that we had just experienced," says von Furstenberg with a laugh and a smile. "It was incredible."

QVC, a publicly traded company, had two key owners. One was Liberty Media, a piece of cable magnate John Malone's empire that was led by his Tele-Communications Inc. (TCI). Two decades after it launched in 1973, TCI had a $1.6 billion cash flow and had acquired, invested in or become a partner in about 650 companies, among those Rupert Murdoch's News Corporation, Ted Turner's Turner Broadcasting System, Bill Gates' Microsoft and AT&T. Malone's reputation as one of the smartest people in the telecommunications business seems well earned, based on his educational background. He was a Phi Beta Kappa and a merit scholar at Yale, where he got a BS in electrical engineering and economics in 1963; the next year he earned a master's in industrial management from Johns Hopkins; three years later, in 1967, he completed a doctorate in operations research from Johns Hopkins. Malone has been called "the Darth Vader of cable" and, in the words of former vice president Al Gore, the head of "the cable Cosa Nostra."

The other QVC owner was Comcast Corp., led by Brian Roberts, who would ultimately come to thwart Diller's attempts at expansion. "In my opinion Dr. Malone is the smartest businessman I've ever met," says Roberts, whose company also owns the Philadelphia Flyers and 76ers along with several arenas. The two brought Diller on board to revamp the network. If anybody could, they thought, he could.

"They said I'd lost my mind," says Diller of people's reaction to his decision to leave the Hollywood hustle for a suburban home shopping network. Here was a mogul who was used to traveling in his own plane who was now, rather suddenly, taking the train to work in the middle of winter. It was quite a change. However, the fifty-one-year-old's track record indicated there was a method to the madness. He made rapid improvements to QVC, recasting the network's image in a significantly hipper light by bringing in celebrities and selling higher-end merchandise. As von Furstenberg says, "Barry can see something way before you can see anything." QVC's stock rose almost immediately upon his arrival, although due to conflicts with Roberts, he departed in 1994.

AS 1997 ROLLED AROUND, DILLER again had his sights set on a familiar prize: Ticketmaster. Only four years earlier Diller had lost QVC's bid for the company to Paul Allen, who had purchased an eighty percent stake. Now Diller, thanks to Malone, was the head of the Home Shopping Network, QVC's biggest rival. The numbers being thrown around for Ticketmaster seemed a trifle compared with the deals Diller had been trying to broker since.

Behind the scenes Allen had become entirely fed up with Rosen, who was showing the owner a minimum of respect and running the company as if it were his own. It was no longer fun for Allen.

Former Ticketmaster COO Tim Wood recalls hearing stories of how "Fred was giving [Paul] such a hard time." And it was rather by chance, in a separate deal, that Allen found a remedy to his situation. "Paul had done a deal for DreamWorks," says Woods. "He was talking to David Geffen and said, 'I've got this great company, but the guy running it drives me crazy.' [Geffen] said, 'I know a guy who can help you — Barry Diller. You need a barracuda.'"

One former Ticketmaster executive thinks that Rosen "really blew it," feeling that "had Fred played his cards right, he could have been Paul's right-hand guy and used Paul's money to propel him to the next level. But Fred never wanted to see himself as working for someone else. He had to be in charge."

Armed with the Home Shopping Network and having witnessed the power of order-by-phone and foreseeing the future of the Internet, Diller the predatory animal could feel "the wind at the back of electronic commerce." That May HSN bought a 47.5 percent stake from Allen in the now publicly traded Ticketmaster for $209 million worth of HSN stock.

By July Diller had bought enough Ticketmaster stock on the open market to gain control of the company with 50.1 percent.

"Barry, at the time, was trying to get a meaningful foothold in the Internet space, and it wasn't easy," says Citron. "Back then Internet valuations were out of sight. I think in that regard, Ticketmaster was probably a good deal because you could buy the company and the Internet site came with it, but the Internet site wasn't driving the valuation like a pure play."

October saw HSN offer Ticketmaster somewhere between $297.2 and $340 million for the rest of its stock. Rosen and others rejected the bid and forced the issue into a Chicago court (the Pritzkers' home turf) in a class action lawsuit that alleged the transaction was bad for shareholders.

"Each of us had a role," said Rosen at the time of his negotiations with Diller. "His role was to buy the company and do the best job he could for his shareholders. I had a job to do and [did] the best job for my shareholders. Obviously that led to some differences of opinion."

By March 1998 Diller had sweetened the stock swap to a value of roughly $400 million, valuating the ticketing giant at approximately $900 million. Ticketmaster agreed. Just five years earlier the entire company had been worth $340 million. With Diller now in charge, Rosen thought it time to start making his way toward the exit.

"I was ambivalent," Rosen suggests now. "Some of [Ticketmaster] was very good, but I had been doing it for sixteen years. When Barry came, we had some candid conversations. Notwithstanding whatever you read, Barry wanted me to stay and I didn't want to stay. When he came to buy the rest of the company, my argument with Barry was never about control; it was about price."

Citron agrees with Diller's wanting Rosen to stay but disagrees otherwise: "Barry would have preferred for him to stay, but the clash was that Fred has to be in charge. Fred isn't the kind of guy who's going to work for anyone — I don't think — so the idea of Fred taking orders from Barry was preposterous to anyone who knew Fred."

Rosen was interviewed by conservative newsman Neil Cavuto on Fox News as his tenure at Ticketmaster was coming to a final close in the spring of 1998. Much had been made of Rosen's leaving, and Cavuto asked him pointedly about Diller.

"Do you like him?"

"I think he's a smart guy," Rosen responded tersely.

"I didn't ask you that. Do you like him?" countered Cavuto.

"I think that's irrelevant," shot back Rosen. "At the end of the day, whether he likes me or I like him is not what this issue should be."

Rosen had tried to assume the same role in leading the company as he had had under Allen but was met with a new reality. "He tried like hell to maintain his role with Diller," says one former Ticketmaster executive. "He walked in and metaphorically punched him in the nose. But Diller had been the head of a studio. He'd seen this personality before. So he did what drove Fred crazy — he ignored him."

Gene Cobuzzi, who worked for Ticketmaster beginning in 1985 and was Ticketmaster's COO prior to Tim Wood, shares a similar sentiment about the change in atmosphere under Diller. "I used to go to [Diller's] Tuesday afternoon meetings with all his CEOs and COOs of all his companies, and those were very interesting," he says. "Those were just two totally different cultures. Barry was business 24/7, so you always had to be on your toes from a business standpoint, but at the same point I made a lot of money from Barry, so I don't have anything bad to say. It was just a different way of doing business."

Even before Rosen left in late spring, the landscape was already rapidly changing around Ticketmaster.

DILLER'S VISION WAS BECOMING CLEAR: he wanted to create a twenty-first century media company with an integrated portfolio that leveraged the Internet. Just months earlier the Home Shopping Network had bought Universal Studios, Inc. from Edgar Bronfman Jr.'s Seagram for just over $4 billion.[1] The main asset in the purchase was the USA television network. Upon regulatory approval HSN merged with USA Networks (so it was technically the latter that purchased the rest of Ticketmaster, not HSN). Since its nationwide launch in November 1996, Ticketmaster's online sales had risen steadily from a monthly average of $100,000 to $9 million, which now represented five percent of the company's overall business.

In the merger process Citron became president and COO of Ticketmaster Multimedia as well as president of USA Networks Interactive. He recalls meeting Diller at the mogul's home in Los Angeles' Coldwater Canyon. Diller's office there was accessed by a long set of stairs behind the house. "I took my marching orders as, number one, to keep growing Ticketmaster online and improving it and, number two, to look for opportunities to improve the Internet services of other companies under the USA Networks umbrella."

Ticketing, up until the Internet, was largely locally focused, given the emphasis on outlets. While the advent of phones opened up easier ways for people to access tickets in other parts of the country, the technology was designed primarily around the notion of convenience. Moreover, Ticketmaster was still set up as eleven separate, regional companies around the country — meaning that the Northwest office couldn't pull tickets for a show in the Southeast. If a customer in Seattle wanted tickets for an event in New York, they needed to call the Northeast number (though, on occasion, outside area codes were blocked from purchasing tickets for high demand shows in an effort to thwart scalpers). Now, with a transactional website, a customer had a one-stop portal: all 30,000 listings for Ticketmaster's 3,750 clients.

"When it was just a phone and outlet business, everything tended to be geared toward the local customer," recalls Citron. "That made the most economic sense. But the Internet allows you to break down those barriers and offer everyone access to everything. So now it's not just about what's playing in your city. If you're traveling, you can look up what's available at your destination." It was simultaneously local and national (just as Ticketron and Computicket had been in the 1960s, although the Web made this much more cost-effective and consumers now had many more event options).

Citron recalls a fortuitous phone call from Diller. "He said, 'I need to meet more people in the Internet space. Who do you think I should meet?'" Suddenly blanking, Citron scrambled for an answer. "I really couldn't think of anyone, but I didn't want to sound stupid," he says, laughing. "In those days I still had a desk calendar with the pages you'd turn each day and looked down at it, and I was scheduled to have lunch with Charles Conn, who ran

Citysearch. It was the only name I saw, so I just blurted out, 'What about Charles Conn? He's interesting.' Next thing I knew, Barry was investing in Citysearch."

CITYSEARCH LAUNCHED ITS INITIAL WEBSITE for the Raleigh–Durham–Chapel Hill metropolitan area in May 1996. Founded by Conn and Thomas McInerney, it soon proceeded with its Web-based CityGuides for Austin, Baltimore, Dallas, Los Angeles, Nashville, New York City, Portland, Salt Lake City, San Diego, San Francisco and Washington, DC, in addition to international cities like Copenhagen, Melbourne, Stockholm, Sydney and Toronto. It typically partnered with a city's local newspaper such as the *Los Angeles Times* or the *Dallas Morning News* in creating comprehensive listings of classified ads, events, businesses and services.

Other Internet properties focused on the local delivery space were Digital City, Sidewalk and Zip2, in addition to city directories provided by Lycos, Excite and Yahoo. In 1998 Citysearch and Zip2 announced plans to merge in an attempt to battle Microsoft's Sidewalk, which at the time was regarded as nearly unstoppable. At the eleventh hour the merger fell apart, and Citysearch made plans to have its own IPO in June. Diller, who already owned 11.8 percent of the company as part of USA Networks and was one of the company's directors, had other ideas. "I think possibly the last frontier of size to be organized on the Internet is the local city site," Diller declared at the time. He convinced Citysearch to withdraw its IPO and merge with Ticketmaster that August.

With Rosen's departure and the Citysearch merger complete, Diller's priority was increasing online ticket sales. On paper Citysearch and Ticketmaster were a perfect fit: two companies focused locally on a national level. Ticketing was inherently local and there was a strong belief that Citysearch's local portals could significantly throttle up Ticketmaster's online sales.

"Barry believed in the whole local business, and he may still believe in it, but I believe from Ticketmaster's perspective that was a shotgun marriage," says Citron. "I don't think anyone in Ticketmaster was especially excited about that or thought that we needed it, and it was a total cultural disconnect between Ticketmaster and the Citysearch people.

Terry Barnes, who was Ticketmaster's then-president and had been with the company since 1983, disagreed: "Obviously it's going to help both companies. Not only is this great for both companies, it's great for our clients."

There had always been a sharp line between Ticketmaster's clients (venues and promoters) and consumers, who utilized the company's services on behalf of its clients to acquire tickets. Once the relationship is in place between Ticketmaster and its client, the venue no longer deals with its patrons' ticketing for the most part, save for perhaps its season ticket holders and sporting events. Taken at face value, it's an odd dynamic: the venue you are going to does not provide you with the ticket.

With online ticket sales rising and the playing field leveling for potential competitors, it was time for the world's biggest ticketing agent to reassess how it did business.

JOHN PLEASANTS CAME TO CITYSEARCH in 1996 at the age of twenty-nine, shortly after the website service launched. He had attended Yale for his undergraduate education and Harvard for graduate school, where he received an MBA. After graduate school he moved to Dallas to work for Frito-Lay, serving as a brand and product manager. Though he wasn't particularly enamored with the company's core business, he enriched his business school education with management skills, coordinating efforts across sales, marketing, manufacturing and product development divisions. "Hub of the wagon wheel kind of thing," he says causally from his Bay Area home.

After four years at Frito-Lay Pleasants found himself increasingly drawn to the Internet, wanting to test his skill set in business's new Wild West. After looking at various companies, Pleasants felt that Citysearch was the right place. "I think it was something fairly easy to understand, coming from a consumer background," he says. "It was a direct consumer product online. It was not some kind of web technology. It's something everyone could understand."

Citysearch was taking a familiar consumer experience — looking through a phone book, classifieds or event listings for information — and putting it online. Each city it focused on was proving a financial success. The task as presented to Pleasants was how to replicate the success more quickly and easily on a global level. "How do you create a rollout team in a military-like fashion?" he recounts. "How do you organize people to get results? A lot of that was a challenge. . . . There were a lot of technical things going on but also a lot of business things going on, so I think it was a pretty good entry point to move into the Internet as a non-technologist."

Two years later, in a dot.com-era twist, Diller carved off the online portion of Ticketmaster into a separate, publicly traded company that merged with Citysearch and had an IPO in December 1998. Ticketmaster Corp., which remained part of USA Networks, would be responsible for call centers, outlets and box office sales, while the newly created company was solely responsible for online ticket sales.

"There was a lot of resentment about it," says Citron of the split among longtime company employees. "At the time it was hard to argue with the idea of doing an IPO. The valuations were so crazy, it was like scooping money out by the fistfuls. On the other hand I don't know that structurally it made any sense."

The newly christened Ticketmaster Online–Citysearch (TMCS) had its December IPO at $14 per share, raising $112 million in gross proceeds. Pleasants was named president and Conn CEO. The former Frito-Lay product manager was thirty-one years old.

THE FIRST PHASE OF PLEASANTS' tenure was devoted to infrastructure. "Online ticketing is a very big, complicated thing, so I don't want to sound like I ever 'mastered' online ticketing," says Pleasants today. "I can tell you that the first six to nine months of that was kind of hell on wheels in terms of just trying to build a system that could stabilize and handle the volume and demand that was coming for online ticketing. When we started this thing, online ticketing was something like two percent of total tickets or some-thing — it was a really small deal — and today I think probably over eighty percent of tickets are now sold online. That curve ramped up really fast in years two, three and four [of my tenure]. It went from that single digit up to forty or fifty percent faster than anybody would have anticipated, and that was a serious scaling effort."

This meant completely overhauling the software and technology. "I think it is fair to say that the regime prior to us going in there had, to some signifi-cant degree, kind of starved the technology," says Pleasants.

Based in Phoenix, Ticketmaster's core system was built on a VAX com-puter operating system. And while everyone agrees the system was extremely robust, the fact of the matter was the VAX computers and hardware were becoming rather obsolete (by 2005 all manufacturing of VAX computers had ceased).

Citron thinks that anyone who looked at the Ticketmaster system in those days would have come to two conclusions: one, that "it must have taken mad geniuses to create it" and, two, "you didn't dare touch it. It was completely pasted together with glue and gum, but it worked. It worked incredibly well," he says assuredly.

"If a VAX went down, I don't know where we even got parts for it — it was in that kind of stage — and the whole system was running on that," recalls Pleasants. "[Ticketmaster] had made the decision along the way to maximize the profitability of the company, it would seem, and they were not investing in technology for quite a long time."

Pleasants' EVP of technology operations was Sean Moriarty, who would eventually take over as CEO once Pleasants left in 2005. "From a technology organization perspective, everything has been meaningfully revamped," says

Moriarty today. "The website was very weak, and we spent an awful lot of time between 1999 and 2002 really building out a high-volume transactional e-commerce site because the share shift from the phone and the outlet channels to the Internet was happening very rapidly. The demand on the Internet channel was extraordinary, and Ticketmaster was a company that at the time didn't have Internet DNA."

From 1999 to 2002 the company spent hundreds of millions of dollars in research and development. What consumers see today came from Pleasants' and Moriarty's teams rewriting the website from scratch, building out the data center infrastructure and building an industrial strength e-commerce solution.

"Don't get the wrong impression," says Pleasants. "Ticketmaster still had the most stable ticketing system that was available commercially, but it was not at all equipped to do any of the new things that we wanted to do." Pleasants estimates that his TMCS team, which inherited six or seven people from Ticketmaster, eventually grew to more than 300 people in those initial two years.

"Chapter one was, 'How fast could we set up systems and drive online ticketing?'" says Pleasants. "We were not that entwined with Ticketmaster, the company that existed for twenty or twenty-five years. We were coordinated. We would coordinate our on-sales, there was lots of operational back and forth, but it wasn't particularly strategic back and forth because we were so busy trying to drive online ticket percentages north."

Citron saw the TM and TMCS split purely as a way to exploit the highly lucrative IPO offerings at the time. "There was never any apparent need for Ticketmaster to have a relationship with a company like Citysearch, and I don't think in reality Ticketmaster ever did that much for Citysearch either."

There was increasing tension between Ticketmaster's two companies over how on-sales should be handled given that, while separate companies, they were both accessing the same ticket inventory. At issue was transaction speed: phone and outlet sales were slower than Internet sales, and as such Ticketmaster argued that TMCS's online sales should be handicapped so that all transaction speeds took roughly the same amount of time.

"I was a big believer that it should just be a complete meritocracy; wherever the population was is where the tickets should be sold," says Pleasants. "My point was, 'You can't even see the demand online. Even if you're only selling twenty percent of your tickets online, you may have had an extra five million people that couldn't get through.' You have more people with computer access than would be on the phone, so we're actually serving people online less well than we are on the phone, even though there's people backed up on the phone. That was kind of a hard thing for people to get their mind around."

Citron thinks that "Pleasants did the best job of all the Citysearch guys of respecting the Ticketmaster culture and learning to peacefully coexist with it." Beyond that, Citron says, everyone followed orders because "Barry thought it was a good idea and we thought Barry was really smart."

Whereas Rosen had, by several accounts, known the names of nearly everyone who worked for Ticketmaster, the new regime and setup was less familial. "You felt like Fred really understood who worked for the company," recalls Oregon-based Ticketmaster licensee Tom Lasley. "We were used to the way Fred ran big company meetings," he says, "where he would stand out in the middle and look at people, talk about them and ask them what they thought." For Lasley the difference between the two cultures couldn't have been clearer than at one of the early meetings under Pleasants that saw the young CEO reading all his remarks from a teleprompter.

Unfazed by any old-guard resentment, the pros typically outweighed the cons for Pleasants when a company broke itself apart so that the individual pieces could focus on specific tasks. "People can't change from inside the system," he offers. "When you break something up, you get much more focus. You get a group of people who are singularly focused on driving a thing, and in this case it was driving online ticketing."

RATHER THAN BREAKING THINGS UP, Dan Afrasiabi and Thomas Gimple began their path to online ticketing by putting things together. Starting in 1996, the pair purchased a dozen companies in the ticketing space over the next two years. Their efforts culminated with the acquisition of Tickets. com, which finally placed its nascent company on the Web. It was a fine match, they joked, because Tickets.com was "a great ticketing company, except they have no tickets."

Afrasiabi put it all in motion shortly after graduating from the University of Southern California's Marshall School of Business. The first deal presented to him, after he moved to a venture capital firm, involved Hill Arts and Entertainment Systems, a ticketing software company out of Guilford, Connecticut. Founded by a former Yale drama school student, Lawrence Schwartz, the company had a client base that included the Kennedy Center, a number of London theaters and Boston promoter Don Law's Next Ticketing. Intrigued by the company's inability to turn a significant profit, Afrasiabi raised a million dollars to purchase it, with the intent of taking Hill Arts (which by then had renamed itself Entertainment Express) from a software licensing business to a ticketing services business.

Afrasiabi soon enlisted fellow USC Trojan Thomas Gimple, and the pair began contacting the Hill Arts customers, hoping to roll up the licensees. They were moderately successful, although they never could convince Don Law to sell, a wise move from his perspective as Next Ticketing became one of his chips in the $90 million sale of his company to SFX in July 1998 (despite the fact that Next Ticketing was still powered by Hill Arts software). In the midst of this Afrasiabi and Gimple found another small software company, Advantix, with a similar variety of clients and made another purchase (and then took on its name as well). A wild spree of simultaneously raising money and then spending it on ticketing businesses followed, with twelve companies swallowed up in the span of twenty-four months. (This included a small Florida ticketing firm coveted by Michael Jackson; however, the entertainer eventually agreed to back off and instead invest in the ever-growing parent company after it made the purchase.) Advantix's largest acquisition came in September 1997 when it bought BASS, which was still running on the Ticketmaster system (this drove a permanent wedge between Fred Rosen and his former partners, BASS founders Hal Silen and Jerry Seltzer).

Advantix foundered a bit because, in its haste to add pieces to the portfolio, it was supporting multiple software applications. Not only did this not allow the company to cut costs, but as Afrasiabi and Gimple aspired to land larger deals, it limited the development of a single, scalable platform. Afrasiabi has described BASS's decision to push away from Ticketmaster as "gutsy," and this proved to be all too true. Doug Levinson, who was then serving as BASS president, states: "We never should have sold the company to them. They weren't ready for us. All of their clients we talked to said it worked fine, but once we went into a live environment, it was crashing and we never seemed to be able to get around and fix it." Afrasiabi acknowledges: "Our guys totally underestimated what it was going to take to convert off the Ticketmaster software. It might have been old and rudimentary, but that was because it worked. There's a saying in software: old code is stable code, and we never really appreciated the scale in taking our application from Hill Arts and putting the BASS volume on top of it. That was weeks and months of pain."

Meanwhile the pace of acquisitions continued at the behest of the Advantix investors. As Jane Kleinberger, cofounder of Paciolan, another target during this period, recalls: "It was clearly an arbitrage concept. 'Let's roll them all up and we'll have mass and might.' That's pretty much what they were pitching."

Two years in, it became apparent that some means was needed to unify all of the platforms, so that Advantix could become something more than a collector of boutique software companies.

"That's when I had this epiphany," Afrasiabi recalls, "that what we had to do was consolidate all the inventory that we'd accumulated on the back end into a branded front end. By this point the word 'portal' had become huge, and portals were getting massive valuations, so I said, 'We have to become the ticket portal.' But the only way we can do it is have a branded front end."

To achieve this goal, with the active support of General Atlantic, the private equity firm that served as lead investor, Afrasiabi approached Jim Caccavo and Tickets.com. Caccavo's company had developed at Idealab, the same business incubator where Citysearch had originated before it was sold to IAC. Tickets.com positioned itself as an information hub, designed to aggregate ticketing event content, allowing consumers to click through and make purchases from either primary or secondary sellers, while Tickets.com collected a commission. However, despite its Idealab pedigree, the Tickets.com business model had yet to prove itself, and the company was perhaps best known for purchasing the national toll-free number 1-800-TICKETS for $1 million in cash plus stock.

The Advantix–Tickets.com merger was announced in late January 1999, with the blended company now branded as Tickets.com, Inc. Gimple remained president and CEO, Caccavo became president of Internet operations and Afrasiabi served as executive vice president of business development.

"In retrospect it's laughable, but overnight it made us an Internet company," Afrasiabi says with a chuckle. "This was the time when you'd announce you had a website and your stock would go up fifty percent. We had approached Morgan Stanley about a strategic round [of financing], and we were talking to AOL, who said, 'We're interested in buying you, but we're not going to do anything over $400 million.' This is when we're probably doing $40 million in revenues and losing $8, $9, $10 million per year. At the same time Morgan Stanley made an introduction to Excite@Home, and George Bell, their CEO, said, 'Why would you want to sell to AOL at a $400 million valuation? We'll invest $40 or $50 million at a $900 million valuation. Take the money and go public.'" This is precisely what Tickets.com did in November 1999, benefiting from the swelling mania for Internet stocks.

PHASE TWO OF PLEASANTS' TENURE was marked by a fundamental change in company philosophy. Whereas Fred Rosen had designed Ticketmaster to be a client-facing company directed toward buildings and promoters, Pleasants took a different approach in his aim to make it a consumer-facing company.

"Fred didn't pay any attention to the company's image. He'd be the first to admit that," says Citron, who served as chairman of TMCS. "Ticketmaster was always set up to get in front of the ticketing issue on behalf of the clients, so it didn't really ever make sense for Ticketmaster to go out and promote itself. It was really there to facilitate the interests of the clients."

With the advent of Internet ticketing, however, clients' interests were changing. While rebates were a given from any ticketing company, venues and promoters were now asking about the quality of the customer experience. Basic logic said that a better transactional experience meant that customers were more likely to return to purchase another ticket. Now, with the core system overhauled, Pleasants set about changing Ticketmaster's consumer experience (though he unequivocally credits Rosen with building "a monster machine of inventory and contracts" that allowed all of this to occur in the first place).

"Everyone still to this day thinks Ticketmaster is monopolistic, or they think it's rigged and everyone's stealing the best tickets," he says. "People get very passionate about this, and they get pretty pissed off, and we really put a premium on, 'We want to be known as a really high-quality service, period, full stop.'" Out of what he describes as hundreds of changes, Pleasants gives three examples off the cuff.

Pleasants explains that he increased the number of full-time customer service employees because call and wait times for phone orders had become increasingly long. "The [prior] philosophy was, and there's some logic to this, but the philosophy was, 'Hey, listen, we're going to sell the tickets anyhow. Why do we care if somebody has to wait on the phone?'" recounts Pleasants. "In a world where Ticketmaster becomes a consumer-facing brand, I thought it was really important for people to have a high regard for that, because eventually your clients are going to take a lot of flak. A consumer can't distinguish between Madison Square Garden and the ticket that they want to get to Madison Square Garden, which is being run by a vendor called Ticketmaster."

In response the company hired approximately fifty percent of its 2,000-person part-time customer service division full-time. It built additional call centers to bring its total to sixteen nationwide and made an effort to train its representatives to answer customer questions versus simply reading generic scripts. While there were still disgruntled customers, the overall experience seemed significantly improved if only for shorter wait times. Pleasants also curbed things like up-selling on phone orders that were typically variations of, "Would you like a subscription to *Sports Illustrated* with your ticket purchase?"

And for the first time — *the first time* — Ticketmaster began leveraging its mammoth database to proactively contact customers about upcoming events they might be interested in attending, based on their previous purchases. (Pleasants estimates that today the company's email database is well over fifty million.) Armed with its newfangled Ticket Alert email system, Ticketmaster could now offer a clear solution for clients to the industry's age-old problem: the biggest reason people don't go to a concert or event is that they simply don't know about it.

"If you sell two percent more tickets in a year for a building, literally, it just dwarfs any amount of economics that might have been negotiated in what the revenue splits are on convenience charges and things like that," says Pleasants. "It's a really big deal because that money is going to the venue and to the artist. These are the kind of things where it's like, 'Well, how are you going to get someone to give you their email?' You'd better give them a lot of value. The whole ticketing experience has to be clean. It has to be transparent."

It was again a very clear split from the old ways of doing things at Ticketmaster. Pleasants and his MBA-educated staff were a different breed from Rosen's scrappy clan. The primary focus on general consumers versus specific clients had a few industry veterans feeling déjà vu. Recalls a former executive, "One of the major people at Ticketmaster said to me at the time, 'Can you believe we haven't called a client in the past three or four years?' I said, 'Welcome to Ticketron.'"

IN MAY 2000 DILLER AGAIN reshuffled TMCS's top ranks. The changes included moving Conn into a largely honorary role as chairman of the board and naming Pleasants, thirty-three years old, as CEO of TMCS, a company now generating half a billion dollars in revenue. Diller, by his nature, was forever trying to fine-tune the company to greater success and fluidity, whether on a micro or a macro level.

"Barry gets involved in details. That's just who he is," says Pleasants. "Would Barry want to get involved and talk about the color of a logo and how it looked? Yes, Barry will do that, because if it's something he cares about, he's going to get involved in what a lot of people would say are minutiae details. On the same hand, did he give me, as the CEO of the company, a lot of responsibility and autonomy? Yeah, he did."

Citron, who had left USA Interactive by this point, says much the same of Diller: "Even though he was a monumental pain in the ass, I respected how hard he worked. I respected how much he sweated the details because I've known a lot of guys who reached his level who started to pull back and were more like absentee landlords. He was the furthest thing from that."

Former Ticketmaster COO Tim Wood says that when Diller took over, he gave employees stock incentives, but they were based on nearly unattainable goals. "It was a game where you hold it just out of reach and tell people to keep jumping," he recounts. Simply put, says Wood, "Barry is not a nice guy, but he's a straightforward guy. He says, 'If you produce, I'll take care of you; if you don't, I'll fire you.'"

In the fall of 2000 USA Networks, the largest shareholder of TMCS at forty-nine percent, announced that it was considering a merger with

Ticketmaster in an attempt to streamline the businesses that were separated two years earlier.

Following its IPO, TMCS's numbers had skyrocketed. Quarterly revenues were up an average of 294 percent from 1998 to 1999, with the company generating more than $440 million in gross sales and taking in $105.3 million in revenue. It had sold ten million tickets online. By 2000 the numbers had practically doubled: $864 million in gross sales, $220.6 million in revenue and nineteen million tickets sold. Despite the impressive numbers, TMCS stock began suffering from the Internet bubble beginning to fully burst. The stock, which had traded as high as $56.38, giving the company a $3.9 billion market cap, was now $9.50.

The reunification of the two halves commenced in November 2000: TMCS was buying the controlling interest in Ticketmaster Corp., a wholly owned, private subsidiary of the publicly traded USA Networks, for $653 million in stock, upping Diller's share holdings to sixty-eight percent of the new company, which would now simply be called Ticketmaster.

All in all, the spin-off and spin-in of TMCS was a rather tenacious move on Diller's part. Spinning off TMCS and raising money from its IPO had allowed him, over the previous two years, to significantly expand his Internet portfolio through a steady stream of acquisitions that all fell under the TMCS umbrella, including Match.com, the One and Only Network, MSN Sidewalk and Hotel Reservations Network (soon to be Hotels.com). It was the earliest incarnation of what is now known as Diller's InterActiveCorp (IAC).

"I didn't get the sense at that time that any of these properties necessarily had anything to do with each other," Citron says. "There was no conversation along the lines of, 'This fits with that, that fits with the other thing.' It felt more like assets Barry thought were interesting on their own."

Citron recalls weekly senior staff meetings that were done via video conferencing. "Listening to the head of USA Networks talk about a negotiation over a TV show, there was sort of a running disconnect," he says. "A lot of this didn't mean anything, so Barry tried to get everyone together and get a sense of community. But we were all in such different businesses that it was awkward."

Diller soon added several more e-commerce sites to his portfolio: Firstauction.com, Firstjewelry.com, Styleclick.com and Fashiontrip.com, NASCAR.com and Sportsline.com, among others. The one acquisition that did work across several properties was the phone call handler Precision Response Corporation, which was purchased for $608 million in USA Networks stock. Merged with HSN and Ticketmaster's call centers, it created a worldwide network of forty call centers capable of handling 160 million calls via 10,000 work stations. By 2000 USA Networks' revenue increased to

$4.6 billion from the previous year's $3.36 billion, though its net loss grew to $148 million.

When Ticketmaster was reunified — "once separated at birth in order to grow the online business, now properly joined with one word: ticketing," said Diller at the time — each lost about half its work force as the businesses were finely streamlined. The now-singular company had a renewed focus on technology as well.

"We had better technology. We really invested in redoing the ticketing system," recalls Pleasants, who was now CEO of the rejoined Ticketmaster. "We had a great core ticketing system, but there was a lot of legacy technology — we had to modularly build around it and put in all the bells and whistles that would enable somebody to really maximize their business, then train our people how to sell that in the face of all kinds of new competition that were coming up with new business models. That was the big achievement of chapter two."

In March 2001 Ticketmaster struck a strategic partnership with AOL, in which Citysearch guides would now offer AOL Moviefone in exchange for the creation of "AOL Box Office by Ticketmaster." It also bought online activity planner Evite.com. At the time Pleasants said: "The combination of Evite.com and Ticketmaster results in a convenient way for users to obtain information about, and access to, events and to take action by inviting others, making reservations or purchasing tickets. It's a perfect fit!" Today, he's less sanguine about it and other synergistic hopes with ticketing.

"I don't want to sound overly dismissive, but all that stuff, at the end of the day, was secondary or tertiary to what happened at Ticketmaster," he says. "Many of those companies, we ended up doing great things with. Match.com went from less than $20 million in revenue to $300 million. These are huge Internet success stories, but the idea that there was this great bouillabaisse, that everything was going to be cross-selling each other and somehow we were going to be selling piles more tickets because people were going to go on dates, and they were going to be buying tickets and Evite-ing each other about tickets, and they were going to see venues on Citysearch and click through and get tickets. There was going to be this great rising tide that basically never occurred — it occurred maybe to the tune of one, two, three, four percent more ticket sales."

Ticketmaster's annual numbers were continuing to climb. In 2001 total company revenues were up to $675.2 million from $606.2 million with 32.1 percent of its 86.7 million tickets sold online. Pleasants declared that by the end of 2002 the company's aim was to sell at least forty-five percent of its tickets online. He got close — the company averaged forty-one percent for the year.

Concurrent with the company's shift to greater Internet sales was another round of software and hardware upgrades to the core ticketing system. From 2003 to 2005 Moriarty, along with a core of Ticketmaster engineers whom he repeatedly credits as some of the best in the business, moved the ticketing system, component by component, off a proprietary operating system that had been running on the VAX machines and over to a Linux-based one utilizing Intel hardware without a loss of functionality during the migration.

With the improvements Ticketmaster began offering a greater array of Web-based tools for its clients: reporting and analytics, group sales and email campaign management, among others. Moriarty, who oversaw many of the technology upgrades, is clear about those impacts: "What was once an inventory management system with phone and outlet retail sales capability became an inventory management system with multi-channel retail capability, including the Internet, and a suite of products for Ticketmaster's clients to understand their business and market to their consumers using the Web." When Moriarty arrived at the company, he estimates that there were perhaps three or four client products. There are now two dozen.

"When you ask, 'How did you get your arms around this thing?' that was really a two-year push, and I think we were really successful at that. It was one of the things that really worked well," says Pleasants. Ticketmaster posted $655.2 million in revenue for 2002.

As the calendar turned over to 2003, USA Interactive (previously known as USA, Inc.), bought the remaining shares of Ticketmaster and spun it back in. It was now a private subsidiary of a publicly held company (Diller also bought the remaining shares of Hotels.com in June and spun it back in). In bolstering the company, Diller once again reorganized his top ranks: Pleasants became president, information and services; Thomas McInerney, president, electronic retailing; and Anne Busquet, president, travel services.

"Now that USA has 10 principal operating businesses, with offices in 196 cities and 26 countries with 26,000 employees, we felt it was more than past time to organize our operations with strong leaders for each of our business lines," said Diller. "We have a very demanding agenda to become the largest and most profitable interactive commerce company and the only way it will move forward is if we can execute effectively."

"As a public company, it was a great run," says Pleasants of TMCS's being publicly traded from 1999 to 2003, during which the company met or exceeded its numbers every year. "The hardest thing about Ticketmaster being public was that our numbers were exposed. So we were in a business where we're negotiating with very major clients for our deals, and when clients can see how much money you're making and they look at their own situation, they see that they're not making as much in profit margin. It makes the negotiations much more intense.

"On the flip side the company was always kind of public in that the major shareholder, what is now IAC and at the time was USA Networks, was a public company, and my board of directors didn't change between when it was private and when it was public. So if Barry wanted profit out of the company, I would have that same tension and dynamic when we were 'private' and owned by a public company versus 'public' with our own ticker symbol."

IT CAN SAFELY BE SAID that Tickets.com did not enjoy a great run as a public company. The Internet bubble burst in March, exposing many businesses that were burning through cash without any foreseeable means to turn an immediate profit. To avoid being delisted from the NASDAQ market, because its stock price had fallen well below $1 per share, Tickets.com shareholders approved an eight-for-one reverse stock split on July 23, 2001.

Meanwhile Ticketmaster was doing whatever it could to facilitate Tickets.com's downfall. Back in the fall of 1998 when SFX and Ticketmaster had gone to the mat over contract renewal, Dan Afrasiabi believed that he had scored the ultimate coup in securing a nationwide deal with the promoter. "I was in Hawaii when they called me and said, 'We want you in New York.' It was our second day in Hawaii, and I told my wife, 'We have to go.' Tom and I went to New York and sat for five or six straight days in a beautiful boardroom two floors above General Atlantic, our main shareholder, while we negotiated the deal of a lifetime. I would have bet my life it was a done deal. In retrospect they were probably playing us the entire time. When I left New York, they said, 'Fantastic! We're going to circulate this, we're going to get approval and we'll get this signed next week.' But next week never came." Ticketmaster, led by Cobuzzi, had hammered out a deal at the eleventh hour with SFX that saw the ticketing giant giving up fifty percent of its service charge to the promoter.

In June 2000 Afrasiabi was again beckoned to New York. This time Major League Baseball Advanced Media (the new entity created by Major League Baseball to handle all online matters) was interested in striking a deal to grant exclusive rights for Internet ticketing. "I was so paranoid the same thing was going to happen with MLB [as what happened with SFX and Ticketmaster]. They called me at my house on a Friday and said, 'Can you be in New York this weekend?' We didn't leave until we nailed it down and they announced it." This agreement, which MLBAM pursued after negotiations with Ticketmaster had fallen apart over the company's insistence on strict terms in its own favor, ultimately proved to be Tickets.com's saving grace.

Relations between the two competitors remained tense as in July 1999 Ticketmaster filed a lawsuit, charging that Tickets.com's practice of "deep linking" to event pages on the Ticketmaster website, bypassing the front page and establishing direct hyperlinks to sales pages, violated copyright and was an act of unfair competition. In effect Ticketmaster was suing Tickets.com for sending it free business. Ticketmaster wanted to engage customers on its own terms through its front page (an issue that would recur in 2007). The court refused to grant a preliminary injunction on the copyright issue, and although the lawsuit lingered for a few years, Ticketmaster never received a definitive judicial pronouncement in its favor. (In July 2001 Tickets.com, which was then focusing on its own inventory, stopped the practice.)

By the year 2000 both companies also began sniffing around TicketWeb. The company, which defined itself as "the Online Ticketing Alternative," was founded in 1995 by Rick Tyler, a twenty-nine-year-old Berkeley, California–based software engineer, whose impetus to leave his job with a telecommunications company and begin a start-up out of his home was frustration with a $17 ticket that came with a $4 service fee. In January 1996, a few weeks after TicketWeb's launch, he explained quite presciently: "It really struck me that this would be a natural application of the Web technology. It's really a no-brainer." Tyler set his fees at fifty cents per ticket plus five percent of face value, with a two dollar cap, securing deals with two local Bay Area clubs, the Bottom of the Hill and Blue Vision.

TicketWeb's founder soon partnered with Andrew Dreskin, who spearheaded the company's business development. As Dreskin remembers: "From the first minute I met Rick and he explained the architecture of the Ticketweb software that he was writing, the lightbulb went off. You didn't have to be a genius to figure out that the idea of a box office on every desktop in the world, whether you're a ticket seller or a consumer, was hugely powerful. When we first started, we were extremely naïve, and I'm not even sure that our service fees covered our credit card processing costs. We knew we were on to something; we just didn't know where it would go. It's like when you're driving and it's foggy and you can only see twenty feet in front of you. That's how it was in the early days of TicketWeb."

By January 2000 TicketWeb boasted more than 500 clients on three continents, including the Louvre, Six Flags Amusement Parks, the Guggenheim Museum and the San Francisco Symphony. Both Tickets.com and Ticketmaster saw the value in acquiring the company, which nonetheless revealed it was "an estimated eighteen months away from profitability." Ticketmaster, in something of a preemptive strike, prevailed in May as TicketWeb changed hands for $35.2 million. (The company retained its autonomy in many respects as a low-cost alternative for smaller venues and clients outside the rock world. Dreskin would go on to launch a new ticketing company, Ticketfly, along similar lines as the original TicketWeb, in 2008).

Meanwhile Tickets.com found itself increasingly hamstrung as it attempted to expand its client base. Afrasiabi contends: "We discovered that Ticketmaster would leverage one part of its presence to get a deal somewhere else. I had to go to war with them over the Concord Amphitheatre. Ticketmaster did everything in its power to destroy us. Concord had a long-time relationship with us but was owned by BGP, which was owned by SFX, and they went behind the scenes and said, 'We're not going to bring concerts in if we don't get the deal.' In other cases, in order to win a contract, they threatened to cut off rebates in another city that a promoter might also be working in. We just couldn't compete."

Ultimately Tickets.com came to the conclusion that its only recourse was to strike back in a legal forum, accusing Ticketmaster of antitrust violations, in a countersuit to Ticketmaster's original "deep linking" case. The judge recommended mediation, at which point Barry Diller put out a call to Fred Rosen, asking him to work on Ticketmaster's behalf. A meeting one evening in early 2003 at a Long Beach restaurant yielded little more than bluster (although at one point Rosen and Afrasiabi went toe-to-toe after the latter delivered what Rosen viewed as an ad hominem attack), and the two sides prepared for a court battle. Afrasiabi recalls, "Just before responses were due, our law firm blew up and filed for bankruptcy." Nonetheless, papers were filed, and on the merits of the case as presented, the judge ruled in favor of Ticketmaster.[2] Tickets.com had exhausted millions of dollars in legal fees at a time when its stock was delisted from the NASDAQ because it lacked tangible net assets of $4 million.

But for the baseball deal the company likely would have shut down. Two years later, in the face of this imminent possibility, MLBAM purchased Tickets.com.

MARCH 1, 2003, WAS A RECORD DAY for Ticketmaster: 1.1 million tickets sold online with another 600,000 sold through venue box office and phone. "The incredible demand we experienced on Saturday validates the strength of Ticketmaster's state-of-the-art technology and gives us a good indication that we are off to a very strong summer season," said co-chairman Terry Barnes.

"The one thing that people didn't understand that they probably won't for several years is the capability of the TM engineering group at its core was extraordinarily good, absolutely up there with the very, very best in global e-commerce," underscores Sean Moriarty. "The things that TM did — managing high volume on-sales, its queue management, its email campaign infrastructure, its active database replication across data centers — many of those things were actually e-commerce firsts."

While Pleasants acknowledges the ingenuity of the company's tech operations, he also credits the company's core business for its e-commerce success: "Ticketmaster is a ticketing company, and ticketing was a killer application for the Internet. It's just that simple.

"I wasn't surprised that [our online ticket sales] got over fifty percent [of our total tickets]. I'm surprised it got to seventy-five percent in less than five years. It's probably the fastest moving category online of any migration that I know of. Books aren't sold seventy-five percent online, right? Airline tickets . . . Go through all the categories; I don't think anything is as high as online ticketing." Indeed online ticket sales tripled in three years, from representing less than ten percent of the company's total tickets sold in 1998 to more than thirty percent in 2001. By 2003 it was over fifty percent; by 2008 it hovered around seventy-five percent.

To that end Ticketmaster saw its revenues and profits continue to steadily climb under Pleasants as its e-commerce services were fully throttled. He estimates that its profits went from approximately $60–$75 million in 1999 (from roughly $440 million in revenue) to around $250 million when he left in 2005 (from $950 million in revenue).

While Ticketmaster's profits continued to go up, there was already a looming storm on the horizon: the Clear Channel Entertainment contract. As the nation's — and by that time the world's — largest promoter, Clear Channel had inherited SFX's exclusive domestic contract with Ticketmaster when it bought the company in 2001. The contract was due to expire in 2008. As Internet and software technology rapidly improved, it made the cost of entry for new ticketing companies significantly easier than just a few short years before. Ticketmaster now had real competition when it came to technology, though clearly it outmatched any in regard to prospective customer databases and the amount of money it could advance against projected rebates.

"I can't remember what percent it was, but [Clear Channel] probably represented fifteen to eighteen percent of Ticketmaster's total tickets, I'm guessing," recalls Pleasants. "There was no one as big as that. The next one was high single digits. That's a big deal; you lose a big client." Years before the contract came up, he says, there was significant friction between the two companies in their jockeying for what would happen when it did.

In preparation Ticketmaster began looking for new revenue streams and, ultimately, a way to reposition itself in the concert industry's value chain. After battling a little band from Colorado with a funny name over its ability to sell tickets directly to its fans, the future of Ticketmaster's ability to stay at the top was clear: it needed to deal directly with artists.

IT IS ONE OF THE more memorable band names to have ever made head-lines: the String Cheese Incident.

Formed in 1993, the quintet of Colorado ski bums combined the broad stroke sounds of bluegrass, rock, reggae and jazz into a heady musical brew all their own. Guitarist Bill Nershi and mandolinist Michael Kang got their start busking on ski slopes alongside long chairlift lines. Soon adding bassist Keith Moseley and drummer Michael Travis, followed by keyboardist Kyle Hollingsworth, the band became a staple of the après-ski party circuit.

By 1996 the band's popularity had begun to expand outside Colorado as their concerts, or "incidents," attracted fans of the Grateful Dead, Phish and Widespread Panic with their unique setlists and heavy amount of improvisa-tion.

At the same time, across the country in Athens, Georgia, Mike Luba and Nadia Prescher had started a boutique booking agency called Madison House. Luba had entered into the business booking bands while attending Emory University and upon graduation had taken a job with Jack Boyle's Cellar Door Productions in Virginia as a booking agent focused on the col-lege circuit. Prescher, who was a talent buyer at the Patio and Ludlow's in Columbus, Ohio, was one of the few to regularly take the young book-er's calls. When both needed a change, the two launched Madison House out of a spare bedroom in Luba's then-girlfriend Mary Armstrong's house (Armstrong, at the time, was helping manage Widespread Panic).

"Anytime we tried to farm anything out to anybody else or tried to work with other people, it would get totally fucked up," recalls Luba of his and Prescher's impetus to start Madison House. "We realized that we could fuck it up just as good ourselves and at least be accountable and hopefully put some mechanisms in place to fix things when they got screwed up."

One of Madison House's first artists was Keller Williams, a singer-songwriter with an affinity for humorous songs, dexterous guitar playing and the Grateful Dead. And it was Williams who one day played a live recording of the String Cheese Incident covering Aerosmith's "Walk This Way" at the Telluride Bluegrass Festival for the budding business duo. "You can literally hear 10,000 people gasping in horror," laughs Luba now, "and that was when we took over as their managers that the whole thing ramped up."

The "whole thing" included moving Madison House to Boulder to be closer to String Cheese and, more importantly, over the next five years building a multifaceted company that combined the elements of management, agency, ticketing, record label, merchandise and travel services into one.

"From there I'd like to claim it was part of some genius plan or that we really had an endgame in sight, but it was really out of self-defense and default that we ended up doing everything," says Luba of Madison House's growing responsibilities for String Cheese's 200-plus shows a year.

By 1998, there were only three bands that had substantial, direct-to-fan ticketing offerings reaching above the typical eight to ten percent allotment: Phish, Dave Matthews Band and the various projects from the remaining members of the Grateful Dead. No other bands — *in any genre* — were doing this. The Grateful Dead's 1991 victory over Ticketmaster emboldened these three to pursue similar fan club ticketing requests for fifty percent of any given show's ticket allotment to sell directly to fans.

"It was management coming to us and saying, 'Hey, look at what Ticketmaster is doing as far as charges and processing fees,'" recalls String Cheese Incident bassist Keith Moseley. "Everyone was pretty fed up with it, and we were looking for a way to provide fans the service without having to pay the exorbitant fees."

While not a Deadhead, though he quickly points out his wife Kristen was a veteran of mail-ordering for their concerts, Moseley feels that String Cheese's ticketing initiatives were indeed born from the Grateful Dead's DIY approach. "We were going to do it our way," he says. "We were not necessarily going to jump through all the hoops that we're supposed to. We're going to forge ahead and create our own path. And I think we had a lot of kinship with the [Grateful Dead] model." String Cheese, however, took its offerings one step further: online.

Led by Jason Mastrine, Madison House and the band financially backed the launch of a new company called SCI Ticketing in December 1998. Two years earlier Mastrine had finished a master's degree in environmental geochemistry at the University of Alabama and moved to Boulder to pursue consulting work. While he was getting his master's, Mastrine was also a DJ on WVUA in Tuscaloosa and had crossed paths with Madison House through interviewing their clients like Edwin McCain and Hootie and the Blowfish. Growing weary of stale consulting jobs, Mastrine approached Madison House about job opportunities when he heard the company was moving its operations to Boulder. Mastrine's first task was shepherding the band's volunteer "Pirate" program before eventually shifting into ticketing and merchandise.

SCI Ticketing was first run on the TicketWeb platform. Launched in 1995 by Rick Tyler (who soon partnered with entrepreneur Andrew Dreskin), TicketWeb was designed to empower venues that wanted to do their own ticketing and didn't want or feel the need to go with a massive company like Ticketmaster. Remotely hosted, it was one of the first Application Service Providers (ASPs) with its ability to turn any PC into a fully functioning box office, complete with call center.

"TicketWeb was willing to help us find a solution that matched what our needs were, which, in short, meant a fully private label experience that matched the look and feel of the new SCI Ticketing," says Mastrine, who now heads a boutique ticketing company called Dais Limited. "But ultimately where they failed was infrastructure. Time again, each tour we put on sale, there was a different set of problems."

Luba recalls a period of time when the system wouldn't survive past the first five seconds of on-sale. "Every time we tried to go on sale, it would blow up the system, and this was a reoccurring theme for years with us," he says. While the band was doing all this with fan-friendly intentions — lower service charges, better seats — Luba acknowledges that it was a "testament to patience and incredible compassion that the fans kept coming back after continually getting dicked."

In June 2000 Ticketmaster bought TicketWeb for $35.2 million worth of Ticketmaster Online-Citysearch stock. While having some reservations, SCI Ticketing was hopeful that with a more robust back end the ticketing snafus would subside. The TicketWeb partnership was a cost-effective solution for a self-sustaining company like SCI Ticketing that was only taking fifty percent of the reduced service charges (TicketWeb took the other half) and didn't have to worry about hardware and infrastructure costs.

"We figured at that point if we were sleeping with the enemy, we might as well commit to them and see if they could kick down some resources that could actually provide us with a solution," says Mastrine. The on-sales, however, continued to be plagued by problems. "[Ticketmaster] seemed like they were willing, but that solution didn't work, and we never really felt like we could trust them to help us do the right thing." Frustration and concerns mounted.

Whereas the Phish and Dead-related fan club ticketing operations were strictly mail-order, and Dave Matthews Band was online with fans needing to pay for a registered password and log-in, String Cheese was offering tickets online to the general public via the Web with zero barriers to entry besides a ticket cap. The one caveat that made it feasible for String Cheese to even attempt this was that all shows were general admission and had one ticket price (versus a reserved seating show with multiple price points).

"We finally felt like we had hit a wall," says Luba of 2001's early ticketing mishaps. "We really, truly had — the band, us, the ticketing guys — the 'come to Jesus' moment where we said, 'If we can't get it right, we've got to stop abusing people like this because we can only push it so far.'" After much discussion it was decided matters needed to be taken into their own hands. "We saw the opportunity to not only offer this to Madison House artists but to go beyond," says Mastrine. In August 2001 SCI Ticketing licensed software from the Australian company Softix/Ticketek and built its own ticketing platform to the tune of $250,000 (Softix was founded by Bruce Baumgart, the computer programmer who helped get BASS off the ground in the early 1970s).[1] The first on-sale for the new system was set for September 11.

"We did this crazy load testing of the new system," recalls Luba. "As we were coming up on the actual on-sale, it got to the point where eight or ten of us hadn't slept in a week, and we realized that to run the final test, we were going to run out of time. Two hours before we were supposed to go on sale, I get a call from my brother saying, 'You've got to turn on the TV set. You're not going to believe what the fuck is going on.' It was like, literally, the world had stopped. I don't want to overdramatize it, but in a very strange twist, if that had not happened, we would have gone on sale, and there's a good chance it may not have worked, and that would have been the end of it. We ended up pushing it three days, and those extra three days enabled us to get it to work seamlessly, and the rest is history."

EVEN BEFORE SWITCHING TO THE new ticketing platform, SCI Ticketing began running into ticket allotment issues as the band mounted its 2001 summer tour, primarily at Clear Channel–owned amphitheaters where Ticketmaster had exclusive ticketing rights. Though SCI Ticketing was technically a Ticketmaster client via TicketWeb, Luba and Prescher were facing periodic obstacles from promoters and venues.

To briefly recap . . . A promoter buys the show from the agent, at which point they become responsible for selling the tickets (one of Madison House's unique features was that it acted as both manager and agent). The promoter essentially owns the tickets. Ticketmaster is simply a vehicle to distribute them; however, Ticketmaster's monetarily incentivized contracts with venues and promoters make them the exclusive ticket provider. The majority of Ticketmaster's revenue is derived from service and convenience charges applied to individual tickets and orders. As such, losing half the inventory of a String Cheese Incident concert at an amphitheater represented a tangible loss of revenue. Multiply that by twenty dates and the numbers add up.

Any show String Cheese agreed to play up to that point was predicated on the band's being allowed a percentage of tickets from the promoter — up to fifty percent — to sell through their own ticketing system (same with Phish, Dave Matthews and the Dead camp). Promoters were, by and large, happy to give the band their desired ticket allocation because the group was willing to adjust their artist guarantee accordingly. The pressure point was between Ticketmaster and its exclusive agreements with venues and promoters.

"Because we were so locked with the band, we were able to cut deals where we weren't beating [promoters] up," says Luba. "That's maybe because, unlike other bands that became really, really focused on what the guarantee looked like, we realized that the Ticketmaster rebate is a huge part of the business, and it's how a lot of the promoters stay in business. So if we were suddenly taking half the tickets out of every show, it was a very significant thing, so we had to factor that in when the deals got made. We were willing to do that."

The numbers didn't lie: from 1996 to 2003, the average price of a concert ticket rose by eighty-two percent, well ahead of the Consumer Price Index for that period, which increased by seventeen percent. The increase is reflected in the fact that while fewer concert tickets were being sold — down to 22 million annually from a high of about 30 million throughout most of the 1990s — overall revenues were up. Exacerbating it all was where that money was going. In 1981, for example, the top one percent of artists took in twenty-six percent of domestic concert revenue; by 2003 that one percent was accounting for fifty-six percent of the revenue.

Thus, by keeping their guarantees (and thus their ticket price) reasonable, the end goal for String Cheese was always a full house. "If a venue could move tickets in a way that was different from us, we weren't going to keep them from selling them," says Mastrine. "So, in fact, in most cases maybe our asks were fifty percent for String Cheese, but it didn't mean we always got it. We gave tickets back frequently — and I don't mean the day before the show. We were actively in conversations with the box office managers and buyers, and we got ticket counts every day, just like they got from us."

Up to this point String Cheese was more or less flying under Ticketmaster's radar. As Ticketmaster began exponentially ramping up its Internet presence as a leader of e-commerce under the new Diller regime, it was only a matter of time before it took notice of the latest round of wooly freaks.

"Here we come as a band that's very much in the same genre as the Grateful Dead and Phish," recalls Mastrine of Ticketmaster's general perception of the organization. "It's a glorified mail order — it's just a bunch of hippies in Boulder selling some tickets — it's fine, whatever. But the more they got to understand our business model and saw the way we could move tickets, the more they started to view it as a threat."

When the band made the jump to larger amphitheaters in the summer of 2001, "I think a lot of factors piled on at the same time," recalls Luba of Ticketmaster's sudden crackdown on the band's ticket allotment. "I definitely feel there was a lightbulb moment of, 'Oh, shit! If we let them get away with it, then the floodgates will open for everyone else.'" Adding to the band's frustration was that other bands, particularly Dave Matthews Band as part of the burgeoning MusicToday business, were getting their regular allocations.

CORAN CAPSHAW GOT HIS START in the music business booking bands for fraternities in the late 1970s while attending the University of Virginia as a business student. Capshaw owned two music clubs in Virginia: Trax in Charlottesville, which opened in the early 1980s, and the Flood Zone, which opened in 1986, and also booked bands around town.

In January 1991 he asked local South African musician Dave Matthews to open for the Indigo Girls. By the fall Matthews had developed a full band, which Capshaw began managing under his newly formed Red Light Management and booking into Trax for a weekly Tuesday night residency.

The group released its first album, *Remember Two Things*, in the fall of 1993, followed by its major label debut, *Under the Table and Dreaming*, on RCA in 1994. The same year Capshaw launched Red Light Communications, a local Internet service provider. By the time the band released the highly anticipated *Crash* in April 1996, *Under the Table* had already sold over three million units.

Red Light Communications bought an ISP competitor in 1997 and rolled out the non-transactional DMB.com for the first time. Dave Matthews Band released the critically acclaimed *Before These Crowded Streets* in April 1998, and the following January Capshaw merged Red Light Communications with his traditional merchandise fulfillment operation, MMF, to form

MusicToday. In just a few short years the band became one of the biggest in the country, in terms of both touring and record sales. Its meteoric rise was intimately tied to Capshaw's grassroots, Dead-like vision of organically growing a strong fan base via taper-friendly policies, cool merchandise and direct artist-to-fan ticketing.

"There was an opportunity to embrace a whole new model," says Capshaw of what became of MusicToday's vision as a hub of online fan club ticketing and merchandise. "I thought we could also create a fan club model, which, in the past, had been something that nobody really focused on. So I tied the ticketing to it, and both at once we put everything online."

By 2000 DMB's Warehouse fan club had more than 80,000 members and had collected over $2 million in membership dues the previous year at $30 apiece. Additionally, MusicToday was providing services for forty-five acts, ranging from Santana and Cheap Trick to Tim McGraw and Insane Clown Posse. It would go on to include such artists as Madonna and Britney Spears.

"I guess it was just right place, right time," says Capshaw in his typically understated and reserved manner. "Then we just started doing all these other things for other artists . . . using what we've learned in the trenches to help a wide array of careers in a multitude of genres."

Fan club ticketing became popular across all genres for two ostensible reasons. One, it was a revenue stream for bands. At $30 to $40 per person, per year, the money made was substantial. In 2005, for instance, U2's fan club, run through its website, had roughly 100,000 people paying $40 apiece. The Rolling Stones charged $95 and had even more members.

Two, fan clubs typically aimed to assure that some of the best seats always got into the hands of true fans versus brokers. This was largely accomplished via a "presale." Fan clubs, generally speaking, priced premium seats on par with the cheapest tickets being offered in the public on-sale. Many times this was realized by lower service and convenience charges — whereas Ticketmaster might charge $15, a fan club would charge $4. (Ostensibly there is also a difference between fan club ticketing and what has now become known as VIP ticketing. Artists control both, but fan club tickets are typically just "low cost" good seats, whereas VIP tickets are premium-priced seats with added value, such as merchandise or a meet-and-greet with the band.)

In May 2000 SFX bought a minority stake in MusicToday with a vision of the company building out Web stores for the promoter's myriad of national artist tours and integrating them with its own SFX.com. By 2002, with Dave Matthews Band as one of the largest touring acts in the country and MusicToday rapidly growing, Ticketmaster saw the band's standard fifty percent ticket allocation as a significant threat and a dangerous precedent. Capshaw confirms, "They tried to shut down the artist-to-fan concept."

Like the Grateful Dead before them, Capshaw and DMB had significant bargaining power through their sheer popularity and fan loyalty. And as with the Grateful Dead, Ticketmaster was faced with a rather stark proposition: did the company want service charges from half a venue or none of it, should the band choose to play in a non-Ticketmaster facility? "There was a series of letters they sent to promoters and venues, some back and forth there," says Capshaw rather opaquely. "But we worked it out."

The deal MusicToday struck with Ticketmaster at the time gave it a "favored nation status" and ensured all their fan club clients would get a ten percent ticket allotment to sell through MusicToday's website. In return Ticketmaster got a cut of the already-lowered service charges. (It made further sense given Ticketmaster's exclusive contract with SFX.) However, there were still a few exceptions to the new mandate — the previous fifty percent allotments for DMB, Phish and the Dead, which MusicToday now handled, remained in place.

Phish, in particular, changed the way it did fan club ticketing when it became a MusicToday client. The Vermont-bred quartet began offering tickets directly to its fans via mail order beginning in the fall of 1995 for its Halloween show at the Rosemont Theater in Chicago, under the guidance of Shelly Culbertson. After the band went on a two-year hiatus in 2000 (with a five year stretch to follow starting in 2004), its ticketing process began to change, beginning with lead singer and guitarist Trey Anastasio's solo 2001 summer tour. As opposed to filling out a form by hand, either from the group's newsletter or acquired online, fans now entered an online lottery for tickets.

"At the time it was controversial," recalls Jason Colton, who served as one of the band's managers and continues to work with the group as part of Capshaw's Red Light Management. "A lot of Phish fans were pissed off that basically the barriers to entry to get tickets had been greatly reduced, and all of a sudden any newbie with a browser could have a shot at the same tickets." Relative to the String Cheese Incident, the demand was significantly higher for Phish tickets. The band's management was extremely hesitant to replicate any of the on-sale failures that SCI Ticketing had experienced and found the easiest way to alleviate most potential systemic failure was a lottery route.

"We wanted to go with a lottery system versus a first come, first served system, and the main reason for that was demand on the server," says Colton. "We thought it could potentially be a meltdown and have a really bad customer service experience if it wasn't done in a lottery where we stressed to people, 'Take your time. You can do it anytime within this window.'"

Still, any initial lottery system required a lot of manual input because of the technology it was shoehorning itself into. Colton had been aware of

MusicToday's services but didn't take a deeper look until it successfully handled a ticket lottery for Radiohead's U.S. tour around its *Kid A* and *Amnesiac* albums in the summer of 2001.

"I walked through the Radiohead system a lot," says Colton. "We said, 'Well, we prefer to do it this way. We want it taken that way. We want to rewrite all the language so it's appropriate.' It was just putting it through the Phish filter of how do we create a ticketing experience where fans feel like they were treated properly."

The first tour MusicToday participated in with the Phish camp was in the fall of 2001 for Oysterhead, a power trio project featuring Anastasio, Primus bassist Les Claypool and Police drummer Stewart Copeland. It worked, and by the time Phish came back a year later in the winter of 2002, the new ticketing process had been properly road-tested in anticipation of the higher volume of traffic the reunited band's ticketing demand would bring.

"I think what it comes down to is how many tickets your flagship band is selling for Ticketmaster and for Ticketmaster clients," says Mastrine. "Dave Matthews Band [for instance] was selling quite a few more, orders of magnitude more, than String Cheese Incident was. Ultimately the power of the ticket sale opens you up to higher-level conversations that don't require earning respect because you've earned it."

Ticketmaster's CEO at the time, John Pleasants, says much the same: "Dave Matthews is a big enough and powerful enough band that you start to get into a tug of war," he says of fan club friction with Ticketmaster. "What if Dave Matthews turns around and tells the Pepsi Center, 'Okay, I'm not going to play at the Pepsi Center?' This is the iteration of ticketing and the entertainment business — who has the leverage over who?"

The String Cheese Incident's spring 2002 tour proved to be the tipping point. "There was no doubt we were being singled out," confirms Mastrine of the band's increasing clashes with Ticketmaster.

IN MAY 2002 TICKETMASTER SENT letters to venues and promoters with whom it had exclusive agreements. The letter stated that Ticketmaster would no longer allow them to provide direct artist-to-fan ticketing with the historical allocations that they previously had been given. Only "legitimate" fan clubs would be allowed an allocation, and to qualify as legitimate, four requirements had to be met: (1) members must pay at least $15 per year; (2) no more than four tickets can be purchased by a member for a performance; (3) tickets are not allowed to be resold; and (4) there must be "meaningful" interaction between the band and the fans.

The new requirements didn't sit well with a band like the String Cheese Incident.

"Our argument, in terms of precedent, was that Grateful Dead were able to do it through mail order since the beginning of time," offers Luba. "We would sit in meetings with Terry Barnes, the chairman of Ticketmaster, who is actually a really decent guy, and I would say to him, 'Terry, all we were doing was ripping off the idea the Dead had with mail order. It's just an email order. That's all it is. You already set the precedent. What's the big difference?' That was a very scary argument to them."

Pleasants saw String Cheese as "waving the flag that there's this evil company that won't let us sell our tickets; they're our tickets," he reflects now. "Basically, you're getting at this emotional issue, which is who owns the ticket? The artist thinks they own the ticket, the building thinks they own the ticket and the ticket actually sits in Ticketmaster's system." But the fact remained — and remains — that an artist does not own the tickets inside a venue it's playing.

Riffing, Pleasants throws out a hypothetical example: "String Cheese struck a deal through their promoter to play in the building, and the inventory is owned by the Pepsi Center, and the Pepsi Center has contractually given it to Ticketmaster. [The band] can raise as much hell as they want to [about receiving their desired ticket allotment]. They're just breaking the law when they do it."

Madison House and the String Cheese Incident were offered what was deemed a viable alternative by Ticketmaster and Clear Channel, the ticketer's biggest client and the country's largest promoter. If the band hired Capshaw's MusicToday — which Clear Channel had a financial stake in via its SFX purchase — to handle its artist-to-fan ticketing, the "legitimate fan club" requirements would be waived and the band would get a twenty-five percent larger ticket allocation. They passed.

Instead String Cheese Incident played very few Clear Channel or Ticketmaster-operated venues in 2002. "I do remember the conversations of, 'Hey, we may be shut out of some of these venues that we want to play if we go this route and decide to fight them,'" recalls the group's Moseley. "'We are going to have to look at playing alternative venues.' Actually we did some of that. The talk was, 'Is that going to be worth it? Is the fan base going to respond favorably to the fact that we're trying to take on Ticketmaster and we're consequently in different kinds of venues than they're used to? Or would the fan base rather see us in the regular venues and go through Ticketmaster to get their tickets? We felt like the fan base was behind us. It didn't matter where we played."

And when the band did play a Ticketmaster venue, they had developed a rather creative way to secure — or ensure, depending on how you looked at it — their desired ticket allotment.

"As the ruling had come down that we can't have a fifty percent allotment anymore, when we'd book a show, part of [the conversation with the promoter] was, 'What's the ticket allotment?'" recalls Luba, increasingly animated. "We'd say, 'We don't want any ticket allotment and fans can buy as many as they want; and there has to be no service charge at the box office.'" The proposed end-around was for SCI Ticketing to parcel out cash to fans and send them to the box office where there was no service charge to buy the necessary inventory themselves, to sell directly back to fans.

"So when we were going to play the Fillmore in Denver, we would say to the promoter, Don Strasburg, who is a really good friend of ours: 'Don, if you don't let us sell the tickets, we're going to send 4,000 kids to the box office and have them each buy eight tickets, and then they're going to come back to our Boulder office. So instead of making all the out-of-town people pay the \$11 service charge, they're going to pay our \$3 service charge.'"

While box office point-of-purchases were at an all-time low, the no service fee policy had long been something Ticketmaster highlighted in response to public criticism over its convenience charges. "For us it was a huge bat they inadvertently put in our hands because we could threaten it," says Luba. "They knew we were crazy enough that we would literally send 1,000 kids with \$240 each to buy 8,000 tickets for the allotment. There was nothing they could do to stop it." (While they never followed through with it, Luba does have a mental picture of parceling out stacks of cash for ticket-buyers: "It might have gotten to the point where we actually took a picture and sent it somewhere and said, 'This is what's happening.'")

As the year wound down, the band's continued conflicts with Ticketmaster became untenable. The internal conversations among Madison House, SCI Ticketing and the String Cheese Incident circled around whether or not they had the resources and willpower to take legal action. The general consensus was that they had neither. The legal costs would be enormous to fight a company of Ticketmaster's size, and String Cheese was a band that thrived on playing concerts to as many people as possible, not one that wanted to deal with labor-intensive tour routing that avoided Ticketmaster by playing less-than-desirable locations à la Pearl Jam. And then, out of the blue, Luba got a phone call from an attorney who said he was interested in helping them.

NEIL GLAZER IS A LAWYER at the Philadelphia-based firm Kohn, Swift & Graf. His résumé is highly polished: BA, summa cum laude, from the University of Pennsylvania in 1990; JD, magna cum laude, from Harvard Law School; clerkship on the U.S. Court of Appeals for the Second Circuit. His areas of litigation include money laundering and terrorist finance, copyright and trademark, international human rights, technology, e-commerce and antitrust. He is also a music fan. So when he received a call from a friend in January 2003 about the ticketing predicament of the String Cheese Incident — a band he had seen years earlier in Telluride — he took particular interest.

"I got involved in the case because a friend called me up and said that the band and its ticketing company were in a struggle with Ticketmaster, and they were very frustrated and needed some help," Glazer recalls in a methodical cadence. From the time of the phone call to Luba, Glazer estimates that it took approximately four months to determine that, yes, legal action against Ticketmaster had merit. From there it took another couple of months to prepare the case. Who the case was against — and what it sought — was not always clear.

"In between one of the tours when Nadia and I started to book it, some executive decision somewhere had been passed down that the game was up, and we weren't going to be able to [get our ticket allotment]," recalls Luba. "We had a moment where we said, 'Do we sue? Is it Clear Channel? Were they the bad guys, or was it Ticketmaster? We ultimately ended up going after Ticketmaster, but it was a toss-up at some point."

"The whole case was going to rise and fall on those agreements and whether those agreements were intended to, or had the effect of, locking out too much of the market," says Glazer of Ticketmaster's exclusive contracts with venues and promoters, which were primarily with Clear Channel. "The case was crafted in a way to drive a stake right into the heart of this particular problem."

Luba remembers sitting in meetings with Ticketmaster chairman Terry Barnes, whom he again underscores as being a "really decent dude," and his understanding the band's plight but being handcuffed. "He said, 'Look, I'm the chairman of a billion-dollar company. I feel for you guys. I probably understand exactly what you're saying,'" recounts Luba. "I felt he really agreed with it, but what could he do? He would look me in the eye and go, 'You have to understand. We are paid to be TicketBastard. We get it. We're the front for the promoters.'"

Barnes went so far as to suggest that Ticketmaster's rebates created a heroin-like addiction among the promoters and venues that received them.

NINE YEARS EARLIER, AT ALMOST the exact same time, Pearl Jam had hired the high-fueled New York-based firm Sullivan & Cromwell to represent them in submitting a complaint to the Justice Department's antitrust division. Glazer feels Pearl Jam's tactic or, rather, the avenue it traveled to try and effect change, was misguided from the beginning.

"Trying to get Congress to do something on an issue like that was probably a strategic mistake on their part," says Glazer of Pearl Jam's Ticketmaster showdown. "It's not appropriate for Congress to say to Ticketmaster, 'We don't like what you're doing,' because Congress's job is to pass laws. They were trying to get the Justice Department to do something — and it's really hard to get the Justice Department to do anything. If you want to get the Justice Department to do something and they aren't already really looking at it, you have to do their work for them." Despite the fact that it was the Justice Department who approached Pearl Jam, there was little, if any, change in Ticketmaster's policy or practice as a result of the highly publicized feud.

"It just struck me that the effort was nice, and they were very passionate and clearly right about the issue, but it just didn't seem to me that what Pearl Jam had done was enough to really get traction with the Justice Department," says Glazer.

One of the key differences for Glazer was that Pearl Jam was simply trying to do its own ticketing. SCI Ticketing, on the other hand, was also doing ticketing for other artists and was seen as a potential competitor to Ticketmaster in the marketplace.

"There was this new market that was only a few years old for artist ticketing that was really starting to flourish, and it was starting to concern Ticketmaster," suggests Glazer. "The number of tickets, if you added all the different artists [SCI Ticketing] was trying to do, I think Ticketmaster viewed them as, 'Well, this is starting to affect our bottom line and we don't like it.' And it had the power to crush [SCI Ticketing] — that was the other element — because Ticketmaster got its tickets by entering into these exclusive agreements. . . . Ticketmaster would contact its clients and say, 'We have an agreement. We have a right to sell all these tickets. You're not allowed to give these artists any tickets.' So it was effectively squeezing SCI Ticketing and everybody else out that was trying to do it."

With Glazer readying a lawsuit, financial support from a silent backer who said they were willing to go the distance and String Cheese committed to the fight, Luba again met with Ticketmaster. He made it clear that, "I will, if it fucking kills me, find a place for String Cheese to play, somewhere else, somehow, and it's just not worth it for you guys. The amount of noise we're going to make, you let this become a pop culture thing, you're fucked."

Moseley confirms the band was on the same page with management. "We were feeling our oats a little bit, feeling powerful, on the rise and selling a lot of tickets," he reflects. "Pearl Jam took a whack at it, and there was no reason we couldn't go to bat against them as well, with our momentum and our ticket sales and the structure we were trying to set up and the legal contacts that we had."

On June 25 Ticketmaster notified SCI Ticketing that it would no longer permit the company to sell tickets for any acts other than String Cheese unless those acts complied with the company's aforementioned fan club rules.

"MusicToday was growing by leaps and bounds, and SCI Ticketing was being frustrated," recalls Glazer. "Why was Dave Matthews able to get as many tickets as he was? It just smelled bad to us. . . . And the whole idea that Ticketmaster could dictate those fan clubs' rules seemed a little inappropriate."

The decision to proceed with the suit was an obvious one for the band. "We have a chance to make a difference. We have a chance here to provide a service to the fans and stick it to the man. Let's do it," recalls Moseley of the basic thought process. "That was an easy choice for us."

SCI TICKETING FILED A CIVIL LAWSUIT in the U.S. District Court of Colorado on August 3, 2003, at 3:12 p.m. The twenty-page document was precise in articulating SCI Ticketing's genesis, the concert industry dynamics that had made its existence so precarious and the resolutions it was seeking. It charged Ticketmaster on four counts: (1) Ticketmaster has entered into combinations and agreements in violation of section 1 of the Sherman Antitrust Act; (2 and 3) Ticketmaster has monopolized and attempted to monopolize or abused its monopoly power in the market in violation of section 2 of the Sherman Antitrust Act; and (4) Ticketmaster had practiced tortious interference with prospective business advantage. Both Clear Channel and MusicToday were named in the suit.

"SCI Ticketing has become the target of an all-out effort by Ticketmaster to foreclose it from competing in the relevant market," the suit argued. "Acting on instructions from Ticketmaster, venues and promoters have refused to continue their practice of supplying SCI Ticketing with reasonable allocations of popular music concert tickets to offer for sale to the public."

It argued, based in part on publicly available *Pollstar* reports, that Ticketmaster clearly had a monopoly within the concert industry. It had exclusive agreements with approximately eighty-nine percent of the top fifty arenas, eighty-eight percent of the top fifty amphitheaters, more than seventy percent of the top theaters and more than seventy-five percent of the top clubs.

In regard to consumer fairness, the suit used the band's shows at the Warfield theater in San Francisco the previous month as one example: the difference in price between a fan buying four tickets to four different shows from SCI Ticketing versus Ticketmaster was just over $85.

The suit also highlighted King Crimson's spring tour earlier that year, which had used SCI Ticketing. All of the promoters signed and returned the ticket allocation agreements except Clear Channel, which indicated that because of pressure from Ticketmaster, it would not be allocating the company any tickets to any shows at Clear Channel venues. SCI Ticketing was forced to issue a letter to fans and was now, it argued, likely to lose King Crimson's and other future clients' business.

A week later on September 11, two years to the day after the company was supposed to launch its wholly owned ticketing service, the band, along with Luba, Mastrine and Glazer, held a press conference in New York.

Mastrine made it clear that, "We are not saying Ticketmaster doesn't have a place in the ticketing business, but we have a different philosophy of doing business, one that caters directly to our fans."

Luba's comments were broader: "The music industry is suffering right now, but there is no reason that the artists and their fans have to go down with it," he told the press. "We hope that the positive ramifications of filing this lawsuit will reach well beyond just the String Cheese Incident and their fans and benefit everyone."

Ticketmaster responded to SCI Ticketing's press conference with a press release the same day. "While it has been our company policy to not comment on pending litigation, SCI Ticketing has so distorted this issue in its public statements that we feel compelled to clarify the record," it began. "Earlier this year a Federal Court dismissed a similar lawsuit brought against Ticketmaster. The claims that have been asserted by SCI Ticketing in this new lawsuit likewise lack merit and we are confident that they will also be dismissed after all the relevant facts are established."

It went on to assert: "By demanding very large allocations of tickets, SCI has attempted to break valid contracts for its own self-promotion and monetary gain. . . . SCI and its ticketing company are trying to step in for a 'free ride' on the many benefits and services Ticketmaster provides its clients. SCI essentially wants to skim the best, most easily sold tickets and leave Ticketmaster and its clients with the job of selling the rest. . . . SCI's unfair leveraging of its popularity to achieve its for-profit ticketing goals is both improper and illegal."

John Pleasants, Ticketmaster's CEO at the time, remembers the lawsuit being "a big deal for about seven days," that it was nothing more than "a piece of noise that flared up." Pleasants, the man responsible for turning Ticketmaster into a consumer-facing company, is surprisingly rigid in recalling his assessment of the situation. "String Cheese, if I remember correctly, was going into Ticketmaster's buildings and were pulling fifty percent of their inventory and selling it to their fan club," he says. "And if they were doing that, that is — in effect — illegal, full stop. There is no debate about whether it is illegal or not — it is illegal. Ticketmaster has a contract that is for exclusively selling every ticket in a particular building. If String Cheese wanted to sell half of their tickets through their website, they should go play in a park or some other place that is not with an exclusive contract with a ticketing company, with Ticketmaster or anybody else." Simply put, he says, "There's a thing called the law, and if I remember correctly, they were breaking it."

TYPICALLY, TICKETMASTER RESPONDED TO LAWSUITS with a motion to dismiss that said, in effect, whatever laws they claim we're violating, we're not. However, in this instance, much to everyone's surprise, Ticketmaster filed what's called an "answer," essentially a countersuit that systematically responded to each paragraph of SCI Ticketing's lawsuit.

As the company noted, "Ticketmaster would prefer to resolve this matter outside of litigation, but now has no choice but to respond to the frivolous claims that have been asserted. Part of that response will be a countersuit by Ticketmaster against SCI Ticketing (and its founders) for intentionally interfering with contracts and relationships in which Ticketmaster has made great investments. The issue here is whether Ticketmaster and its clients have the right to contract for ticket distribution services or whether SCI Ticketing can free-ride on those relationships by exerting pressure on Ticketmaster's clients to breach their contractual commitments."

Glazer saw the countersuit as Ticketmaster "throwing down the gauntlet and saying, 'Two can play at that game.'" Whereas large corporations typically delay trials through requests to dismiss, this was different. "It indicated to me that we really had something that they were taking very seriously," suggests Glazer. "What I took away was they didn't necessarily want this to be a big public battle over big meaty questions of law."

"We were trying to be nice and be artist-friendly," says Pleasants. "I didn't want to go out and sue String Cheese. I wanted to say, 'Listen, let's figure something out. We understand — we want you to have a fan club.' But a fan club selling six percent in the corner, we can kind of look the other way. You taking the inventory everywhere you go? We're not going to look the other way. Why? Because then everybody's going to take half the inventory, and our business is destroyed because we're not standing up to our law. Either you defend the law or you don't."

National newspapers like the *New York Times*, popular culture magazines like *Rolling Stone* and publications like *Mother Jones* all covered the story. It was typically framed as Pearl Jam, Round II. But while the String Cheese Incident was certainly righteous in its decision to fight Ticketmaster, it didn't really talk about it from the stage the way Eddie Vedder had during Pearl Jam's fight.

As fall gave way to winter, behind-the-scenes conversations between the band, SCI Ticketing, Madison House, Ticketmaster, Clear Channel and various others continued. As a group whose success was dependent upon touring, there was concern about String Cheese's future livelihood in regard to upsetting promoters with whom they had longstanding relationships. There was concern over legal costs. There was concern that no other band or organization had stood up in support. As the band began making tour plans for 2004, the strains of the fight were increasingly being felt.

"We got hamstrung enough to the point where it became so distracting that, at the end of the day, as willing as we were to go pretty fucking far, these are dudes who just wanted to make music," says Luba now of the band's growing uncertainty about a protracted battle. "This was taking over everyone's life."

The band and management's persistence, however, was paying off. As time wore on and the fight faded from the papers and the public eye, Ticketmaster became increasingly willing to negotiate with SCI Ticketing by early 2004.

"The reality was — and we were really clear about it — all we wanted to do was be able to sell fifty percent of the tickets to our fans," says Luba. "It got to the point where they came back and said, 'Okay, look us in the eye and tell us you've been lying to us the entire time, or we're going to give you everything that you need and go do what you need to do." In addition SCI Ticketing would also be allowed to resume sales for other clients, though the allocated allotments would be at or below previous percentages, likely in the ten percent range, which was in line with most of MusicToday's clients.

As part of the proposed settlement agreement, SCI Ticketing, Madison House and the band would have to agree that there would be no fanfare or press releases; there could be no announcements of how they beat Ticketmaster.

Says Glazer, "There were a lot of meetings, a lot of conversations, a lot of soul-searching because the band had staked out a very strong position and had decided to carry the torch on behalf of themselves and everybody else out there, and all of a sudden this was just going to disappear."

Mastrine, for his part, as head of ticketing, was not in favor of settling. "I think ultimately there was the determination that there could still be a business model based on an out-of-court settlement, and that was not where I stood on it," he says. "I love those guys dearly and care about them a lot — and still do work with them — but there was a difference of opinion there internally. Mine was that ticketing is my professional life, and getting involved with an antitrust lawsuit with Ticketmaster is significant; it's career changing in a lot of ways. If we're going to do it, let's do it." Mastrine's bottom line was that if "you take on a lawsuit, you do it because you're going to take it all the way. You don't do it because you want an out-of-court settlement."

Luba's opinion was that if Ticketmaster was giving SCI Ticketing exactly what it wanted, what was the case? "Neil and I were sitting there," he recalls, "and the Ticketmaster lawyer was going, 'Look, we're all big boys. As soon as we stand up in front of the judge and say we've given in to everything you guys asked, obviously this suit is about something else.' We were like, 'Yeah, they're probably right.'"

THERE'S NO QUESTION THAT THE SUIT was framed to be about more than just SCI Ticketing getting its ticket allocations. From the beginning Glazer had always intimated that the suit would shed light on the rather shadowy nature of the concert business — that the relationships and dealings between Ticketmaster, Clear Channel, MusicToday and artists would be exposed.

"I was hired by SCI Ticketing, and I needed to get the best result I could for SCI Ticketing, but it was painfully obvious that this was potentially a big precedent," the lawyer says today. So after much deliberation, it was decided that the best result — for SCI Ticketing, Madison House and the String Cheese Incident — was to settle.

"We didn't really want to be on a crusade," says Luba. "It wasn't meant to be like, 'Fuck the man' or 'Fuck Ticketmaster.' We just wanted to be able to sell tickets and control our own ticket price."

For Moseley the settlement was a bit of a letdown. "You want to go out and brag about beating the giant, but the flipside to that was, 'Hey, in reality we're getting what we want here. We may not be able to get all the press about it and so forth, but the bottom line is our fans are going to be able to get the ticket service from us, [and] we thought all along we could provide better service at a lower cost.'"

Though the band and its ticketing company's well-being were the priority, Mastrine saw the potential to affect the entire concert industry if the case had gone to trial. "I just personally feel like we had an opportunity to really take them the full length and uncover some stuff and really help restore some balance to the industry," he says. "The only way you can do that is by bringing the promoter and venue to it, and if you would have done that, they would have in turn brought the artist back in and you would have gotten everyone at the table at once. To point the finger at Ticketmaster, that's the easiest thing you can do."

With SCI Ticketing allowed to ticket as it had before, free of Ticketmaster's fan club rules, and the String Cheese Incident once again getting up to fifty percent of its ticket inventory, the lawsuit went away quietly. To this day if one looks for details about the lawsuit's resolution in the press, there is nothing beyond passing mention of a settlement.

"We're talking about having shed at least some light on some very dark and secret practices in terms of how money was flowing and who was paying who and how it was all working," says Glazer. "So all the more reason for a defendant in that kind of position to say not only the terms of the settlement have to be kept confidential, but we have to talk about what it is you're allowed to say about the whole thing."

In that regard Mastrine wishes more defendants had been named. "Quite frankly, my biggest regret in that case was that we took the unusual step of filing an antitrust lawsuit against Ticketmaster and we didn't include Clear Channel," he laments. "I think that showing the collusion that existed between those two companies was the key thing that would have brought this thing down. We were close; we just weren't there, and it takes deep pockets."

"It was a quiet victory," says Moseley. "I remember us having the talk of, 'Hey we can accept this offer from them or we can continue to try and fight it and possibly get more publicity about it, but in the end we may not really get what we want, so we should probably take their offer.' It was a bittersweet victory. We definitely got what we wanted, but we didn't get a lot of press about it."

Contributing to SCI Ticketing's decision to settle was the lack of support from perceived allies. "When we stood up, I was expecting people to rally around it," says Luba. "And it didn't happen. I think I had a moment where I was like, 'No one gives a shit about us,' and when we got what we needed for our fans and felt like we moved the ball down the field, it was someone else's turn."

HERE'S WHAT IS SO REMARKABLE about the story of the band with the funny name: they fought Ticketmaster and won. The whole reason Ticketmaster took the String Cheese Incident and its ticketing company on was that it feared a precedent would be set for artist ticketing. As Pleasants puts it, "We couldn't let these people run around with other ticketing companies." Yet, within approximately six months, Ticketmaster acquiesced. So, despite the ticketing giant's best efforts, SCI Ticketing *had* set a precedent.

"It wasn't like a big, brilliant explosion that would have happened had we won at a trial, but it nevertheless set a precedent within the industry," concurs Glazer. "It did open things up. It generated a lot of awareness, and a hell of a lot more artists and managers started looking at artist ticketing that hadn't even been thinking about it before. . . . We all felt good about that, and I think it made that final decision a little easier at the end of the day." However, there was a sincere belief that other artists would follow in a similar fashion.

"What we were hoping was that the message, without being overly righteous about it, was that if a bunch of twits from Boulder could figure out how to do it — and it was very clear that we were able to still sell tickets, and a lot of them on our terms — we hoped someone would come up behind us and pick up the mantle," says Luba, nonplussed. "Which, ultimately, as fucking crazy as it is, no one did — to this day."

"I think we carry a sense of pride from our accomplishments there," says Moseley. "It was certainly a big effort." More than anything, he sees it as a continued victory for fans. When Moseley was interviewed in February 2010, tickets for the String Cheese Incident's first headlining concerts in three years had gone on sale through SCI Ticketing. The band sold out three nights at Red Rocks amphitheater and three nights at Horning's Hideout outside Portland, Oregon. "We're looking at being able to sell half the Red Rocks tickets through our own ticketing company and all of Horning's Hideout and knowing that we're getting fans a better deal. They're paying less in service charges and hopefully getting better service from the band."

Pleasants, who left Ticketmaster in 2005 and went on to serve as CEO of Revolution Health Group, COO of video game company Electronic Arts and now CEO of social game developer Playdom, is fairly ambivalent about String Cheese's impact. "In the picture of the last ten years of my knowledge of what's happened in this industry, this was a complete non-event," he says. "It only signals that artists have leverage and that Ticketmaster has to be careful in terms of how it works with artists, but at the end of the day, the law is on the side of the building — the contract with Ticketmaster. This is a little Mexican standoff that happens from time to time. Pearl Jam was one in Fred's day; String Cheese was one in my day."

Indeed, for Luba, Pearl Jam's defeat and quick capitulation to Ticketmaster were major factors in how much impact the SCI Ticketing victory had. "In a lot of ways [Pearl Jam's case] was really hurtful to everyone else who followed after them because it was seen as a huge defeat," he says. "It empowered Ticketmaster to say, 'Okay, Luba, you won String Cheese. Who gives a fuck? Look at what we did to Pearl Jam,' who at the time were the most popular band in the world. It was really damaging on a lot of levels. It was good they created an awareness for it, but the way it ended up and the way their next tour which went out had a huge Ticketmaster and Clear Channel logo, it was kind *wah-wah*."

It's ironic, then, that one of String Cheese's tangential impacts was on what Pearl Jam fought so loudly over: lower service and convenience fees. Luba and the band routinely illustrated how artists could easily keep fee charges down simply by charging the promoter less money, something Pearl Jam, for all of its hullabaloo, was not willing to do. For instance, if a Clear Channel promoter was going to get $3 from a $6 convenience charge at a 5,000-seat venue that it would split with Ticketmaster, String Cheese could instead reduce its artist guarantee by approximately $15,000 and cap the extra fees at $3.

A significantly bigger impact of the lawsuit, which both sides agree on, is that it catalyzed Ticketmaster's self-evaluation of its role in artist ticketing. "There are a thousand little things that come out of this," confirms Pleasants. "Every band has an artist fan club, and every artist fan club pulled tickets out of the inventory system and sold them as bundled premium packages for every concert that's out there. And yeah, that may only be 200 or 300 tickets per building, but that's a lot of tickets when you add it up over time. There are lots of reasons why Ticketmaster would want to get into that business. These things were already happening — it was about how could we enable them better."

Which leads him to the rhetorical question of what do you do if you're Ticketmaster facing this new reality: "You say, 'The only way I wouldn't care if [artists] sold twenty percent of the inventory through this fan club is if *we* ran the fan club.'"

While Pleasants still sees the SCI Ticketing lawsuit as a "non-event," he does credit it and the conversations surrounding it with getting the company to the "lightbulb" moment for its future: "I wanted to have a relationship with the artists' management."

Ticketmaster wanted to provide more services to artists because artists were the ones who ultimately controlled the ticket inventory, decided if they wanted to tour and decided what venues they wanted to play in. "The most important headline in this is we ended up doing the Front Line deal," says Pleasants of Ticketmaster's initial investment in Irving Azoff's Front Line Management in 2004. "We wanted to have a relationship with artists. We wanted to be in the business that MusicToday was in [though not necessarily involved with merchandising]. For us it was about [ticket] inventory."

And, as always, artist profit was at the center of it. "How do you get more money for the artist? Who deserves it?" asks Pleasants. "Of course, Ticketmaster, being capitalistic, wants some too and would take more middlemen out of the equation. So it all felt right, and it all felt like a smart thing to do, so we invested in Front Line Management, which was the largest management company out there. It gave us a relationship in a different part of the value chain."

In just a few short years the industry's entire value chain would be revaluated as Ticketmaster, Front Line and the new face of Clear Channel Entertainment, Live Nation, would join forces to completely reshape the concert industry.

CHAPTER 10

Secondary Education

BROOKLYN KINDERGARTEN TEACHER BY DAY, Manhattan ticket maven by night, Shelley Lazar became the guardian of the guest list. When musicians such as Bruce Springsteen, the Rolling Stones, Billy Joel and Neil Diamond needed someone to coordinate their friends and family tickets, they turned to Shelley.

Starting in the early 1970s, Lazar found her niche while occupying a variety of roles. She was a ticket taker and a front of house manager and even provided backstage catering at the Fillmore East, Academy of Music, Palladium and eventually in arenas and amphitheaters. Throughout all this she remained in the school system and even pursued the postgraduate work necessary to obtain her principal's license.

"What I used to say was I worked with chronological children during the day and psychological children at night, and it was really the same," she says. "It was, 'Okay, guys, everybody's eating; okay, class, get in a line.' The only difference was I didn't zip zippers for the guys at the rock shows. That they could do themselves."

Like students creating nicknames for their favorite teacher, musicians have done the same for Lazar. Bob Dylan calls her Shelvis. However, Keith Richards may have bested the Bard in describing her as "The Mothafuckin' Ticket Queen." It's a title she references in her email handle.

Eventually Lazar parlayed her access, trustworthiness and sheer creativity into a related endeavor that became the first of its kind: the VIP ticketing package.

"I said to the artists, 'These are your great fans and these are your great tickets, so why not give your great fans the great tickets?' That way they don't have to go to what we at the time called scalpers. We didn't talk about secondary ticketing; we didn't call them brokers — they were scalpers."

Lazar's story raises a significant distinction. Just when did scalpers become brokers and who edited the lexicon, bestowing the far less pejorative term "secondary ticketing" on the practice, which represents a multi-billion dollar industry today?

The answer can be traced in no insignificant way to two Stanford MBAs who saw a market inefficiency and sought to "disintermediate brick and mortar ticket brokers by creating a liquid market for the exchange of event tickets." Strike that. The effort was plotted by *one* Stanford MBA and *one* Stanford graduate student who was enticed to drop out of school after his first year to run the company, earning an eight-figure bonus check in the process. Along the way strategies shifted, legislation was flouted and a ticketing leviathan may well have been felled in the process.

ERIC BAKER ENTERED THE STANFORD Graduate School of Business in the fall of 1999. Four years out of Harvard, Baker had been an associate at Boston's Bain Capital, a private equity firm run by future Massachusetts governor and Republican presidential candidate Mitt Romney. He arrived at Stanford with the express intent of utilizing the institution's knowledge base and contact network as a platform to launch a business. Where he differed from many of his equally ambitious classmates is that he already had a viable idea in mind.

Earlier that year, at his girlfriend's request, he had made plans for them to attend *The Lion King*, which was still a hot ticket more than a year after its opening on Broadway. "I had to use a broker, and it was an exorbitant price and a pain in the ass," he now recalls. "This was around the time that eBay was taking off, and I started thinking, 'Why aren't people reselling these seats over the Internet?' And what I found was that while eBay's got a great marketplace — it's phenomenal for tons of different goods — it wasn't very good for time-sensitive items. If I buy an antique table and it's not delivered in time or it's chipped or the wrong color, I can get my money out of escrow, give the seller negative feedback and buy another table next week. But that wouldn't work for tickets.

"As for companies like Ticketmaster that worked with the venues to issue the original ticket and sell it, there seemed to be huge channel conflicts when dealing in the after-market. You can imagine from the point of view of a fan who wants Britney Spears tickets and is informed that they're all sold out. That person is already wondering how they sold out in ten seconds, which seems suspicious enough. But wait, 'Over here in door number two we can sell you the same ticket for three times the original price.' It just seemed like there was going to be a problem with consumers."

If Baker was interested in launching an online business, then he had landed in the ideal locale. Silicon Valley was flush with venture capital firms supporting existing Internet companies with astronomical valuations (some would say *aspirational* valuations, while others preferred *implausible* valuations). In December 1999 *New York* magazine trumpeted the 1990s as the "e-Decade," the heyday of the Pets.com sock puppet, when an online grocery business like Webvan.com would go public and then burn through a billion dollars to develop a national distribution system on the fast track to bankruptcy.

"Those were the go-go days," Baker says, laughing, "when Solarpowered-flashlights.com was worth a billion dollars. You could throw a rock and hit a trillionaire with a moronic idea in Palo Alto."

At Stanford Baker met someone with no such dim view of *his* idea. Jeff Fluhr graduated summa cum laude from the University of Pennsylvania in 1996 with dual degrees in finance and engineering. From there he moved into investment banking in New York City at the Blackstone Group, relocated to San Francisco to join the private equity investing team at Thomas Weisel Partners and then decided to pursue his MBA.

In late January 2000 the two were among a group of Stanford Graduate School of Business students who flew to Las Vegas over Super Bowl weekend. There Baker shared his vision for the company with Fluhr, and their animated dialogue soon drifted from the theoretical to the practical. This was a heady time for anyone contemplating an Internet business, as seventeen of the thirty-six ads that ran during the Super Bowl were purchased by dot-coms.[1]

Back in Palo Alto, Fluhr was so taken with Baker's idea that he wanted to expand upon it to draft an entry for Stanford's upcoming E-Challenge business plan competition. Baker consented, but as a means to preserve his rights, Fluhr signed a "ticket venture partnership agreement" on February 2, 2000. Here he acknowledged that "Eric H. Baker was the originator of the concept that is reflected in my entry (Needaticket.com) to the E-Challenge 2000 at Stanford Business School. In recognition of the substantial work that Eric did in originating, researching and developing the concept, Eric shall be designated as a founder and will be entitled to 20% of the founder's equity of Needaticket.com (or any similar/related ticket business that I may choose to eventually launch)."

As events would unfold, it's quite possible that Fluhr bristled at such future declarations, particularly as the business moved through additional iterations, and their next contract would have combustive implications four years into the future.

The Needaticket.com executive summary received high marks. Defining the company as "a centralized Web-based auction site addressing the currently inefficient secondary market for event tickets," it assessed that potential market in the vicinity of $10 to $12 billion. The entry advanced to the next round.

However, the lure of that $10 to $12 billion beckoned with increased urgency. Rather than take the top slot in an academic exercise, even one that came with a five-figure reward check, the pair increasingly believed that a larger prize loomed. They decided to withdraw from the E-Challenge and pursue another avenue of competition.

By June 2000 they were well on their way to raising the first round of capital. Needaticket.com had become I-drenalin.com, itself a placeholder entered for purposes of incorporation (Baker quips, "I-drenalin sounds like some chemical that Mark McGwire would be using"). This name then gave way to LiquidSeats. The .com was jettisoned by necessity at the same time that stockholders began doing the same to their Internet holdings, as the tech-heavy NASDAQ composite index fell from a high of 5000 in March to below the 2000 level by the end of the year. "This ended up being valuable to us," Baker explains, "because it forced us to build a sturdy business and figure out how we would make money. You were dealing with the days when people would go from a concept on a napkin to an IPO in nine months. Stuff like Theglobe.com [which saw its stock price drop from $97 on the day of its 1998 initial public offering to a nickel three years later]."

Thus, rather than rely on soon-to-be defunct delivery services such as Kozmo.com or UrbanFetch — named in the initial business plan — Fluhr struck an essential deal with the stable, if less chic, Federal Express to integrate with its system ("Some people thought it didn't look like we had a sexy Internet business because we were moving these physical tickets all over the place, but it was a key to our success. We knew when tickets were picked up, dropped off, and where they were at a given time"). The shift in the capital market also helped the start-up avoid some potential long-term legal entanglements as the business plan also projected that the company would acquire a million dollars of inventory in each launch city to seed its marketplace. Instead LiquidSeats would become a pure platform for others to list tickets, which eventually would help insulate the business from state-based anti-scalping legislation.

The I-drenalin.com business plan was subtitled, "Life, liberty and the pursuit of a consumer-driven market for the exchange of event tickets," and while this reflected the breezy and somewhat cavalier attitude of the founders, the pair also moved forward with a measured, analytical approach. Shortly after classes ended, Fluhr enlisted a Washington, DC law firm, Wiley, Rein

& Fielding, to conduct a survey of the existing anti-scalping regulations. There was no applicable national law because the federal government left that responsibility to the states, and as of June 2000, there was little uniformity. Ticket resale was altogether unfettered in twenty-two states. Hawaii, Indiana and Maryland were similar except for limitations that applied exclusively to boxing matches. Four other jurisdictions (including California) only restricted sales in the immediate proximity of event facilities. The remaining states did impose price-based restrictions, and almost half of them mandated that all resellers secure licenses.

Baker and Fluhr were not daunted. As the latter now explains: "We were aware of the legislative issues in a few states. So we made sure that we had a user agreement that said that all buyers and sellers had to know and obey the laws of their state. We also were not involved in setting the price of the tickets, which was the relevant part of the transaction when it came to those laws. Finally, there was a gray area around the question of which state might have jurisdiction because the transaction on the Internet had a buyer, seller, venue that could be in three separate states: a New York Yankees game with a New Jersey season ticket holder selling to someone in Connecticut. On top of that our servers and employees were based in California, a fourth state. Over time, as we spoke with the attorneys general, we found that most of them were focused on crime, on child predators, not on somebody selling a ticket for $50 more than they should be."

Still, from the outset the two recognized they also were battling what Fluhr characterizes as "the age-old imagery of a street scalper in a trench coat, selling gold watches and tickets out of the trunk of his car." In response they made an effort to redefine the nomenclature. As Baker explains, "Jeff and I, if nothing else, our contribution is we coined the term 'secondary ticketing.' We couldn't say 'online scalping,' 'online touting,' 'the black-market' . . . We thought of 'recycled tickets,' 'ticket resale' . . . but eventually we came up with 'secondary ticketing.' 'Primary ticketing' would be Ticketmaster, and we were secondary ticketing."

However, unlike the Gershwin tune, it wasn't simply a matter of potato or potahto (and as *Seinfeld*'s George "Coco" Constanza learned all too well, you can't give yourself a nickname). The phrase "secondary ticketing" eventually gained traction, particularly within business circles, but for the wider public it would take time.

"Oh, it's the scalper guys!" Washington Redskins owner Dan Snyder greeted Baker and Fluhr at *Street & Smith's SportsBusiness Journal*'s World Congress of Sports in March 2002. Shortly afterward outside a conference room at New York City's Waldorf-Astoria hotel, Snyder made a show of proclaiming, "The Washington Redskins would never be associated with online ticket scalping."

Four years later the team signed a promotional agreement with StubHub, and a link appeared on the Redskins website directing the team's fans to the marketplace. "Obviously Dan Snyder got religion," an early LiquidSeats staffer offers. The fact that the deal was worth "several million dollars to the team" may have accelerated the conversion process.

Back during the summer of 2000, however, Baker and Fluhr were working out of empty Stanford classrooms, and while they agreed that they needed to push forward, Baker was committed to completing his second year of graduate school and receiving his degree. The agreement the two eventually reached was that Fluhr would withdraw from school to run the day-to-day operations of the company. In exchange he would receive the majority of the founder's equity, although it wouldn't vest for four years. As Baker looks back, he acknowledges with a strained chuckle, "It might have been the most expensive MBA anyone ever received."

Fluhr set up shop in an industrial warehouse space located deep in San Francisco's funky, affordable Mission neighborhood. Baker returned to school, although he did so on his own terms, which allowed him the freedom to visit New York and Los Angeles in search of funding: "I figured out the best thing to do was never show up so you'd never be on a seating chart, and there would be no way to track your attendance. I'd do all the work remotely and send it in. So I never went to class, and I pulled that off for about two quarters until there was a whole brouhaha, but the great thing is I was able to travel. I could not have done that if I was in med school. If you train doctors who are ill-prepared, they'll kill people. If you train MBAs who are ill-prepared, you'll just have a lot of Dilberts running around."

The business school dropout and the truant maintained a steady course. They were bright, affable and able to connect with their former colleagues at Blackstone and Bain, who supplied the seed capital. With that in place and a business model that mirrored one of the few ongoing Internet success stories in eBay, LiquidSeats completed a $2.1 million Series A financing in early 2001, a round that included Alanis Morissette's then-manager Scott Welch, BEA Systems cofounder Edward Scott and retired San Francisco 49ers quarterback Steve Young. In a subsequent meeting of prospective investors, Young joked, "As an expiring asset myself, I can appreciate what these guys do with tickets." They matched the sum a year later with commitments from New York investment firm Allen & Company, former HBO chief executive Michael Fuchs and others.

The company's initial focus was on partnerships. Rather than building a destination website or a consumer brand, LiquidSeats sought to work with sports teams and media properties to power their secondary ticket marketplaces, known as StubHub Exchanges. These were revenue-sharing deals because, in reaction to the recent dot-com flameouts, "we were maniacal about not spending up-front money." Fluhr elaborates: "We didn't want to spend a bunch of money on advertising that may or may not pay off. We didn't want to give AOL a million dollars for a partnership which might force us to go out of business."

So LiquidSeats' business development personnel made the rounds in an attempt to pitch the company as something of a white label software vendor facilitating branded exchanges for the teams. Jeff Berman, vice president of business development during this era, remembers: "It took almost a full year of evangelizing the opportunity: 'It's happening with or without you. It's a good thing for your season ticket holders. It will help them retain their season tickets, and they will renew every year at a higher rate.' I can still do my pitch in my sleep, but we kept getting stonewalled by people on the ticketing side who irrationally and incorrectly kept thinking we were going to be cannibalizing primary sales."

In February 2001 the NHL's Phoenix Coyotes became the first team to establish a StubHub Exchange. A larger prize followed in June when Major League Baseball Advanced Media, the same folks who saved Tickets.com, granted LiquidSeats the exclusive rights to be the online reseller for Major League Baseball. With eighty-one home games for each of baseball's thirty teams, this was a plum opportunity, even if the Seattle Mariners and the Arizona Diamondbacks were the only two to make an initial commitment. A smattering of other professional sports organizations followed, including the Seattle Supersonics and the Los Angeles Clippers.

Then in July 2002 LiquidSeats announced an agreement with MSN to power its secondary ticket marketplace. In the accompanying press release, trumpeting the arrival of MSN StubHub, Fluhr declared: "StubHub is a great fit with MSN and offers users a valuable new feature. Our relationships with sports teams, performing artists and Broadway theatres will give MSN users access to premium tickets not available through traditional ticket outlets."

The only wrinkle in all this was that to share revenue, LiquidSeats needed to generate revenue — which meant ticket sales. Back when he had drafted the original Needaticket.com executive summary, Jeff Fluhr had maligned the efforts of "ticket 'scalpers' who existed only because of the inefficiencies inherent when disparate sellers and buyers had no way of contacting each other."

However, to establish a vibrant marketplace, he now needed an infusion of inventory. As a result, the company that would brand itself as a "fan-to-fan ticket exchange" extended an olive branch and some potent software tools to ticket brokers.

After twenty consecutive years of buying and reselling tickets to the game, boasting a perfect record in terms of annual cash flow, Doug Knittle contemplated retiring his Rolodex. In April 2001, after making yet another killing at the Masters Golf Tournament, he set off for Europe. In between trips to Monte Carlo for the Grand Prix and Milan for the Union of European Football Associations Champions League final, he contemplated what might pull him out of his malaise.

Like many brokers before him and plenty yet to come, he found reason to hope in the Internet. When his wife joined him in Portugal, a few weeks into his wanderings, the forty-three-year-old Knittle explained, "The time is right to take what we're doing and move it online. If we can build this the right way, we can own the secondary market."

Knittle's instincts for such matters had landed the couple a multi-million dollar Bel-Air mansion. Any doubters were unfamiliar with Knittle's two decades as one of the nation's most prosperous ticket brokers, which is how he preferred it.

In the mid-1970s Knittle began an apprenticeship, of sorts, at Troy Ticket Service in Pico Rivera, California. "I worked for a bookmaker who, in trying to hide his bookmaking operations, started a ticket office. After school I would go into his office to see what concert tours were coming to southern California. I was about seventeen years old, I was going to see anything I could afford and I kept running into this guy that owned the ticket office. Then, when I was eighteen, I went to go work for him."

Troy Ticket Service was run by Dominick "Sonny" De Falco. In an April 6, 1976 *Los Angeles Times* article on brokers, De Falco looks every bit the part of a bookmaker/ticket broker, standing in front of his board of upcoming events, donning a blaring, patterned shirt unbuttoned to expose a dangling gold medallion necklace, a complementary hat and a pinkie ring. In the piece, entitled "Ticket Brokers: A Service or Rip-off?" he defended his efforts by explaining, "Go watch the way the kids are treated in line. You wouldn't like that. You'd pay $20 over the price not to be treated like that." De Falco revealed he had observed this kind of treatment while shepherding caravans of kids to arena box offices to secure inventory: "We treat them good, buy them gas and lunch, give them free tickets." As a result, he boasted of selling more than 7,000 tickets to The Who's concert the prior month at Anaheim Stadium.

Beyond carpools there were other ways to secure inventory during this era. Some box offices had not yet committed to Ticketron, and, as Knittle recalls, "Places like Liberty Ticket Agency would have outlets in furniture stores, and someone would call in on the phone and then write up a voucher that would be turned in on the night of a show for the tickets. So it was very easy for box office managers to wheel and deal." Ticketron outlets offered an alternative because "instead of working with the box office, you had the ability to make a contact with somebody that had a store, and you could even buy a store that had a Ticketron machine in it. In New York I knew guys who had machines. They might own record stores or whatever, and they'd get all the tickets."

There was a more direct route as well. Knittle recalls De Falco negotiating with Jerry Weintraub, who was then managing Bob Dylan, Neil Diamond, John Denver and the Carpenters. "They got into this big argument," he recalls. "He would have given us tickets, but we had to pay $1.50 apiece, and at the time we could get them for seventy-five cents, so Sonny didn't take them. Back then the reason you paid vig [the sum above face value] was to return the tickets; it wasn't to buy tickets. Anyhow, it was a mistake because he would have been getting in with one of the leaders in the industry at the time, and the prices just started to go up."

Weintraub wasn't the only one cutting deals, as any number of managers (one assumes, in most cases with the knowledge of their clients) recognized the going rates of choice seats on the secondary market and sought to direct some of these funds toward the performers. Pioneering booking agent Tom Ross, former head of CAA's music division, acknowledges: "Rod Stewart definitely was one of the ones. He's Scottish, he counts his pennies every day and he was always pressing for more. They [managers Arnold Stiefel and Randy Phillips] were among the first people to start to siphon off monies to the brokers. [Manager] Howard Kaufman was the first, and then they learned that business, figured out how to get a part of that market, go to the brokers direct and how they would disseminate it."

A longtime promoter confirms: "Howard Kaufman with [Jimmy] Buffett, Rod Stewart, so many of them scalp their own tickets. Before a show went on sale, they'd say, 'Give me 200 tickets,' and you'd send it to them. You knew what was going on.' What they used to do was give them to one broker in L.A. who would sell them to brokers all over the country." The industry vet also suggests that the "general consensus" is Kaufman went to great lengths to earmark prime seats for this purpose, and on at least one occasion "put in extra rows at Dodger Stadium for Elton [John], and those were his tickets to sell to the brokers."

Still, many managers were *willing* to leave that money on the table (or in the briefcase as it turned out). Back when he was working with Aerosmith during the group's 1990s heyday, Tim Collins was offered $2 million cash in exchange for 2,500 of the best seats each night for a tour. "Two million in a Halliburton briefcase in a house in Beverly Hills," Collins remembers.

"They said, 'This is what we want. [We'll give you $2 million plus the] face value of the tickets. You can [decide whether you want to split any of this] with the band.' And I'm looking at $2 million in cash, and I literally went into the bathroom — I'm not a deeply religious person, but I do have a spiritual nature. That's why I was able to maintain my sobriety from drug addiction for the last twenty-three years — and I said, 'All right, God, if you're out there, if you fucking exist, I need you now, because this is more tempting than chocolate cake or a beautiful naked young body,' which are my other two vices in life, or were. And I literally washed my face, washed my hands, and I walked out the door. I never said goodnight. They tried to call me four or five times, and I just never took their call. I never heard from them again."

The band may well have had a different take on this decision, as it is worth noting that after parting ways with Collins, Aerosmith eventually settled into a long-term relationship with Kaufman's HK Management, and these days, one concert industry insider suggests, "None of their good seats ever go on sale to the public — they are all sold directly to ticket brokers or the fan club or VIP travel companies."

Promoters faced their own temptations, particularly as artists' guarantees continued to rise, seeking out revenue streams beyond what would appear on a settlement sheet at the end of the night. Tracy Buie, who began her tenure in the business working for Los Angeles–based promoters Avalon Attractions in the early 1990s, can pinpoint the moment that she raised an eyebrow about some potential behind-the-scenes relationships. "I think it was the Christmas that we got this enormous box of incredible fruit from South America that was from the local ticket broker. I was going, 'We're getting Christmas presents from a ticket broker? This is *so* not good.' I think that's what really got it home. I know a lot of the major promoters deal tickets with brokers. It's another income stream. They feel the bands take all their money, and they've got to do what they've got to do to make what they consider an appropriate wage. If you think about it, promoters are on the line for a lot of money. If you make a bad decision on an arena show, you could lose $150,000 in the bat of an eye. If you make money, at least back then, you're making $35,000 to $50,000, which wasn't much. You could take some serious, serious hits on those shows."

Colorado promoter Barry Fey was particularly conflicted. He helped secure the passage of a Denver law that limited the resale of tickets beyond face value. He recalls once policing the line before Neil Dimond tickets went on sale: "A guy was there who didn't look like a Neil Diamond fan, so we went up to him and said, 'What's your favorite Neil Diamond song?' He said, 'I have no idea. I'm in line for my mother.' So we took him to a pay phone. He called his mother. I got on the phone; it was okay, so we put him back in line. We'd do anything to try and stop the scalpers."

However, when it came to shows he produced outside his home market, he took a different tack. There, he acknowledges, "I'd do what everybody else did. Brokers would be consistently calling me, and I said yes, and I'd get a high price, at least $25 or $50 a ticket over face value. I never sold them the best seats, never. They never got a front row out of me. But I did it. Christ, I wish I would have made some of the money some of these other guys did."

Still, when Doug Knittle set out on his own in 1977, leaving Troy Tickets for a storefront in Hermosa Beach (followed by locations in Anaheim, the San Fernando Valley and downtown L.A. in anticipation of the 1984 Olympics), he began to shift his personal focus away from rock music. "To cultivate the promoters took time and energy," he remembers. "At times, I'd stick my nose in, but I never took a tour. People would make a deal with the promoter or the manager of an artist and get the tickets for an entire tour." Instead, he increasingly worked with major corporate clients for high-profile sporting events.

"I'd sell Super Bowl tickets ten months before the game. Football season hadn't even started, and we sold them to Merrill Lynch, Coca-Cola, Pepsi-Cola. We had all the big accounts because they knew we could get the tickets. So they might say, 'Get me 200 tickets between the thirty yard lines at $4,000 apiece.' The key to success in the ticket business is not your ability to get tickets. The key to success is your ability to sell them. Distribution is critical. It's the only thing that matters. I was able to get all these tickets because I would sell them."

And just how would he get them?

Some of them he acquired from season ticket holders. But not your average season ticket holders. "One ticket office I ended up buying in the late '80s, this guy had come out from New York in the 1950s, and he had had about 700 USC season tickets at tunnel 7, which is the fifty yard line. Nowadays you might have to give $25,000 to $100,000 to USC to buy one of those tickets. He also had about 1,500 season tickets to the Rams [Los Angeles' NFL franchise, which left for St. Louis in 1994]."

Others came from savvy planning. One of Knittle's mentors was Harold Guiver, a former sports agent and later a Rams executive. "He and another guy started the Rose Bowl tours in the 1950s. They'd bring in all these folks from the Midwest to come to the Rose Bowl, and when the Rose Bowl expanded, they sold these bonds, and if you put the money up for these bonds, you were able to buy Rose Bowl tickets for the next twenty years at face value. He went to all these banks and explained it was a can't-lose deal, and he ended up with about 800 tickets, although he wanted about 5,000 of them. And the thing ran beyond twenty years — it ran for about forty."

Guiver, who had preceded Knittle as reigning monarch of Super Bowl tickets (and eventually would share the crown with him), was named by Oakland Raiders owner Al Davis during a deposition when Davis brought suit against the NFL in 1980 for refusing to allow him to move the team to Los Angeles. Davis alleged that L.A. Rams owner Carroll Rosenbloom had worked with Guiver to funnel thousands of tickets to brokers, with the height of the practice coming in 1977, when as Super Bowl host team for the game at the Rose Bowl, the Rams were allocated 30,000 tickets, many of which passed through Guiver's hands. Davis also charged (and Guiver later confirmed) that three years later, after Rosenbloom had passed away, his widow, Georgia, sold Guiver 1,000 seats to the 1980 Super Bowl, honoring a promise made by her late husband.

In the wake of these events the stream of tickets was stanched a bit. This lull was not destined to last, however, as one broker explained in a 1981 *Sports Illustrated* piece: "The Super Bowl is the single biggest scalping event since Little Bighorn. It's a single event scheduled at least two years in advance to take place in a certain city on a certain day. It can't be rained out. And it's a national event, the single most popular sporting spectacle of the year."

It soon fell to Knittle, who began working with Guiver, to help restore the flow. Eventually he did so by finding a way to ingratiate himself: "I was good at being able to figure out how to do something and present it in a way that folks could say yes." So he regularly helped defray the costs for the teams and players to entertain family and friends in exchange for the right to buy some of their tickets.

It all worked quite well, but as the years passed, the repetitive nature of the business began to take its toll on Knittle. So, after giving it a few months of thought and discussion, it was on to a new challenge. Knittle placed an ad for a chief technology officer on Monster.com and eventually hired someone out of Singapore to help him build his new site. The initial focus was his own inventory, as by this time Knittle owned a number of regional ticket agencies. One of these, San Francisco's St. Francis Theater Ticket Service, had been founded in the 1950s, allowing the new site to post on its About Us page that it "has been a leader in ticket brokering for sports since 1958."

As for a name, Knittle was looking for something a little less on the nose. "Every broker uses the word 'tickets.' I didn't want a name with what we do in it. We were looking for something different, something that people would remember, and so we came up with RazorGator. Actually my technology guy came up it." The fact that someone from a foreign country was responsible for the company's appellation likely adds clarity for some critics who remained confounded by this selection. Still, Knittle, who had run his company for many years under the radar with the generic title Special Events, has his own instincts for such matters.

Beyond company-owned inventory RazorGator soon sought to build a more robust marketplace by broadening consumer options. So Knittle turned to the founders of two broker-to-broker exchanges that had been operating quietly for nearly a decade.

In 1992 Pat Toole was running a small business selling computer components in Southern California, when one of his colleagues mentioned that a local broker was looking for someone to develop a software program to handle inventory control, customer maintenance and back office accounting. Toole agreed to create such a package gratis with the promise that he would be introduced to other potential clients. This eventually led to the widespread dissemination of his MasterBroker program, which eventually acquired 250 licensees over the next few years. In 1997 Toole expanded his reach with the creation of MasterBroker Exchange, allowing clients to access his server via their dial-up modems to share inventory details with the other ticket brokers on the system. A Web plug-in followed a few years later, as did a client base that approached 400.

Knittle recognized the value of MasterBroker and acquired it in the early days of RazorGator. He also purchased the other major broker exchange, Ticket Trader. By the fall of 2002, as Knittle inked a deal to become the secondary ticketing provider for FOXSports.com, RazorGator was swiftly becoming both well established and well stocked.

The LiquidSeats team looked on and recognized that their site needed a corresponding upgrade as well. So the company's engineers went to work developing software tools that could interface with existing inventory control systems such as MasterBroker. The new bulk upload programs allowed brokers to place their inventory on the StubHub exchange en masse with the click of a mouse.

LiquidSeat's user base and revenues accelerated accordingly.

2004 WAS A WATERSHED YEAR for Eric Baker and Jeff Fluhr.

The commitment to bulk upload software had secured a steadily rising volume of sales. Although brokers initially were wary about the competitive impact on their own bottom lines, former vice president of business development Jeff Berman suggests: "We were bringing them a massive audience, allowing them to cut back on marketing expenses and move their tickets at a much higher volume and much lower cost. This allowed them to focus on the things they were good at: acquiring tickets, pricing tickets and working the back-end office."

Ram Silverman, who cofounded Georgia's Golden Tickets in 1988, agrees with one qualification. "We started selling a lot of tickets, and the good side of it is it allowed us to cut our advertising budgets," he says. "We used to spend a million a year on advertising. That was a big part of our budget, and now they're spending that money for us and they're getting the business for us. But in return they're making a pretty big percentage for doing so." The rate eventually became fifteen percent from sellers and ten percent from buyers.

Starting in late 2002, Fluhr also began to experiment with Google's new paid search platform. "Jeff was able to manage that aggressively," Baker commends. "And this was before everyone and their brother had caught on to the fact that you could use AdWords to build a business."

Fluhr explains: "We realized after a period of paid search experimentation that we could drive a lot of traffic to our site, and we could track with surgical precision the profitability of that revenue. Since we knew how much we were paying, we could control it like a volume knob, and the beauty was we didn't have to share revenue with everybody. We had to pay for the customer acquisition, the marketing, the awareness-building, but once we got that customer, there'd be repeat usage, and they would tell their friends, so we had that viral marketing piece. Plus, we now had the relationship and we could market to that customer without any question about who owned the data, which was always a very sensitive piece of the negotiation with MSN and AOL."

So as 2003 came to a close, the company decided it was ready to implement a new strategy. The name LiquidSeats was dropped in favor of StubHub, which now became a consumer-facing website.

This shift made Jeff Berman's life much easier on the business development side, as he returned to many of the same teams that had once rebuffed him, cast a wide berth around the ticketing office and approached the sponsorship and advertising departments. Rather than a prospective revenue share, Berman was looking to purchase sponsorships (from folks who sold them on commission). Berman's pitch made it much more palatable for the organizations as well: "I brought them guaranteed marketing dollars, which allowed them to make money off the secondary market, but it also permitted them to take a step back and say, 'We have an arm's-length relationship with the secondary market. We are promoting it, but we are not the ones exchanging tickets.'"

By January 2005 StubHub had tripled its workforce (to nearly 100), its site visitors (attracting close to 1.5 million uniques per month) and its ticket sales (which approached $40 million). The company had announced deals with, among others, AOL, the Portland Trailblazers, the Detroit Lions and the University of Southern California Athletic Department and an arrangement with the Museum of Television & Radio that included charity auctions for live tapings of the *Tonight Show*, *American Idol* and the *Survivor* finale. However, as the new year arrived, the man who first envisioned the business was no longer part of its growth story.

After Eric Baker graduated from Stanford in May 2001, rather than join his cofounder in the San Francisco office, he opted to return to his home in Los Angeles, where he focused on corporate development, fundraising and communications, while Fluhr directed the day-to-day operations of the company ("Jeff was Mr. Inside; I was Mr. Outside"). "These guys had complementary strengths," Berman offers. "I don't think anyone can raise funds the way Baker can, and Jeff was really good at facing inward and downward." Still, the lack of physical proximity reflected an interpersonal and professional fissure, which only widened as the company expanded.

The abyss became non-navigable after Fluhr moved PR out of Baker's hands, relocating it to StubHub headquarters, under the domain of the new vice president of marketing, Anthony Rodio, a veteran of both Microsoft and Amazon ("[Rodio] wanted to oversee PR," Fluhr remembers, "and I thought we should give him a shot and that Eric should talk to the press when opportunities arose to do so, but that we should let this guy be the spokesman"). Baker was incensed by the decision and ultimately, Fluhr concluded, the tension had become too disruptive at a critical period for the company. Since Fluhr's founder's stock had finally vested in mid-2004, the CEO now retained a substantial controlling interest in StubHub, along with the ability to dismiss anyone from service, including the company's cofounder and president.

Baker was removed from the board and departed without any form of a severance package, both of which became critical to his next course of action.

"I think it was September 13 when I got canned officially, and then in November I was talking about taking a trip through Europe, when it struck me, 'Gee, they have tickets in Europe . . .' Since I had no severance and no employment contract, I could do what I wanted. I could have started HubStub across the street, but they figured, correctly, that I owned a double-digit chunk of the company, so that would be destroying my own value. So I never thought I would remain in ticketing until that moment two months later, when it occurred to me that the whole concept of ticket resale is not uniquely American and StubHub was in no position to go international. I was let go without a non-compete, and if they'd kept me on the board, I would have had a fiduciary responsibility to the company. So the fact that my exit wasn't handled the way I believe most people traditionally would have handled it turned out to be a blessing and a cautionary tale on how not to terminate people."

Baker moved to New York in January 2005, opened a London office a year later and in August 2006 launched his second secondary marketplace, Viagogo. "We needed a name that was easy to remember, easy to spell, had a URL available and didn't offend anyone in any language because we're in fifteen European countries," he offers. Baker then announced he had raised more than $20 million in funding and had signed exclusive deals with soccer powerhouses Manchester United and the Chelsea Football Club to establish official ticket exchanges.

Fluhr admits that he received some inkling of his former partner's plans in early 2005: "Initially there was some surprise and concern that faded over time. Going into '05, shifting into our consumer-driven strategy, we were hitting our stride, and since he wasn't really bugging us, I decided it would be a distraction for me to worry about it."

A week after Baker launched Viagogo, Fluhr received news that likely quelled any residual anxieties. *Inc. Magazine* ranked StubHub as the eighth fastest growing private company in America on its annual "Inc. 500" list. The magazine charted sales growth by StubHub over the preceding three years that topped 3,000 percent. The year 2006 would end with over $400 million of tickets sold on the site, representing more than $100 million in revenue.

However, StubHub's status as one of the nation's most rapidly accelerating private businesses was not destined to last, as it would join a public company within five months. In 2005 eBay concluded that the online ticket sales business was transitioning from pure auctions to fixed prices. At the same time StubHub was still gaining market share, although it was taking twenty-five percent of the ticket price as compared with six to eight percent on eBay. StubHub remained an acquisition target for well over a year because, as eBay's Greg Bettinelli explains, "There were multiple leadership teams, and eBay was pretty good at moving executives around, so you had a really short window where you could make a bet." Eventually that moment arrived, and in January 2007 terms were reached on a deal to buy the company. Eric Baker, Jeff Fluhr and the rest of the stockholders were cashed out to the dulcet tune of $310 million.

Ticketmaster was goosed into action.

THE SO-CALLED "FIRESIDE CHAT" TOOK place on Tuesday, May 13, 2008, at the Palms Casino Resort in Las Vegas. More than 100 ticket brokers who placed their inventory on the TicketsNow secondary marketplace had been invited to a closed door discussion with the company's relatively new CEO,

Cheryl Rosner, and Sean Moriarty, the chief executive of Ticketmaster, which had acquired TicketsNow for $265 million four months earlier.

The brokers were wary as TicketsNow had been founded by one of their own, who was then discharged of his duties shortly after the sale.

In the fall of 1992 Mike Domek, a recent dropout of Southern Illinois University in Carbondale, Illinois, decided to dabble in ticket resale. Back in high school the budding entrepreneur, who grew up on a farm sixty miles northwest of Chicago, had built a small but steady business as a hay broker: "We had one ad in the paper buying and one ad selling. We'd find deals, mark the hay up a quarter per bale and then try to make a quarter times a couple hundred bales." He came to apply this same idea to the ticketing space, starting with $100 of seed capital, working out of his apartment with a second phone line under the name VIP Tour Company. "I bought a music on hold adapter from Radio Shack, and we had an old computer that didn't work, so we'd be punching on the keyboard pretending we're computerized and we'd put callers on hold. They'd called an 800 number, so they had no idea we were just a bunch of dumb kids in the back of my apartment. Perception is everything." That perception became reality through the cultivation of a corporate clientele, and by January 1997, when the Green Bay Packers appeared in their first Super Bowl in nearly thirty years, Domek chartered an L-1011 aircraft to fly 350 clients down to New Orleans. "It was a nice business. We grew it to about $7 million in gross sales by the time we went online in 1999. I would say ninety-five percent of what we sold was somebody else's inventory."

The online marketplace that Domek launched in 1999 was purely broker-driven, as TicketsNow only permitted approved partners to upload listings, starting with sixteen brokers and ultimately reaching upwards of 500.[2] TicketsNow's success came through its broker relations and also through an early adoption of paid search, all of which was handled by Domek's team of self-educated self-starters: "Bob Kopsell was an out-of-work auto parts manager who helped bring me online. We had a superior broker sales guy, Nick Bucci, who was a concrete contractor before he came to work for me. My brother, who ran the search engine side, hung drywall and did custom plaster jobs. So I got my concrete guy, my drywall guy and my auto parts manager, and we did the transactional marketing better than anyone. StubHub did the brand marketing better than anyone, but we did the transactional marketing better than anyone." TicketsNow's gross sales support his contention, as they doubled annually for a few years, eventually reaching $300 million by 2008.

However, in mid-2007 some board members installed by venture capitalists who had recently invested in TicketsNow encouraged Domek to step aside as CEO while remaining as chairman ("I thought this was the next level of management. I'm an entrepreneur by definition, and entrepreneurs are not good at running large operations"). Cheryl Rosner's name was then brought to Domek's attention: "We found her through a search firm. She referenced pretty well and she could interview like you wouldn't believe." Rosner had no prior experience in ticketing but came from the world of finance and marketing.

The appointment of someone from outside the brokers' immediate circles proved unsettling to its community. However, the company's investors welcomed a CEO who could unlock TicketsNow's value through a sale or a public stock offering.

This feeling was underscored in the initial press release announcing Rosner's hiring, which emphasized, "Cheryl's solid experience in leading burgeoning companies, including her participation in Hotels.com's successful IPO in 2000, will serve to further accelerate TicketsNow's extraordinary corporate growth." In addition to her stint at Hotels.com, she had more recently served as president of Expedia Corporate Travel, and both companies, perhaps not entirely coincidentally, had been owned by Barry Diller's IAC group, which also owned Ticketmaster.

Today Moriarty offers three clear reasons for the TicketsNow purchase: "One, we were losing traction in the category because we were straitjacketed by the industry and legal landscape for a long time. Two, we knew that the StubHub acquisition by eBay would signal to the industry that, 'Look, this is coming and we need a solution to it.' And three, we liked the TicketsNow asset and the value we thought we could unlock by our ownership of it."

The online ticket resale market had seen an influx of would-be executives from MBA programs enter the space in recent years, and the long-standing brokers did not entirely trust the newbies. As Greg Bettinelli, the former director of eBay tickets, himself a business school graduate, offers: "I'm kind of bored by the MBA guys because they look at it as there's an inefficiency in the marketplace, and it's a complex math problem that needs to be solved. They got into the business tangentially because they saw a PowerPoint presentation that highlighted operational inefficiencies and the opportunities to consolidate a market.

"Meanwhile, the brokers are more blue-collar guys, gamblers, but they're incredibly sharp and this is their livelihood. If the power grid went out and we had to go old-school, I'd want to hang out with a broker versus somebody who's got an MBA because they're going to figure out how to survive and flourish. They figured out how to make a lot of money the untraditional way and get very protective when someone tries to take it away."

This is precisely what the purchase of TicketsNow represented to the brokers, an encroachment on their territory by a company (Ticketmaster) that often acted as their nemesis, blocking their ability to secure tickets and at times even confiscating them. Now that very same entity would have back-end access to the brokers' inventory and might raise some questions about how tickets were secured. The fact that Ticketmaster had systematically replaced Mike Domek and his longtime executives with new faces in the days and weeks following the sale did little to allay anxieties.[3]

The brokers also were troubled by the TicketExchange platform, which ostensibly allowed for the resale of tickets first purchased via Ticketmaster. However, in recent months some of the best seats in the house for various high-profile tours had been placed on TicketExchange at premium prices just minutes after the initial on-sale. Artists such as Beyoncé, Van Halen, Bon Jovi, Neil Diamond, Lynyrd Skynyrd/Hank Williams Jr. and the Eagles all seemed to be using the platform in such a manner, which many of the brokers believed was cutting into *their* business.

Moriarty's audience additionally sought clarification regarding computer technology that some brokers utilized to help acquire inventory. In April 2007 Ticketmaster had filed a lawsuit against RMG Technologies Inc., a company that had created TicketBrokerTools.com, a website that enabled its users to flood Ticketmaster.com with ticket requests, "in effect allowing them to cut in line," as characterized by Ticketmaster vice president and assistant general counsel Joseph Freeman.[4] Eliminating the use of automated ticket buying software, or "bots," as they were commonly referred to in the press, had become something of a cause célèbre in the wake of the Hannah Montana Best of Both Worlds Tour, which kicked off in the fall of 2007.

"All hell broke loose with Hannah Montana," Arkansas chief deputy attorney general Justin Allen explained at the time, as he vowed to investigate the matter. "The tickets were gone in 12 minutes and when people turned around, they were selling at online sites for sometimes as much as 10 times the face value."

As Greg Bettinelli recalls: "That was great for StubHub and a big headache for Ticketmaster. It was a real catalytic event. The one person you don't want to piss off is a parent because they don't buy a lot of tickets and don't understand how the game works. If Disney Channel was advertising that tickets go on sale at 10:00 a.m., it wasn't advertising that tickets would be sold out at 10:01. In the real world if someone says that a sale starts at 10:00, you can still go to the Nordstrom at 11:00. A lot of moms had promised their kids, 'Oh yeah, I'll get you tickets to Miley Cyrus,' but by the time they checked, the tickets were all gone. Then when they Googled 'Miley Cyrus Tickets,' they could see them on sale for $300 at another site. It was an audience that had no problem with calling their attorney general, and it was a win-win situation for the politicians because who wasn't going to support moms over ticket scalpers and Ticketmaster?"

Ticketmaster had indeed taken the brunt of the heat after most of the Hannah Montana concerts sold out so quickly, only for tickets then to appear immediately on secondary sites. It all just seemed suspicious to people who were not familiar with the present-day particulars of online sales. *USA Today* reported, "The whiplash speed with which Hannah Montana tickets disappeared prompted grumbling from many parents, folks who in many cases hadn't bought tickets to a concert since the days when Pearl Jam was a little-known band from Seattle." The piece then outlined the means by which some desperate parents had resorted to scalping, buying tickets for distant locales and then reselling them at elevated prices to fund the purchase of seats to local venues. As Bettinelli noted, it was a boon for StubHub, which in early December announced that the Best of Both Worlds Tour had already generated more than $10 million in sales on its site.

In part to restore public relations and also out of a genuine frustration (the RMG suit had after all preceded the Hannah Montana contretemps), Ticketmaster pledged increased vigilance when it came to users that it believed were employing bot technology, threatening to block any users from its site that it suspected of the practice.[5] Meanwhile brokers who employed a range of online tools, including some relatively innocuous ones that simply trolled the Ticketmaster site looking for any "ticket drops," which often followed the initial on-sale, wanted some clarity regarding potential bans from Ticketmaster.com.

These issues all simmered as Sean Moriarty picked up a microphone to offer some brief remarks before fielding questions from a slightly restless audience. Attendees had already sat through a presentation by Henry Harteveldt of Forrester Research on the impact of "digital channels" on the secondary ticket market, as well as the latest TicketsNow marketing campaign, introduced by Rosner (the ticket monkey radio spot didn't play so well).

"Someone told me there was going to be a dunking booth here, and I'm glad I don't see one," Moriarty began somewhat awkwardly, eliciting minimal response from the stone-faced brokers.

Then he got down to business, attempting to engage the assembly by cutting to the crux of the meeting's purpose: "I feel like we've been in the same business for a long time but approaching it from different ways. The question on everybody's mind is, 'How are our worlds coming together? How is this going to work?' And, ultimately, 'What's in it for me?' which is a fair question to ask."

It was such a fair question that it was rephrased and redirected at Moriarty seven minutes later by Gary Adler, lead attorney for the National Association of Ticket Brokers (an organization founded in 1994, following public outcry after extensive fraud surrounding the resale of tickets to that year's Rose Bowl). Adler picked up a microphone and queried, "Tell us, why is this good for our members of a growing community?"

"I touched on that a bit in the opening remarks . . ." Moriarty swiftly responded, with a hint of exasperation and also resignation about the session to follow. He then circled back for another take on his initial assertion: "We never would have bought a business that we fundamentally didn't believe we could make better, make more valuable and service the clients who drive that business."

There was something of a culture clash in the room because, while the brokers wanted to hear his specific position on a range of topics and situations, Moriarty tended to offer generalities and MBA-speak. This became apparent after the questions began rolling in regarding the use of TicketExchange. He did acknowledge that some performers were indeed placing their own inventory on the platform, explaining, "What you're seeing now very clearly are the principals saying 'I want to participate in my own initial public offering.'" Still, he refused to offer any additional details: "I'm not in the business of disclosing the individual client practices to the general public. I think that's bad practice, and I don't think anyone in this room would like their business put forth in front of the general public. I don't think it makes any sense."

Moriarty also was reluctant to provide any specificity when it came to illicit computer technology. Instead, rather than providing any narrow definitions, which might allow for circumvention once the boundaries were tightly drawn, he emphasized that any automated devices designed to overload the Ticketmaster site would be unacceptable (and in June the California District Court judge assigned to the RMG lawsuit gave credence to the company's self-policing efforts by ruling in Ticketmaster's favor[6]).

Despite what was interpreted by some attendees as caginess on these two issues, Ticketmaster's CEO did win over a number of the skeptical brokers during the two hours that followed by expressing interest in two of their suggestions: to open dedicated TicketsNow box office windows at venues and to establish a dedicated broker hotline for Ticketmaster-related administrative issues.

However, he induced groans and a few hisses when he characterized the company's legislative efforts: "We've been fighting for unencumbered resale rights from the very, very beginning."

Greg Bettinelli takes issue with this assertion and has the souvenirs to back his position up: "When I was at eBay, I used to put Ticketmaster cease and desist letters on my wall as a badge of honor. They ran their business based on trying to protect their contracts, and they were trying to scare the marketplace into not wanting to work with anyone else for fear they would get sued. Early on they tried to take the principles of the primary market and apply it to the secondary market, pushing for exclusivity in the laws so that the ticketing company had the sole rights on the secondary, but the legislators weren't going to give them another monopoly."

Eric Baker concurs: "Sean's a really nice guy, but I'll tell you what their playbook was. They tried to get legislation passed that said resale should be illegal unless it's done with the blessing of the team or by the team's ticketing provider. I don't blame them. That would be a great rule if you're the team's ticketing provider, but that just didn't fly."

"If you look back to the first few years of the decade, Ticketmaster had its own hamstrung environment that went above and beyond the law," a former company executive recalls. "We were working with teams on the primary side and there was a perceived conflict of interest from a lot of our clients: 'We want you to focus on selling our ticket the first time, not the second time,' which allowed the other businesses to ramp up. We were also a public company, and while StubHub could be a bit more cavalier about local laws, we did business in those states. So for a mix of legal reasons and client conflict reasons, we sat on the sideline until the picture clarified and the teams came to recognize that this was happening with or without their participation."

The first team that came to this conclusion was the NHL's Columbus Blue Jackets. Starting in January 2002, season ticket holders were permitted to log on to a website and sell their seats to the public at a price predetermined by the team, in this case five percent above face value. In her article on the new enterprise, the *Wall Street Journal*'s Julia Angwin opened, "Meet the newest competition for ticket scalpers: Ticketmaster." This line likely didn't play so well in either corporate office, but what eBay and StubHub soon pointed out was that Team Exchange wasn't a free market for consumers because tickets were never allowed to be priced below face value (which was certainly a relevant factor in this instance since the Blue Jackets held the worst record in the NHL's Western Conference that season).

The next phase of Ticketmaster's efforts to move beyond its traditional distribution model came the following June. The company debuted an auction platform for a few seats at the Lennox Lewis–Vitali Klitschko heavyweight championship fight at the Staples Center in Los Angeles. That fall the format was used for a Sting concert at New York's Hammerstein Ballroom, with proceeds going to UNICEF. This charitable component then fell by the wayside in many instances as artists authorized auctions of certain tickets to test and taste the value of primary tickets sold at secondary market prices. As Moriarty then explained: "We're creating an opportunity whereby fans have the ability to get tickets to the shows they want at prices they're willing to pay in a safe, open and transparent environment. And the industry — the artists and producers and promoters who have worked so hard to bring their offering to market — have the opportunity to truly capture the value of the experience they're offering. That's a much better option, a much more fair one, for the parties involved."

Madonna, Tim McGraw and Faith Hill, Shakira, Kelly Clarkson, Red Hot Chili Peppers and Roger Waters were among the artists who opted for the "fair" approach and participated in Ticketmaster auctions. *Pollstar*'s Gary Bongiovanni offered his own critique of the auctions, which "move the concert market even further from its roots: music for the people. Concerts are supply and demand, and the person with the most coconuts gets the prize."

Ticketmaster had extended its Exchange platform beyond season ticket holders and into the concert setting by the time that eBay purchased StubHub in January 2007, but sales were still lagging far behind many of the secondary sales sites. In an effort to remedy this and maintain its status as a market leader, Ticketmaster began thinking of an acquisition. As one observer recalls: "They were positioning to go public, to do a spin-off [after spinning the company back in, IAC would spin the company back out in the summer of 2008]. So they needed a growth story and needed to pump up international and secondary as avenues for growth because their core business, which was great, just wasn't growing. They needed something in their portfolio just to tell Wall Street that they were going to be playing in this high-growth secondary market." A Ticketmaster employee adds: "Our secondary software had limitations. The architecture worked fine for season ticket holders, but it was inadequate to support large numbers of individual sellers because of the way it was all tied to bar codes."

Ticketmaster believed it had identified a suitable target in mid-2007 when it entered into talks with Doug Knittle's RazorGator. This was not the first time that Ticketmaster considered such an expansion, as in mid-2001 Sean Moriarty had been part of a fact-finding mission that had carried him, along with John Pleasants and a team of six to eight business development executives and lawyers, into San Francisco's Deep Mission for a dialogue with StubHub. Jeff Fluhr remembers, "This was shortly before we launched our deals with Arizona [Diamondbacks] and Seattle [Mariners]. We knew it was early to sell the company and we weren't interested unless they were going to offer a very compelling price. I don't remember that there was much price discussion, but they decided not to do it, and within a year they launched Team Exchange."

Six years later, motivated by the eBay acquisition, Ticketmaster was game for a move of its own. However, the company's accountants couldn't quite wrap their heads around RazorGator's financials. The strength of the company was less its broker marketplace than its own inventory sales, which exceeded $100 million per year, representing more than half the volume on the site. Knittle offers, "You have to remember that to do what we were doing was much harder than what everybody else was doing, but our profits were sixty to one hundred percent more." The company also ran a lucrative hospitality business for corporate clients focused on such major events as the Super Bowl and the NCAA Final Four. In 2006 RazorGator rolled out its TicketOS software, signing on Bank of America as the first licensee. The goal was to help large-scale business entities manage their inventory, which in the case of sponsorship deals with teams or tours could represent thousands of tickets. One additional TicketOS element was a "concierge" feature that "leverages RazorGator's industry connections for Hard-to-Get tickets to easily access in-demand events beyond company-owned tickets."

Ticketmaster and RazorGator remained in the due diligence phase for well over three months, hung up on just how RazorGator accounted for those "Hard-to-Get tickets." There were two elements here, as Knittle points to the challenge of "financial reconciliation, which is the hardest piece, to be able to scale to $200, $300 or $400 million of owned inventory and reconcile them in real time." He also admits: "At the time we were buying a lot of tickets from Ticketmaster using other people's credit cards. We don't even do that anymore, and it was a part of the problem, but it wasn't that important of a business channel to lose."

Another industry exec adds: "RazorGator had long-standing relationships with a lot of the teams' owners and presidents, and when it came to Super Bowl tickets, you'd see big cash outlays, but you wouldn't have anything documented about what that money was used for. So while ticket brokers might do great business, from an accounting perspective it's not the type of business that's necessarily suitable for a publicly traded company." This was the conclusion that Ticketmaster ultimately reached as well.

Sean Moriarty and his executive vice president, Eric Korman, swiftly regrouped and directed a newfound ardor to TicketsNow, which had been ramping itself up for such an opportunity. The only other company on the shortlist was TicketNetwork, a burgeoning secondary empire founded by Don Vaccaro in 2002. As an August 28, 2009 *New York Times* profile reflects: "Mr. Vaccaro seems to pride himself on bridging the generations. He got his start 30 years ago in classic Damone fashion [*Fast Times at Ridgemont High's* resident reseller, Mike Damone] when he snagged 20 tickets for a Jethro Tull concert at Madison Square Garden, and he built his brokerage the old-fashioned way. 'I bought and sold tickets on the street for years,' he said."

In this spirit, at its outset TicketNetwork's focus was on smaller brokers and affiliates, often drawing in partners that wanted to move into the space but needed help with back-end development. Along the way Vaccaro added such ancillary businesses as the TicketNews informational website and the Ticket Summit, a conference and trade show devoted to the secondary market. As Ben Sisario wrote in the *Times*, "Everything in Don Vaccaro's world is called ticket something-or-other" (including the company's mascot, a feline named Ticket, and her kittens, Stub 1 and Stub 2). The ticket network's 2007 revenues topped out at $83.8 million, earning it slots on the annual list of growth companies published by Inc.com and Deloitte.

TicketsNow, however, nearly tripled that figure. The Illinois-based business now run by former IAC employee Cheryl Rosner was deemed to have better technology along with a broader audience. So on January 14, 2008, Ticketmaster announced that it would buy the company for $265 million.[7]

One Ticketmaster alumnus contends: "When eBay bought StubHub, it purchased a company with a lot more resources in terms of cash and positive public perception. I think Ticketmaster overreacted by saying, 'We can't do this ourselves. We need to buy TicketsNow.' The purchase price was about the same as what eBay paid for StubHub, but StubHub was three times bigger. It was a defensive move."[8]

Greg Bettinelli, admittedly no Ticketmaster cheerleader, contends, "I would argue that the secondary market is the reason why Ticketmaster eventually put itself up for sale [to Live Nation] because they made bad bets, worried about the wrong people, focused on the wrong things and spent a lot of time thinking about problems they didn't need to think about."

What can be said with certainty is that over an eighteen month period beginning in the spring of 2007 with the acquisition of echomusic, an online marketing and fan club business, and extending through the fall of 2008 with the purchase of a controlling interest in Irving Azoff's Front Line Management, Ticketmaster moved well beyond its origins as a venue-attentive ticketing provider. Two weeks after buying TicketsNow, Ticketmaster added a European exchange with the purchase of Get Me In! (Viagogo's Eric Baker immediately responded, "As the largest secondary ticketing exchange in Europe, we are always excited to see the further validation of the industry.")

Then in late April 2008 the company moved into the specialized realm of VIP packages when it added "The Mothafuckin' Ticket Queen" Shelley Lazar's SLO Limited to the portfolio.

IT ALL STARTED WITH THE little scraps of paper.

By the mid-1970s Shelley Lazar had established herself as the New York City point of contact for beleaguered road managers eager to turn over their collection of used matchbooks, torn hotel stationery, wrinkled business cards and other detritus covered with hastily scribbled names. Lazar's daytime gig was in an elementary school classroom at Brooklyn's PS 277. (Chris Rock was one of her third grade students, and future Scandal vocalist Patty Smyth was in her kindergarten class.) By night she handled the band guest lists for many of the major acts making the pilgrimage to Manhattan. There was an unparalleled, manic energy to artists' New York dates, where Lazar recalls, "We didn't get a representative from Columbia; we got Walter Yetnikoff. We didn't get a representative from Atlantic; we got Ahmet Ertegun." So with all else going on, the road managers were relieved to know that promoters such as Bill Graham and Ron Delsener had deputized Lazar to collect the names and coordinate the appropriate tickets, wristbands or stick-on passes.

Lazar had arrived at this position through persistence, organizational skills and versatility, working from the front of house ("When I ripped people's tickets, they'd say, 'Give me the bigger half,' and I being the teacher would say, 'There's no such thing as a bigger half,' knowing full well they just wanted the name of the artist that they were going to see") to the backstage ("In order to have the food ready for dinner when I was catering, I would give lessons to my class on cooking certain foods that I would then bring backstage and serve to the artists. So I would go to school and say, 'Okay, class, today we're going to make sweet and sour meatballs.' Billy Joel loved my sweet and sour meatballs. I would teach the kids, and with their dirty hands from the sandbox they would come in and help me make the food that I would then bring in and heat up."). From her various perspectives, Lazar came to know the musicians, managers and agents rather well, starting at a moment in the early 1970s when the business of rock had not yet become altogether professional and commodified, where a party atmosphere often predominated and a steady, reliable presence was all the more appreciated.

After a few years of struggling to decipher the handwriting on various odds and ends, she took a step toward formalizing the process. "I said to the artists and road managers, 'Rather than these little pieces of paper, how about we do it more organized? You give people my phone number, and they'll call me, and you'll tell me that they're calling and we'll try to put some order in all of this.' That's how I came up with the idea of making a business. I had to get paid, so I told the artists I would be working with, 'I'll charge a service charge, and that'll be my fee. It'll be $2.50 or $3.50 or $5 dollars [per ticket]," and people would pay me in cash and go off to the show. And then I started supervising all the credentials. I was gathering more moss, and I saw there was a need to be doing the artists' friends and family ticketing."

Increasingly she found herself doing just that, working for the Rolling Stones, Elton John, Neil Diamond and Rod Stewart when they came through the Tri-State Area. Then in August 1981, before classes started, Lazar joined an act on the road for the first time, traveling to Los Angeles with Bruce Springsteen for his seven shows at the Sports Arena. She recalls, "I organized all the guest ticketing in LA, and I remember Jackson Browne coming to pick up tickets from me at the hotel, saying, 'This is a great fucking idea. They've got you, Shelley, and you know who needs to sit where. You know where the record company people need to sit. You know who's friends, who's not friends.'"

By the mid-1980s Lazar decided it was time to make new friends of her own by hosting pre-show dinner parties that came packaged with some of the best seats in the house. These were special events that she coordinated either at the venue or at a nearby restaurant that also often included a back-stage tour and a piece of commemorative merchandise. She successfully lobbied many of the acts to supply her with the tickets that provided the main selling point for these packages, pitching, "These are your great fans and these are your great tickets, so why not give your great fans the great tickets?" (Some artists passed, believing that the price point would lock out many of their great fans.) Lazar's initial customers came through the group sales offices at venues, who contacted corporate clients that normally pur-chased tickets to sporting events and sold them on her VIP concert experi-ences. The response was significant, and the profits were split by Lazar, the group sales staff and the artists.

"Then I started calling the special events people. I would call Don Law's office and deal with the man there who handled charitable events and the people he knew, the high rollers who always came to the promoter's office to buy tickets. From there it was the record companies — 'Let's do a dinner party before the show and escort people to their seats.'"

The music industry became her full-time employment in the summer of 1988, after an incident in the classroom left her rattled. "I had put in twenty years, but things had changed. I was assaulted by a parent in June, and I said, 'Next time she's going to have a gun or a knife, and I'm going to be dead. This is crazy, and it's not what it was.' So I left. I went out on the Amnesty tour and I never came back." (Lazar's old friend Bill Graham produced the 1988 Human Rights Now! Tour in support of Amnesty International, which featured Bruce Springsteen and the E Street Band, Sting, Peter Gabriel, Tracy Chapman and Youssou N'Dour.)

By the mid-1990s Lazar had a thriving business, offering "experiential packages" that typically included backstage tours, soundchecks and/or meet-and-greets along with front row seats in her highest-end offerings. Her clients included performers such as Paul McCartney, Bob Dylan, Barbra Streisand, the Eagles, The Who, KISS, Tina Turner, Paul Simon, the Police and more recently Lady Gaga, Robert Plant and Alison Krauss, John Legend and Conan O'Brien's "Legally Prohibited from Being Funny on Television" Tour.

Meanwhile she has continued to offer friends and family ticketing services to many of these acts and some others who won't commit to VIP allotments. Lazar has also been hired to handle seating arrangements for the MTV Music Awards and Movie Awards as well as two papal masses ("They called *me*, a little Jewish girl from Brooklyn . . . I said to Pope John Paul II, 'Good yontif, Pontiff,' and Pope Benedict said to me, 'My boss is Jewish too.'")

A few years ago Paul McCartney pulled her aside. "I don't understand, Shelley," he queried. "We're sold out and we don't have any tickets, and then somebody comes and we need more tickets, and you're always finding tickets. Where are these tickets coming from?"

"Well, Paul," she responded, "I blow the fire marshal in every building, and when you blow the fire marshal, the fire lanes get narrower and you can add seats."

At the end of the tour Sir Paul gave her a pair of autographed kneepads.

So just where did she find seats on the McCartney tour?

"I blew the fire marshal," she reiterates with a laugh. "Listen, there's always ways to find more seats. There's no such thing as a sold-out show."

This may well be the case, although, for members of the general public lacking the wherewithal or the disposable income, "sold out" is often a definitive pronouncement and one that comes far sooner than they expect.

VIP ticketing is the antithesis of the secondary market in certain respects as it allows performers to sell seats directly to fans while reaping the benefits that otherwise would accrue to brokers. However, it does further constrict the pipeline of quality seats available through the initial on-sale to the general public. Typically, weeks before a given tour is even announced, Lazar (or any of her growing list of competitors) estimates how many packages are likely to sell in each city, contacts the box office, receives a seat map and makes inventory requests. As long as there are no competing holds (more on that in a moment), the tickets are allocated for VIP sales. Lazar points out that she is conscious of not taking an entire front row of seats (and if she can't sell some portion of her allocation, she releases that back to the box office a week or two before the show). Still, there is no question that in some instances upward of 500 choice tickets are directed to this channel.

As for holds, particularly when it comes to amphitheater shows, VIP tick-eters will often run headfirst into season ticketing conflicts. Unlike the box seats that typically ring the rear of the front section in most outdoor venues, these subscriptions focus on the first few rows of the venue. While one imag-ines that some corporate clients would take an interest in such opportuni-ties, the overwhelming portion of season ticket holders are brokers. In some facilities, such as Shoreline Amphitheatre in Mountain View, California, the entire first row of seats can be taken in this manner. Greg Bettinelli, who in 2008 moved from eBay to Live Nation, where he crunched the numbers for season ticket sales, remembers: "I spent a lot of time on pricing strategy because a lot of the guys who bought season tickets were ticket brokers. You want them to make a little bit of money, but you don't want to leave money on the table."

In 1999 New York's Bureau of Investor Protection and Securities issued a report entitled "Why Can't I Get Tickets?" One section, subtitled "Seats That Are Never Available to the General Public," outlined the existence of ticket clubs, by which participants could secure inventory. The first of these, run by promoters Ron Delsener and Mitch Slater, included 400 fee-paying members who were permitted to receive two tickets per concert.

Delsener's long-standing competitor John Scher professes: "Look, I com-pete with somebody who ran an amphitheater that happens to be out on Long Island, and there was a show [in 1996] where it turned out that every single ticket in the first ten rows got scalped. It was for a Hootie & the Blowfish show. Well documented. *Daily News* or the *Post* did a huge exposé. Nothing happened to the promoter; the box office guy took the fall . . . I can tell you this — and I'll take a lie detector test — I've never scalped a ticket in my life — never once, ever, of my own shows, ever, ever, ever, not one time, not one ticket. And you know what? I'm a schmuck."

This may be technically accurate (the scalping not the schmuck designa-tion). However, the report also indicates that his Metropolitan Entertainment club maintained 100 to 200 members.

Lazar once had her own Executive Ticket Club, which she says she has since closed. "That was created for the people coming up to me asking for favors, all of my doctors, for instance. So I said, 'If you want access to Shelley's Rolodex, whether it's a tour I'm working on or not, you want to go to the Super Bowl, you're asking me to do you a favor, you have to join my club. Just like if you want to play golf at the Olympic Club, you have to join the club.' People paid dues and had access to anything I could get tickets for, and I would say I'm pretty successful. The hardest for me is usually the NCAA Final Four because so many tickets go to the school and the brokers, but the Super Bowl, Wimbledon . . . Sir George Martin got tickets to the rugby finals in South Africa from me because I know people in ticketing from all around the world. But too many people wanted to join, and we had too many members who were entitled to buy as many tickets as they wanted. So now, if people buy tickets through me, they pay a service charge, which I never charged before."

As for the incident Scher references regarding Hootie, this took place at Jones Beach amphitheater during the summer of 1996. It was exposed because the group was particularly vigilant in its egalitarian ticket distribution practices. Manager Rusty Harmon recalls: "That summer the three biggest shows were us, Dave Matthews and Melissa Etheridge. While Melissa and Dave were charging $32 to $40 a ticket, our ticket prices were $17.50 to $22.50. We tried to keep tickets as low as we could for the longest time because our theory was that a year ago you could see us in a club for $7 to $10, so why would we go to $40 now? We also wanted to keep it fair to the fans. So with that in mind we had a policy that promoters couldn't take tickets out of the first twenty rows for promo or specialty items or gold circle or anything like that. We wanted to make sure that real fans could get the best seats in the house."

Acting on a tip, the group's tour accountant, Michael Loric, discovered that all of the tickets in the first eleven rows for the group's performances on August 3 and 4 had been placed into a hold status by the box office before the general on-sale and were later scarfed up and directed to brokers. A month before the show, at the behest of the New York attorney general's office, the band announced that due to box office misfeasance, it would issue refunds for tickets in the first *ten* rows, with state officials later questioning anyone who arrived with seats in row 11, hoping to uncover inculpatory evidence (no fruitful leads were found).

According to former CAA agent Tom Ross, who led the company's music division, rumors about Jones Beach had been circulating that summer. "Everyone knew what they were doing, and every manager would go to the box office and say, 'Look, we know . . .' The response was, 'What are you talking about? Would we do that to you? We've been doing shows here . . . We make a nice living. We don't need to do that.' They blamed it on the brokers. They blamed it on the fans that could get online and buy six tickets and sell four."

Ultimately, after a grand jury hearing, the box office manager pleaded guilty to second-degree grand larceny and third-degree computer tampering and was sentenced to sixty days in jail but never implicated anyone else.

Seven years before the Jones Beach incident, promoter Michael Cohl faced allegations that he had directed large numbers of tickets to the secondary market. Cohl acknowledges that he made very aggressive efforts to monetize the Rolling Stones' *Steel Wheels* tour to cover his tremendous overhead, which included unprecedented guarantees he made to the band. However, he does not acknowledge direct sales to brokers.

Instead one of the means he used to generate new revenue streams was the first large-scale VIP ticketing operation. By 1989 Shelley Lazar had stepped away from the classroom and was ready to ramp up her business. "So I said to Michael, 'We can do it. Let's dip our toes in the major markets. The worst that can happen is we don't sell any and we release those tickets to public sale.' But it was a huge success."

Lazar's VIP ticketing was just one of the means Cohl employed to maximize his return. He also allocated an estimated 70,000 tickets to Event Transportation Systems, a Canadian company that packaged seats with a bus ride to the show (although many fans purchased the seats at the premium price and then drove themselves). In November 1990 *Rolling Stone* reported that many of these tickets were funneled through a range of middlemen to brokers across the country. Tom Ross, who is quite willing to call out any questionable practices, defends the travel packages: "When you'd go and tour Canada with a big act, there was a guy who would go to all the outlying areas, outlying cities, and he would put together bus tours for the bumpkins in the small cities. He'd buy tickets for whoever the artist was, and they would provide you with good tickets in the first third of the house, a bus ride, a party, a local radio guy, a keg of beer on the bus . . . and they made a nice profit putting together the package. They were very successful, and it went on for years and years."

Nonetheless, going back to *Steel Wheels* dates, Ross suggests that Cohl pitched acts on his ability to access the resale market. "He was probably the first promoter who used that to lure acts into the national tour business or the world tour business by saying, 'This is twenty-five percent of your revenue that we can make bigger, because either you're sharing in this secondary market that other people are making money on or you're not sharing in it at all.' He wasn't wrong. People unconnected with the show and unconnected with the business are sitting at home smoking cigars and making five times more than the promoter."

With the rise of the Internet's secondary markets, artists increasingly began to appreciate this point. While many of the questions that the brokers directed at Sean Moriarty during the fireside chat revolved around musicians, such as Neil Diamond and the Eagles, who seemed to be placing their own inventory on Ticketmaster's TicketExchange, what few in the room likely knew was that Céline Dion had very much changed the model in 2007 when her management solicited bids to handle the "premium ticketing" aspect of her tour, pitting Ticketmaster against StubHub, with the former company emerging victorious. She was followed by Bon Jovi, Van Halen, Billy Joel and Elton John, and Britney Spears. Another broker, who held season tickets in the fifth and sixth rows at the DTE Energy Center in Michigan, complained that he was having his seats pulled back and sold for major acts such as Jimmy Buffett. Again Moriarty steadfastly refused to provide any specifics, beyond indicating that "our clients have chosen in some cases to use auctions and use Exchange as a way to sell tickets for the first time to the general public."

Two weeks before the meeting in Vegas, Ticketmaster had signaled that it was inclined to revisit its traditional business model with the purchase of Shelley Lazar's SLO Limited. While she had not been actively looking to sell, Lazar recognized that it might be the right time for such a strategic alliance since the Internet had lowered the entry point for competition. She had seen some of this firsthand when she began working with Dell Furano and his Signatures merchandise business, only to see Furano later break off and begin approaching artists on his own. Promoter AEG established its own VIP ticketing division (and was so aggressive at times that it seemed the only way to buy tickets to a Black Eyed Peas show was via the four available VIP packages). Meanwhile younger competitors arose such as Dan Berkowitz, former tour manager for the Disco Biscuits, who used his connections in the jamband world to create CID Entertainment, which services music festivals like Coachella and Bonnaroo and artists like the Black Crowes, Maxwell and the Kings of Leon. (Another artist client was the Dead in 2009, where CID offered packages with seats in the first few rows. Things had come a long way since Calico and Steve Marcus examined the envelopes and index cards on the floor of the GDTS offices, searching for anomalies.)

SLO Limited's biggest rival was founded by a former client: Irving Azoff. Lazar worked with the Eagles for three tours until the manager decided to launch his own service, I Love All Access, to offer premium packages for his Front Line Management clients.

When Lazar received her offer from Ticketmaster in the spring of 2008, Live Nation had countered with one of its own. However, she signed with Ticketmaster because, "I felt it kept me more neutral. I thought if I worked with one promoter, it might take my business away from other tours."

Her status shifted on Tuesday, February 10, 2009, when Ticketmaster and Live Nation announced their plans to merge.

Not only did a promoter now own SLO, but given that Irving Azoff and Howard Kaufman's Front Line Management was owned by Ticketmaster, Shelley Lazar was competing with I Love All Access, a property held independently by Azoff, who had become CEO of Ticketmaster.

Things were about to get messy.

CHAPTER 11

It's a Live Nation

IN 2005 TICKETMASTER AND CLEAR Channel Entertainment began making strategic moves as their exclusive agreement, signed in 1998, was due to expire at the end of 2008. At the heart of it all was a desire by each to have a greater, more direct relationship with artists.

Coming out of the String Cheese Incident settlement in early 2004, Ticketmaster began actively looking at how to reposition itself in the value chain. The same year Irving Azoff relaunched Front Line Management Group with his longtime friend Howard Kaufman, this time rolling up other major management companies into an unrivaled management group. For the effort he raised $100 million from investors that included, among others, Ticketmaster, Warner Music Group and Cablevision. Front Line quickly became the industry's biggest management company with approximately 200 clients that included the Eagles, Jimmy Buffett, Neil Diamond, Van Halen, Fleetwood Mac, Christina Aguilera, Aerosmith and Steely Dan, and nearly 100 managers, whom some estimate as accounting for perhaps forty percent of the top-tier acts (nearly double Front Line's closet rival).

Since emerging in the 1970s as the Eagles' manager, Azoff had become an undisputed force within the industry. He took over the struggling MCA Records in 1983 and set it back on course. (Not without controversy, as reputed East Coast mobster Salvatore Pisello worked out of the company's Los Angeles offices, swindling wholesalers in deals for "cut out," discounted records. The Feds, after years of investigation, ultimately found no legal wrongdoing.)

In righting MCA's ship, Azoff also created a concert division in the mid-1980s that he oversaw, partnering with PACE and waging turf battles against longtime promoters like Barry Fey in Denver.[1]

Leaving MCA in 1989, Azoff went on to head Giant Records, a division of Warner Music, for nearly a decade until he sold his fifty percent share in 2001 to focus strictly on management.

The concert industry had dramatically changed since Azoff had left MCA, and — the story goes — he found it difficult to get the deals he wanted from Clear Channel. So, taking matters into own his hands, he reformed Front Line because his experience had taught him, "The only way to fight big is with big." Ticketmaster saw a direct relationship with Front Line and its stable of artists as the key to its future success.

"We created an artist services label called Blend, we did the deal with Front Line — we were moving in and around all kinds of things like this — and on the horizon was the end of the Clear Channel contract," recalls former Ticketmaster CEO John Pleasants of the company's repositioning. "[The contract] probably represented fifteen to eighteen percent of Ticketmaster's tickets. There was no [other client] as big as that. The next one was in the single digits. That's a big deal."

Pleasants, who left Ticketmaster in 2005, says that he "was in negotiations with Clear Channel about lots of things that could happen. There were many other discussions that happened with other clients about things that could happen, and Clear Channel was on the verge of what ultimately happened — going into a [ticketing] deal with CTS Eventim." Before the CTS deal would be completed two years later, in December 2007, Clear Channel Entertainment had some internal restructuring to do.

When thirty-six-year-old Michael Rapino took over Clear Channel's spin-off of Clear Channel Entertainment — renamed Live Nation in 2005 — he was the division's fifth CEO in as many years. Like former CEO Brian Becker, he was deemed to have the potential to turn the company around.

Rapino had gotten his start at Labatt Breweries in the music sponsorship department in 1988. As a newcomer to the business in his early twenties, fresh out of college, Rapino cut his teeth under Michael Cohl, whose CPI was then a division of Labatt. (It financed Cohl's *Steel Wheels* deal in 1989.) He became director of marketing and entertainment before leaving in 1998, when Labatt divested its concert assets, and started his own promotion company with Steve Herman called Core Audience Entertainment, the second largest Canadian promoter at the time behind CPI. The company was sold to SFX in 2000, shortly after Clear Channel announced its acquisition. Prior to being tapped to run Live Nation, Rapino was Clear Channel Entertainment's chairman of European music.

Six months after taking over, in March 2006 Rapino delivered the keynote speech at the Concert Industry Consortium, an annual gathering of all the concert industry's key players. "In my early days in the business, I idolized — as did everyone else who worked in the business in Canada — Michael Cohl, Arthur Fogel and Donald Tarlton," he said. "They were the evangelists."

He went on: "[Cohl's] words of wisdom have remained with me. He said: 'If you want to be a promoter you can either keep working with the same model, or you can try to invent a new one.' When I got the Live Nation CEO job, my first question was, 'How can I change this model?'"

In just a matter of years, Rapino would be waging an inner company war with his old mentor over the future of what some deemed the music industry's new model — the 360 deal — while fighting a very public battle with Ticketmaster over ticketing.

And it all could likely have been avoided had Rapino been able to close on a deal he thought was as good as done: the acquisition of Front Line Management Group.

TICKETMASTER AND LIVE NATION WANTED to renew their contract. It was just a matter of figuring out terms they could agree on. After years of on-and-off negotiations, the time had come to make a decision.

"I think Michael Rapino was very candid about saying, 'I have a lot of things in my business that need to be fixed. I have a money-losing promotions business and a very thin margin venue business," says Sean Moriarty, who was Ticketmaster's CEO at the time and had previously been Pleasants' right hand for technology operations since the Citysearch days. "[Rapino's thought was,] 'I want to understand who my consumers are, and I want to be able to serve them better, and I want to be more involved in the ticketing process.'"

Moriarty, along with longtime Ticketmaster negotiations point person Terry Barnes, met Rapino at the Palm steak house on Santa Monica Boulevard in West Hollywood, a few blocks from Ticketmaster's headquarters and about a mile away from Live Nation's, to discuss matters as the window for negotiations became increasingly smaller.

Once seated and after a few pleasantries, Ticketmaster slid a piece of paper across the table to Rapino with their offer on it. They advised him to take the offer or else, no hard feelings — and business being business — they were going to crush him. Rapino shrugged off the threat and suggested that it wasn't the best tactic if they wanted to get the deal done. They needed to negotiate.

"They had an aggressive culture," says one person of Ticketmaster who was privy to the talks. "[Like] 'We do what we want, we're the biggest, we'll write a check and get this deal done. Nobody has ever left us because it's too scary when you look over the edge." Internally Rapino's staff gradually convinced him that Live Nation could leave Ticketmaster. Somebody had to stand up to the longtime bully, they argued, and they were the ones to do it because overnight they would become the second largest ticketing company in North America, owing to their venue portfolio.

As it continued strained negotiations with Ticketmaster, Live Nation let it be known to other ticketing companies that the deal was far from complete. After a flood of applications Live Nation narrowed down the field to a possible five: Paciolan, Audience View, Vertical Alliance, CTS Eventim and, still, Ticketmaster.[2] Live Nation sent a team to each company for a week to look over its code and programming, with the end result typically being a 100-page-plus report on that company's ticketing system.

After much analysis it was clear that German-based CTS Eventim, with its sophisticated architecture and proven performance under heavy load demands, was the only other company that could go head to head with Ticketmaster. (CTS cited its flawless service for the World Cup in 2006, where it handled thirty million inquiries in the first hour.)

Still, Live Nation wasn't quite ready to break up with its longtime partner.

There were several issues that the two, after protracted discussions, could not agree on. One was a service charge schedule: Ticketmaster always set a schedule in advance with its clients to determine what service charges would be levied for what price points and what the rebate back to the client would be. Live Nation wanted the unilateral right to decide what, if any, service charges there would be. It was an untenable request for Ticketmaster, given that their entire business was predicated on collecting an expected amount of money from each ticket sold.

"I don't think the deal broke down over any one thing," says Moriarty, who declines to be much more specific. "I think it was a consequence of them wanting to actually get into the Ticketmaster business and just using our platform to do it." To that end the insurmountable hurdle came down to a fundamental question: whose customer was it? The answer would determine who controlled one of the most valuable pieces of the ticketing business: customer data.

Live Nation vehemently argued it was their customer, and, as such, all transactions should be done through their site. Ticketmaster conversely argued that it made no sense to not sell its biggest client's tickets on its own website. Live Nation's compromise was to allow Ticketmaster to list the on-sale tickets but then, when it came time for the actual transaction, send customers back to Live Nation's website. As someone familiar with the situation described it, "Ticketmaster thought Live Nation was their customer; Live Nation thought Ticketmaster was their customer."

Despite taking a less adversarial approach than it initially had, Ticketmaster still hadn't persuaded Live Nation to renew. The subtext of the conversation, to Live Nation, was Ticketmaster's passive-aggressively saying "Ticketing is a really hard business. Look how complicated it is. We have to develop and maintain all this because, in case you forgot, we sell 100,000,000 tickets a year," says one person involved with the deal. Live Nation argued it only needed a system that could handle a fifth of those numbers.

"The reality is much easier said than done," says Moriarty of any large-scale ticketing operation. "Not only does the public misunderstand Ticketmaster, I'd say that even clients of Ticketmaster don't know how devilishly hard it is to do what Ticketmaster does and how well Ticketmaster does it relative to other options."

By early summer 2007 it was official: Live Nation would not be renewing its Ticketmaster contract. Live Nation's deal with CTS was green-lighted, and over the next few months the two hammered out the details. As the year came to a close, a deal breaker presented itself. CTS's founder, Klaus Schulenburg, wanted a joint venture, while Live Nation wanted a licensing deal. Negotiations reached such an impasse that Live Nation resumed talks with an earlier candidate, Vertical Alliance, and indicated to CTS that they were more than willing to go in another direction if an agreement could not be reached in the immediate future. Schulenburg assessed the situation and agreed to a licensing deal — cents from every ticket sold — predicated on CTS's being the exclusive ticketing agent for all of Live Nation's European properties, which were significant. The two signed a ten-year deal in early December and announced the partnership to the world the following month.

Meanwhile the jockeying between Live Nation and Ticketmaster was just getting started.

In March Ticketmaster announced its acquisition of echomusic, an online fan club and brand management company. Behind the scenes Live Nation had also gone after the company, and former employees suggest they drove the price up from $10 million to somewhere in the vicinity of $28 million.

Between May and July of 2006, Live Nation went on a spending spree, buying up Michael Cohl's latest version of CPI and a fifty percent stake in his Grand Entertainment for $123 million in stock and $10 million in cash, House of Blues (a Ticketmaster client whose contract would expire at the end of 2009) for $350 million and the majority stake in Coran Capshaw's MusicToday.

By the spring of 2007, Live Nation and Ticketmaster were again competing with each other, this time for a much more coveted prize: Front Line Management Group. Azoff entertained offers from both sides, though it's not clear if either knew they were competing with each other.

"We had almost done a deal to buy Front Line," confirms Cohl, who participated in some of the Live Nation conversations. "Michael [Rapino] had been in close negotiations with Irving, and then Irving skipped off and did the deal with Barry [Diller]." Diller was CEO of IAC, Ticketmaster's parent company.

The deal, according to insiders, would have "transformed Live Nation." So close was the deal, they say that Rapino thought it was as good as done on a Friday, only to get a call from Azoff the following Monday saying, "I hate to tell you . . ."

Ticketmaster announced its majority stake in Front Line in mid-May.

"We thought one of the ways we could bring innovation to the market is by having direct conversations with the artists," say Moriarty, echoing Pleasants' earlier comments. "The big challenge for us was not that we didn't have the tools for dynamic pricing, resale, innovative online marketing campaigns . . . it was that we didn't have the buy-in or support. With Front Line we felt that we would have direct influence with artists."

In the wake of losing the Front Line deal, Live Nation hardened its resolve to develop a new business model. That October the company announced the arrival of Artist Nation with a news-making headline: a ten-year, $120 million deal for all of Madonna's future music and music-related businesses, which included everything from her touring, merchandise and fan club to new studio albums, sponsorships and branding (save for publishing).

Ten years in the making, Michael Cohl's vision of Grand Entertainment had finally come to fruition.

"OUR PARTNERSHIP IS A DEFINING moment in music history," declared Rapino in trumpeting the Artist Nation announcement. "I am thrilled that Madonna, who is also now a shareholder in our company, has joined with us to create a new business model for our industry."

While Madonna was not the Rolling Stones, she was in the upper echelon of global superstars. "The paradigm in the music business has shifted and as an artist and a business woman, I have to move with that shift," she said. "I've never wanted to think in a limited way and with this new partnership, the possibilities are endless. Who knows how my albums will be distributed in the future? That's what's exciting about this deal — everything is possible."

Indeed Artist Nation offered artists lucrative opportunities in becoming part of a one-stop shop: tour rights, publishing, albums, merchandise, media rights, digital rights, fan club management, website servicing and sponsorship.

While SFX's proposed Rolling Stones deal in 2000 was the blueprint of a large-scale 360 deal, it wasn't until two years later that the first major 360 agreement was announced: British pop star Robbie Williams signed a $160-million contract with record label EMI, which entitled them to revenues from his recordings, publishing and performances.

The term "360" refers to the all-encompassing nature of this type of arrangement, that all of an artist's rights were now potential revenue streams. They're also called "unified rights" deals.

Artist Nation was propelled by Cohl along with a team that included Arthur Fogel, whom Cohl had hired in the 1980s to run his world tours; renowned producer Bob Ezrin; Larry Peryer, who ran UltraStar; and Mike Luba, the former head of Madison House, the multi-faceted company that managed the String Cheese Incident.

The company, when it began, was Cohl's idea of Grand Entertainment from the late 1990s fully realized. Despite it being seen as a new model, Cohl argues that the concept of the 360 deal is really quite old. "If you go back to the Dick Clark Caravan or the early '50s, you'll find that the record company owned everything," he points out. "The way I remember it was that they not only owned everything, but eventually they became limited in their scope — they let the merchandise rights go; they let the touring rights go. The old tours were the record company trying to sell records. Nobody thought they were going to make [money] of any substance [from touring]."

In short order Artist Nation signed U2 in March for approximately $100 million (in a twelve-year deal for exclusive tour rights, merchandising rights, image licensing, website and fan club rights); Jay-Z in April for $150 million (a ten-year deal for tours, recordings, publishing, management and record label businesses, endorsements); and in July Shakira for $70 million (a ten-year deal for touring, records, merchandise) and Nickelback for $50–$70 million (three albums and subsequent touring cycles).

Wall Street did not react well to the company's new strategy. Between the Madonna deal in October 2007 and the U2 deal in March 2008, Live Nation's stock fell from $23.36 to $11.83 per share.

"Was I surprised?" asks Cohl rhetorically of the market's reaction. "Not really. I was hoping that they wouldn't, but it was a new idea . . . People tend to be afraid of and cynical and wary of things that are new, different, and that they can't put their finger on and predict."

Relations within Live Nation became strained as the company's valuation plummeted. "In the coming up with the idea [for Artist Nation] is of course the seeds for the discontent amongst the parties," says Cohl now of the internal struggle.

Primary points of contention with Artist Nation were the development of a record label, its large overhead and the volume and scope of its future artist signings. "As I started to live and breathe it, I realized that you should be in everything," Cohl says. "You don't necessarily want to have a warehouse and manufacture whatever form of music it is, but you want to be in the record business, absolutely," he asserts in reference to the various forms of digital music servicing. "This started the hugest friction because on the surface Rapino and Arthur saw that as folly and insanity."

Cohl and his team were very much convinced that they wanted to be in the baby band business, too — groups that they would begin working with in their infancy and that had the potential to grow into major stars. "I thought it was crucial," he says. Their first baby band signings were Zac Brown Band and Paolo Nutini. Before any of the Artist Nation signings — seven in all — had any significant business cycles, Cohl and his team were sacked. The catalyst for what Cohl describes as "the nuclear explosion within the Live Nation/Artist Nation family" was Mötley Crüe.

Rapino and Fogel disagreed with Cohl's vision of a diversified roster. "What the hell are you doing with Mötley Crüe?" the duo questioned, as Cohl recalls. "What are you doing with Zac Brown? Who the hell is he? And Paolo? You're a lunatic! Look at all the people you've hired! Look at the leases you've signed!"

Cohl pauses.

"It was folly — they'd approved everything — so it had to be something else."

Resigning as chairman of Live Nation in June, Cohl walked with a lump sum payment of $4.5 million, shackled with a ten-year non-compete clause that excluded the Rolling Stones, Barbra Streisand and Pink Floyd along with a limited number of Broadway shows. (Cohl is the producer of *Spider-Man: Turn Off the Dark*, the most expensive Broadway production to date.) So while Jay-Z thought he'd "turned into the Rolling Stones of hip-hop," the architect behind the Stones' modern success had been ousted by his own protégé.

"Everybody put out a friendly press release that I was moving on," he says. "I thought of it as a philosophical difference and a loss occurred on their part."

Beyond the Mötley Crüe deal, Cohl says there were dozens of acts lined up who wanted to explore what Artist Nation could do for their careers. "We were becoming part of the vernacular. We were part of the discussion in management offices and record labels."

Mike Luba feels much the same of the fallout. "They chicken-shitted out. There's no way around it," he says of Live Nation. "But their hands may have been tied [in that] to really, fully manifest our plan, there had to be some scale to it, and we had to put some systems in place to service the deals that we had done. Those first four or five deals weren't ever meant to be stand-alone deals. It was only going to work if we got to forty or fifty deals."

Shortly after Cohl's departure, Rapino steadfastly indicated "Live Nation's strategy and execution remain on track. We are committed to acquiring additional artists' rights beyond the concert tour, including unified rights with select artists. . . . We will continue to build our integrated model as we selectively look to add more artists that feed our concert pipe." Beyond the Shakira and Nickelback deals, which Live Nation announced the following month in July 2008 — deals that were well under way when Cohl left — Live Nation has not signed another client to a unified rights deal as of early 2011.

Rapino says that he and Cohl never debated the overall strategy. "[But] he thought we should move faster and sign more artists quicker," he suggests. "And we never had a strategy to sign more than four or five in the first year. . . . So when we got Madonna, U2 and the three or four others, my plan was always, 'That's enough. Now we've got to execute. We'll entertain new deals as the opportunity comes.'"

Cohl, for his part, isn't quite as sanguine about it. "My mistake in all of this — and it's the only way I can reflect on it — is that I trusted Michael," he says today. "In doing that, I found myself in a corner where I went, 'Oh, crap — there's no way.'"

Today, he says the difference between what's become of Artist Nation and what he envisioned it to be is more than just apples and oranges. "It probably needs something even more different because those are too close," he offers. "There's no comparison that one can do; they've taken it and used it in a completely different way than what we were going to do."

Navigating the rather turbulent waters of Cohl's departure and Wall Street's negative reaction to its artist deals, and preparing to launch its own ticketing service in January 2009, Live Nation's stock took a further beating. By December it had fallen more than seventy percent since the beginning of the year, hovering just above $4. Matters weren't helped when U2 cashed in its first stock options at year's end — Live Nation guaranteed the band a minimum of $25 million for 1.6 million shares (about $15.63 per share). It now had to come up with roughly $19 million to cover the difference.

In fortifying its new ticketing position, Live Nation announced a three-year deal with Blockbuster movie stores, giving its 500 outlets "exclusive blocks" of tickets. It also entered into a future ticketing agreement with Ticketmaster's second largest client at the time, SMG, one of the world's leading venue management companies. The five-year agreement called for Live Nation to handle ticketing for all 216 of the company's venues, starting in late 2009. (However, many had remaining years left on their exclusive Ticketmaster contracts.)

Ticketmaster in turn solidified its full acquisition of Front Line Management Group in October, installing Irving Azoff as the CEO of the combined company, newly christened as Ticketmaster Entertainment.

With Azoff now fully involved, scenarios for what 2009 might look like for the concert industry were played out by a variety of parties. Shortly after the Front Line announcement, Randy Phillips, CEO of AEG Live, the country's second largest promoter behind Live Nation, told an industry panel that already, "I know a lot of amphitheater tours where [Azoff has] come to me to try and figure out the economics to keep out of [Live Nation] amphitheaters because he does not want [Live Nation] handling the tickets." Phillips estimated that Front Line's 200-plus acts accounted for about thirty or forty percent of Live Nation's amphitheater season.

"You're naïve if you think this isn't going to be a battle."

HIPPIE JAMBANDS HAVE POPULATED the history of modern concert ticketing with a surprising frequency. First there was the Grateful Dead and its own ticketing service, which thwarted Ticketmaster and led the way for other artist fan clubs. Then there was the String Cheese Incident, who fought Ticketmaster and quietly won. And on January 30, 2009, Phish crashed Live Nation's new ticketing system. While the Vermont-bred quartet had yet to perform its reunion shows that March, it had put part of its forthcoming summer tour on sale that winter day.

Never mind that CTS Eventim's system said it could serve three million clients simultaneously by displacing the load over 15,000 servers around the world — a remarkably robust system that under normal circumstances would never have to operate at such levels. But at ten o'clock that fateful Friday morning, the system was instantaneously barraged with approximately one million hits, maybe more according to various sources.

The volume was driven by the secondary market knowing that tickets to the band's summer tour would be highly sought after. Multiple broker sources utilized bots — computer programs that can make hundreds to thousands of automated requests in a matter of seconds — to try and secure tickets. "It was an ungodly number that was off the charts," says a former Live Nation employee. "It was all bots."

In an earnings call that March Rapino addressed the fiasco: "The weekend where we absolutely dropped the ball was when we put Phish on sale — and God bless Phish, a huge band." He suggested that Live Nation's front door and CTS's back door were not communicating as well as they should have. After engineers spent the weekend making adjustments, the problem did not recur. "We're now confident these platforms can handle the load." It would prove to be the system's only black eye.

Four days after the Phish meltdown and just a month after Live Nation had entered the world with its own ticketing system, news of an unexpected development reverberated throughout the industry: Live Nation and Ticketmaster were going to merge.

Bruce Springsteen, often cast as a workingman's musician, immediately lashed out with his manager, Jon Landau, in an open letter posted on his website: "The one thing that would make the current ticket situation even worse for the fan than it is now would be Ticketmaster and Live Nation coming up with a single system, thereby returning us to a near monopoly situation in music ticketing. Several newspapers are reporting on this story right now. If you, like us, oppose that idea, you should make it known to your [congressional] representatives."

If artists and consumers reacted negatively, Wall Street initially reacted positively, as each company's stock rose nearly fifteen percent, though within a month they would fall nearly thirty-eight percent. On Tuesday, February 10, 2009, they made it official: the two companies were merging in a $2.5-billion all-stock deal.

On a conference call the morning of the announcement with investment analysts, IAC CEO Barry Diller gave the opening remarks. "There are times for everything," he began. "I have been trying and mostly consistently failing to put these companies together for many years now. The economic difficulties and the uncertainties of this moment, [with] probably lots more moments to come, [are] actually the second reason to do this now."

Indeed, up to the very end of their contract, the two companies were trying to make something work. In June of the previous year, shortly before being ousted as chairman and six months before Live Nation was to launch its own ticketing service with CTS Eventim, Cohl and vice chairman Randall Mays each met with Barry Diller to talk about the future of Live Nation and Ticketmaster's relationship.

"At the end of the day we weren't in the ticket business yet," says Cohl. "I was sitting with Barry Diller, who was telling me how he was going to bury us. We were talking about, 'Well, we should talk about going together,' but Michael [Rapino] felt threatened by that, so he wanted to stay in the ticket business himself. We all supported that, rather than doing some merger with Ticketmaster, which people thought wouldn't be approved by Justice."

A short while later on the conference call, Ben Mogil from Thomas Weisel Partners asked for some perspective on Live Nation's competitors who were also Ticketmaster clients.

Azoff responded with typical bravado and candor, sounding almost impatient as he offered the group an analogy: "If you look at the entertainment business, there's four broadcast networks, there is plenty of room for plenty of promoters and artists have loyalties to them — past, present and future — and it will be business as usual if not better. We think that it will be a more level playing field."

If Live Nation Entertainment was like one of the four television networks, who were the other three? And how — even to the most open of minds — was this merger going to create a more level playing field? Or was this all in response to the plummeting values of each company? From August 2008 to the merger announcement, Ticketmaster's stock had fallen by seventy-four percent. Live Nation's stock had dropped over seventy percent in value in the six months prior to the merger announcement and in the six months following it dropped another forty-four percent.

After two rounds of congressional hearings and a yearlong investigation by the Justice Department, the U.S. government would decide the answers to those questions and much, much more.

THE DAY OF THE MERGER announcement, the Justice Department gave notice that it would be launching a full and vigorous investigation. Two congressional hearings were also immediately scheduled for later in the month to explore the impact of the merger. The first was to be held before the Subcommittee on Antitrust, Competition Policy and Consumer Rights, part of the Senate's Committee on the Judiciary. The second was to be held before the Subcommittee on Courts and Competition Policy, part of the House of Representatives Committee on the Judiciary. Azoff and Rapino appeared at each with various promoters, law experts and industry professionals filling out the panels.

But before Ticketmaster and Live Nation appeared before Congress, the heat was already on. New Jersey representative Bill Pascrell and New York senator Chuck Schumer — both of whom would appear at the congressional hearings — quickly demanded a federal investigation into the deal even before it was officially announced. The Springsteen ticketing snafu with Ticketmaster and TicketsNow — which both Pascrell and Schumer had raised issues with — had happened only days earlier. The incident, which ignited considerable press coverage, occurred when unsuspecting Springsteen fans were offered secondary tickets on Ticketmaster's homepage via TicketsNow after primary tickets for fourteen of the Boss's shows that May and June sold out in a matter of minutes.[3]

Most significantly, a day before the first hearing began, President Obama announced his nomination of the new assistant attorney general to head the

Department of Justice's Antitrust Division: Christine Varney. Having previously served as a commissioner at the Federal Trade Commission during the Clinton administration, one of the areas in which Varney had made a name for herself was vertical monopoly enforcement.

What made the Live Nation–Ticketmaster merger ripe for scrutiny was that it possessed attributes not only of a horizontal monopoly — two competing companies in the same business merging (in this case ticketing) — but a vertical monopoly as well. The concerns of a vertical monopoly are about different businesses (ticketing, management, promotion) within the same general market (the concert industry) joining together in such a way that it would unfairly raise the barriers of entry for competitors in any of the individual businesses. Vertical monopoly enforcement, generally speaking, is tougher than clear-cut horizontal monopoly enforcement and, as such, has seen less scrutiny at the behest of pro-market, pro-business interests.

During the previous Bush administration, there had been little enforcement of anticompetitive business. In fact, during its eight years the Bush administration did not pursue a single investigation under Section Two of the Sherman Act — the section pertaining to monopolies. Varney's nomination was a clear signal that times were changing.

THROUGHOUT THE TWO CONGRESSIONAL HEARINGS four major concerns were continually addressed:

1. The merger would prevent the entry of other ticketing companies to compete and/or rival Ticketmaster. The quick acquiescence of Live Nation's ticketing efforts a month after it began, critics suggested, seemed to be clear proof.
2. The merger would diminish competition in the secondary market because Ticketmaster and Live Nation would give unfair advantage to its own secondary seller, TicketsNow.
3. Non-Live Nation promoters who used Ticketmaster would be at a competitive disadvantage because their biggest competitor would have access to highly sensitive information.
4. The merged Live Nation and Ticketmaster would use its considerable assets to leverage artists and venues into exclusively working with them.

And of course a concern threaded throughout the hearings: what was the consumer going to be paying?

Those testifying against the merger argued the points thoroughly and convincingly. Notable among them were David Balto, a senior fellow at the Center for American Progress, who had previously served as a trial attorney for the Antitrust Division and as policy director at the Federal Trade Commission; Robert Doyle, an antitrust lawyer who had previously served on the Federal Trade Commission; Ed Mierzwinski, director of the U.S. Public Interest Research Groups; Jerry Mickelson, cofounder of Jam Productions in Chicago; and Seth Hurwitz, owner of IMP Production in Washington, DC.

The merger's proponents — Azoff, Rapino along with Comcast-Spectator CEO Peter Luukko, Vanderbilt professor Luke Froeb and artists, venues and ancillary businesses that submitted written letters of support — addressed the proposed concerns but did little to provide concrete answers to assuage them.

While the two hearings generated an enormous amount of press, the end results provided scant assurance to either side as to whether the merger might be approved. At their best the hearings provided insight into how a complicated and often misunderstood industry operated. At their worst they reinforced false assumptions of how the concert business worked. And somewhere in the middle was a plethora of statements and assertions that lacked merit, evidence and consistency.

IN HIS FIRST ORAL STATEMENT Azoff addressed the impact of the secondary market on primary ticket sales. "An artist only benefits from a first sale," he said. "[The artist's first sale comes from] placing the ticket on sale via Ticketmaster's regular channels, or by offering it for sale as a higher priced VIP or Platinum ticket or through a licensed broker." This was the first time that a manager, promoter or ticketing agent had publicly acknowledged that artists willingly — and regularly — allow the sale of their tickets directly to the secondary market.

As would be partially elucidated six months after the hearings, with the antitrust division's investigation in full swing, Azoff had a long, well-known history of working with ticket brokers. The *Wall Street Journal* broke a story that August about Azoff meeting with a handful of brokers and representatives from AEG and Madison Square Garden Entertainment in the summer of 2007 with the hope to "crush Live Nation" and "make lots and lots of money."

At the meeting, which took place at Ticketmaster's headquarters in West Hollywood, Azoff suggested that if business went well, then IAC, Ticketmaster's parent company, would acquire each broker company for up to $25 million in addition to giving them seats on its board.

The trial run for the more formalized business relationship, dubbed "Project Showtime," was for a fall tour by Van Halen, one of Azoff's clients. The six brokers divided 500 of the best tickets from each of about twenty shows, with the revenue split above the face value as thirty percent to the brokers, seventy percent to the band. As a result, Van Halen netted an extra million dollars. It's unclear why, based on the success of the venture, the deal was not pursued further.

Equally illuminating was a lawsuit brought that September by New Jersey–based broker Chuck Lombardo, founder of Elite Entertainment, against Ticketmaster, TicketsNow and Front Line. Surprisingly, Elite was not one of the companies Azoff had met with for Project Showtime, but the testimony nonetheless documented Ticketmaster's foray into the secondary world and again confirmed Azoff's direct work with brokers.

The suit, in part, stated, "For their initial consulting services, Plaintiffs managed, priced and sold premium tickets for Ticketmaster for the 2008 Van Halen, Def Leppard, Kanye West, Steely Dan, George Michael, Journey, New Kids on the Block and Neil Diamond tours on Ticketmaster's secondary/premium ticketing platforms, TicketsNow, TicketExchange (a.k.a. Platinum Seating) and TicketNetwork." (Recall Azoff's mention of "Platinum ticket" above and the note of it here.) The majority of the artists mentioned are part of Front Line management.

The broker further asserted that he entered into an agreement with Front Line to handle tickets for Azoff's most famous client, the Eagles, for the group's *Long Road out of Eden* tour in 2008–09 through sales on Ticketmaster's TicketExchange and other secondary sites. "Plaintiffs purchased the Eagles tickets from Front Line above face value and then priced and offered them for sale on TicketExchange and other secondary websites," the suit contends. "In exchange, Front Line agreed to reimburse plaintiff for the cost of the tickets plus a share of the profits earned from the sale of those tickets." After agreeing to buy Elite Entertainment, Lombardo said, Ticketmaster reneged and he was essentially "blackballed" in the industry from getting tickets (Lombardo and Ticketmaster settled out of court in 2010).

Neil Diamond, also an Azoff client, was the lead in another article published by Ethan Smith in the *Wall Street Journal* that dealt with artists selling their tickets directly to brokers. He cited Ticketmaster CEO Sean Moriarty's meeting with brokers in Vegas (the "fireside chat"), during which Moriarty confirmed that the company's TicketExchange — billed as "fan-to-fan" — sold 160 Diamond tickets for two shows on behalf of the artist. Other artists known for direct sales to scalpers include Bon Jovi, Céline Dion, Van Halen and the Billy Joel–Elton John tour.

Smith reported, "According to several managers of top artists and Ticketmaster executives, the company routinely offers to list hundreds of the best tickets per concert on one of its two resale Web sites — and divides the extra revenue, which can amount to more than $2 million on a major tour, with artists and promoters."

These were just the recent instances and allegations that had come to light since Azoff relaunched Front Line and headed Ticketmaster, to say nothing of his storied past.

Later, in the second hearing, Azoff found himself again candidly answering questions about ticketing, this time from Representative Brad Sherman of California:

> Sherman: "If there are 10,000 seats in the arena and you are doing the event, are you selling 10,000 seats or are you often selling 7,000?"
>
> Azoff: "Never the former. I would say on average we might see 80 or 85 percent of the seats."
>
> Sherman: "When you don't get the 15 percent, are those bad or good seats that you are not getting?"
>
> Azoff: "The vast majority, they are the best seats in the house. They go to building holds, sponsor holds, band holds, record company holds. They go out the door, you know, multiple places."
>
> Sherman: "So if I want to pay $800 for a ticket, I probably am getting one of those and you probably never touched it?"
>
> Azoff: "I would say that is correct, yes."

This is further confirmation that some of the best seats on secondary ticket sites are acquired by brokers not through the use of bots or sophisticated computer software but rather through direct sources such as the artist (i.e., its management), the venue or the promoter.

Indeed, as Lombardo's suit noted, "When Plaintiffs contacted Beyonce's management regarding obtaining her artist 'hold' tickets for resale through TicketExchange or TicketsNow, Ticketmaster contacted Plaintiffs via email informing Lombardo to 'step down and away from Beyonce please. We [Ticketmaster] have a comprehensive deal with her.'"

If he was up-front here, then it was Azoff's condemnation of the secondary market and Ticketmaster's purchase of TicketNow that would prove overstated, as he clearly had encouraged their existence.

"Personally, I don't believe there should be a secondary market at all," Azoff testified to Senator Schumer. "I believe that scalping and resales should be illegal." He confirmed that, were he at Ticketmaster at the time it purchased TicketsNow, he would not have bought the secondary ticketing company.

"I think what raised eyebrows was not that Irving had conversations with brokers — which I would argue certainly were within his rights . . . but the hypocrisy of him publicly saying that he thinks there should be no scalping and that he wouldn't have bought a resale business," says one source familiar with Azoff's history, who had a close working relationship with him. "If you dig deeper, I think that brokers would say that over thirty years, he's been one of their largest suppliers."

The *Wall Street Journal* quoted Azoff as saying that when ticket brokers resell tickets without permission from artists or promoters, it "drives up prices to fans, without putting any money in the pockets of artists or rights holders." It suggests that, for Azoff, as long as artists were capturing the money from the secondary ticket sales, then whatever inflated cost fans paid over face value was a reflection of the real ticket value.

In subsequent written testimony, Azoff told Senator Schumer that Ticketmaster "believes brokers get their tickets a number of different ways" and went on to list such sources as season ticket holders, artist fan clubs and promotional pre-sale opportunities. He never mentioned that artists, with the help of their managers, regularly funnel tickets directly to the secondary market for considerable profit.[4]

Another point he made was that "sometimes brokers do not have actual tickets in-hand but nevertheless post listings on multiple resale websites. . . . This is an unfortunately all-too common practice in the resale world, and one we are committed to curtailing at the TicketsNow site."

Clearly, one way to help facilitate that would be for Front Line and its massive management family to strike deals directly with the brokers that utilized TicketsNow to list their tickets — just as Azoff had with Project Showtime and Elite Entertainment — for tighter control over them and higher profit margins in return for guaranteed access to tickets.

Azoff also noted, to his continued dismay, "Regrettably some unscrupulous individuals also use illegal software programs to bypass Ticketmaster's sophisticated security systems and 'cut to the front of the line.'"

He assured Senator Schumer, however, "We continue to invest significant resources and cooperate with law enforcement to do everything possible to ensure that the illegal and unethical behavior of a few does not thwart fans' fair access to tickets."

ONE OF LIVE NATION'S ARGUMENTS made throughout the hearings was that it only had a thirty-eight percent market share of concert promotions. Time and again Rapino underscored this figure. It wasn't until the end of the first hearing that Jam Productions cofounder Jerry Mickelson called the figure into question. "That is not true," Mickelson rebutted. "In 2000 *Pollstar* said SFX promoted 150 of the top 200 tours. In 2001, Clear Channel promoted 161 of the top 200 tours. . . . They dominate the arena level for ticket sales. They control and have all the amphitheaters so that not one of us really can compete."

Mickelson's written testimony laid out how Live Nation controlled forty-seven amphitheaters, making it impossible for another company to effectively compete for outdoor shows during the summer months.

As for Tickemaster's market share, Azoff confirmed in subsequent written testimony that, "While Ticketmaster neither contributes to nor can attest to the accuracy of *Pollstar*'s statistics, with respect to the *Pollstar* Top 100 concert arenas, amphitheaters, stadiums, theaters and clubs in the U.S., Ticketmaster provided ticketing services to 87 of those venues in 2007, and 84 of those venues in 2008."

Despite their best efforts to obscure the fact, it was clear that Live Nation and Ticketmaster controlled the majority of the country's premier venues. It was in Live Nation's DNA — the original business model behind SFX was predicated on the company having enough venues to sell sponsorship from the promoter side. Live Nation, with its purchase of House of Blues, operated even more venues domestically than SFX did.

These dynamics played themselves out among Balto, Rapino and Mickelson when Senator Amy Klobuchar asked about competition among promoters.

"You must recognize that what compels these companies to reduce prices is competition, and both of these firms are dominant firms in the market," said Balto. "Nothing after this merger is going to force them to lower prices. It is only rivalry that does that."

While that holds true in most scenarios, the concert industry has, in fact, demonstrated the reverse. The highest bidder wins, and the cost in turn trickles down to the fan.

Rapino went on to make much the same point that former Ticketmaster CEO Fred Rosen had made over a decade earlier before Congress. "The true monopoly, as you know, is the artist," he countered. "There is only one Aerosmith. So Aerosmith's ticket price goes up because Aerosmith gets to call Seth, Jam and I. The agent calls us and says, 'Who is going to bid the most for my tour?'"

But here was where the flaw in Live Nation's argument was exposed. Again, it was Mickelson — who had been in the business for thirty years and nearly sold his business to SFX — who corrected Rapino.[5]

"Aerosmith did not call me; they did not call Seth. U2 did not call us. Shakira did not call us. Coldplay did not call us. And I can go on and on and on about the tours [Live Nation] bought that the independent promoters did not get a call on because they have paid so much money to buy that tour."

He was right. It's what was at the heart of a small margin business Rapino would later describe to Representative Sherman.

"We do 1,000 concerts at our fifty amphitheaters," he offered. "We lose $70 million at the door. That means the price of the talent versus the ticket price. That is ten million tickets being sold. In theory, if I had any control of those ticket prices, you would assume I would charge $7 more a ticket to cover my $70 million loss. The artist takes the door, and we end up making the money on peanuts, popcorn, parking and ticket rebates."

As much as Rapino was seemingly admitting the flawed dynamics of the concert industry, it was what he *wasn't* saying that painted a clearer picture of what was wrong with the concert industry. Or rather what was wrong with Live Nation.

Why would Live Nation willingly lose $70 million on artist guarantees when, by its own admission, it wasn't turning a profit? Didn't a promoter pay an artist based on the number of tickets it thought it could sell at a given price? Wouldn't logic suggest that if a promoter was losing an average of $70,000 a concert, they were overpaying artists by a known quantity? Didn't Live Nation have two easy options — pay artists less or don't book them? Couldn't that, right there, help make them more profitable?

The answer goes back to when Bob Sillerman first rolled up enough promoters to control the summer amphitheater circuit. It's worth repeating an elucidating remark of veteran promoter Jack Boyle, founder of Cellar Door Productions in the 1960s, who for a time helped run Clear Channel Entertainment after selling his company to SFX: "When SFX [started] going around and grabbing all the venues, everyone thought they'd get a break because people couldn't afford not to play for them. As it turned out, the trio, as I call them — Howard Kaufman, Irving Azoff and Howard Rose — realized [that the SFX rolled-up promoters would] have to pay more money because they *had* to put artists into these amphitheaters. Whatever they thought was the strength of these big companies turned out not to be so much a strength as a weakness."

As the artist guarantees got higher and the revenue splits lower, SFX and its future incarnations came to rely upon ancillaries as their primary source of revenue. The idea that they'd make up the massive overhead and debt from synergistic sponsorship and advertising never materialized in a significant way and was derailed shortly into Clear Channel's takeover.

"Sillerman had always touted himself as doing what's best for the customer and the industry, finding ways to use this newfound power for the benefit for everyone," wrote Seth Hurwitz to the committee. "The word 'synergy' became famous here. Synergy? Synergistic? Synergistic opportunities for synergy? It was all pitched, when the only synergy that was ever intended, in my opinion, was between Robert Sillerman and his bank account. Yes, I blame him for starting this. But he is no longer the one perpetrating it."

Live Nation, now responsible for all of SFX and Clear Channel's contracts, was on the hook for all the amphitheater and venue properties that it either owned or had long-term leases with. (As of 2009, that included forty-seven amphitheaters, forty-six clubs and eleven House of Blues clubs among its 140 domestic venues.) Every night that they were empty meant they were not making money on alcohol, food and parking. They couldn't let that happen. So they overpaid artists for entire tours in return for guaranteeing themselves some (hopefully) small margin revenues on ancillaries.

As Rapino said, openly admitting for the first time that Live Nation now gave artists straight door deals, "The artist takes the door, and we end up making the money on peanuts, popcorn, parking and ticket rebates." (He earlier testified that the company made an average of $12 to $15 per person from ancillaries and an average of $4 per person on every $100 worth of ticket sales.) So now, with artists getting door deals and 100 percent guarantees, weren't they really the ones to blame since they were taking the money?

"Yes, of course, the bands could have said no, just like my kids could say no if I put ice cream in front of them for dinner," testified Hurwitz. "The idea of blaming the artist for ticket prices is completely out of context. The offers come from the promoters who are supposed to know their market, and in Live Nation's case, they are the self-proclaimed leader of the concert world who claim, then and now, to know what is best for everyone."

Without a hint of irony, as Azoff sat next to him, Rapino offered his assessment: "We believe the only way you can try and get output in the future is do two things: make the artist more money other ways, so if the artist wants $700,000 a night for a guarantee, you have got to find it other ways than the primary ticket. That is the problem with the business," he said, stopping short of providing a second option.

It would have been more accurate for Rapino to say, "That is the problem with *our* business." The business of Live Nation and Front Line — the business that was Clear Channel, the business that was SFX.

It was Kaufman and Azoff, who first got into business together running Front Line Management from 1974 to 1983 and reformed it in 2005, who famously persuaded SFX and Clear Channel to give Jimmy Buffet a 105 percent guarantee because of the amount of alcohol sales they knew his fans would generate. They were, and are, leaders in driving the hardest of bargains for their artists.

Former New England promoter Frank J. Russo, who sold his business to rival Don Law in 1992, traces Azoff's impact on escalating ticket prices to the Eagles' 1994 *Hell Freezes Over* reunion tour. Indeed it was the first time that the $100 mark had been reached for the face value of a concert ticket for a major concert tour (that same year Barbra Streisand, touring for the first time in twenty years, had $350 tickets but only performed twenty-two shows in six cities). "Had those Eagles dates stiffed, you would have seen a different transition," posits Russo of price trending. "You never would have seen corporate America in the music business; you never would have seen corporate America come in and offer promoters retirement money." He notes that many of the amphitheatres currently earn their profits via concessions, so that nowadays, "You're in the delicatessen business — you're no longer selling tickets for a living."

Now Azoff was trying to save the business he and his business partners had, by many accounts, irreparably damaged for their own gain.

Alex Cooley, the Atlanta-based promoter who ran Concert/Southern Promotions with Peter Conlon, compares Azoff's longtime business partner to Conan the Barbarian. "Rape, pillage and leaving nothing unburned, no dollar untaken," he says of Kaufman's business practices. "That's always been his philosophy, and I'm not telling you anything that's a secret. I think if you called him right now, he'd tell you that's his philosophy. . . . While that's good for Howard and good for the individual artist, for the overall benefit of the business, it's been a disaster."

So, as much as Azoff and Rapino tried to paint a picture of an entire industry in dire financial shape, it was Live Nation that was on the verge of collapse. It wasn't as if all concert promoters were losing millions annually. Hurwitz and Mickelson weren't — if they had been, they wouldn't have been in business. Former BGP execs Gregg Perloff and Sherry Wasserman with their recently launched Another Planet weren't. Bowery Presents in New York, led by former Live Nation exec Jim Glancy wasn't. Live Nation's biggest competitor, AEG Live, led by former Rod Stewart manager and record exec Randy Phillips, didn't seem to be (or, if they were, certainly weren't broadcasting their woes). No, just one concert promoter, the only one that was a publicly traded company, was losing millions annually: Live Nation.

So if Ticketmaster was in decent financial shape, why would it want to tether itself to a company like Live Nation that had never made money? Wouldn't it have made more sense to partner with the privately owned AEG Live, backed by billionaire Philip Anschutz? Clearly it was something Azoff had considered, as reports peg him talking to the company at the same time Live Nation was, shortly before the merger announcement.

"I'm sure someone would tell you [the merger] was the [the result of Live Nation] sniffing out that Ticketmaster, Diller and Azoff were talking to AEG and that scared them," says Michael Cohl. "This is only a story I hear — I don't know anything — I'm long gone. I'm not part or privy to those discussions."

If Azoff had no qualms about blindsiding Rapino during the Front Line deal in favor of Ticketmaster, what would keep him from doing a deal with AEG, which was clearly in better financial shape than Live Nation?

As SEC documents would later reveal, Rapino and Azoff got $3 million and $2 million bonuses, respectively, upon completion of the merger and would make $2 million a year in salaries plus seven-figure bonuses.

In addition, in a deal that was supposedly struck before the merger announcement, Ticketmaster agreed to pay $36.4 million to Azoff's family trust. The merger filing noted that, "After an initial payment of approximately $1.7 million on February 1, 2010, the outstanding principal amount of the note will be approximately $34.7 million and the note will vest and pay equal monthly installments of approximately $835,000 on the first day of each month beginning on March 1, 2010 through and until October 1, 2013."

The much touted savings projection from the combined companies' efficiencies that Rapino and Azoff both noted on several occasions during the merger hearings — $40 million — was roughly the same amount as bonus payouts to the company's executives.

THE OVERRIDING QUESTION PERMEATING the hearings — why did Live Nation and Ticketmaster want to merge? — was never answered with any specificity by either Azoff or Rapino.

"We've grown the right way but the current economic climate has still taken its toll," Rapino asserted in the written testimony of Live Nation. "Our stock has declined by nearly two-thirds. Our real estate holdings have been gutted. Our hard work is not producing the rewards it should. We face the very real possibility that if we don't find a solution, we could ultimately be bought by a foreign-owned entertainment conglomerate like the majority of the major record labels.

"I have two choices," he continued. "I can hope the economy gets better or I can seek a more proactive approach to protect our employees, reward our shareholders and grow our company. That is the motivation behind this merger."

The three reasons given have nothing to do with giving consumers a better product — whether by design or price — nor do they necessarily have anything to do with serving artists better. Yet throughout the hearings Azoff and Rapino repeatedly emphasized the merger was in the best interests of artists and consumers — that they were the real winners. And in fact, when the time came for his oral testimony, Rapino repeated the same statement verbatim as his written one save for a few slight modifications, including replacing the phrase "grow our company" with "better service for artists and fans."

As Rapino made his case for the dire financial shape that Live Nation was in, his testimony about how well the company was performing seemed contradictory.

"We are not overleveraged," Rapino testified in his opening remarks to the Senate Judiciary. "We have managed our balance sheet carefully. We have grown our business three years in a row."

And yet two days later, in his next round of opening remarks to the House of Representatives Judiciary, Rapino testified: "Last year our market share was approximately 35 percent and has declined for five years straight. Our market cap is $250 million and we are carrying $700 million in debt."

Rapino later noted: "We invest $2 billion a year with artists. We made $160 million in EBITDA [Earnings Before Interest, Taxes, Depreciation and Amortization] last year but we had negative cash flow. We actually didn't make a dollar." And yet, throughout the course of the hearings, Rapino testified about the company's strong financial performance.

In written questions submitted later, Senator Herb Kohl asked Rapino for clarification: "Doesn't this excellent financial performance and your own statements during [the Q3 2008] earnings call contradict the claim that Live Nation's merger with Ticketmaster is necessary to give you the financial strength to grow and improve your business?

"I see no contradiction here," Rapino wrote back. "As I have testified, our stock has declined by nearly 90 percent over the last year and a half; the value of our real estate holdings has dissipated substantially; and our existing debt levels mean that we have scant access to capital. As a result, we cannot invest to move forward the way we should."

Representative Hank Johnson also asked Rapino for a clear answer: "Can you explain in detail the grounds on which this merger is necessary for Live Nation to survive as a U.S. company?"

Rapino responded by talking about how they'd rebuilt Live Nation from Clear Channel's "failing business model" only to face an uncertain future in tough economic times. However, he said, "We believe that we can continue our model with or without Ticketmaster. This is not about us going broke and needing a solution. This is about excelling in the race to try and solve these problems that Peter [Luukko] outlined."

It's unclear how that reconciled with his submitted testimony for the day, which suggested, "We face the very real possibility that if we don't find a solution, we could ultimately be bought by a foreign-owned entertainment conglomerate."

Azoff and Rapino's choice of words like "innovate," "experiment," "new" and "solution" proved vague and vacillated from being applied to the music industry as a whole to the concert industry to the combined companies to Live Nation by itself. Neither Azoff nor Rapino offered a single concrete example of what the merged company could do that the two companies, separately, could not have done. The clearest reason for the merger given to

Representative Johnson by Rapino was, "We want to excel in our chance to innovate this market."

Senator Kohl, irked two days earlier by similar generalities, took the CEOs to task.

"You both certainly do expect your companies together will be bigger, better and more profitable than ever before; otherwise, you wouldn't be doing this," he said sternly. "You have not addressed that at all. And you are not serving your shareholders unless you can make that claim. But in your statements, you do not make that claim at all. You would not be talking with each other unless the combination were bigger, better and more profitable than the individual businesses. And you have every right to do that, and we have every right to challenge it."

He paused ever so briefly.

"But I am, I must say, disturbed by your unwillingness to discuss the main reason for your merger."

LIVE NATION AND TICKETMASTER SUBMITTED thirty-seven letters to the House of Representatives Judiciary from artists, promoters and ancillary businesses that supported the merger. Of the six submitted by artists, five — Shakira, Seal, Billy Corgan, Journey and Alejandro Fernandez — had ties to Live Nation or Front Line. The only one that apparently didn't was an unsigned artist named Robert Shulze.

Out of the remaining thirty-one letters from venues, promoters and ancillary businesses like hotel and security firms, all but three were largely written from a form. The letters typically began, "I'm writing to you in an effort to lend our support for the proposed Live Nation/Ticketmaster merger." The first paragraph usually ended with the belief that "any changes that result from the merger will have a positive effect on my business and other businesses in the community."

Depending on how it was edited, the second or third paragraphs would include the assertion that, "From what I have heard about the merger, many in the industry are supportive of it and believe it will improve ticketing options and increase event attendance."

The letter's last paragraph almost always began with the line, "I urge you to defend the merger between Live Nation and Ticketmaster."

In their efforts to push the merger through, public records indicate that Live Nation and Ticketmaster spent a combined $1.62 million on congressional lobbying during 2009.

The merger's seemingly biggest hurdle — Christine Varney — was confirmed as the assistant attorney general for the Antitrust Division of the Department of Justice on April 20. On May 11 she delivered her first speech, entitled "Vigorous Antitrust Enforcement in This Challenging Era," to the Center for American Progress.

She announced that the Antitrust Division had withdrawn the previous department's report on Single-Firm Conduct Under Section 2 of the Sherman Act, a report that had previously guided the department's response to possible monopolies.

"While there is no question that Section 2 cases present unique challenges (for example, in the fashioning of injunctive remedies), the Report advocates extreme hesitancy in the face of potential abuses by monopoly firms," Varney told the audience. "We must change course and take a new tack."

"In short, while preserving the right of firms with market power to continue to compete, we cannot allow them a free pass to undertake predatory or unjustified exclusionary acts," she continued.

She concluded with something of a holistic view as to how the Antitrust Division under her guidance would begin its tenure: "The current economic challenges raise unique issues for antitrust authorities and private sectors," she acknowledged. "We are faced with market conditions that force us to engage in a critical analysis of previous enforcement approaches. That analysis makes clear that passive monitoring of market participants is not an option. Antitrust must be among the frontline issues in the Government's broader response to the distressed economy. Antitrust authorities — as key members of the Government's economic recovery team — will therefore need to be prepared to take action. The Antitrust Division will be ready to take a lead role in this effort."

ON JANUARY 25, 2010, NEARLY A YEAR after the Department of Justice began its investigation, it approved the Ticketmaster–Live Nation merger contingent upon a multitude of conditions.

"The Department of Justice's proposed remedy promotes robust competition for primary ticketing services and preserves incentives for competitors to innovate and discount, which will benefit consumers," said Varney. "The proposed settlement allows for strong competitors to Ticketmaster, allowing concert venues to have more and better choices for their ticketing needs, and provides for anti-retaliation provisions, which keep the merged company in check."

Ticketmaster was required to license a copy of its software to its client AEG, which was then allowed and encouraged to market its own ticketing system. Within five years AEG would either have to purchase the software or develop its own system.

Another part of the settlement called for Ticketmaster's divestment of Paciolan, a ticketing company it had acquired in 2008. It already had a buyer in Comcast-Spectator, Peter Luukko's company, which owned its own ticketing company, New Era Tickets, powered by Paciolan software.

Live Nation and Ticketmaster were also forbidden from retaliating against any venue owner that chose to use another company's ticketing service or another company's promotional services. Finally, firewalls to protect confidential and valuable competitor data from the company's promotion and management business were also required.

What surprised many was that Ticketmaster's secondary ticketing properties — TicketsNow and TicketExchange, among others — were left alone and allowed to remain part of the merged companies' infrastructure.

"After a rigorous investigation, we concluded that the transaction, as originally proposed, was anticompetitive," Varney told reporters the day of the announcement. "We were prepared to litigate this case, and I told the parties that. The required divestitures and behavioral prohibitions alleviate our concerns. Specifically, if approved by the court, this settlement will preserve competition in primary ticketing and maintain incentives to innovate and discount, thereby benefiting consumers. This is the right result."

Seth Hurwitz, the Washington, DC–based promoter who had battled SFX, Clear Channel and Live Nation and used Ticketmaster, Tickets.com and most recently Ticketfly, saw the decision as a positive step toward a better concert industry environment.

"The department seems to understand the issues, our concerns and the fears the entertainment industry hold about Live Nation's and Ticketmaster's predatory and uncompetitive behavior," he said, thankful that it appeared the companies were now being viewed under a microscope by the government.

"The Department of Justice has dictated a consent decree that Live Nation and Ticketmaster can't engage in anticompetitive behavior on any level going forward — and if that's true, it'll be a better world for everyone."

Isn't it pretty to think so?

Full Circle

LIVE NATION'S EMPLOYEE IDENTIFICATION CARDS resemble the laminates worn by artists and their crew — the ones that often say All Access. For the company's Bay Area division — the remaining legacy of Bill Graham Presents — the ID cards have a quote from their founding father: "My philosophy has always been 'How would I want to be treated if I bought a ticket?' Everything evolves from there."

The ticket buying process has evolved considerably since Graham personally collected tickets from patrons in a basket, only to resell some of them to last-minute fans who were hoping to catch a piece of the action. It was, it seemed, a relatively benign transgression — it's just what promoters did by nature (the Stones once famously played Winterland Arena in San Francisco and told Graham they wouldn't go onstage unless the top balcony was empty — the only sure way they could know that he wasn't overselling the venue). One manager mentioned that Graham was still back-dooring people into shows late into his career — but Graham being Graham, the manager politely asked him to refrain with little fanfare.

It's hard to know what Graham would make of the paperless ticket, the latest innovation in the concert industry. On its surface it portends a future of better ticketing equality — scalpers would be thwarted from buying seats in bulk to resell at exorbitant prices. Tickets would have a better chance of going to the fans, advocates say, because they must be retrieved at the gate with the same credit card that purchased them (and matching ID required in many instances).

Poke around a bit more, though, and you'll quickly hit a wasp nest of critics buzzing about the policy. Its opponents — led by ticket brokers — argue that it's far too restrictive for consumer freedom. What if somebody buys a ticket and can't attend the concert and either wants to sell it or give it to a friend? What if parents want to buy their child a pair of tickets for a birthday present (or conversely, if a young, credit card–less fan needs their parents to buy them the ticket)? Fluid answers to these fundamental questions have not been provided as of yet.

Larger issues reveal themselves, however, when one recognizes that the company driving paperless ticketing is Live Nation Entertainment (the new Ticketmaster–Live Nation entity). Critics suggest LNE is attempting to place another stranglehold on the industry since all of its paperless tickets, as of now, remain on the Ticketmaster platform. It's as if the company has put a leash on the concert ticket so that no matter where it goes, it's never that far from home. Each time that ticket is transferred or changed — in a similar fashion to what happens in the airline industry — there is an associated cost.

"The fight is not over," assured the National Ticket Brokers Association's counsel, Gary Adler, after the Live Nation–Ticketmaster merger was approved. "Our efforts to protect the rights of the consumer by exposing Ticketmaster's anti-consumer activities, including the use of paperless ticketing and excessive fees, are still priority number one." That Adler said this with the support of such heavy-hitting consumer advocacy groups as the National Consumers League, the Consumer Federation of America and the U.S. Public Interest Research Group is reflective of just how much the lines have been blurred between primary and secondary tickets sales.

The other new development in ticketing is dynamic pricing. This method, again much as in the airline industry, sets a sliding scale, taking into account seat location, date of purchase in relation to the event and, of course, demand. As one might suspect, front row tickets, like first class seats, are very expensive, allowing the seats in the upper levels to be more economically priced for fans on a budget. This concept has been floated within the industry for years and, for whatever reason, has yet to gain real traction in the primary ticketing market (the periodic ticket auction comes closer, although that's predicated on bidding). This will likely change in the near future as the multi-billion dollar secondary market is like a large, blinking highway billboard clearly indicating that primary tickets have been inefficiently priced — the primary justification managers like Irving Azoff have always had for dealing directly with brokers. One point nearly everyone in the industry agrees on is that over the last decade, the most desirable seats have been chronically undervalued, while the worst seats have been overvalued.

The tide of primary ticketing is clearly shifting, likely the beginning of a major and overdue pricing correction. A quick glance at performers like Paul McCartney sees some of the best seats in the house fetching $1,000 apiece. In less than a decade since Azoff broke the $100 mark for popular rock concerts with the Eagles, another zero has been added. Thus the question: if primary tickets are priced like secondary market prices, what happens to the secondary market?

Indications are that it has reached a relative peak. While there will always be a demand for tickets after the general on-sale, the secondary market may well shrink as that money is captured more efficiently by the primary market.

RazorGator founder Doug Knittle believes, "The brokers are toast. It's over. A broker might be able to make living if he buys some season tickets to basketball and baseball and stuff like that, but it's like we're going full circle. The concert business has been taken off the table. Now we're back to sports and theater, which is where we started in the early '70s."[1]

Meanwhile the summer concert season of 2010 proved to be one of the worst attended of all time. Shows with proven tracks records — American Idol, the Eagles and Tom Petty — all faced soft ticket sales and a smattering of canceled dates. After U2, Christina Aguilera and Limp Bizkit also decided not to follow through with announced tours, citing health and creative reasons, Live Nation, in scrambling for cash flow, put shows for sure-sell acts like Lady Gaga on sale for dates ten months out, just to generate dollars. If the needed cash flow gets too thin for the company with its massive overhead — the synergy works both ways with all those properties — Live Nation's ship may finally run aground.

Moreover, promoters' shortsighted, desperate actions these past few years — largely Live Nation's efforts to fill its amphitheaters during the summer — have been detrimental in conditioning consumers to wait for a better deal on concert tickets. Far too frequently Live Nation, in an effort to drive ticket sales in the face of low ticket counts, slashed prices weeks before a concert in an effort to capture ancillary revenues from attendance.

Throughout the summer of 2010, for instance, Live Nation launched ticket promotions ranging from "fan appreciation day," "no service fee Wednesdays" to $10 lawn tickets applied to concerts months after their general on-sale. While it's great for the two fans who were able to see the Jonas Brothers for $20, how do their friends feel, who bought a pair of tickets for the original face value of $100?

Indeed, a conversation that increasingly occurs between consumers and primary ticket sellers goes something like this:

"When do the tickets for the show go on sale?" asks the buyer.

The operator responds, "They're on sale."

"No," says the buyer. "When do they go on *sale?*"

In a presentation to Wall Street in July 2010, Live Nation Entertainment showed a variety of graphs and charts depicting how they were driving business despite a down economy. One of the illustrations highlighted the difference in the number of tickets sold for ten concerts on a normal day and a day they offered a $10 ticket promotion: 338 versus 24,075.

Several slides before that, it broke down the cost of an average ticket priced at $55.65. After paying approximately thirty percent to show costs and sixty-five to ninety percent to the artist and tax, a promoter's profit was $3. (Oddly there was no accounting for the clearly delineated $14 service charge to the promoter's bottom line, given that Live Nation and Ticketmaster would traditionally split it; there was also no mention of the instances in which the thirty percent show cost was met with a ninety percent guarantee.) So how do the numbers jibe when a $55 ticket is reduced to a $10 ticket, when by the company's own admission it owes the artist anywhere from $34 to $47 from it? What does the secondary market's proliferation and constant price reduction of primary ticket sales say about the state of the industry?[2] Several promoters, agents and managers have likened Live Nation Entertainment's vertical integration of the concert business to a Ponzi scheme — implying that it's just a matter of time before the cash runs out and it all comes crashing down like Bernie Madoff's empire. As Michael Cohl says, "The money doesn't necessarily pervert the music, but the price can pervert the business."

There is no question the business of rock and roll has shifted considerably over the past few decades. Revenue streams once deemed ancillary have become primary to support increasingly debt-ridden corporate entities. It often seems as if the music fans themselves have become mere afterthoughts, their loyalty expected but rarely nurtured in the way Bill Graham was so famous for doing.

Sherry Wasserman, one of Graham's longtime employees and right hands, founded Another Planet with fellow longtime BGP employee Gregg Perloff when the two defected from Live Nation's Bay Area office in 2003.

On her desk sits a framed note that Graham handwrote in 1991. It reads:

Lower the guarantees, so that we can lower the ticket prices, so that we still can afford to rock & roll . . . cheers.

"That was his mantra going into 1992 had he lived to fight the fight," she says. "The rest is history."

CHAPTER 1

1 The UNIVAC, which derived its name from "Universal Automatic Computer," could fill a one-car garage at a seven-figure price tag (although it's fair to say both the military and corporate America found more climate-controlled facilities for their $1.5-million investments). The significance of the machine was that the UNIVAC stored programs on tape, rather than relying exclusively on operators to input punch cards. This allowed for much more flexibility of usage and resulted in the emergence of software developers working independently of engineers servicing mainframes.

In the preface to his 1962 book *Electronic Business Systems*, which otherwise focused on practical business applications, programmer Richard Sprague looked back at the initial giddiness that continued to animate the pioneers of the emerging software industry: "When each of us first heard about the remarkable new machine, the electronic computer, visions came to mind of a completely automated world. The stories and articles on automation, predictions of the automatic factory, anticipation of the automatic electronic office — all stirred our imaginations. In most of these visions, the so-called Push-Button Age seemed to be made possible by the electronic computer."

2 The development of this building had been guided by Sam's older sister, Phyllis.

3 This interest was later a pursuit of his son Edgar Jr., a songwriter by avocation, who acquired Polygram Records for Seagram in 1999 and became CEO of the Warner Music Group in 2004.

4 Born George Warren Goldberg, the producer was the son of Rube Goldberg, best known for his cartoons that depicted complex contraptions performing simple tasks, so in terms of lineage one could fairly call Ticketron a Rube Goldberg invention.

5 During World War II he had demonstrated a fair share of leadership while serving as a

naval lieutenant and the commanding officer of an all-black minesweeper. Upon returning home he began a four-year stint at National Cash Register (NCR would soon move from accounting machines to business computers and somewhere in-between with its Post-Tronic, which despite its futuristic-sounding name, was more accounting machine than computer).

6 In *A Few Good Men from Univac*, David Lundstrom tracks these events, starting with the rumor, "soon confirmed by a cryptic notice on the company's bulletin boards," on through a period of exodus where "senior Univac engineers would leave in ones and twos to join Control Data. Because the two companies were separated by the Mississippi River, the defectors to Control Data were known around Univac as wetbacks."

7 Much, much later he would be fired from his role as director of the Texas Lottery by Governor George W. Bush's appointed lottery chair, Harriet Miers, in the wake of his allegations regarding improper campaign contributions, which subsequently would help torpedo Miers' Supreme Court nomination.

8 If this happened, it is more likely that it took place when demonstrating a TRS "Computer Controlled Ticket Vendor," a precursor of the ticket kiosks that debuted in the 1990s. The company brochure highlighted the TRS V-1, which looked impressive in all its metallic sheen but never reached the production phase beyond a prototype.

9 Di/An would go on to produce successful printer units for more than forty years, and the company's founder, Robert D. Kodis, holds the designation of receiving patents over a longer time span than any other inventor, including Thomas Edison.

10 Mayo focused on producing and directing, while Blair eventually gravitated to television, where her extensive résumé includes a 1971–72 stint opposite Henry Fonda on a family drama called *The Smiths*, where their son was portrayed by Ron Howard.

11 A CSC interoffice memo reflects a somewhat surprising inability to discover much information about Ticket Reservation Systems beyond its status as a Delaware corporation. TRS had filed its papers in that state to take advantage of its sympathetic corporate laws.

12 Hankenson began his career at the San Francisco Opera on a Ford Foundation Grant, serving as an assistant to general director Kurt Herbert Adler, where one of his responsibilities was in the box office, coordinating with remote bureaus that sold vouchers for the individual performances. This slightly cumbersome process necessitated agents providing patrons with vouchers and then sending the box office notification to set aside tickets that could be picked up prior to a given performance. One day, after Hankerson read in the paper about a new computer-facilitated approach to selling subway tickets, it occurred to him that a similar solution might serve the opera as well.

"They were in the midst of a big hullabaloo about creating the Bay Area Rapid Transit Service," he remembers. "They announced that IBM was going to be able to have ticket machines at each stop. You'd be able to purchase your ticket from these machines, and it would charge you just for where you were going from that point. I was fascinated because I thought that if we could implement this technology with our bureaus, patrons would be able to get their tickets immediately and know what seating they would have when they bought their tickets. At the time I even didn't recognize its great accounting value."

With Adler's consent Hankenson secured a meeting with a mid-level IBM executive, where he outlined his proposed system. However, as he remembers: "I explained my idea but they pooh-poohed it. They said that the entertainment industry and the opera and theater industry in particular wouldn't generate sufficient revenue to sustain the cost required to set it up. I couldn't convince them otherwise."

Hankenson also recalls that the transition to computerized ticketing at Saratoga wasn't necessarily a smooth one: "[Eugene] Ormandy was being presented the key to the city and I was part of the ceremony up on the platform. Well, at one point I noticed an expression of horror on Ormandy's face. He was looking with alarm behind me, where I discovered this little old lady coming at me with an umbrella. 'What had I done with her tickets?' Apparently, when we computerized our inventory, I had messed up her season tickets.

13 The Computer Sciences Corporation then repurposed the Computicket resources, using the IBM 360/50 mainframes to help secure a contract providing off-track betting services for New York City. Unfortunately for CSC this ended badly as well because the company's technology was not up to the task, resulting in a series of outages that led the Offtrack Betting Corporation to shut down telephone wagering and rely on a manual system for days at a time. Control Data then offered its assistance, and by early fall 1971 Ticketron began operating a series of OTB terminals. Ultimately neither company would remain on the job for long, with a new vendor, AmTote, winning the sweepstakes. In the interim some Computicket employees moved over to Ticketron (including Howard Erskine and future senior vice president Robert Gorra), while Nick Mayo was invited to become the general manager of the new Shubert Theater then being constructed in Century City.

14 Quinn departed to potables and poetry at the Cork 'N Bottle on December 29, 1970, with the commemorative tickets billing the event as "Goodbye Jack: Starring the Mighty Quinn" and produced by "The House That Jack Built."

CHAPTER 2

1 The Beginner's All-purpose Symbolic Instruction Code was created at Dartmouth College in 1964 by math professor (and future Dartmouth president) John George Kemeny along with Thomas Eugene Kurtz from the college's computing center. Their goal was to create a language "simple enough to allow the complete novice to program and run problems after several hours of lessons." In practice this amounted to two hours of instruction before setting students loose on Dartmouth's mainframe. Eventually many high schools and even junior highs offered introductory classes in BASIC, the language supported by the early Apple computers and some of the initial Microsoft programs.

2 Wojtulewicz would later be able to boast, "I saw my first demo of Select-A-Seat in their dining room and I saw my first demo of Ticketmaster on Albert Leffler's backyard patio."

3 Minneapolis was the home of Control Data, which was never able to break into its own market, a fact that some in the industry attributed to a reluctance on the part of CDC to align itself with the volatile rock world in its backyard. But former CEO Bob Price explains: "The market driver

in the Twin Cities was Dayton's department store, and they had no interest in Ticketron. It was pretty simple. We couldn't get the customer interested."

4 It is worth noting that while the *Literary Digest* was renowned for its polls, the next year the magazine made headlines via a "straw ballot" that predicted Republican presidential candidate Alfred Landon would take fifty-seven percent of the popular vote in his race against incumbent Franklin Delano Roosevelt, who would go on win in a landslide.

5 His authority similarly cleared him to plop a skater with a movie camera atop his head into the fray to support the filming of the vérité documentary *Derby*. Roger Ebert gave the film a four-star review, and it made *New York Times* critic Vincent Canby's Top 10 list for 1971, even if it does not always show its subjects in an appealing light. After the film opened, its central figure, a lothario who longs to leave his wife and two young children at least temporarily to attend Derby school, joined the pro ranks, becoming something of a draw, if not a virtuoso player.

6 Another parallel between the two worlds: Derby mainstay, green-haired aggressor Ann Cavello and her teammates referred to their breasts as "tickets" because "that's what put people in the seats."

7 Tandem was founded by former HP employees in 1974, who would sell the company to Compaq in 1997 before things came full circle in 2002 when HP acquired Compaq.

8 McLaughlin, however, was still in demand. Diamond's Department Stores had operated Select-A-Seat outlets in Phoenix, and the company was eager to keep the system active. Margie Bliss had become a Diamond's employee and McLaughlin joined her. Around this time the Dayton Hudson Corporation, which owned Diamond's, wanted its own proprietary ticketing software and, given the complications with Select-A-Seat's legal status, asked Bill Bliss to develop a new system. (Dayton Hudson didn't want McLaughlin involved, to ensure that the software would be an independent creation.) Shortly after he completed the basic programming, Bill Bliss passed away. McLaughlin came on board in 1978 and finished the work on the new system, which then supplanted Select-A-Seat. The service took on the mildly absurd name of Seat-o-Matic, although most referred to it by the department store that offered it, initially Diamond's and later Dillard's, after that company purchased the Diamond's chain in 1984.

CHAPTER 3

1 Two engineers with MIT affiliations, setting out to build mainframe alternatives, founded DEC in 1957, delivering a prototype, the PDP-1, two years later ("PDP" was an acronym for Programmable Data Processor). The company first achieved sales success in the middle of the decade with the PDP-8, while its successor, the PDP-11, carried the manufacturer into the 1970s.

2 One such early demonstration provides Gunn with a lasting memory of the process: "Pete had a dry sense of humor. We wanted him to help us show how you could easily set different prices for a single event. Well, he came up with a ticket and it was for '6 Lions Devour 50 Christians.' I remember the cheap seats were up front."

3 The 1970s saw its share of disturbances during ticket sales for certain popular acts. A few years later, when Elton John tickets went on sale at a Meir & Frank store in Portland, Oregon,

customers charged up the escalators in reverse, put cigarettes out on the carpet and caused such a general ruckus that future major sales were banished to the Meir & Frank parking booth across the street.

4 In January 1975 Boston mayor Kevin White revoked the license for a Led Zeppelin concert at Boston Garden after 2,500 fans, who had been allowed to congregate in the lobby of the building on the night before an on-sale, broke into the facility, vandalized the concession stands and tossed beer bottles onto the Garden ice below.

5 Kanter's strategies so rankled the Internal Revenue Service that in 2008, more than seven years after his death, the IRS was still trying to collect taxes (unsuccessfully) on a 1973 transaction resulting from a commission paid by A.N. Pritzker, after Kanter helped the family secure a management contract for what would become San Francisco's Hyatt Embarcadero.

6 Nearly thirty years later Rosen looks back with considerable warmth at the man who gave him this opportunity: "Jay was a mentor, a second father to me, and I was extremely fond of him."

7 The fact that the Hyatt chain was continuing to expand in pace with the family fortune never hurt in terms of relationships or perceptions of the company's prospects. The Pritzkers ultimately invested $12 million in Ticketmaster, although when it suited his needs, Rosen occasionally insinuated that the numbers were higher for purposes of intimidation relative to how far Ticketmaster could take a deal.

8 This reference would come to be flipped, as reflected in a 1994 *Billboard* piece entitled "Ticketmaster Is Under Fire: How David Became the Industry's Goliath."

9 Box offices did this on occasion, adding to their otherwise limited bottom lines by selling seats and then providing the purchasers with location passes rather than hard tickets, so that no stubs would be available to count.

10 Axl's proclivities are noted in a classic Barry Fey story regarding a Guns N' Roses/Metallica show he promoted at Mile High Stadium. Although the commonly received account has it that Fey brandished a .357 magnum at Rose after the singer walked off stage during his performance, the truth isn't far off. After discovering that Rose had commandeered a limo following the opening song and was headed back to his hotel, Fey explains: "I immediately went to the head of the limo company, Big John, and I said, 'Let me tell you something. You don't work for him. You work for me. If you ever want to see another dime from this company, you get that limo back here, and the only way he's leaving is if he jumps out, and if he jumps out, you leave him in the street, but you get the car back here.' Meanwhile [Guns N' Roses] had sent an emissary into Metallica's dressing room to say, 'Can you come on the stage and jam with us?' And [Metallica drummer] Lars [Ulrich] says, 'You bozos don't have enough money in your collective bank accounts for me to go back on that stage.' So then the car comes back, and he's in it. Before this, I had gone to *my* car and out of my glove compartment got a .357 and put it in my back pocket. Before he was going to go again, I was gonna shoot him, or I was going to put it in his face. He comes back, talks to his manager, and he goes back up on the stage, and they start to play again. I put three bad asses at the top of the stage and two Denver cops at the bottom, and I say, 'The only way he leaves the stage is that way,' pointing out that he had to walk through the crowd."

11 Another story from this era suggests the divisions within the corporate culture. Upon

taking a new position with Ticketron in Dallas, Matt Whelan discovered that all seven people who worked for him carried a gun. So he called Bob Gorra in New York and asked, "What's the deal with the guns?"

"What do you mean?"

"Everyone in this office including my secretary carries a gun, and they're prepared to use it if they get into trouble."

"I'll call you in an hour or two," Gorra responded. Then he immediately stepped away from his desk, took a cab to LaGuardia Airport and flew to Dallas.

Four hours later he phoned Whelan from the Dallas airport.

Upon arriving in the office, Gorra announced, "Mr. Whelan called me today and he was very upset and he claims that everyone in the office is carrying a gun. Is that true?"

The staff said it was.

"Well, what are you going to do with those guns?"

One employee answered, "Well, if somebody comes up behind me and asks me for the money, I'm protecting the company's assets."

"No, no, no. We're insured. We're not having a shootout. Just give them the money."

Gorra then hosted what he referred to as a "gun turning-in ceremony."

Back at the airport a few hours later, while sharing a beer with Whelan, Gorra said, chuckling: "I've had to explain a lot of things to Control Data, and they don't understand us, but they try to work with us. I just don't know how I'd explain my little account rep having a shootout in Dallas over $10,000. I don't think those engineers up in Minnesota would get it."

12 Ticketmaster had severed its relationship with Chargit a few months following the US Festival, as an experience with a Chicago Cubs on-sale led Rosen to conclude that Chargit was misrepresenting its ability to handle high-volume events.

13 As Rosen testified before Congress during the Pearl Jam hearings, after submitting the affadavits Ticketron had filed with the Justice Department in 1991: "What these affadavits show is as follows: Ticketron had lost $2 million in 1988, $2 million in 1989, $7.5 million in 1990, and were projecting a loss of $8.5 million in 1991. . . . Unfortunately, because Ticketron neglected to segregate their clients' funds from their operating accounts, if Ticketron had been allowed to file bankruptcy, the public, the buildings, the arenas, and the entertainers would have suffered a loss of somewhere between $13 and $16 million. Such losses would have been a black eye to the entire ticketing industry."

CHAPTER 4

1 Around this time a disproportionate number of VW buses carried bumper stickers that questioned, "Who are the Grateful Dead and why do they keep following me?"

2 In the documentary film *Last Days of the Fillmore*, Bill Graham described him in a somewhat convoluted manner as "the big papa bear of what rock music should have been. I think he and the group stand for what the utopia that never was, is."

3 Weldon, Williams & Lick was founded in 1898 by Chauncey A. Lick, a printer who had

moved from St. Louis to the relative frontier of Fort Smith, Arkansas. Lick opened a general printing shop above a saloon but found a new direction when pressed into service by the manager of an opera house, who could no longer wait for the tickets he had ordered from an eastern printer. Over the first decades of the twentieth century, the newly focused ticketing concern expanded into circus, carnival and rodeo tickets. The company later added sports and museum clients and in recent years has diversified even further by producing custom hangtags, ID cards, parking permits and admission credentials. Walcott, the great grandson of Chauncey Lick and the fourth generation to head the company, has been president since 1985. And while the close-lipped executive might wince to find the details in print, the company has prospered under him, with more than 300 employees now generating an excess of $40 million in annual sales in a 190,000-square-foot facility.

4 As for her name, the story has it that one day at the Hog Farm someone stood on the edge of a field, calling for their missing cat, and she appeared instead, thereafter becoming Calico. If that wasn't sufficiently unconventional, Calico took on a new identity at GDTS: Ruby Begonias. The idea was to maintain a sense of anonymity from Deadheads, so that staffers who communicated directly with fans by answering the telephone problem line acquired aliases. Forest Schofield was Sherman, named after the sidekick to the cartoon canine time traveler on *Rocky and Bullwinkle*. Tom Reed became known as Bamm-Bamm. ("A woman named Annie, who later married [sound engineer] John Cutler, started to work in the ticket office a week before I did, and she was given the names Pebbles. So the next unfortunate boy who came along had to match up with Pebbles.") Joanne Wishnoff, who headed up the customer service line, was known as Pearl Problem.

5 On the subject of industry feuds, strained relations also exist between Scher and promoter Ron Delsener, which resulted from Scher's decision to promote shows in New York City. Howard Stein, who ran his own Capitol Theater, this one just outside Manhattan in Port Chester, New York, had stepped into the breach after the Fillmore closed, opening the Academy of Music, later known as the Palladium. However, Scher recalls: "He sort of self-destructed pretty earlier on in his career. He let his ego completely get in the way and actually started thinking people were seeing the shows because he was promoting them. I learned a long time ago if it says 'John Scher Presents John Scher,' very few people are going to come, and the ones that are coming will ask for comps." Promoter Ron Delsener, who had worked with the Beatles at Forest Hills Tennis Stadium in 1964 and had started a summer series at Wollman ice skating rink in Central Park, believed that he was the rightful heir. So when Scher bought into the Ritz nightclub during the 1980s and began promoting shows at the Beacon Theater and Carnegie Hall, mutual acrimony ensued, which persists to this day.

Steve Marcus believes he was the collateral damage of this antipathy. After Jerry Garcia's death Marcus began a brief and unsuccessful run as head of Bob Dylan Ticket Sales. Delsener promoted Dylan in New York, and Marcus remembers receiving a vituperative dressing-down from the promoter based on his relationship with Scher. Marcus also alleges, "The first shows I did with Delsener were the Theater at Madison Square Garden [which began life as the Felt Forum]. I got 500 tickets and sold them all. Then I get a call from [Dylan manager] Jeff

Kramer saying, 'You took all our guest tickets.' I said, 'What are you talking about?' And he said, 'Ron Delsener sent you all our guest list tickets for the mail order.' I said, 'That's not the agreement we had,' and I even had a letter in writing that said our tickets were on top of the guest list. We'd already sold our tickets and they were gone, and Delsener had done a setup for me so I'd look really bad."

Ultimately Marcus's stint with Dylan lasted less than two years and somewhat improbably left Marcus in a financial hole. He attributes this to a lack of support by the organization. He was allowed to sell taper's tickets, but Dylan reserved the right to change his mind and rescind permission on the night of the show. ("I said, 'Forget it. It doesn't work that way.'") Beyond that Marcus contends he never received sufficient lead time to conduct a proper mail order. "One thing I told Jeff Kramer was that the Dead used Grateful Dead Ticket Sales as a meter to see how much advertising would be needed for a show. Sometimes we would be out eight weeks before it went on sale to the public. That way the promoter would know two or three weeks before the show if we sold out our allotment, and they might not have to advertise. I explained that to him but he never utilized it. It didn't matter to him. By the end of my working with the Bob Dylan organization, I lost $5,000. There was no excuse for it, and it was because Jeff Kramer wasn't willing to give me the backing I had with the Grateful Dead."

CHAPTER 5

1 Estimates suggest the band could have made an additional $2 million in 1993 had their tickets and merchandise been competitively priced higher.

2 Jane Kleinberger explains: "We did not found Paciolan deliberately; it was just a wonderful accident." Back in 1980, two years out of school as an accounting major, she became the assistant to Cary Thomas, the vice president of finance at a small computer firm in Southern California. Thomas's wife worked in business affairs at the University of Southern California, and as Kleinberger recalls, "their ticket manager of thirty years had just retired, things were in a bit of an upheaval and we built them a name and address database." Along with co-worker Thomas McQuade, who had taken the lead on the software development, the three began moonlighting under the company name Paciolan, a nod to Italian monk Luca Pacioli, a fifteenth-century mathematician and the first to document the double-entry method of accounting. When they were still unsure of what might follow, "suddenly San Diego State called and said they wanted to look at our ticketing system. We all looked at each other and put the phone down and said, 'They called it a system!'"

Paciolan soon became a stand-alone operation, mostly servicing college athletic programs, offering ticketing software with robust accounting features. "It wasn't until the late '90s that we gave a name to our model, but we called it the 'enablement model.' We enabled teams, venues, organizations to sell their own tickets to their own clients under their own branding. It was not about a consumer brand; we were pure play venue enablers." Paciolan expanded from the university setting into performing arts and eventually would power a few regional ticketing operations, including New Era and Tickets West.

By 2000, with twenty consecutive years of profitability and not a dime of outside capital, Paciolan became quite appealing to outside suitors. The company did welcome in a few investors but rebuffed attempts at purchase until Ticketmaster made a successful bid in the summer of 2007. Two and a half years later, as a result of the Justice Department's antitrust investigation, Ticketmaster was required to divest itself of the company, which had been rebranded Ticketmaster Irvine. The name Paciolan returned under the new ownership at Comcast-Spectacor (which, under the leadership of President and COO Peter A. Luukko, had previously invested in Paciolan with the thought of eventual acquisition but had not been able to best Ticketmaster's offer in 2007).

3 In Tic-X-Press, Inc. v. Omni Promotions Co. of Ga., 815 F. 2d 1407 — Court of Appeals, 11th Circuit 1987815 F.2d 1407 (1987), both a US District Court and a federal Court of Appeals sided with Tic-X-Press. The courts awarded damages of $30,273.21 to Tic-X-Press but more importantly issued an injunction barring the Omni from conditioning its facility rental upon the use of the SEATS ticketing service.

For whatever reason (whether it be ignorance of the ruling, unwillingness to pursue costly legal means or other considerations), beyond Leiken and Fastixx, other, similarly situated ticketing companies failed to harp on the case.

4 Black wasn't just any lobbyist — he was one of the most influential. Beginning in the early 1990s, he was instrumental in defending Philip Morris and big tobacco. As the dangers of secondhand smoke became more apparent and the clear solution became banning smoking indoors, Black helped move the issue away from the Environmental Protection Agency to the less threatening Occupational Safety and Health Administration, suggesting it focus on all potential indoor pollutants and better ventilation.

Moreover, in 1991, in a well-documented strategy, Black devised a plan to, as he wrote, "raise the Philip Morris profile in a favorable manner in the Executive Branch of the federal government." Simultaneously, he proposed raising the company's profile within the Republican Party. Taken together, he hoped to set up meetings between key company representatives and influential members of the administration. The aim was to "establish independent personal relationships between the PM representatives and the official visited." If Black had successfully maneuvered big tobacco out of (temporary) legal detriment, he surely had a good shot at doing the same for Ticketmaster.

5 The sixty-three seat swing in favor of the red states in 2010's midterm election has since trumped it.

CHAPTER 6

1 Speculation was that Sony would eventually leverage Sony Music artists for primary slots at the venues. At the time, however, Sony corporate was said to be facing antitrust concerns given they were one of the leading manufacturers of CD players and owned a record label that sold millions of CDs. Sources have said that to avoid further concern, it divested its stake in Pavilion and its purchase of Bill Graham's former merchandise company Winterland and

scuttled plans to get into the ticketing business for its venues with Blockbuster.

2 In its January 1904 issue, *Out West* magazine ran a feature on the newly erected building. It noted, in part:

> In its natural site, its use for dramatic representations, its architecture, the character of its surrounding scenery – with the Pacific Ocean in the foreground and the Berkeley hills rising behind, and the blue sky of California for a canopy, the new amphitheater may be said to be true to the Greek ideal.
>
> The amphitheater presents a striking spectacle when filled with people from its topmost row of seats to its lowermost, the gay colors of ladies' dresses gleaming in the sunlight, their ribbons lightly fluttering in the sea-breeze, while the waving fringe of green trees framing the top forms a charming background.
>
> The audience now sits under the open sky, as in the days of old Greece; the absence of summer rains making this practicable. It is possible, however, that an awning may be stretched across the auditorium, after the upper colonnade has been built to afford a rest for the supporting poles.

CHAPTER 7

1 Cohl and his friend Ricky Brown were sitting around their Toronto apartment in 1969 deciding what to do with their lives. Cohl was employed part-time by his father, a clothier, working in the shipping room, wrapping boxes and delivering them to stores in the family station wagon. Brown's father was a dentist. They were certain they didn't want to go into their families' businesses. But what to do?

"I've got it," said Brown one day, smoke likely wafting in the air as a record crackled away on the turntable. "We're going to open a strip club."

"But why are they going to come to our strip club?" Cohl countered, noting that Sam's was already the destination of choice for those wanting to see some skin in their city.

It didn't matter. Brown would not be dissuaded, and Cohl, while not committed to the business venture — for one thing neither of the young men had any formal business training — entertained the idea. Still, he kept asking Brown, "Why are they going to come?"

Bolstering the young entrepreneurs' confidence was the low employment rate in Canada, one that was kept in check by the government's seeming ability to employ just about anybody who needed a job. So after much investigation it was decided the country's capital city of Ottawa needed its own strip club. As the two were doing some research at another local establishment, the answer to his question suddenly struck Cohl.

"Ricky, I've got it!" he declared. "We're going to be so successful, it's unbelievable."

Brown looked at him, waiting for the answer.

"We're going to tell the girls to take off their pasties and G-strings," said Cohl, beaming.

The two triumphantly strolled into a bank on Eglinton Avenue in Toronto and, after a brief explanation of their business plan to the branch manager, were promptly given a $10,000 business loan. They quickly hooked up with Harvey Glatt and Harold Levin, Ottawa's biggest concert promoters at the time, who contributed $5,000 each to the endeavor.

Before the club, which they'd named Pandora's Box, could have its grand opening, Brown and Cohl burned through the $20,000, leaving no money for marketing. The two convinced a local printer to print up their "Come to our undress rehearsal" flyers on the promise of paying him four times over should they be in business the following week.

The opening was a success — if scandal-fueled national news coverage is any measure — and after a few arrests and painful hurdles in subsequent months, Cohl decided to shift his focus in the live entertainment business to concerts.

2 By the late 1980s CPI had expanded its reach considerably. Rather quietly, the company had invested in several, smaller American promoters: Barry Fey's Feyline Productions in Colorado, CC Productions in South Carolina and Randy Levy's Rose Productions in Minnesota. "Our strategy was to tap into the local expertise if it was there," says Perryscope cofounder Riley O'Connor, who led CPI USA. "We could learn more about [the individual market] by having [a local promoter] involved. It was not about taking somebody out [of the market]; it was about bringing somebody in. That was always our philosophy."

Ballard and Cohl partnered with Labatt Ltd.'s BCL Entertainment in 1987, selling the company a forty-five percent stake in CPI the following year as it became CPI's parent (CPI had previously partnered with Molson three years earlier). Part of the Labatt's deal saw the sale of Donald K. Donald Productions to BCL.

"I seem to remember that I found myself in the middle of a Michael Cohl vision," says Tarlton. "He and the CEO of Labatt Brewery had a strategy of one united concert company from coast to coast in Canada that I would run, and he would focus with Arthur Fogel on how to grow his global touring vision."

The idea, says Cohl, was much bigger than what it eventually became. "It was just my own version of what ultimately became SFX, but we didn't have the time," he suggests, referencing the promoter rollup of the late 1990s that transformed the industry. "We sat and agreed on the concept with Labatt's in '87 — they were supporting me — and toward the late '80s there was this huge collapse in real estate and this huge recession. It set the principals in Labatt's way back." The company was part of a vast Canadian business empire whose holdings were largely tied up in real estate and construction.

However, Cohl notes, even if his vision had come to full fruition, it would have been done in a much quieter way than Bill Graham or SFX went about their business. "I never had a show that said, 'Michael Cohl Presents,'" he says by way of example. "I never put my name out there, and I never thought that was the way to go about it. Whether we were the Antichrist or the anti-Graham, we were the opposite. We liked to sneak our way around. And I'm cocky enough to believe that, had the real estate bust of the late '80s not happened, we would have been . . ." his voice trails off for a moment. "Not SFX [per se] but [similar, albeit] in a different economic way. Though I admire Bob Sillerman — he's the king as far as I'm concerned — I was going to go around buying things for nickels and dimes and trying to grow it, make it bigger, hopefully smarter and therefore better."

3 Peter is the son of Allan Bronfman, the brother of Samuel Bronfman, who built the Seagram alcohol empire and whose son Edgar founded Ticket Reservation Systems.

4 AMFM owned CapStar Broadcasting, which Sillerman had originally sold SFX Broadcasting to for $2.1 billion.

CHAPTER 8

1 Edgar Sr. was the original investor behind Ticket Reservation Systems.

2 On March 7, 2003, the United States District Court for the Central District of California granted Ticketmaster's motion for a summary judgment and dismissed the case before trial (a decision later affirmed by the 9th Circuit Court of Appeals). The court ruled that, even if it assumed the conclusions reached by Tickets.com's expert economist to be altogether accurate (and they had been challenged by Ticketmaster's own expert), there was no valid antitrust claim.

To this end the court granted: "In the relevant market as described, TM has by far the dominant share of the business. In 31 of the 41 regional areas, of the larger arenas, TM has exclusive contracts which cover 75% of the tickets sold. In 25 of the regional areas, TM's market share was about 90%."

Nonetheless it held: "Size alone or heavy market share alone does not make one a monopolist (or in danger of becoming one). To qualify as a monopolist or have a dangerous likelihood of becoming one, one must have either the power to control prices or to exclude competition. In fact, the power to exclude competition is almost a necessity to be able to charge prices above competitive levels. There must be evidence of the ability to control prices or exclude competitors. The evidence here establishes that these conditions do not exist because of the bidding nature of the competition, in which TX [Tickets.com] is fully able to join, that the venues have the bargaining power to prevent being taken advantage of, that prices cannot be unilaterally raised because of the long term contracts controlling the prices, and that there are no meaningful barriers to entry by TX if it can convince venues that it can provide better service or a better price."

Judge Harry L. Hupp also concluded: "TX's major point is that long term exclusive contracts with large venues narrows the immediate field for competition for such contracts for TX. Undoubtedly, this is true. The question here, though, is whether such contracts are commercially reasonable. The evidence points very strongly to the conclusion that the venues themselves prefer long term exclusive contracts for their own reasons, that they have the economic power to resist long term contracts if it were in their interests to do so, and overwhelmingly, they prefer the long term contracts and prefer them to include the retail outlets, the telephone centers, and the internet connections. This can be for a number of reasons. Where the venues run their own box office at the venue site, the computers need to be compatible with the computers at the other sites, which means that changing ticket servicers every few years means retraining staff on new computers and software. Changing servicers often also means changing retail outlets (with which their customers become accustomed to) and also changing telephone and (perhaps) internet addresses. If the ticket servicer has reasonable performance and price, continuity leads to customer usage and satisfaction. Costs can be fixed for a longer, more predictable future. But by far the most important reason why venues prefer long terms contracts is that this is the method by which they can obtain cash upfront from the ticket servicer, but at the cost of a long term contract, so that the ticket servicer may amortize the cost with the expected income over the years of the contract. Often, the large up-front payment is obtained to build the venue or to remodel it, to the mutual benefit of the ticketing service and the venue, but a long term contract is then needed to support the cash payment demanded by the venue. Some venues prefer exclusive contracts because it simplifies their bookkeeping and reduces the cost of renegotiating the contracts every few years. Virtually no venues have complained about long term contracts or felt forced into them against their desires. Both TX and TM [Ticketmaster] use the long term exclusive contract to accommodate their customers' desires, to their mutual benefit. So does Paciolan and TX with licensing software. Thus, the evidence shows that the long term exclusive contract is not for the purpose of excluding competition, but for the mutual economic benefit of both competitors. It is a mutually desired reasonable business practice from which no antitrust inferences may be drawn." (Case citations removed.)

CHAPTER 9

1 Baumgart sold Softix to Australian media tycoon Kerry Packer in 1987. Of that deal Baumgart remembers: "I would say Fred Rosen essentially clinched my deal with Kerry Packer. At the last minute Fred said I'll pay you twice what Kerry's paying. But I knew that Rosen only wanted to shut the company down, and Kerry Packer continued to run it."

CHAPTER 10

1 These ads mostly benefited ABC, as the seven-figure price tag did not serve as a Hail Mary to such advertisers as Lifeminders.com, an "email reminder service," and online stationery company OurBeginning.com. With the dot-com bubble set to burst in three months, the absurdity of this moment is registered in a Salon.com account from the following day, which shares the following jargon-heavy, substance-light dialogue from ad agency execs watching the game: "'Is it a purchasing portal, or a commerce network?' someone asks of Computer. com. 'It's a purchasing portal that aggregates content across a vertical commerce network.' 'No, that's Epidemic.com' 'I thought that was a real-time, cross-platform purchasing portal.'"
2 This was somewhat akin to opening the MasterBroker exchange to public eyes, which Pat Toole contends is exactly what happened, as he assisted Domek with an upload tool and then watched his own clients gravitate to the new site. After Toole sold his company to Doug Knittle, RazorGator filed a lawsuit against TicketsNow, which was settled out of court. Domek acknowledges Toole's assistance and has kind words for him but suggests that TicketsNow had to develop alternative software after Toole's proved insufficient and that this new programming led brokers to switch allegiances.

3 Domek explains that following the sale, "I wanted to be around, and I was led to believe I would be around, and two days later I had a very different conversation with Cheryl Rosner. Sure enough, it wasn't only me but they got rid of anybody who knew what made our company successful. Those people just didn't have a place there."

4 Ticketmaster's court filings contended that RMG technology users "are bombarding Ticketmaster's website with millions of automated ticket requests that can constitute up to 80 percent of all ticket requests made." The suit identified one user who made 600,000 ticket requests in a single day and a second who made 425,000 requests.

5 The company's frustration also led it to break from general policy, in detailing some of the particulars regarding available inventory. Ticketmaster's Joseph Freeman pointed out, for example, that for the December 3, 2007 show at the Sprint Center in Kansas City, Missouri, out of 11,000 possible seats, only 8,400 were available for the initial on-sale, with half of those going to the Miley World fan club and the other 4,200 placed on sale through Ticketmaster. The remaining 2,600 seats were held by sponsors, the promoter, the record label and other insiders. This information led to a new hue and cry for state legislation to ensure that a higher percentage of tickets were made available to the general public (although no laws came close to passage).

6 On June 25, 2008, the U.S. District Court for Central California in Los Angeles ruled on behalf of Ticketmaster. Following up on a preliminary injunction issued the previous October, Judge Audrey B. Collins permanently banned RMG from developing software that would help users access inventory on Ticketmaster.com. The court also ordered RMG, which by then was near bankruptcy, to pay $18,000,000 in damages to Ticketmaster.

One other interesting tidbit that came out of the case is that although the software created by RMG unleashed a flood of requests onto Ticketmaster.com, when it came to outwitting the CAPTCHAs, which required users to interpret distorted letters and enter them into a field, RMG outsourced this task to India, where a room of workers furiously typed for $2 per hour.

7 Two significant changes would follow over the course of the year. On June 17, in an effort to compete more directly with StubHub, the site began allowing fans to list tickets for sale. This transformation to a consumer ticket exchange angered brokers who feared that prices would drop, quashing much of the cooperative spirit nurtured at the fireside chat.

A few months later on December 8, with the sale to Ticketmaster long since completed (and questions mounting regarding the future of TicketsNow, which still had not dented StubHub's market share), Cheryl Rosner stepped down as president and CEO.

8 Speaking of defensive moves, eBay itself entered the initial bidding, with the thought of icing Ticketmaster out of the market or at least raising the sales price, which it succeeded in accomplishing.

CHAPTER 11

1 When Seagram acquired MCA in 1995, MCA's Music Entertainment Group was renamed Universal Music Group. Canadian-based BCL Entertainment — owned by Seagram CEO

Edgar Bronfman's cousin Peter — and including Michael Cohl's CPI family of businesses — was also purchased.

2 Audience View had been included out of respect for its new CEO, Fred Rosen, although its software was not deemed scalable, and Rosen himself, who had joined the company, sensing an opportunity to reenter the business and work directly with venues once again, soon departed.

3 Ticketmaster would settle with the Federal Trade Commission a year later, agreeing to give refunds for the difference between those tickets purchased on TicketsNow and their original face value.

4 Azoff also quietly acknowledged a longtime practice within the industry that had rarely, if ever, been discussed in public: "In that service charge are the credit card fees, the rebates to the buildings, rebates sometimes to artists, sometimes rebates to promoters."

Ticketmaster, on a case-by-case basis, is willing to increase the service charge on behalf of the artist. An accepted rule of thumb is that any amount above about $10 on a service fee is, generally speaking, the artist's own add-on.

5 JAM Productions, founded by Jerry Mickelson and Arny Granat in the early 1970s, became Chicago's premier concert promoter. Unbeknownst to many, it was extremely close to selling to SFX in the late 1990s.

According to sources, the deal was essentially done to the point of handshake agreements with the meeting adjourned. As those present were exiting, JAM asked what would be done with the Park West Theater. JAM's contention was that given it had just sunk a sizable sum of money into acquiring the theater — they had promoted there for years — it had contributed zero to their bottom line and therefore should not be part of the deal (i.e., its real value had not been realized).

SFX CEO Robert Sillerman responded by saying something to the effect of, "We're buying your company — it's one of the assets — you can't pick and choose. You cannot operate this on your own." JAM contended that the building alone was worth several million dollars, and they weren't going to walk away from that money.

"If it's worth more as a parking garage, then sell the building off before we close the deal," Sillerman suggested. "You can't use it as a concert venue. If you're saying the building is worth $3 million and the value is not reflected in your numbers, we're not going to pay you an extra $3 million. We're buying your business — it is what it is."

Mickelson in particular said, "Not a chance."

Had SFX been willing to come to terms for the Park West Theater, it's unlikely that JAM would have become such an ardent and vocal critic of the concert industry's consolidation as orchestrated by SFX, Clear Channel Entertainment and Live Nation. Nor is it likely that Mickelson would have testified before Congress against the Live Nation–Ticketmaster merger.

JAM itself was the subject of a $3-million antitrust suit in June 1982 brought forth by fellow Chicago promoter Flip Side Productions. The suit alleged that JAM conspired to control the city's major venues in an effort to squeeze out Flip Side. According to Mickelson, the suit was dismissed "six years and $400,000 later."

1 A few months after he said this, on July 15, 2010, the company he founded but no longer operated, RazorGator, announced it would cease selling its own inventory and function exclusively as a commercial ticket exchange.

2 At least one individual views all this upheaval as a moment of opportunity. In October 2010 Fred Rosen reentered the ticketing world as the newly named CEO of Outbox Enterprises. Unlike the company he led to prominence, Outbox offers "white label" services, providing venues with an alternative to centralized ticketing systems, allowing them to market and sell tickets directly from their websites.

SOURCE NOTES

PROLOGUE

"So if you": Quoted in http://twitter.com/irvingazoff, August 4, 2010.

"If they could": Quoted in 'Live Nation: Future of Ticketing" http://money.cnn.com/video/fortune/2010/07/23/f_bst_live_nation_ticketmaster.fortune

CHAPTER 1

This chapter draws on the authors' interviews with Roy Bellman, Kurt Devlin, Harvey Dubner, Howard Erskine, Craig Hankenson, Larry Litwin, Andrew Mayo, Faye Nuell Mayo, Bob Price, Jane Quinn, Bill Schmitt, Peter Schniedermeier, Matt Whelan, Harvey Wineberg and others. In addition it utilizes the secondary sources listed below:

"I'd always loved": Quoted in Edgar M. Bronfman, *Good Spirits: The Making of a Businessman* (New York: G.P. Putnam's Sons, 1998).

"Whether we were": Quoted in Edgar M. Bronfman, *Good Spirits: The Making of a Businessman*.

"A computerized ticket": Quoted in Howard Taubman, "How To Civilize Ticket Sales," *New York Times*, May 23, 1965.

"One could obtain": Quoted in Paul E. Ceruzzi, *A History of Modern Computing* (Cambridge, MA: The MIT Press, 2002).

"Control Data Widens Line," *Business Week*, October 2, 1965.

Harvey Dubner and Joseph Abate, "Ticketron — a successful operating system without an operating system." AFIPS — *Conference Proceedings, Volume 36*.

"All other reserve": Quoted in "System Description: TRS Ticket Issuing and Control."

"TRS is the": Quoted in Louis Calta, "Computers Speed Box-Office Sales, *New York Times*, July 7, 1967.

"Millionaires: How They Do It," *Time*, December 3, 1965.

"The Teleticket system": Quoted in Walter T. McHale, "An Analysis of the Teleticket Concept."

"Each sturdy unit": Quoted in "Computicket Is Here!"

"The new computer": Quoted in *New York Times*, October 16, 1969.

"Here we are": Quoted in Cecil Smith, "Computers Battle for Ticket Sales," *Los Angeles Times*, May 17, 1968.

"Dedicated to the": Quoted in "Computicket Is Here!"

"When *Happy Time*": Quoted in John L. Scott, "Automation Comes to the Aid of Ticket Buyers," Los Angeles Times, February 11, 1968.

"Both companies are": Quoted in "No SRO at Computer," *Business Week*, March 23, 1968.

"We have yet": Quoted in Paul Zimmerman, "Computers Poised To Solve Sports Ticket Problems," *Los Angeles Times*, March 31, 1968.

"The name of": Quoted in John Hall, "A Loaf of Bread . . . a Jug of Wine . . . and 2 Tickets to a Dodger Game?" *Los Angeles Times*, January 11, 1968.

"Polite, edgy hostility": Quoted in "Automation Has Come to Broadway," *Palm Beach Post*, December 14, 1969.

Some of the bitterest": Quoted in "Just the Ticket," *Newsweek*, April 1, 1968.

"Jack Kent Cooke," Quoted in *Los Angeles Times*, May 5, 1968.

"It is inevitable": Quoted in *Wall Street Journal*, March 15, 1968.

"New York bound?": Quoted in *Los Angeles Times*, December 8, 1968.

"All network terminals": Quoted in "Computicket Is Here!"

"Bernard B. Zients": Quoted in Louis Calta, "Computers Speed Box-Office Sales, *New York Times*, July 7, 1967.

"Personally, I've never" Quoted in Jeannie Mandelker, "A Business of Reservations," *New York Times*, July 18, 1976.

"I allocate 25-percent": Quoted in Milton Esterow, "Box Office, Mail, Parties, Scalpers — Playgoers Use All Sources," *New York Times*, May 21, 1964.

"By eight o'clock": Quoted in George Dolby, *Charles Dickens As I Knew Him* (London: T. Fisher Unwin, 1887).

"We are at": Quoted in John Forster, *The Life of Charles Dickens* (London: Chapman and Hall, 1874).

"The Jenny Lind Fracas," *Christian Secretary*, July 11, 1851.

"The box office": Quoted in "The Circus," *New York Times*, March 26, 1908.

"Gougers and ticket": Quoted in "Sees Plays in Grip of Ticket Brokers," *New York Times*, July 15, 1927.

"The existence of": Quoted in Milton Esterow, Ticket Scalping Netting Millions To Be Bared at Theater Inquiry," *New York Times*, December 2, 1963.

"The annual take": Quoted in "Broadway: The Icemen Melteth," *Time*, July 17, 1964.

"Experience has shown": Quoted in "System Description: TRS Ticket Issuing and Control."

"Outlying areas of": Quoted in "Sam Zolotow, "Computickets Due Here at Year-End," *New York Times*, April 1, 1968.

"Walter O'Malley": Quoted in "Just the Ticket," *Newsweek*, April 1, 1968.

"As Edgar M. Bronfman": Quoted in James J. Nagle, "Seagram Aide Gets Share of the Chores," *New York Times*, December 8, 1968.

"The red ink": Quoted in Larry Townsend, "Tickets, Tickets Everywhere," *Chicago Tribune*, December 26, 1969.

"Convinced me that": Quoted in Percy Tucker, *Just the Ticket* (Johannesburg: Jonathan Ball Publishers, 1997).

CHAPTER 2

This chapter draws on the authors' interviews with Bruce Baumgart, Roy Bellman, Dan Deboer, Barry Fey, Peter Gadwa, Tom George, Gordon Gunn, Keith Krokyn, Albert Leffler, Doug Levinson, Bob Machen, Dorothy McLaughlin, John Pritzker, Frank Russo, Charlie Ryan, Peter Schniedermeier, Jerry Seltzer, Hal Silen, Terry Wojtulewicz and others. In addition it utilizes the secondary sources listed below:

"You know, Seltzer": Quoted in Frank Deford, *Five Strides on the Banked Track* (Boston: Little, Brown & Company, 1971).

"Upside down": Quoted in Frank Deford, *Five Strides on the Banked Track* (Boston: Little, Brown & Company, 1971).

"That by itself": Quoted in Frank Deford, *Five Strides on the Banked Track* (Boston: Little, Brown & Company, 1971).

"That's definitely true": Quoted in Keith Coppage, *Roller Derby to Rollerjam* (Santa Rosa: Squarebooks, 1999).

"The largest one": Quoted in Frank Deford, *Five Strides on the Banked Track* (Boston: Little, Brown & Company, 1971).

Stewart Brand, "Spacewar: Fanatic Life and Symbolic Death Among the Computer Bums," *Rolling Stone*, December 7, 1972.

"At 9:30 there": Quoted in John Blatt, *Rage & Roll: Bill Graham and the Selling of Rock* (New York: Birch Lane Press, 1988).

"Seemed to have": Quoted in Bill Graham and Robert Greenfield, *Bill Graham Presents* (New York: Doubleday, 1992).

"Total, wall-to-wall, gonzo": Quoted in Bill Graham and Robert Greenfield, *Bill Graham Presents* (New York: Doubleday, 1992).

"Bill would stand": Quoted in Bill Graham and Robert Greenfield, *Bill Graham Presents* (New York: Doubleday, 1992).

"I remember he": Quoted in John Blatt, *Rage & Roll: Bill Graham and the Selling of Rock* (New York: Birch Lane Press, 1988).

"We were able": Quoted in *Last Days of the Fillmore*, Rhino Records, 2009.

"Frank Barsalona virtually": Quoted in Dave Marsh, "Concert Master — Marsh on Music," DMusic.com, March 24, 2002.

"When I first: Quoted in "Frank Barsalona: The Lisa Robinson Interview," *Billboard*, August 18, 1984.

"If I got": Quoted in Fred Goodman, *The Mansion on the Hill* (New York: Times Books, 1997).

"He brought a": Quoted in "Something Must Happen," *Billboard*, November 14, 1970.

"To me, one": Quoted in "Frank Barsalona: The Lisa Robinson Interview," *Billboard*, August 18, 1984.

"When I started": Quoted in "Promoters Proffer Frank Thoughts," *Billboard*, August 18, 1984.

"Fotomat has three": Quoted in *Fotomat Corporation Study*, October 1978.

CHAPTER 3

This chapter draws on the authors' interviews with Lou Baumeister, Richard Beatty, Roy Bellman, Ralph Beyer, Bill Birdsall, Gary Bongiovanni, Alan Citron, Gene Cobuzzi, Tim Collins, Dan Deboer, Al Dejardin, Kurt Devlin, Howard Erskine, Neil Feltz, Nick Flaskay, Mark Fleishman, Wayne Forte, Peter Gadwa, Gordon Gunn, Bruce Houghton, Peter Jablow, Tom Lasley, Albert Leffler, Dave Leiken, Doug Levinson, Larry Litwin, Jack Lucas, Jerry Nelson, Andy Nyberg, Jim O'Chery, Bob Price, Vince Rieger, Fred Rosen, Claire Rothman, Mike Rowe, Charlie Ryan, Bill Schmitt, Peter Schniedermeier, Jerry Seltzer, Hal Silen, Patricia Spira, Michael Walthius, Matt Whelan, Charlie Williams, Tim Wood and others. In addition it utilizes the secondary sources listed below:

"To do a": Quoted in Steve Wozniak, *iWoz: Computer Geek to Cult Icon: How I Invented the Personal Computer, Co-founded Apple, and Had Fun Doing It* (New York: W.W. Norton, 2006).

"Ticketmaster Joins 'Us!'": Quoted in *Los Angeles Times*, March 27, 1983.

"Ticketmaster is another": Quoted in *Fotomat Corporation Study*, October 1978.

"Relevant topics such": Quoted in http://iaam.org/Governance/hist.htm

"Ticketron is the largest": Quoted in *Fotomat Corporation Study*, October 1978.

"Several times a": Quoted in Kurt M. Devlin, "Automated Ticketing: A Case Study."

"We've pulled the": Quoted in John Rockwell, "Stones Tour Is On and So Is Ticket Rush," *New York Times*, May 2, 1975.

"The city and": Quoted in Jeannie Mandelker, "A Business of Reservations," *New York Times*, July 18, 1972.

"The mother of": Quoted in Luke Ford, "Phyllis Carlyle — Producer of *Se7en*, *Accidental Tourist*," www.lukeford.net/profiles/profiles/phyllis_carlyle.htm

"It was a small business": Quoted in Leslie Helm and Chuck Philips, "The ticket king's path to power: As Pearl Jam just learned, Ticketmaster's Fred Rosen gets what he wants," *Los Angeles Times*, June 17, 1995.

"Press estimates of": Quoted in Steve Wozniak, *iWoz: Computer Geek to Cult Icon: How I Invented the Personal Computer, Co-founded Apple, and Had Fun Doing It* (New York: W.W. Norton, 2006).

"Welcome to Ticket": Quoted in Michael London, "Just the Ticket for Healthy Competition," *Los Angeles Times*, May 13, 1983.

"If we made": Quoted in "Rosen Reflects on Ticketmaster," *Amusement Business*, May 25, 1998.

"If the only": Quoted in Leslie Helm and Chuck Philips, "The ticket king's path to power: As Pearl Jam just learned, Ticketmaster's Fred Rosen gets what he wants," *Los Angeles Times*, June 17, 1995.

"A hard-bargaining": Quoted in Joe Holley, "Allen J. Bloom, 72; Promoted 'Greatest Show on Earth,' Musical Acts," *Washington Post*, February 1, 2008.

"Complimented him on going": Quoted in John R. Emshwiller, "Ticketmaster's Dominance Sparks Fears," *Wall Street Journal*, June 19, 1991.

"In the extreme": Quoted in "Instant Ticket to the Leisure Market."

"Betting on bigness": Quoted in "Control Data Tackles the Giant," *Business Week*, June 28, 1969.

"I've been in": Quoted in David Vise, "Bitter Bout for the Box Office; Abe Pollin, Carlyle Group Beef Up Ticketron for Grudge Match with Rival Ticketmaster," *Washington Post*, February 25, 1990.

"[Pollin] is going": Quoted in David Vise, "Bitter Bout for the Box Office; Abe Pollin, Carlyle Group Beef Up Ticketron for Grudge Match with Rival Ticketmaster."

"I gave birth": Quoted in Rick Pearson, "Donald Stephens Mayor of Rosemont," *Chicago Tribune*, July 25, 1999.

CHAPTER 4

This chapter draws on the authors' interviews with Frankie Accardi, Bob Barsotti, Gary Bongiovanni, Calico, Shelly Diamond, Bruce Ede, Jeff Hecker, Hal Kant, Morey Koretsky, Keith Krokyn, Carol Latvala, Doug Levinson, Ian Mackaye, Steve Marcus, Dennis McNally, John Pritzker, John Rhamstine, Fred Rosen, Alan Rossi, John Scher, Forrest Schofield, Cameron Sears, Lee Ann Vick, Jim Walcott, Bob Weir, Joanne Wishnoff and others. In addition it utilizes the secondary sources listed below:

"The pipeline for": Quoted in Dean Budnick, "Phil Lesh and the Alchemy of a Quintet," Jambands.com, November 19, 2001.

"This is not"; Quoted in Greil Marcus, "The Who on Tour/Magic Bus," *Rolling Stone*, November 9, 1968.

"Ruthlessly efficient": Quoted in Jane Gross, "'Deadheads' in an Idolatrous Pursuit," *New York Times*, May 18, 1988.

CHAPTER 5

This chapter draws on the authors' interviews with Alan Citron, Tim Collins, Gary Condit, David Cooper, Bertis Downs, John Edgell, Jane Kleinberger, David Leiken,

Ian Mackaye, David Marsh, Fred Rosen, Claire Rothman, Peter Schniedermeier, Matt Whelan and others. In addition it utilizes the secondary sources listed below:

"Conversely as Chuck Philips reported": Quoted in Chuck Philips, "Pearl Jam Takes Ticket Complaints to Capitol Hill," *Los Angeles Times*, June 30, 1994.

"It was necessary for us": Quoted in "Pearl Jam's Antitrust Complaint: Questions About Concert, Sports, and Theater Ticket Handling Charges and Other Practices," U.S. Government Printing Office, July 11, 1995.

"Ticketmaster fought us in Detroit": Quoted in Steve Morse, "Pearl Jam Adds Third Local Date," *Boston Globe*, March 16, 1994.

"The minute they became": Quoted in Chuck Philips, "Pearl Jam Takes Ticket Complaints to Capitol Hill."

"We take a lower": Quoted in Alec Foege, "Green Day," *Rolling Stone*, December 28, 1995.

"This could be our": Quoted in Allan Jones, "I'm Not Your F***in' Messiah," *Melody Maker*, May 21, 1994.

"It doesn't cost them": Quoted in Fred Moody, "Battle of the Band," *Seattle Weekly*, November 2, 1994.

"What Pearl Jam is doing": Quoted in Chuck Philips, "Pearl Jam–Ticketmaster Dispute Rocks Concert World," *Chicago Sun-Times*, June 9, 1994.

"Change the way tickets": Quoted in Bob Herbert, "Ticket Trust Busters," *New York Times*, June 5, 1994.

"The White House is impressed": Quoted in Chuck Philips, "Pearl Jam Takes Ticket Complaints to Capitol Hill."

"This summer, if Ticketmaster's gonna": Quoted in Kim Neely, *Five Against One* (New York: Penguin Books, 1998), p. 270.

"This thing has been": Quoted in Chuck Philips, "Pearl Jam Takes Ticket Complaints to Capitol Hill."

"The day before Sullivan & Cromwell": Quoted in Melina Newman, "Pearl Jam Postpones Summer Tour of U.S.," *Billboard*, May 7, 1994.

"Kurt died right at": Quoted in Chuck Philips, "Pearl Jam Takes Ticket Complaints to Capitol Hill."

"We'd spent so much": Quoted in Kim Neely, *Five Against One*, p. 282.

"The Ticketmaster thing came": Quoted in Eric Weisbard, "Ten Past Ten," *Spin*, August, 2001.

"We would have settled": Quoted in Fred Moody, "Battle of the Band."

"The billion-ticket figure was": From Anthony Ramirez, "Ticketmaster's Mr. Tough Guy," *New York Times*, November 6, 1994.

"Validates the idea that": Quoted in Chuck Philips, "Pearl Jam Tries New Approach to Tickets," *Los Angeles Times*, December 22, 1994.

"Pearl Jam doesn't just": Quoted in Chuck Philips, "Pearl Jam Tries New Approach to Tickets."

"Certain Pearl Jam impetus": Quoted in Ralph Blumenthal, "Oddities Continue with Ticketmaster and Pearl Jam," *New York Times*, August 23, 1995.

"In any way connected": Quoted in Bill Holland, "Groups Unite for Ticket Reform," *Billboard*, April 1, 1995.

"Disseminating false and misleading": Quoted in Alan Citron, "Ticketmaster Cites Distortions in Consumer Group Remarks; Refutes False Rhetoric About Ticket Pricing, Access," *PR Newswire*, March 21, 1995.

"Pearl Jam is back": Quoted in Chuck Philips, "Pearl Jam Finds a Way to Tour," *Washington Post*, April 4, 1995.

"The band has fought": Quoted in Chuck Philips, "Pearl Jam Finds a Way to Tour."

"We're frustrated and disappointed": Quoted in Adam Sandler, "Pearl Jam Cancels in Fee Flap," *Daily Variety*, April 24, 1995.

"After this tour, we": Quoted in Chris Riemenschneider, "Pearl Jam To Reconsider Its Ticketmaster Boycott," *Los Angeles Times*, June 14, 1995.

"I regret to say": Quoted in Chuck Philips, "Pearl Jam Throws in Towel in Crusade Against Ticketmaster," *Los Angeles Times*, June 15, 1995. Also quoted in Chuck Philips, "Pearl Jam Ends Ticketmaster Boycott," *Washington Post*, June 15, 1995.

"Jeff and Eddie were": Quoted in Robert Hilburn, "Vedder Lowers the White Flag," *Los Angeles Times*, June 19, 1995.

"The difficulty the band": Quoted in Jennifer Bowles, "Ticketmaster's Pearl Jam Battle Highlights Agency's Legal Woes," *Journal Record*, June 30, 1995.

"We nonetheless remain troubled": Quoted in Linda Himelstein and Ronald Grover, "Will Ticketmaster Get Scalped?" *Business Week*, June 26, 1995.

"We were afraid there'd": Quoted in Eric Weisbard, "Ten Past Ten."

"That was a day we": Quoted in Robert Hilburn, "Working Their Way out of a Jam," December 22, 1996.

"The whole thing was": Quoted in Eric Weisbard, "Ten Past Ten."

"We weren't trying to break": Quoted in Hélène Schilders, "Still Alive," *Guitar World*, April 1998.

"We thought there was": Quoted in Greg Kot, "Regrouped," *Chicago Tribune*, February 8, 1998.

"We haven't lost anything": Quoted in Hélène Schilders, "Still Alive."

"As a teenager and": Quoted in Greg Kot, "Regrouped."

CHAPTER 6

This chapter draws on the authors' interviews with Brian Becker, Jack Boyle, Tracie Buie, Gene Cobuzzi, Alex Cooley, Barry Fey, Seth Hurwitz, Tom Ross, Steve Schankman, John Scher, Steve Sybesma and others. In addition it utilizes the secondary sources listed below:

"If this was an Orson Welles movie": Quoted in Harry Hunt, III, "The New King of Rock-and-Roll Concerts," *U.S. News & World Report*, April 27, 1998.

"He was the consummate salesman": Quoted in Kevin Gray, "Ticketmaster," *New York Magazine*, November 15, 1999.

"Multidimensional youth-marketing business": Quoted in Harry Hunt, III, "The New King of Rock-and-Roll Concerts."

"There were enough kids there": Quoted in Jim Sullivan, "When It Comes to Pop Concerts, He Is the Player," *Boston Globe*, May 16, 1999.

"Strong sense of social consciousness": Quoted on website, "About the Sillerman Center," *Sillerman Center for the Advancement of Philanthropy*.

"A product of the '60s": Quoted in Harry Hunt, III, "The New King of Rock-and-Roll Concerts."

"I suppose if you were a psychiatrist": Quoted in Andy Serwer, "The King's Business: The Man Who Bought Elvis," *Fortune*, December, 12 2005.

"Bob can sell igloos": Quoted in Andy Serwer, "The King's Business: The Man Who Bought Elvis."

"Bob buys the bakery": Quoted by Andrea Adelson, "Radio Entrepreneur Mixes Fun and Money," *New York Times*, July 4, 1988.

"After you shake hands with Bob": Quoted in Dean Johnson, "SFX Grows into the New Monster of Rock," *Boston Herald*, May 5, 1998.

"Losing the House in '94": Quoted in Eric Boehlert, "One Big Happy Channel?" *Salon*, June 28, 2001.

"Lobbyists have seldom met": Quoted in Edmund L. Andrews, "House Panel Acts To Loosen Limits on Media Industry," *New York Times*, May 26, 1995.

"There are numerous provisions": Quoted in Jon Healey, "Provisions: Telecommunications Highlights," *CQ Weekly*, February 17, 1996.

"While this acquisition is immediately attractive": Quoted in "SFX Broadcasting To Acquire Leading Concert Promotion/Production Company," *Business Wire*, October 16, 1994.

"When we bought Ron Delsener": Quoted in Dean Johnson, "Music Firm Wants To Work in Concerts with Entertainers," *Boston Herald*," July 5, 1998.

"If we can control these events": Quoted in Elizabeth A. Rathbun, "SFX Expands into Concerts," *Broadcasting & Cable*, October 21, 1996.

"We anticipate realizing": Quoted in "SFX Agrees To Buy Indianapolis-based Concert Promotion Company," *Business Wire*, March 10, 1997.

"The industry in general": Quoted in Jo Sharp, "Sunshine Promotions, Inc. To Be Sold to New York's SFX Broadcasting," *The Indianapolis Star and News*, March 11, 1997.

"We have no grandiose ideas": Quoted in Jo Sharp, "Sunshine Promotions, Inc. To Be Sold to New York's SFX Broadcasting."

"I'm particularly pleased": Quoted in Elizabeth A. Rathbun, "CapStar/SFX Merger Detailed," *Broadcasting & Cable*, September 1, 1997.

"I wonder if Congress knew": Quoted in Paul Farhi, "Texas Firm Craft Biggest Radio Group in U.S.," *Washington Post*, August 27, 1997.

"They overpaid for us": Quoted in Kevin Gray, "Ticketmaster."

"I think part of it may be": Quoted in "Radio Group To Buy Concert Promoters," *New York Times*, December 16, 1997.

"These guys hated each other": Quoted in Kevin Gray, "Ticketmaster."

"I was sort of astounded": Quoted in Ray Waddell, "SFX: More Than Just a Promoter?" *Amusement Business*, July 13, 1998.

"If you look around": Quoted in Ray Waddell, "SFX Caps Off Aggressive Year with PACE Purchase," *Amusement Business*, January 5, 1998.

"The Irving deal": Quoted in David Segal, "Calling Almost Everyone's Tune," *New York Times*, April 24, 2010.

"The concert industry [is] similar": Quoted in Richard Harrington, "Cellar Door Joins the Band," *Washington Post*, August 14, 1998.

"Disney's relationships with corporate sponsors": Quoted in Harry Hunt, III, "The New King of Rock-and-Roll Concerts."

"These are people voting with their feet": Quoted in Kevin Gray, "Ticketmaster."

"What they are attempting": Quoted in Ray Waddell, "SFX: More Than Just a Promoter?"

"Remember that magical moment": Quoted in Kevin Gray, "Ticketmaster."

"100 percent of it was regional": Quoted in Richard Harrington, "A Concert Promoter Out To Steal the Show?" *Washington Post*, August 28, 1998.

"There was an outcry": Quoted in Jim Sullivan, "When It Comes to Pop Concerts, He Is the Player."

"It's all we can do": Quoted in Kevin Gray, "Ticketmaster."

"I think they're the enemy": Quoted in Richard Harrington, "A Concert Promoter Out To Steal the Show?"

"We will serve different functions": Quoted in Ted Drodowski, "Concentrated Rock," *Worchester Phoenix*, March 20–27, 1998.

"It is virtually impossible": Quoted in Ray Waddell, "SFX: More Than Just a Promoter?"

"They'll say, 'We'll give you": Quoted in Melinda Newman, "Indie Concert Promo Biz Reshaped by SFX's Rise," *Billboard*, September 4, 1999.

"See where the jury's still out": Quoted in Melinda Newman, "Indie Concert Promo Biz Reshaped by SFX's Rise."

"I said, 'Of course": Quoted in David Segal, "Calling Almost Everyone's Tune."

"It's very, very tasty": Quoted in Melinda Newman, "Indie Concert Promo Biz Reshaped by SFX's Rise."

"I make millions on the road": Quoted in David Wild, "Tom Petty Is Pissed," *Rolling Stone*, October 23, 2002.

"SFX's long-term interests": Quoted in Adam Sandler, "Corporate Rock in Concert," *Variety*, March 9, 1998.

"This is lightning": Quoted in Ray Waddell, "SFX: More Than Just a Promoter?"

"It flatters me that": Quoted in Kevin Gray, "Ticketmaster."

"Here's what we created": Quoted in Dean Johnson, "Music Firm Wants To Work in Concerts with Entertainers."

"It was like Moses": Quoted in Jim Sullivan, "When It Comes to Pop Concerts, He Is the Player."

"It was amazing": Quoted in Jim Sullivan, "When It Comes to Pop Concerts, He Is the Player."

"I never founded a company": Quoted in Jim Sullivan, "When It Comes to Pop Concerts, He Is the Player."

"The people in our industry": Quoted in Kevin Gray, "Ticketmaster."

"Do leopards change": Quoted in Ray Waddell, "SFX: More Than Just a Promoter?"

"The leopard doesn't change": Quoted in Kevin Gray, "Ticketmaster."

"A lot of people expect": Quoted in Jim Sullivan, "When It Comes to Pop Concerts, He Is the Player."

"People are charging": Quoted in Ray Waddell, "Concert Tickets Selling Despite Record Prices," *Amusement Business*, June 21, 1999.

"I want people to think": Quoted in Jim Sullivan, "When It Comes to Pop Concerts, He Is the Player."

CHAPTER 7

This chapter draws on the authors' interviews with Brian Becker, Jack Boyle, Michael Cohl, Alex Cooley, Steve Martin, Lawrence Peryer, John Scher, Steve Sybesma and others. In addition it utilizes the secondary sources listed below:

"We consider this acquisition": Quoted in Reed Bunzel, *Clear Vision* (Albany: Bright Sky Books, 2008), p. 73.

"It was a groundbreaking tour": Quoted in Jerry Weintraub, *When I Stop Talking, You'll Know I'm Dead* (New York: Twelve, 2010), p. 82.

"He was simply too big": Quoted in Jerry Weintraub, *When I Stop Talking, You'll Know I'm Dead*, p. 83.

"Many of us did not necessarily agree": Quoted in Melinda Newman, "Colleagues Recalls Hullet's Cutting-Edge Tour Biz Work," *Billboard*, August 14, 1993.

"Basically we did": Quoted in Melinda Newman, "Colleagues Recalls Hullet's Cutting-Edge Tour Biz Work."

"I became the most hated man": Quoted in Jerry Weintraub, *When I Stop Talking, You'll Know I'm Dead*, p. 84.

"Every local promoter wanted": Quoted in Jerry Weintraub, *When I Stop Talking, You'll Know I'm Dead*, p. 84.

"It was the largest-grossing tour": Quoted in Bill Graham and Robert Greenfield, *Bill Graham Presents* (Cambridge: Da Capo Press, 2004), p. 365.

"We realized that what": Quoted in Bill Graham and Robert Greenfield, *Bill Graham Presents*, p. 366.

"It took me and the company": Quoted in Bill Graham and Robert Greenfield, *Bill Graham Presents*, p. 367.

"I agreed to forego": Quoted in Bill Graham and Robert Greenfield, *Bill Graham Presents*, p. 368.

"Our strategy was to tap": Quoted in Larry LeBlanc, "Industry Profile: Riley O'Connor," *Celebrity Access*, July 24, 2009.

"I seem to remember": Quoted in Jane Cohen and Bob Grossweiner, "Industry Profile: Donald Tarlton," *Celebrity Access*, April 12, 2002.

"Excuse me, young man": Quoted in Andy Serwer, "Inside the Rolling Stones, Inc." *Fortune*, September 30, 2002.

"'They're going to go on tour'": Quoted in Bill Graham and Robert Greenfield, *Bill Graham Presents*, p. 521.

"If these people owned the tour": Quoted in Bill Graham and Robert Greenfield, *Bill Graham Presents*, p. 524.

"You tell me the money": Quoted in Bill Graham and Robert Greenfield, *Bill Graham Presents*, p. 529.

"I've never seen greed": Quoted in Steve Morse, "Rock Promoter Titans Clash over Stones Dates, *Boston Globe*, July 13, 1989.

"We're sorry it's not going": Quoted in Bill Graham and Robert Greenfield, *Bill Graham Presents*, p. 529.

"I think Michael would admit": Quoted in Andy Serwer, "Inside the Rolling Stones, Inc."

"It was a deal where": Quoted in Andy Serwer, "Inside the Rolling Stones, Inc."

"During the months after": Quoted in Bill Graham and Robert Greenfield, *Bill Graham Presents*, p. 530.

"Cohl would later acknowledge": Quoted in "Satisfaction, Guaranteed," *Washington Post*, October 3, 2002.

"SFX was formed by aggregating": Quoted in Kelly Barbieri, "Q&A: Brian Becker," *Amusement Business*, December 25, 2000.

"If anyone said": Quoted in Christine Y. Chen, "The Bad Boys of Radio," *Fortune*, March 3, 2003.

CHAPTER 8

This chapter draws on the authors' interviews with Dan Afrasiabi, Alan Citron, Gene Cobuzzi, Andrew Dreskin, Jane Kleinberger, Tom Lasley, Doug Levinson, Sean Moriarty, John Pleasants, Fred Rosen, Tim Wood and others. In addition, it utilizes the secondary sources listed below:

"Ticketmaster is an important vehicle": Quoted in "Ticketmaster Sale Confirmed," *Chicago-Sun Times*, November 22, 1993.

"In the flesh, he was power incarnate": Quoted in Dawn Steel, *They Can Kill You but They Can't Eat You* (New York: Pocket, 1994).

"I was 28 and he was 33": Quoted in Lesley Stahl, "Profile of Interactive Corp. CEO Barry Diller," 60 *Minutes*, June 10, 2007.

"I thought, 'This is the dumbest'": Quoted in Lesley Stahl, "Profile of Interactive Corp. CEO Barry Diller."

"I was struck": Quoted in Lesley Stahl, "Profile of Interactive Corp. CEO Barry Diller."

"The Darth Vader of cable": Quoted in Patrick Parsons, *Blue Skies* (Philadelphia: Temple University Press, 2008), p. 575.

"They said I'd lost my mind": Quoted in Lesley Stahl, "Profile of Interactive Corp. CEO Barry Diller."

"Barry can see something": Quoted in Lesley Stahl, "Profile of Interactive Corp. CEO Barry Diller."

"The wind at the back": Quoted in Farrell Kramer, "Diller Plans Ticketmaster Takeover," *Associated Press Union*, May 21, 1997.

"Each of us had a role": Quoted in Neil Cavuto, "CEO Ticketmaster Group Interview," *Cavuto Business Report*, March 12, 1998.

"Do you like him?": Quoted in Neil Cavuto, "CEO Ticketmaster Group Interview."

"When it was just a phone": Quoted in Athena Schaffer, "Online Ticketing Continues To Gain Ground," *Amusement Business*, September 14, 1998.

"Obviously it's going to help": Quoted in Michael Gannon, "CitySearch Merges with Ticketmaster," *Venture Capital Journal*, October 1, 1998.

"Once separated at birth": Quoted in Clare Saliba, "Two Ticketmasters To Merge," *E-Commerce Times*, November 21, 2000.

"Now that USA has 10": Quoted in "USA Interactive Names Leaders of Its Three New Principal Areas," *Business Wire*, December 12, 2002.

"The incredible demand": Quoted in "Ticketmaster Announces Top Selling Day in History," *PR Newswire*, March 6, 2003.

CHAPTER 9

This chapter draws on the authors' interviews with Jason Colton, Neil Glazer, Mike Luba, Jason Mastrine, Keith Moseley, John Pleasants and others. In addition it utilizes the secondary sources listed below:

"There was an opportunity": Quoted in Chuck Salter, "Way Behind the Music," *Fast Company*, February 1, 2007.

"I guess it was just": Quoted in Chuck Salter, "Way Behind the Music."

"They tried to shut": Quoted in Chuck Salter, "Way Behind the Music."

"There was a series": Quoted in Chuck Salter, "Way Behind the Music."

CHAPTER 10

This chapter draws on the authors' interviews with Gary Adler, Eric Baker, Jeff Berman, Greg Bettinelli, Tracy Buie, Tim Collins, Mike Domek, Barry Fey, Jeff Fluhr, Rusty Harmon, Mike Janes, Doug Knittle, Shelley Lazar, David Lord, Sean Moriarty, Tom

Ross, John Scher, Ram Silverman, Pat Toole and others. In addition, it utilizes the secondary sources listed below:

"Disintermediate brick and": Quoted in "LiquidSeats: Executive Summary."

"Ticket Venture Partnership Agreement": February 2, 2000.

"A centralized Web-based": Quoted in "NeedATicket.com Executive Summary."

"StubHub is a": Quoted in StubHub press release, July 11, 2002.

"Ticket 'scalpers' who": Quoted in "NeedATicket.com Executive Summary."

"Go watch the": Quoted in Barbara Isenberg, "Ticket Brokers: A Service or Rip-off?" *Los Angeles Times*, April 9, 1976.

"The Super Bowl is": Quoted in William Nack and Robert Sullivan, "Football's Little Bighorn?" *Sports Illustrated*, January 26, 1981.

"All hell broke": Quoted in Ellen Rosen, "In the Race to Buy Concert Tickets, Fans Keep Losing," *New York Times*, October 6, 2007.

"The whiplash speed": Quoted in Marco R. della Cava, "Web scalping boosts ticket prices and frustration," *USA Today*, November 6, 2007.

"Meet the newest": Quoted in Julia Angwin, "Ticketmaster takes on scalpers, eBay with Online Reseller System," *Wall Street Journal*, April 5, 2002.

"We're creating an opportunity": Quoted in Richard Harrington, "Ticket Auction Trend May Cost You," *Washington Post*, June 2, 2006.

"Move the concert": Quoted in Jefferson Graham, "Ticketmaster uses auctions to fight online scalpers," *USA Today*, May 22, 2006.

"Leverages RazorGator's industry": Quoted in RazorGator press release, September 26, 2006.

"Mr. Vaccaro seems": Quoted in Ben Sisario, "Pssst! Want a Ticket? Hey, I'm Legit. Really," *New York Times*, August 28, 2009.

"As the largest": Quoted in Ray Waddell and Tom Ferguson, "Ticketmaster Buys U.K. Online Ticket Reseller secondary ticketing," www.billboard.com, January 29, 2008.

"Seats That Are": Quoted in "Why can't I get tickets?" report on ticket distribution practices, Office of New York State Attorney General Eliot Spitzer, 1999.

CHAPTER 11

This chapter draws on the authors' interviews with Michael Cohl, Alex Cooley, Mike Luba, Sean Moriarty, John Pleasants, Frank J. Russo and others. In addition it utilizes the secondary sources listed below:

"The only way to fight": Quoted in Ethan Smith, "Can He Save Rock 'n' Roll?" *The Wall Street Journal*, February 21, 2009.

"Our partnership is a defining moment": Quoted in "Madonna Joins Forces with Live Nation in Revolutionary Global Music Partnership," *PR Newswire*, October 16, 2007.

"Turned into The Rolling Stones of hip-hop": Quoted in Jeff Leeds, "In Rapper's Deal, a New Model for Music Business," *New York Times*, April 3, 2008.

"Live Nation's strategy and execution": Quoted in Bob Grossweiner and Jane Cohen, "Michael Cohl Out as Chairman of Live Nation," *TicketNews*, June 20, 2008.

"[But he] he thought we should": Quoted in Ethan Smith, "Live Nation Has Ticket to Blockbuster Success," *The Wall Street Journal*, July 13, 2008.

"I know a lot of amphitheater tours": Quoted in Mitchell Peters, "Live Nation, AEG Reps Discuss Azoff Deal," *Billboard.biz*, November 21, 2008.

"The weekend where we absolutely": Quoted in "Live Nation, Inc. Q4 2008 Earnings Call Transcript," *Seeking Alpha*, March 2, 2009.

"There are times for everything": Quoted in "Live Nation and Ticketmaster Entertainment To Combine in Merger of Equals To create World's Premier Live Entertainment Company Call Transcript," February 10, 2009.

"Throughout the two Congressional hearings": in reference to and subsequently quoted from: "The Ticketmaster/Live Nation Merger: What Does It Mean for Consumers and the Future of the Concert Business," hearing before the Subcommittee on Antitrust, Competition Policy and Consumer Rights of the Committee on the Judiciary United States Senate, February 24, 2009.

"Competition in the Ticketing and Promotion Industry," hearing before the Subcommittee on Courts and Competition Policy of the Committee on the Judiciary House of Representatives, February 26, 2009.

"The *Wall Street Journal* broke a story": Quoted in Ethan Smith, "Big Ticket Seller Tried Deal with Scalpers," *Wall Street Journal*, August 28, 2009.

"Another high profile Azoff client": Quoted in Ethan Smith, "Concert Tickets Get Set Aside, Marked Up by Artists, Managers," *Wall Street Journal*, March 11, 2009.

"Six years and $400,000 later": Quoted in John Barron, "Promoter Kings," *Chicago Sun-Times*, April 30, 1995.

"The Department of Justice's proposed": Quoted in Christine Varney, "Justice Department Requires Ticketmaster Entertainment, Inc. to Make Significant Changes to Its Merger with Live Nation, Inc.," US Department of Justice press release, January 25, 2010.

"The department seems to understand": Quoted in Ray Waddell, "Reaction to Live Nation–Ticketmaster Merger," *Billboard.biz*, January 25, 2010.

EPILOGUE

This book's epilogue draws on the authors' interviews with Michael Cohl, Doug Knittle, Sherry Wasserman and others. In addition, it utilizes the secondary source listed below:

"The fight is not over": Quoted in "Ticketdisaster.org Statement on DOJ Settlement in Ticketmaster–Live Nation Merger," Ticketdisaster.org, January 25, 2010.

Dave Abbruzzese: drummer for the band Pearl Jam, 1991–1994.

Frankie Accardi: Grateful Dead ticketing service manager.

Gary Adler: president of the National Association of Ticket Brokers.

Dan Afrasiabi: executive vice president of business development for the Tickets.com ticketing service, 1998–2003.

Paul Allen: Microsoft cofounder and principal Ticketmaster owner, 1993–1997.

Jeff Ament: guitarist for the band Pearl Jam.

Irving Azoff: manager of the Eagles and cofounder of Front Line Management Group; executive chairman of Live Nation Entertainment.

Eric Baker: cofounder of StubHub, founder of Viagogo.

David Balto: senior fellow at the Center for American Progress who testified at the Live Nation–Ticketmaster hearings in 2009.

Terry Barnes: chairman of Ticketmaster.

Frank Barsalona: booking agent, founder of Premier Talent, "the Godfather of the rock tour industry."

Bob Barsotti: Bill Graham Presents staffer and later executive.

Lou Baumeister: president of California Sports, which ran the L.A. Forum.

Bruce Baumgart: programmed the BASS system while pursuing a Ph.D. in artificial intelligence at Stanford; later founded Softix.

Richard Beatty: longtime Ticketron vice president.

Brian Becker: Texas-based concert promoter and principal of PACE Entertainment, who sold to SFX in 1997; CEO of Clear Channel Entertainment, 2000–2005.

Roy Bellman: Computicket employee who later spearheaded Fotomat's Fototicket project.

Dan Berkowitz: founder of CID Entertainment, a music-based travel and VIP entertainment company.

Jeff Berman: former StubHub vice president; later moved to TicketsNow and Ticketmaster.

Greg Bettinelli: while at eBay helped engineer StubHub acquisition; later moved to Live Nation.

Charlie Black: government lobbyist for Ticketmaster, during first half of 1990s.

Judy Black: government lobbyist and senior vice president, governmental affairs of Ticketmaster, 1995–1998.

Bill Bliss: Dorothy McLaughlin's brother-in-law, who ran business operations at Select-A-Seat.

Margie Bliss: Dorothy McLaughlin's sister and Bill Bliss's wife, who cofounded Select-A-Seat.

Allen Bloom: longtime Ringling Bros. and Barnum & Bailey Circus promoter.

Eric Boehlert: investigative journalist whose work has appeared in *Salon* and *Rolling Stone*, among other publications.

Gary Bongiovanni: editor of concert industry trade publication *Pollstar*.

Jack Boyle: founder of Virginia-based concert promotion company Cellar Door Productions, who sold to SFX Entertainment in 1998.

Edgar M. Bronfman Sr.: president of Joseph E. Seagram Sons, whose Cemp investment fund was the lead investor in Ticket Reservation Systems.

Peter Bronfman: Canadian business mogul who owned Labatt brewery among other lucrative businesses and became financial partners with Michael Cohl, beginning with the Rolling Stones' 1989 *Steel Wheels* tour.

Maura Brueger: executive director of Consumers Against Unfair Ticketing, a non-profit coalition begun in 1995.

Tracie Buie: general manager, Northwest for Bill Graham Presents. Also worked at Avalon Attractions.

Calico: Grateful Dead ticketing service staffer.

Coran Capshaw: manager for the Dave Matthews Band and founder of MusicToday.

Alan Citron: senior vice president of New Media for Ticketmaster, 1995–1997; president of USA Networks Interactive, 1997–1999.

Kurt Cobain: lead singer of the band Nirvana, who committed suicide in April 1994.

Gene Cobuzzi: joined Ticketmaster in 1985 as regional controller, became chief operating officer.

Michael Cohl: Canadian concert promoter and principal of Concert Promotions International (sold to MCA in 1995); cofounder of the Next Adventure (sold to SFX in 1998); CEO of Concert Productions International (sold to Live Nation in 2006); CEO of Live Nation Artists.

Jay Coleman: founder of music sponsorship firm EMCI.

Tim Collins: manager for Aerosmith, who testified at the Pearl Jam–Ticketmaster hearing in 1994.

Jason Colton: Phish co-manager.

Gary Condit: Democratic member of the U.S. House of Representatives from California, who headed the Pearl Jam–Ticketmaster hearing in 1994.

Peter Conlon: Atlanta-based concert promoter who cofounded Concerts/Southern Promotions and sold the company to SFX in 1997.

Charles Conn: cofounder of the website CitySearch, which merged with Ticketmaster Online in 1998.

John Conyers: Democratic member of the U.S. House of Representatives from Michigan, who was present for the Pearl Jam–Ticketmaster hearing in 1994 and the Live Nation–Ticketmaster hearings in 2009.

Tre Cool: drummer for the band Green Day.

Alex Cooley: Atlanta-based concert promoter who cofounded Concerts/Southern Promotions and sold the company to SFX in 1998.

David Cooper: ticketing contractor who ran Pearl Jam's self-ticketing initiative as part of ETM and later Fillmore Tour & Ticketing.

Cecil Crawford: early Ticketmaster investor.

Kelly Curtis: manager for the band Pearl Jam.

Dan Deboer: BASS employee from the 1970s who joined Ticketron in early 1980s.

Ron Delsener: New York City–based concert promoter who cofounded Delsener/Slater and sold to SFX in 1996.

Kurt Devlin: Ticket Reservation System/Ticketron Employee and Executive 1969–1991, then moved to Shubert Ticketing; wrote his master's thesis on automated ticketing.

Barry Diller: CEO of Ticketmaster's parent company, IAC (and its predecessors), 1995–2010.

Mike Domek: founder of TicketsNow.

Bertis Downs: attorney for the band R.E.M.

Robert Doyle: antitrust lawyer who testified at the Live Nation–Ticketmaster hearings in 2009.

Andrew Dreskin: principal in TicketWeb ticketing service, which sold to Ticketmaster in 2000; founder of Ticketfly ticketing services.

Harvey Dubner: Computer Applications Incorporated vice president, who helped develop Ticket Reservations Systems software.

John Edgell: congressional staffer for the Information, Justice, Transportation and Agriculture Subcommittee who instigated the Pearl Jam–Ticketmaster hearing in 1994.

Mike Ferrel: SFX Entertainment president and CEO, 1997–2000.

Barry Fey: Colorado-based promoter who founded Feyline; partnered with Michael Cohl and Bill Graham Presents.

Jeff Fluhr: cofounder of StubHub.

Arthur Fogel: Canadian concert promoter and principal at Concert Promotions International; cofounder of the Next Adventure, which was sold to SFX in 1998; chairman of global music and CEO of global touring for Live Nation.

Luke Froeb: Vanderbilt professor who testified at the Live Nation–Ticketmaster hearings in 2009.

Peter Gadwa: programmed initial Ticketmaster system and remained with the company for two decades.

George W. George: Broadway producer (and son of Rube Goldberg) who funded the feasibility study that resulted in the formation of Ticket Reservations Systems.

Thomas Gimple: CEO of Advantix and its subsequent entity, the Tickets.com ticketing service, 1996–2001.

Neil Glazer: lawyer who represented SCI Ticketing in its lawsuit against Ticketmaster.

Ned Goldstein: vice president and general counsel for Ticketmaster, 1987–1998.

Bob Gorra: Ticketron senior vice president.

Stone Gossard: guitarist for the band Pearl Jam.

Bill Graham: founder of San Francisco-based concert promotion company Bill Graham Presents, who died in a helicopter accident in 1991.

Phil Gramm: Republican senator, Texas.

Arny Granat: Chicago-based concert promoter who cofounded Jam Productions.

Jim Guiernot: manager of such acts as No Doubt, Nine Inch Nails and Social Distortion.

Gordon Gunn: cofounded Ticketmaster with Albert Leffler; focused on business development.

Charley Hamby: early Ticketmaster investor.

Craig Hankenson: attempted to enlist IBM in computer ticket project in 1962; later helped TRS create a user-friendly system while working at the Saratoga Performing Arts Center.

Rusty Harmon: Hootie & the Blowfish manager during Jones Beach ticket larceny.

Bob Herbert: columnist for the *New York Times.*

Steven Hicks: cofounded SFX Broadcasting with Robert Sillerman; executive chairman of CapStar, which bought SFX Broadcasting in 1997.

Tom Hicks: cofounder of Texas-based investment firm Hicks, Muse, Tate & Furst, which backed CapStar's purchase of SFX Broadcasting in 1997.

Robert Hilburn: music critic for the *Los Angeles Times.*

Stephen Horn: Republican member of the U.S. House of Representatives from California, who was present for the Pearl Jam–Ticketmaster hearing in 1994.

John Hoyt: founder of Seattle-based Pyramid Communications, who helped launch Consumers Against Unfair Ticketing in 1995.

Tom Hulett: cofounder of concert promotion company Concerts West.

Seth Hurwitz: Washington, DC–based concert promoter and founder of IMP Productions, who testified at the Live Nation–Ticketmaster hearings in 2009.

Peter Jablow: Ticketron president, 1989–90.

Hank Johnson: Democratic member of the U.S. House of Representatives from Georgia, who was present for the Live Nation–Ticketmaster hearings in 2009.

Hal Kant: Grateful Dead attorney.

Burt Kanter: tax attorney who purchased Ticketmaster in 1980 and brought on Fred Rosen as adviser.

Howard Kaufman: manager for Jimmy Buffett and cofounder of Front Line Management.

Tom Keenan: founder of Portland record chain Everybody's Records and partner with Dave Leiken in Fastixx ticketing service.

Tim Klahs: director of investor relations for SFX Broadcasting and SFX Entertainment.

Jane Kleinberger: cofounder of Paciolan ticketing service, which was bought by Ticketmaster in 2008 and divested to Comcast-Spectator in 2010 to meet governmental compliance for the Live Nation–Ticketmaster merger.

Amy Klobuchar: Democratic senator from Minnesota who was present for the Live Nation–Ticketmaster hearings in 2009.

Doug Knittle: longtime ticket broker, founder of RazorGator.

Herb Kohl: Democratic senator from Wisconsin, who was present for the Live Nation–Ticketmaster hearings in 2009.

Keith Krokyn: point person on tickets for Jack Boyle at Cellar Door.

Jon Landau: manager for Bruce Springsteen.

Tom Lasley: Oregon-based Ticketmaster licensee.

Carol Latvala: Grateful Dead Ticketing Service staffer.

Don Law: founder of Boston-based concert promotion company Don Law Company, who sold to SFX in 1998.

Shelley Lazar: founder of SLO Limited, a VIP ticketing company.

Albert Leffler: employee Number One at Ticketmaster.

Dave Leiken: founder of Portland-based concert promotion company Double Tee Concerts.

Bob Leonard: Ticketmaster president during Fred Rosen era.

Doug Levinson: vice president of operations, later president of BASS.

Pam Lewis: manager for Garth Brooks, 1987–1994.

Ben Liss: CEO of North American Concert Promoters Association.

Larry Littwin: Ticket Reservations/Ticketron employee and executive, 1969–1989; took over technical leadership after Harvey Dubner departed.

Prince Rupert Loewenstein: financial adviser to the Rolling Stones.

Chuck Lombardo: ticket broker and founder of Elite Entertainment.

Mike Luba: cofounder of Madison House, home to SCI Fidelity and SCI Ticketing; part of Live Nation's initial Artist Nation team under Michael Cohl.

Dave Lucas: Indianapolis-based concert promoter and founder of Sunshine Promotions, who sold to SFX in 1997.

Peter Luukko: Comcast-Spectator CEO who testified at the Live Nation–Ticketmaster hearings in 2009 and whose company also owns New Era Tickets.

Bob Machen: business manager of the Phoenix Suns who placed the team's inventory on Select-A-Seat.

Ian Mackaye: lead singer for the punk band Fugazi.

John Malone: founder of Liberty Media and financial partner with Barry Diller in Silver King, HSN and IAC.

Steve Marcus: headed Grateful Dead Ticketing Service.

Dave Marsh: music journalist.

Steve Martin: president, North America for The Agency Group.

Jason Mastrine: head of SCI Ticketing.

Nick Mayo: president of Computicket, 1967–1970.

Lowry Mays: founder of Clear Channel Communications.

Mike McCready: guitarist for the band Pearl Jam.

Mike "Goon" McGinley: tour accountant for the band Pearl Jam.

Walter T. McHale: pitched idea for what would become Computicket to Computer Sciences in 1966.

Thomas McInerney: cofounder of the website CitySearch, which merged with Ticketmaster Online in 1998.

Dorothy McLaughlin: programmed Select-A-Seat.

Dennis McNally: Grateful Dead publicist and biographer.

Jerry Mickelson: Chicago-based concert promoter who cofounded Jam Productions and testified at the Live Nation–Ticketmaster hearings in 2009.

Ed Mierzwinski: director of the U.S. Public Interest Research Groups, who testified at the Live Nation–Ticketmaster hearings in 2009.

Michael Milken: Wall Street financier.

Sean Moriarty: Ticketmaster CEO, 2005–2009.

Chuck Morris: manager of the Nitty Gritty Dirt Band; Colorado-based concert promoter who worked for Feyline and Bill Graham Presents.

Bruce Morrow: radio DJ known as "Cousin Brucie," who partnered with Robert Sillerman in the radio company Sillerman-Morrow Group.

Keith Moseley: bassist for the band the String Cheese Incident.

Kim Neely: author of Pearl Jam biography *Five Against One*.

Jerry Nelson: Arizona real estate developer and early Ticketmaster investor.

Bill Norris: founder of Control Data Corporation.

Andy Nyberg: Ticketron employee and executive, 1974–1990.

Riley O'Connor: Canadian talent buyer and cofounder of Perryscope Productions, who partnered with Michael Cohl's CPI and Donald K. Donald Productions in 1977.

Major Owens: Democratic member of the U.S. House of Representatives from New York, who was present for the Pearl Jam–Ticketmaster hearing in 1994.

Bill Pascrell: Democratic member of the U.S. House of Representatives from New Jersey, who was present for the Live Nation–Ticketmaster hearings in 2009.

Greg Perloff: CEO of Bill Graham Presents, who cofounded Another Planet after nearly thirty years at Bill Graham Presents.

Norman Perry: Canadian concert promoter and cofounder of Perryscope Productions, who partnered with Michael Cohl's CPI and Donald K. Donald Productions in 1977.

Larry Peryer: president of UltraStar artist fan club and subscription service.

Collin Peterson: Democratic member of the U.S. House of Representatives from Minnesota, who was present for the Pearl Jam–Ticketmaster hearing in 1994.

Chuck Philips: investigative reporter whose work has been featured in the *Los Angeles Times* among other newspapers.

Randy Phillips: CEO of AEG Live.

John Pleasants: Ticketmaster CEO, 2000–2005.

Nadia Prescher: cofounder of Madison House, home to SCI Fidelity and SCI Ticketing.

Bob Price: succeeded Bill Norris as president of Control Data Corporation.

Jay Pritzker: Hyatt Hotel head who purchased Ticketmaster in 1982.

John Pritzker: Hyatt Hotel heir whose father purchased Ticketmaster in 1982.

Jack Quinn: president, Ticket Reservation Systems, 1966–1970.

Michael Rapino: CEO, Live Nation Entertainment.

Joe Rascoff: managing director and cofounder of the music business firm RZO, which handles finances for the Rolling Stones and David Bowie among many others.

Janet Reno: United States attorney general, 1993–2001.

Danny Rifkin: Grateful Dead manager.

Eliot Roberts: manager for Neil Young and CSN&Y.

Fred Rosen: CEO of Ticketmaster, 1982–1998.

Tom Ross: head of music division for Creative Artists Agency.

Cheryl Rosner: TicketsNow president, 2007–2008.

Claire Rothman: general manager of the Los Angles Forum; later joined Ticketmaster.

Mike Rowe: general manager of the Meadowlands complex from the mid-1980s through the mid-1990s.

Charlie Ryan: ran Ticket Hub hard ticket service in Memphis, later merged with Ticketmaster.

Steve Schankman: St. Louis–based concert promoter and cofounder of Contemporary Productions, who sold to SFX in 1997.

John Scher: New Jersey–based concert promoter and founder of Metropolitan Entertainment.

William Schmitt: Ticketron president from the mid-1970s through the late 1980s.

Peter Schniedermeier: worked for Ticket Reservation Systems, Select-A-Seat and BASS, and later served as president of ETM.

Chuck Schumer: Democratic Senator from New York, who was present for the Live Nation–Ticketmaster hearings in 2009.

Cameron Sears: Grateful Dead manager.

Jerry Seltzer: former Roller Derby commissioner who cofounded BASS and later became Ticketmaster vice president of marketing.

Brad Sherman: Democratic member of the U.S. House of Representatives from California, who was present for the Live Nation–Ticketmaster hearings in 2009.

Hal Silen: California lawyer who worked with Roller Derby and cofounded BASS.

Robert Sillerman: cofounder of SFX Broadcasting and founder of SFX Entertainment.

Mitch Slater: New York–based concert promoter and principal in Delsener/Slater, who sold to SFX in 1996.

Ethan Smith: reporter for the *Wall Street Journal.*

Larry Solters: longtime Ticketmaster publicist.

Charlie Spencer: assistant director of the Boise State Pavilion.

Arnold Stiefel: manager of Rod Stewart.

Bart Stupak: Democratic member of the U.S. House of Representatives from Michigan, who was present for the Pearl Jam–Ticketmaster hearing in 1994.

Chuck Sullivan: owner of the New England Patriots and promoter of the Jacksons' *Victory* tour in 1984.

Steve Sybesma: principal partner in Indianapolis-based concert promotion company Sunshine Promotions, who sold to SFX in 1997.

Donald Tarlton: Canadian promoter and founder of Donald K. Donald Productions.

Craig Thomas: Republican member of the U.S. House of Representatives from Wyoming, who was present for the Pearl Jam–Ticketmaster hearing in 1994.

Karen Thurman: Democratic member of the U.S. House of Representatives from Florida, who was present for the Pearl Jam–Ticketmaster hearing in 1994.

Pat Toole: founder of MasterBroker, acquired by RazorGator.

Rick Tyler: founder of TicketWeb ticketing service.

Don Vaccaro: founder Ticket Network, Ticket Summit and TicketNews.

Nicole Vandenberg: publicist for the band Pearl Jam.

Christine Varney: assistant attorney general, 2009–present.

Eddie Vedder: lead singer for the band Pearl Jam.

Diane von Furstenberg: fashion designer and wife of Barry Diller.

Jim Walcott: president of ticket designer and printer Weldon, Williams & Lick.

Michael Walthius: Ticketron employee in mid-1980s, who joined Ticketmaster in 1991.

Sherry Wasserman: Bay Area–based concert promoter who cofounded Another Planet after nearly thirty years at Bill Graham Presents.

Jerry Weintraub: cofounder of concert promotion company Concerts West and movie producer.

Scott Welch: manager for Alanis Morissette.

Dave Werlin: owner of Great Northeast Productions.

Matt Whelan: vice president of Ticketron's New England region in the late 1980s and founder of TicketPro.

Charlie Williams: Ticketron employee, 1972–1991.

Harvey Wineberg: vice president, Midwest region, Ticket Reservation Systems, 1968–1970.

Tim Wood: joined Ticketmaster in 1983; departed as chief operating officer in 2005.

Lynn Woolsey: Democratic member of the U.S. House of Representatives from California, who was present for the Pearl Jam–Ticketmaster hearing in 1994.

Terry Wojtulewicz: ASU athletic department ticket manager, who agreed to use Select-A-Seat and later worked for Dillard's tickets and ETM.

Steve Wozniak: co-creator of Apple Computers, founder of US Festival.

Irv Zuckerman: St. Louis–based concert promoter and cofounder of Contemporary Productions, who sold to SFX in 1997.

Bill Zysblat: cofounder of the music business firm RZO, which handles finances for the Rolling Stones and David Bowie among many others.

Acknowledgments

FIRST AND FOREMOST WE WISH to thank Jack David, Jen Hale and everyone at ECW for understanding our vision and exhibiting patience while it came to fruition. Thanks as well to Martin Townsend for his deft touch and Sarah Dunn for her enthusiasm.

We also owe a deep gratitude to Peter Shapiro, Rachel Baron, Mike Greenhaus, Dale Hirschman and the *Relix* home team.

We'd like to thank everyone who shared their time and insight with us while we wrote and researched the book, along with those individuals who helped facilitate the interviews.

We also wish to acknowledge those writers and reporters who inspired us and also helped lay the groundwork for this book: Fred Goodman, Robert Greenfield, Ray Waddell, Ethan Smith, William Knoedelseder, Steve Knopper, Larry LeBlanc, Bob Grossweiner, Julia Angwin, Sarah Lacy, Bill Carter, Chuck Philips, Melinda Newman and many others.

Dean also wishes to thank (for fellowship, good advice and the occasional lovely beverage): Randy Ray, David Steinberg, Jefferson Waful, John Patrick Gatta, Brian Robbins, John Zinkand, Jesse Jarnow, Craig Judkins, Dave Kingdom, Larry Bloch, Butch Trucks, Jon Topper, Robert DiFazio, Bert Holman, Joyce Dollinger, Jonathan Healey, Tommy Faulkner, Jim Walsh, Alec Gowan, David Piacitelli, Joan Myers, Manny Sinnegan, Bob and Joan Budnick (Steve, Pia and Debi too), Lynne Barrett (and all associated Barretts and Burnhams, even those who occasionally feel the need to alter the seating arrangements or flee the table altogether).

Josh also wishes to thank: my parents (forever, thank you) and family (Barons, Otto, Berliner and otherwise), my new family (the extended Seiden clan), my Brooklyn crew (*esprit de corps*), lifelong friends (Irvine), fellow officemates Dan Berkowitz, Matt Busch, Jeremiah "Ice" Younossi and Matthew "Chewy" Smith for offering their ears and insight, mentors Richard Flacks and Jaan Uhelszki, my transcriber Chris Steffen and to all those who repeated those six terrifying (but gratifying) words: "I can't wait to read it."